ENGLISH BIOGRAPHY IN THE SEVENTEENTH CENTURY: A CRITICAL SURVEY

Although biography is one of today's most flourishing literary genres, its early history has attracted much less attention than that of other forms, a neglect that is especially apparent in the case of the formative period of English biography, the seventeenth century. This new work by Allan Pritchard fills the scholarly void by providing a wide-ranging and comprehensive survey of this period's biographical writings.

After charting the growth of seventeenth-century biographical writing, Pritchard explores the ways in which traditional forms of religious biography and lives of princes and other secular figures were adapted to, and transformed by, the crises and revolutions of the period. He then considers the development of less traditional biographical types and analyses the emergence of a 'new biography,' concerned essentially with individuality and with private as well as public life.

The richness and diversity of texts examined in *English Biography in the Seventeenth Century* make this work an essential survey of the field.

ALLAN PRITCHARD is a professor emeritus in the Department of English at the University of Toronto.

English Biography in the Seventeenth Century

A Critical Survey

ALLAN PRITCHARD

UNIVERSITY OF TORONTO PRESS
Toronto Buffalo London

© University of Toronto Press 2005
Toronto Buffalo London
utorontopress.com

ISBN 978-0-8020-3889-0 (cloth)
ISBN 978-1-4426-1033-0 (paper)

Library and Archives Canada Cataloguing in Publication

Pritchard, Allan
English biography in the seventeenth century :
a critical survey / Allan Pritchard.

Includes bibliographical references and index.
ISBN 978-0-8020-3889-0 (bound).–ISBN 978-1-4426-1033-0 (pbk.)

1. England–Biography–History and criticism. 2. Biography as a literary form.
3. English prose literature–17th century–History and criticism.
I. Title.

CT34.G7P74 2005   820.9'4920042'09032   C2005-900428-2

University of Toronto Press acknowledges the financial assistance to its publishing program of the Canada Council for the Arts and the Ontario Arts Council.

This book has been published with the help of a grant from the Canadian Federation for the Humanities and Social Sciences, through the Aid to Scholarly Publications Programme, using funds provided by the Social Sciences and Humanities Research Council of Canada.

University of Toronto Press acknowledges the financial support for its publishing activities of the Government of Canada through the Book Publishing Industry Development Program (BPIDP).

Contents

Acknowledgments vii

Introduction   3

1 The Growth of Biographical Writing   9

2 Lives of the Protestant Saints   30

3 Patterns in Religious Biography   53

4 Izaak Walton's Lives   78

5 Lives of Public Figures   91

6 Lives of Writers: Scientists and Antiquaries   114

7 Lives of the Poets   128

8 Brief Lives: Thomas Fuller and Anthony Wood   145

9 Brief Lives: John Aubrey   170

10 Biography as Family History   199

11 Roger North: Lives of the Norths   219

Notes   243

Bibliography   279

Index   289

Acknowledgments

My interest in seventeenth-century English literature was first stimulated by Roy Daniells at the University of British Columbia. At the University of Toronto, Norman Endicott through his enthusiasm for George Carleton's life of Bernard Gilpin drew my attention to the English biography of this period. I am indebted to the Canada Council, during the time when research in the humanities was part of its responsibility, for supporting the present study at an early stage, and I am indebted to the University of Toronto for allowing me a period of leave for the work. I owe special gratitude to the British Library and the Bodleian Library, where I carried out most of my research.

ENGLISH BIOGRAPHY IN THE SEVENTEENTH CENTURY

Introduction

Biography is today one of the most flourishing and vital English literary genres. Few other forms attract so much interest or so many readers. Yet the early history of biographical writing in England remains a surprisingly neglected subject. Developments in the eighteenth century, particularly the distinction of Samuel Johnson and James Boswell as biographers, have tended to obscure the prior history of the form, almost as if English biography had suddenly emerged from nothing or at best had produced only a few isolated earlier works of note. The extensive biographical writings and developments in seventeenth-century England, well in advance of Johnson and Boswell, have received much less attention than they deserve.

Little has been done to follow up Donald Stauffer's pioneer survey over seventy years ago: *English Biography before 1700* (1930).[1] This is an admirable work, but since Stauffer ranged over the medieval period and the sixteenth century as well as the seventeenth century, and included autobiography as well as biography in a single volume, his scope was too great to permit comprehensive treatment or detailed analysis. He took little note of some of the most innovative types of seventeenth-century biography, for example the brief life and biography written as family history. He provided only a few rather dismissive sentences on John Aubrey, in many ways the most original figure among seventeenth-century English biographers. Later literary historians and critics have given more attention to autobiography than to biography proper.[2] Aubrey's *Brief Lives* have often continued to be undervalued, while the only other figures among seventeenth-century biographers who have subsequently attracted much interest have been Izaak Walton and, more recently, Roger North, and they have not been adequately considered in the context of other developments in biographical writing during the period.[3] More than almost any other area of seventeenth-century English literature, biography still remains in fact a practically unexplored territory.

One evidence of this neglect is the lack of good editions of seventeenth-century biographies. There are scarcely any modern scholarly editions even of the most important works. Walton's lives, revised and enlarged over many years, have a very complicated textual history which no editor has thus far attempted to deal with. The last scholarly edition of Aubrey's *Brief Lives*, which have survived in manuscripts difficult to read and interpret, was Andrew Clark's in 1898, over a hundred years ago. Modern editions of North's biographies, which their author similarly left in a series of manuscript versions, have also been slow to appear, although parts of this gap have gradually been filled in recent years. Many of the most interesting biographies published in the seventeenth century have never been reprinted and are available only in the rare book rooms of a few major research libraries. Unless one is prepared to read a great deal in microfilm or an electronic medium, one must go to the British Library in London or the Bodleian Library in Oxford to find copies of many of the texts.[4]

While the lack of modern editions of the texts has meant that much of the biographical writing has not been widely or easily accessible to readers, another reason for neglect is the fact that such texts as have been published in later times have often been scattered among historical society publications less familiar to literary students than to specialist historians. For example, Gervase Holles's *Memorials of the Holles Family*, a masterpiece of the biographical writing that emerges from family history during the period, was published from manuscripts for the first and only time in a Camden Society series in 1937 – too late, incidentally, for Stauffer's survey. Other works interesting in relation to the development of biography have tended to be overlooked because they have unpromising titles or are disguised in unlikely forms, for example Thomas Stanley's *History of Philosophy*, which contains a fine series of lives, and Richard Gough's *Antiquities and Memoirs of the Parish of Myddle*, which incorporates brief biographies and character sketches in the context of parish history. One also needs to take into account the fact that the number of biographies published during the seventeenth century is much greater than is apparent from such bibliographies as the Short-Title Catalogues, because many, including a high proportion of the best, were printed as prefaces to writings by their subjects.

The neglect of seventeenth-century biography is the more surprising in view of the strong modern interest in literary and artistic forms of the period that have affinity with biography. The development of the portrait in sixteenth- and seventeenth-century England, for example, which was once a similarly neglected subject, has attracted much interest from art historians in recent years. The neglect of biography stands in striking contrast to the intense modern study of such literary developments of the period as the emergence of the novel, a genre with which it has significant links. The neglect of this field by literary students arises partly no doubt from the sense that biography is an 'impure' or mixed form, belonging as much to the history of scholarship as to that of literature; but on the other hand biography is a branch of writing full of human interest, and it has a cultural importance that is more than simply literary, as Jacob Burckhardt, the great historian of the Italian Renaissance, recognized.

Burckhardt first conceived the idea of his *The Civilization of the Renaissance in Italy* while reading a series of early Florentine biographies. In that seminal work he attached importance to the development of biographical writing as a manifestation of the emergence of the individualism he believed to be at the heart of the Renaissance.[5] His views have often been criticized on the ground that he did less than justice to the earlier cultural developments of the Middle Ages, and they have been more recently disputed on the ground that he conceived of individualism as essentialist, as prior to history, when really it should be seen as a construction of political, religious, economic, and social forces. But as a modern historian has commented, 'Burckhardt's view of the Renaissance may be easy to criticize, but it is also difficult to replace.'[6] However much his theories may be debated and modified, whether individualism is viewed as a liberating development, associated with great intellectual and artistic achievements, and ultimately with the emergence of democracy and concern for human rights, or seen more negatively as a bourgeois construct tied to class oppression, Burckhardt was clearly right to emphasize the link between individualism and biography.

Indeed the term 'individual' is difficult to avoid even in dictionary definitions of biography. The first of the definitions given by the *Oxford English Dictionary* is 'the history of the lives of individual men, as a branch of literature.'[7] The extreme postmodern view that individual identity, the self, is no more than a fiction seems difficult to reconcile with any interest in biography: if the reality of individual identity and difference is altogether denied, there would appear to be little reason to read or write biography, and little reason for the form to have developed beyond narrow limitations as a didactic or political instrument. But the fact that such questions and issues have sometimes been made the subject of postmodern debate is all the more reason to study the emergence and development of biography as a genre.

Much in the history of this genre in seventeenth-century England confirms Burckhardt's view that biography is one of the key exemplars in a historic shift from concern with persons as members of classes to concern with them as individuals. This is not of course to deny either that social groups continued to be important or that many biographers during the period still worked within older traditions deriving from the Middle Ages. Biographers of religious figures, following long-established hagiographical traditions, commonly sought to discern and display not so much individuality as similarities, correspondences between their subjects and ideal models. But during this century newer types of biography emerged less concerned with similarities and more fully concerned with the differences between one individual and another.

This seventeenth-century divide between older and newer types of biography is well exemplified by the contrast between Izaak Walton and John Aubrey. Although Walton is influenced by newer developments, he makes no radical break with older hagiographical traditions: in many respects he represents the finest flowering of those traditions. He attempts to assimilate his subjects with ideal models and to a large extent works deductively from those ideals. Aubrey on the other hand is primarily concerned with the most individual aspects of his subjects, the ways in which each differs from the others, and he works by an empirical method on the basis of the observations he has made and the information he has gathered. His biographies give the sense of a fascinated exploration of the variety of human characters and lives.

This central concern with individuality, the ways in which one character differs from another, is well developed in some other biographers in the later seventeenth century, including Roger North. In his life of his brother Francis, Lord Guilford, North emphasizes that the biographer must display in his portrait 'the peculiar features whereby the subject is distinguished from all others.'[8] Thus many decades in advance of Samuel Johnson he places the same emphasis on individuality as appears in Johnson's classic definition of the biographer's business: 'to give a complete account of the person whose life he is writing, and to discriminate him from all other persons by any peculiarities of character or sentiment he may happen to have.'[9]

For biography, just as for science and a number of other fields, the seventeenth century holds the special interest that attaches to a formative period. The gradual emergence during the century of a radically new type of biography amidst the older types makes biographical writing one of the most interesting fields for the study of cultural change, fundamental shifts in values. It demonstrates profound epistemological changes of the kind attributed to the seventeenth century by Michel Foucault, and it exemplifies Douglas Bush's view that at the beginning of this century the culture of England was more than half medieval and in the later part more than half modern.[10]

The development of the newer biography represents the kind of gradual movement and change in values that cannot be precisely dated, but most of the radically new works belong to the second half of the century: they begin to appear in the 1650s. John Aubrey, who is highly conscious of his own position as an innovator in biography, comments in his *Natural History*: 'Till about the year 1649 'twas held a strange presumption for a man to attempt an Innovation in Learning.'[11] This mid-century date, to which Aubrey assigns the beginning of experimental philosophy or science in England, and which coincidentally marks the most revolutionary political event of the century in England, the execution of the monarch and inauguration of the republic, might be taken also as marking as closely as any single date could the beginning of a revolution in English biographical writing.

Virginia Woolf has commented that to judge by the history of biography and autobiography, 'Interest in our selves and in other people's selves is a late development of the human mind.'[12] But biography that offers much to satisfy modern standards begins to appear in England earlier than has often been supposed. Rather than awaiting the era of Johnson and Boswell, crucial developments in the genre occur a hundred years earlier. Nor is the innovative new biography coeval with the novel, as has sometimes been held. There are close parallels in the ways biography and the novel separate from hagiography and romance, but biography runs in advance of the novel in England and helps prepare the way for it, as is evidenced by the fact that early novels commonly present themselves as biographies or autobiographies.

The present study is primarily concerned with lives seventeenth-century English biographers wrote of contemporaries and near-contemporaries, figures from the same century and the later part of the previous one. Seventeenth-century lives of persons from earlier periods have generally been excluded, since writers could rarely gain enough information to write true biographies of figures very much earlier than their own time, because of the relative scarcity of first-hand testimony and private correspondence and the difficulty of obtaining access even to official records, but occasional reference has been made to exceptional seventeenth-century works concerned with earlier periods, such as Thomas Stanley's *History of Philosophy.* While 1700 has been adopted as the general terminal date, the study concludes with Roger North, whose biographical writings extend from the late seventeenth century well into the eighteenth century. Special attention is given to biographical innovation, but the traditional kinds of biography are also examined, including the religious biography of the period, which remains a remarkably neglected subject in comparison with the extensive study given to medieval hagiography. The traditional types deserve consideration not only for their intrinsic importance but also because they often provide the norms against which innovation can be measured.

The first chapter of this study examines in general terms the growth and expansion of biographical writing during the course of the seventeenth century in England. The next three chapters are concerned with the most widely practised traditional form, religious biography: they examine the ways in which hagiographical traditions are adapted or replaced in this century, and culminate in an analysis of Walton's lives.[13] The fifth chapter analyses the second important traditional type, biographies of princes, statesmen, and other public figures, and surveys its development in response to the great political crises and revolutions of the period. The remaining six chapters consider the development of newer, less traditional biographical types: innovative secular lives of scientists, scholars, and writers, often published as prefatory biographies, brief lives, including those of Aubrey, and biographies shaped as family history, including those of North, whose work provides an appropriate conclusion.

CHAPTER 1

The Growth of Biographical Writing

I

Biography was so relatively rare and so imperfectly established a form in England before the seventeenth century that the author of an anonymous life of Sir John Perrot, a Tudor Lord Deputy of Ireland, written about 1600, felt it necessary to defend the genre: 'Yet some perchaunce will say, that to write the Lives of particular Men, is a Thinge as unnecessarie, as it is unusuall.' Francis Bacon in *The Advancement of Learning* in 1605 listed biographical writing among the most neglected areas of learning and issued a call for its development beyond the limitations he found at that time. He expressed wonder that so few lives of eminent men were written: 'For although there be not many soveraigne Princes or absolute cõmanders ... yet there are many worthy personages, that deserve better then dispersed report, or barren *Elogies*.'[1]

Bacon's appeal proved to be well timed, for English biographers in the new century responded as if they had been waiting for such a call. During the course of the century an enormous increase took place in the number and forms of biographies and in the range of biographical subjects. A complete list of sixteenth-century English biographies would be short, but a complete list of seventeenth-century biographies would be so long that no one has yet ventured to compile such a bibliography. In the sixteenth century biographies rarely moved beyond the two traditional types developed in the Middle Ages, the lives of saints, and the lives of princes and other great personages to which Bacon referred. In the seventeenth century biographical coverage extended far beyond figures of exalted rank and position to many members of the gentry and middle classes and to a wide range of professions and occupations.

This expansion of biographical writing in seventeenth-century England may be seen as occurring in three different but interrelated ways. First, there was a great enlargement and broadening of the two traditional types, the lives of saints and other notable religious figures, and the lives of princes and other great secular figures, stimulated both by the aftermath of the sixteenth-century religious revolution and by the seventeenth-century conflicts that culminated in the Civil War. Second, biographical elements were developed increasingly in various established literary forms that had not previously contained much biographical component, ranging from sermons to histories. Third, a number of forms were developed that had little earlier precedent in England and can be regarded as distinctively new seventeenth-century types of biography, including the prefatory life and the brief life.

The greatest increase in the number of lives took place in the field of religious biography, in works that can be seen as this period's adaptation or replacement of the ancient form of the saint's life. Biographies, whether of clergy or lay persons, written in the service of religion and church outnumber primarily secular examples even in the later part of the century. Their proliferation reflects the fact that the movement which had begun in the previous century to provide England with distinctively Protestant versions of biography reached its culmination in the seventeenth century.

While Roman Catholic biography remained very much alive in England after the Protestant Reformation, and indeed was stimulated by the religious crisis, it was driven underground. The persecution suffered by Catholics in Protestant England gave rise to a fine series of lives of Catholic martyrs, including biographies of Thomas More by William Roper and others, an anonymous life of John Fisher, and a life of Edmund Campion, but such lives could rarely be published openly or safely in England, except during the short period of the reign of Mary I. Many remained long in manuscript before their publication could take place. In contrast to the surreptitious continuation of Roman Catholic biography in England, the official encouragement of the Anglican church and state was for the development of a Protestant tradition in biography, which replaced those aspects of the older hagiographical traditions rejected by Protestants and served the purposes of the new religious establishment.

The Protestant revolution in England had as one of its consequences a great broadening of religious biography beyond the confines of the traditional category of the saint's life. Protestants rejected the Roman

Catholic definition of the saint as a figure marked by miracle-working powers and specially recognized by canonization, and opened biography to larger and more loosely defined classes of persons distinguished by the nature of their religious beliefs and by the sanctity of their lives. In Protestant redefinitions of sainthood, the saints could be seen as the whole company of believers, as all those who possessed the true faith, or all those who were saved.

In the view of many Protestants, including such prominent and influential Puritans as Richard Baxter, the number of saints worthy of biographical commemoration was very large. In his funeral sermon for Elizabeth Baker in 1661 Baxter emphasized that he was not about the 'Popish' work of making a wonder of a saint as a phoenix. He declared that while for Roman Catholics saints must be canonized, and they say Protestants have none, he rejoiced in the many he had known. In his preface to Samuel Clarke's great collection of religious biographies, *The Lives of Sundry Eminent Persons in this Later Age* (1683), Baxter wrote that it should not be supposed that among such Protestants as this volume commemorated saints were so rare that they should be marked by canonization. He maintained that they were so numerous that it would be an endless work to list them all.[2]

Since Baxter's view was shared by many, both Puritan and Anglican, the publication of religious biographies so proliferated during the course of the seventeenth century that it became common for clergy and other pious persons to recommend the reading of such works, and the diaries of the period often record the reading of 'good lives.' In accordance with the Protestant emphasis on the equality of all believers, these biographies were by no means confined to persons of high social class or worldly prominence. John Shawe expressed a common viewpoint when in *Mistris Shawe's Tomb-Stone* in 1658 he advocated the writing of the lives of God's precious saints 'how private so ever their station be.' A high proportion of the biographies published were of clergymen, but many had as their subjects lay persons of a wide range of classes and occupations, including otherwise obscure country gentry and city merchants. As well as lives of men, there were many lives of women, and as well as lives of adults there were lives of children. So many biographies appeared even within this last special category that the anonymous biographer of Margaret Andrews, who died in 1680 at the age of fourteen, records her delight in reading the lives of children.[3]

The religious conflicts of the period stimulated the writing of lives in ways that demonstrate how productive of biographies eras of disruption may be. During the later sixteenth and early seventeenth centuries Anglican biographers wrote with the special purpose of establishing the legitimacy and authority of the Church of England and defending their church against Roman Catholic attack. When internal conflicts grew increasingly strong among Protestants as the seventeenth century advanced, Anglican biographers commonly wrote to defend the Church of England against Puritan attack, and to uphold their particular conception of that church, whether Laudian or Latitudinarian, 'High Church,' 'Broad Church,' or 'Low Church,' against rival views. Likewise, Presbyterians, Independents, and adherents of other sects wrote biographies designed to provide polemical support for their religious groups. The religious conflicts and controversies of the period generated a vast amount of biographical writing, even while they made it difficult for biographers to achieve detachment and objectivity. Some of these developments and problems will be considered in the next three chapters.

In the great seventeenth-century conflict between Anglicans and Puritans, Royalists and Parliamentarians, that culminated in the Civil War, religious and secular political issues were so closely linked as to be inseparable. Hence the two traditional categories of the lives of saints and lives of princes and other great public figures became in effect amalgamated or fused together. The older type of the life of the prince was no longer possible after the beheading of the reigning king. Accordingly, in Royalist biographies the executed monarch Charles I is represented as a martyred saint and as a Christ-figure, while in Puritan biographies his great opponent Oliver Cromwell is compared to such biblical figures as Moses.[4] The biographies reflect the fact that while such secular statesmen as Cromwell were fundamentally driven by religious motives, many of the leading political figures in the conflict like Archbishop Laud were churchmen. As will be noted in the discussion of biographies of public figures in chapter 5, the most important seventeenth-century works of political biography include lives of ecclesiastical statesmen, such as the 'High Church' Anglican Archbishop Laud, the moderate Anglican Archbishop Williams, and the Puritan leader John Preston.

It would be difficult to exaggerate the impact of the Civil War upon the development of English biography in the seventeenth century. Like Cavendish's life of Wolsey and Roper's life of More in the previous century, some of the most notable seventeenth-century biographies were written to commemorate and defend members of the party apparently defeated in the conflict. Defence of the Church of England during its period of defeat and affliction was a major motive of Izaak Walton's lives. His first life, that of John Donne, was published in 1640 before the war, but he added hostile references to the Puritan regime in later editions, and the biographies he wrote during the Interregnum and after the Restoration were shaped as defences of Anglicanism against Puritanism.

The result and aftermath of the Civil War provided many biographers not only with the motive for writing but also with the necessary leisure, arising from the disruption of their previous activities. During the Interregnum of the 1650s a remarkably large number of Anglican clergy prohibited from exercising their ministerial functions and Royalist gentlemen deprived of their estates and public roles devoted themselves in their enforced leisure to the writing of biographies. Among the clergy, Thomas Fuller, who had carried out local researches during his marchings as a chaplain with the Royalist armies during the war, worked during the 1650s on his great series of brief biographies published as *The History of the Worthies of England* in 1662, and during the same period John Hacket wrote a voluminous biography of Archbishop Williams, a prelate he considered had been unjustly discredited during the conflicts of the 1640s. The Royalist gentleman Gervase Holles, driven into exile in Holland, occupied himself during the 1650s in writing a family history which embodied a fine series of biographies and character sketches, including prose elegies for relatives who had fought and died in the Royalist cause. Another gentleman, Thomas Stanley, employed his leisure during this period in writing a biographically remarkable *History of Philosophy* (1655–62).[5]

Some of the ways in which the Civil War continued to affect and stimulate biographical writing in the later part of the century long after the Restoration are illustrated by the cases of John Aubrey and Anthony Wood. The war took place during the formative period of their youth, and their view of life was permanently affected by the conflict. The phrase 'before the war' occurs again and again in Aubrey's writing. The sense that the war had suddenly swept away the world of his youth gave him a sense of the fragility of the human record and stimulated the antiquarian interests and special quality of historical imagination that led to his *Brief Lives*. Wood, who shared Aubrey's antiquarian interests and possessed much stronger prejudices, High Anglican and Royalist, continued during the 1680s and 1690s to the end of his life to fight the ideological battles of the Civil War in the biographies of his *Athenæ Oxonienses*, just as the Earl of Clarendon fought the battles again in his great *History of the Rebellion*, which is really a work of collective biography as well as a history. The biographies written in the later seventeenth century leave us in no more doubt than the histories that the Civil War was the central event of the century in England.

II

In addition to expansion and enlargement of the traditional areas, the saint's life and the life of the public figure, biography in the seventeenth century assumed many new forms and invaded many literary genres. The growth of biographical writing in this century has often been underestimated partly because of the employment of too narrow a definition of biography. The situation is similar to that of autobiography during the period. It has sometimes been concluded that there is little development of autobiography during the seventeenth century, but really, although formal autobiography may be slow to emerge, the literature of the period is full of elements of autobiography and self-portraiture: personal essays in the Montaigne tradition, diaries such as those of Samuel Pepys and John Evelyn, and intimate letters such as those of Dorothy Osborne. Works like Sir Thomas Browne's *Religio Medici* and Robert Burton's *The Anatomy of Melancholy* have strong elements of self-portraiture, and forms such as religious meditations in the hands of Donne and Traherne assume a decidedly autobiographical caste. Everywhere one looks in the poetry of the period too one finds writers developing if not literal autobiography at least the illusion of intensely personal self-revelation, as in the lyrics of Donne and Herbert, and in Milton the epic voice is infiltrated with the personal and autobiographical. Many parallels to these autobiographical developments occur in biography.

Just as in the seventeenth century the autobiographical impulse reaches far beyond works that are formally autobiographies, so also biographical elements are omnipresent even in works that are not formally biographies. Biography emerges as a significant aspect of many established literary forms: sermons, national and local histories, family genealogies and chronicles, journalism, and popular literature. It has links with such developments as the fashion for the Theophrastian character, as appears in writers like Fuller, who places side by side in his *Holy State* and *Profane State* (1642) characters representing types of humanity and brief biographies of individuals. Like autobiography, elements of biography invade even poetry, as is apparent in the prominence of verse character sketches in the political and satiric poetry of Andrew Marvell, Samuel Butler, and John Dryden.

Some of these subjects, such as the biographical evolution of genealogy and family history, are best reserved for later chapters, but one may take here, as an example of the way in which biography invades established genres, the most widely practised of all seventeenth-century literary forms, the sermon, and consider the biographical development of the funeral sermon. The funeral sermon is an ancient type, with such patristic precedents as Gregory of Nyssa's oration on the death of Basil, which underwent unprecedented development and expansion during the seventeenth century. In the Middle Ages the notable examples recorded are of funeral sermons for monarchs and princes, for example Thomas Brinton's sermon on the death of the Black Prince in 1376. This tradition continued into the sixteenth century with the famous example of John Fisher's sermon on the death of the Lady Margaret, the mother of Henry VII, in 1509, and in the later part of the century several funeral sermons were published in commemoration of peers, prelates, and great officers of state, for example Sir Henry Sidney, but very rarely for persons of lower rank.[6] In the seventeenth century, however, the number of recorded and published funeral sermons greatly increased, and it became common for members of the gentry and middle classes as well as those of higher rank to be commemorated in this way. These sermons deserve some attention here, despite their inherent limitations, partly because they were the only form of biographical commemoration granted to many persons in the period, and reached the widest audience, including even the illiterate.

Records of such families as the Verneys and Holleses show that among the gentry and middle classes during the course of this century the practice became widespread of leaving sums of money in wills for the preachers of funeral sermons: typically Penelope, Lady Osborne, who died in 1695, left £5 to a scholar from Oxford to preach her funeral sermon. It became increasingly common for the sermons to be published. Thomas Sparke in his funeral sermon for the Earl of Bedford in 1585 declared he had given in to urgings to publish despite his initial reluctance: 'yet, in this, loe, I am overcommed.' The seventeenth-century preachers frequently allowed themselves to be 'overcommed' in this way, by urgings of families wishing published commemorations of their relatives, by belief in the exemplary value of godly lives, and no doubt sometimes for more self-interested reasons of career advancement. While a single funeral sermon was the sole publication for many a clergyman, some preachers such as the Anglican Nathaniel Hardy and the Presbyterian John Howe published ten or more, and some of the sermons achieved great popularity in print: one of Edmund Calamy's ran through at least seventeen editions, and another was pirated, so that 'bad' quartos exist for funeral sermons as well as for plays. Preachers sometimes indeed seem to have conceived these sermons as rival attractions to the drama. Anthony Walker issued this summons to his sermon on the death of the eminently pious Mary Rich, Countess of Warwick, in 1678: 'I may without *Hyperbole* invite you, as the Cryer us'd to call Spectators to the secular Plays: Come see those Shews.'[7]

No complete bibliography of the seventeenth-century funeral sermon exists, but probably the largest single collection ever assembled was that formed by Sir William Musgrave in the later eighteenth century, and given by him to the British Museum in 1799. These sermons are now dispersed among the holdings of the British Library, but the Library possesses Musgrave's manuscript catalogue of his collection.[8] This lists about five hundred funeral sermons published between 1600 and 1700. It shows a gradual increase in numbers in the earlier part of the century, a large increase in the 1650s, and then after a temporary decline in the 1660s an increase to large numbers again in the remaining decades of the century. Computer analysis of the on-line English Short-Title Catalogues, which has been undertaken in recent years by social historians interested in the sermons for what they reveal about attitudes toward death, raises the total number of surviving funeral sermons published before 1700 to as many as eight hundred, but shows the same pattern as Musgrave's catalogue.[9]

The persons commemorated in these sermons are drawn from a wide range of social levels and occupations. Among the earliest published sermons honouring country ladies and gentlemen of ordinary rank are two sermons by William Harrison and William Leygh on Katherin Brettergh (1602) and Richard Eaton's sermon for Thomas Dutton (1616). Early examples of sermons for middle-class citizens and wives include Roger Fenton's on John Newman, a London grocer (1616), and Stephen Denison's on Mrs Elizabeth Juxton (preached 1619, published 1631).[10] Among the professions the clergy are particularly well represented, as one would expect, but during the course of the century various sermons were published also commemorating lawyers and physicians, soldiers and diplomats, scholars and schoolmasters, scientists and poets.

The amount and value of the biographical information provided by these sermons vary widely. Andreas Hyperius in *The Practis of Preaching*, published in an English translation in 1577, stated that, while Gregory of Nazianzus and Ambrose followed the custom of pagan funeral orations and the rules of ancient rhetoricians, rehearsing all their subjects' lives from childhood to old age, the modern preacher should seek the profit of the living rather than praise of the dead but might say something of the character and life of the person commemorated.[11] These principles are restated and followed by many seventeenth-century English preachers. Some preachers provided no eulogies or biographical elements at all, but most, both Anglican and Puritan, included some biographical information, at least an exemplary character and an exemplary account of the death, and many provided a fuller narrative of the life. The Presbyterian Simeon Ashe states that he gives a biographical account of the persons commemorated in his funeral sermons in 1654 and 1655, because 'I know it is expected.'[12] The Anglican John Donne and the Presbyterian Edmund Calamy are both alike in dividing their funeral sermons into two parts, and turning at the dividing point from, as they term it, one text to another, that is from the biblical text of the sermon to the exemplary life and character that are its occasion. This two-part division became a conventional feature of the sermons.

The funeral sermon was of course subject to obvious limitations and abuses. Some widely publicized sermons, such as Bishop (later Archbishop) Williams's on the death of James I, published in 1625 with the title *Great Britains Salomon*, became notorious for flattery. Throughout the century the abuses of such sermons were widely recognized and frequently deplored. Edward Boteler in his funeral sermon on Edmund, Earl of Mulgrave, in 1659 declared that the complaint of the prophet, 'Who hath believed our report?,' was the fittest text for a funeral sermon, and that 'Here Lyes' should be inscribed on the preacher's pulpit. At the end of the century Philip Stubbs, who gave his funeral sermon for Thomas Wright (1700) the subtitle 'Wherin are some Occasional Reflections on the Abuse of Funeral Sermons,' declared that false and flattering sermons were common and did a great disservice to religion, and he condemned those who canonized atheists, deists, and debauchees. In fact funeral sermons acquired such a bad reputation for dishonesty and flattery that the Puritan minister John Carter forbade the preaching of a sermon on his death in 1635, and Fuller records similar prohibitions in his *Worthies*.[13]

Despite this widespread awareness of their defects and limitations, the potential biographical value of the funeral sermon was well recognized in the seventeenth century. Fuller in his *Worthies* frequently drew upon these sermons for biographical knowledge and he sometimes referred his readers to published sermons for fuller information than he had space to provide. Anthony Wood in his *Athenæ Oxonienses* criticized Clement Barksdale for publishing lives 'scribled' from funeral sermons, but he made much use of them himself: in many instances they provided his chief biographical source. For example, he praised Robert Parsons's funeral sermon on the Earl of Rochester as 'excellent' and much admired, and he drew extensively upon Zacheus Isham's sermon on the death of John Scott and referred the reader to the published version for more information. He expressed regret that he had never managed to see one of the rare copies of Anthony Burgess's funeral sermon on Thomas Blake: 'otherwise I might have been more large of our learned Author.'[14] John Aubrey in correspondence with Wood sometimes drew attention to the biographical value both of published and unpublished sermons: on 7 August 1680 he commended Simon Patrick's sermon on Samuel Jacombe, published in 1659, 'wherin are a great many Remarques of his Life,' and on 5 July 1690 he praised Anthony Horneck's unpublished sermon on Theodore Haak for providing 'many eminent remarques of his Life,' and expressed the hope that it might be printed.[15] The biographical compilations of Wood and others could not have appeared on such a large scale as they did in the later seventeenth century without the biographies already embodied in funeral sermons, and in the eighteenth century it was for their biographical value that Sir William Musgrave made his great collection of these sermons.

The seventeenth-century funeral sermons best known to literary students are the eloquent and moving tributes of John Donne to Lady Danvers and Jeremy Taylor to Lady Carbery, with their grand meditations on life and death, but many lesser-known sermons actually provide more biographical information. Examples from early and late in the century that better show the biographical value of the funeral sermon are George Abbot's sermon on Thomas Sackville, Earl of Dorset (1608), and Robert Parsons's on the Earl of Rochester (1680). Abbot provides an account of the various phases of Sackville's life, his activities in youth as scholar, traveller, courtier, and author of *A Mirror for Magistrates*, and in maturity as ambassador, councillor, and great Elizabethan officer of state, Lord Treasurer, and he analyses his private virtues: his kindness to his wife and children, his hospitality, his religious devotion, and his charitable works. Parsons's sermon on Rochester, the Restoration poet and rake, is worthy of the praise it received even from the usually critical Wood. It is not now so well known as Gilbert Burnet's life of this figure but it provides as fine a tribute to Rochester's wit and learning and as vivid a representation of his great sins and his final repentance.[16]

Two other notable examples that show the biographical value of the funeral sermon are John Buckeridge's sermon on Lancelot Andrewes (1631) and George Rust's on Jeremy Taylor (1668).[17] Buckeridge provides an admirable short biography of Andrewes, a good narrative of the life (although lacking dates) and a fine analysis of Andrewes's piety, learning, and charity. He writes from personal knowledge as one who loved and honoured Andrewes for thirty years. Together with Henry Isaacson's life it is one of the two indispensable early accounts of Andrewes, to which all later biographies are much indebted. Rust's sermon on Taylor deserves for the eloquence of its tribute to rank with the great seventeenth-century funeral eulogies by Donne and Taylor himself, and it incorporates a brief but valuable narrative of Taylor's life and analysis of his character, with a particularly fine picture of him as the handsome, eloquent young preacher at St Paul's. Like Buckeridge's sermon on Andrewes, it is written from long and close knowledge. As Taylor's modern admirer, Logan Pearsall Smith, has stated: 'Our most intimate glimpses of Jeremy Taylor as a man are derived from his funeral sermon.'[18]

As well as providing one of the foundations for the biographical collections and dictionaries that began to appear in the later part of the seventeenth century, throughout this period funeral sermons frequently served as the starting point for fuller biographies. In published versions, although the preachers sometimes omitted personal and biographical elements that had been delivered orally, they more often expanded these aspects, as their title-pages and prefaces make clear. For example, John Gauden in publishing his funeral sermon on Robert Rich (1658) states that he has much enlarged it 'beyond the Horory limits' of a sermon, and provides a biographical account extending together with a discussion of funeral ceremonies to 124 pages. Gauden's funeral sermon on Ralph Brownrig, Bishop of Exeter, is an even more extreme case of such expansion: in the version published in 1660 the sermon is followed by 'Memorials of the Life and Death' of Brownrig, running altogether to 245 pages, and preceded, as is not uncommon in such publications, by a portrait frontispiece of the bishop.[19] This close seventeenth-century link between the funeral sermon and biography may sometimes be regretted as resulting in lives that are excessively reverential and eulogistic, but much of the biographical writing probably would not have taken place at all if it had not been for the starting point of the funeral sermon.

III

In addition to the biographical invasion or evolution of such established older forms as the sermon, during the seventeenth century important new forms of biographical writing emerged and flourished in England, most notably the prefatory biography and the brief life. These two types were not entirely without precedent, but they underwent such development and acquired such importance in this century that they deserve to be seen as distinctively new forms. A high proportion of the biographies that will be considered in subsequent chapters fall into these two categories. Furthermore, the development and popularity of the brief life is inextricably linked with the appearance in the later part of the century of numerous biographical collections, some of them very large in scale, prototypical biographical dictionaries, formed on a variety of different principles.

Antecedents for the seventeenth-century English prefatory life are to be found in publications on the Continent, where the practice was well established of providing biographies in this form for editions, especially collected works in large folios, of writings of the church fathers and great classical authors. In sixteenth-century Europe prefatory lives were also attached to some publications of modern divines, including Protestant reformers and theologians. In England the prefatory life was likewise developed at first primarily for publications of eminent religious authorities, particularly posthumous editions of their collected works. The first notable seventeenth-century example is Daniel Featley's life of John Jewel, who was presented as a modern Anglican equivalent of the ancient church fathers, prefixed to a posthumous edition of Jewel's *Works* in 1609.

During the course of this century a large number of prefatory lives were attached to collections of sermons and other religious writings in England. They included as well as many short biographies some very substantial ones: for example, an anonymous life prefixed to the *Works* of Joseph Mead (or Mede) in 1664 extends to seventy-six closely printed folio pages. Many of the most important religious biographies published during the century appeared in this form, among others John Fell's life of Richard Allestree, prefixed to Allestree's *Forty Sermons* (1684), as well as most of Izaak Walton's lives.

The practice of publishing prefatory lives of notable religious figures had already become so well established in England before the middle of the seventeenth century that Walton in 1640 was moved to write the first of his biographies, that of Donne, by the thought that it would be a pity if Donne's collected sermons appeared without such a life, after Sir Henry Wotton, who had planned to provide one, died.[20] Four out of five of Walton's biographies were first published as prefatory lives. The growing importance of the prefatory life is indicated by the fact that, while the life of Donne occupied only seventeen pages of the massive folio of the *LXXX Sermons* in 1640, the last of Walton's lives, that of Robert Sanderson, was almost as long as the tracts to which it was prefixed in 1678 and was given the priority on the title-page: *The Life of Dr. Sanderson, Late Bishop of Lincoln. Written by Izaak Walton. To which is added some short Tracts or Cases of Conscience, written by the said Bishop.*

While most of the early prefatory lives in England were of religious figures, there was a gradual expansion into secular areas. This movement began even before the end of the sixteenth century, with Thomas Speght's life prefaced to his edition of Chaucer's *Workes* in 1598, and it gained momentum in the middle and later part of the seventeenth century. Prefatory lives appeared of figures in a wide range of secular fields. Some of these lives of philosophers, scientists, and antiquaries, including William Rawley's life of Francis Bacon (1657), Abraham Hill's life of Isaac Barrow (1683), and White Kennett's life of William Somner (1693), will be considered in chapter 6. There were notable examples too of prefatory lives attached to political and economic treatises, such as John Toland's life of James Harrington (1700). Lives of eminent lawyers, including Sir Thomas Littleton in 1628 and Sir John Vaughan in 1677, were prefaced to legal treatises and law reports. Lives were even prefaced to library catalogues and cookbooks. Thomas Smith's Latin life of Sir Robert Cotton was attached to a catalogue of Cotton's library in 1696, and W.W.'s brief life of Robert May was prefaced to May's culinary work, *The Accomplisht Cook*, in 1660.[21]

A field in which the prefatory life gradually acquired special importance during the course of the seventeenth century is literary biography. Speght's life of Chaucer in 1598 was not followed for some time by the biographies of more contemporary poets. We might know much more than we do about Shakespeare's life if by the time of the publication of the first folio in 1623 the practice had become established of honouring modern poets and dramatists with prefatory lives as well as with such commendatory verses as Ben Jonson's. Walton's life of Donne prefaced to the *Sermons* in 1640 was naturally designed to commemorate the preacher rather than the poet, but by the middle of the century prefatory lives of poets who had recently died began to appear, for example Ursula Quarles's brief account of Francis Quarles in 1645 and John Davies of Kidwelly's fine and detailed life of John Hall of Durham prefixed to Hall's *Hierocles* in 1657. Examples later in the century include brief prefatory lives of the Earl of Rochester, Aphra Behn, and John

Cleveland, as well as much more substantial biographies of Abraham Cowley and John Milton.[22] The most important of these prefatory biographies of literary figures, Davies' life of Hall, Thomas Sprat's life of Cowley, and the lives of Milton by Edward Phillips and John Toland, will be considered in chapter 7.

As well as the important early biographies of Milton in the format of the prefatory life, there are two lives of the poet, by John Aubrey and Anthony Wood, that belong to that other widely practised seventeenth-century biographical form commonly known as the brief life. The brief life has in a sense existed as long as any kind of biographical writing has been known, but it became established as specially characteristic of this period in England. It found its historical moment in a period which had reacted against the copious Ciceronian and Spenserian styles of the previous century and developed a series of highly concentrated forms, ranging from the lyrics of Donne and Jonson to the essays of Bacon. Attempting at its best to extract the essential and discard the inessential, it includes biographies like Wood's notable for their scholarship, biographies like Fuller's notable for their style, and biographies like Aubrey's notable for powers of observation and understanding. It is particularly important as marking a great expansion of life-writing into new areas, extending coverage to a wide range of classes and types of persons beyond those that had been traditional in biography.

Fuller's *History of the Worthies of England* (1662) is distinguished not only by its witty style but by its large scope. It incorporates brief biographies of notable persons of the whole of England and Wales arranged by county, and is radical in its social inclusiveness. Fuller reaches far beyond such conventional categories as princes and prelates: he brings in not only courtiers but a court porter, alchemists, theatre people, and many other classes of persons who had previously been ignored by biographers, even a blacksmith. While Wood's *Athenæ Oxonienses* (1691–2) is specially valuable for the factual information it provides about its subjects, such as dates of events and lists of writings, it is remarkable too for its wide range. Wood's primary subject was the prelates and writers of Oxford University, but he found means to bring in many Cambridge figures and others who had attended neither university, and he not only interpreted the category of writer very broadly but employed various strategies to include many who had written nothing at all. He constantly pushed his work in the direction of comprehensive national biography.[23]

Wood furthermore encouraged his friend Aubrey to produce the biographical writings now known as the *Brief Lives*, which remained in manuscript largely unprinted until the nineteenth century. As well as being more original, perceptive, and distinguished in their literary qualities than Wood's own work, these lives further extended the range of biographical coverage. As will be seen in the discussion of the *Brief Lives* in chapter 9, Aubrey brought to the writing of biography the wide interests of a Restoration virtuoso, a special concern with figures like William Harvey and Thomas Hobbes who belonged to the new world of mathematics, science, invention, and radical thought, and an endless fascination with all the varieties of human individuality.

As the work of Fuller, Wood, and Aubrey illustrates, an important development in the later seventeenth century is the production of collections of biographies, various models of biographical dictionaries, and anthologies of lives. There are a few slight earlier English precedents, such as the compilations of John Leland and John Bale in the mid-sixteenth century and of John Pits at the opening of the seventeenth century, concerned primarily with the lives and works of medieval authors,[24] but it was not until the later seventeenth century that a large number of biographical collections appeared, including substantial and important ones. Some were essentially the work of a single heroic author, as in the cases of Fuller, Wood, and Aubrey, while others were gatherings of biographies by various authors. They were formed and organized on a wide variety of principles.

As one might expect in an era of acute conflicts and controversies, some of the collections were formed primarily in terms of religious and political affiliations. David Lloyd's *Memoires* (1668) provides biographies of Anglican and Royalist loyalists of the Civil War and related conflicts.[25] It is enormous in scale, a thick folio volume, which claims to include over a thousand lives. Lloyd was a compiler more than a scholar, and he was charged by Wood and others with plagiarism; his work, gathered from a great many sources, displays frequent marks of haste and carelessness but contains valuable material not obtainable elsewhere, on literary as well as political figures. Lloyd was a special admirer of George Herbert, whose verse he frequently quotes, and he included in the *Memoires* accounts of numerous poets and other writers. Thus it is as loyalists to the Royal cause that many seventeenth-century poets were given their first biographical treatment. His lives of such figures as Robert Burton, Sir John Suckling, William Cartwright, John Cleveland, Abraham Cowley, and Richard Crashaw would probably be better known than they are if the *Memoires* had been less chaotic in its organization and better indexed.

On a smaller scale, Clement Barksdale's *Memorials of Worthy Persons* (1661, 1662, 1663) is another primarily Anglican work, subtitled in the 1663 version *Lights and Ornaments of the Church of England*, but it includes a few lives of Roman Catholics and persons of the 'Genevan' persuasion. Lives of nonconformists were of course less publishable during much of the Restoration period than lives of Anglicans, but Samuel Clarke's large and important collections of biographies by various authors primarily of Puritan figures, which began to appear in the 1650s, culminated in *The Lives of Sundry Eminent Persons in this Later Age* (1683). In the freer time of the 1690s and early in the next century, Edmund Calamy published his accounts of dissenting clergy who were silenced and persecuted during the Restoration regime, which can be seen as a Puritan counterpart of works like Lloyd's *Memoires*.

Other biographical collections were formed and organized in terms of place or institution or profession. While Fuller in his *Worthies* attempted to provide biographical coverage for all the counties of England and Wales, John Prince confined himself to a single county in *The Worthies of Devon* (1701), and Richard Gough limited himself to a single parish in the biographical sketches of his *Antiquities and Memoirs of the Parish of Myddle*, written mainly in 1700–1. Wood's *Athenæ Oxonienses* is the largest and most notable of collections centred on an institution. The collections based on profession or vocation include a series of biographical dictionaries of writers: Edward Phillips's *Theatrum Poetarum* (1675), William Winstanley's *The Lives of the Most Famous English Poets* (1687), and Gerard Langbaine's *English Dramatic Poets* (1691), although these are rather slight productions and the last is really more a bibliographical than a biographical work. There were even collections that combined profession and place, such as Thomas Guidott's *A Discourse of Bathe ... With an Account of the Lives and Character of the Physicians of Bathe* (1676).

The appearance of biographical collections and compilations in large numbers in the later part of the century reveals the extent of the cumulative development of life-writing during the period. Large works of collected biography like Wood's could not have been formed if many lives had not previously appeared as funeral sermons or prefaces or in other forms. Wood in fact relied mainly on written sources, to a large extent on sources already in print. Thus such collections demonstrate the maturing of biographical writing during the century, even as they point the way to further developments in the eighteenth and nineteenth centuries that culminate during the 1880s and 1890s in the great *Dictionary of National Biography*.

IV

The biographical collections of the later seventeenth century provide impressive evidence how far biography moved in the course of this century beyond the traditional areas of the saint's life and the life of the great public figure to provide accounts of persons of many classes and occupations. By modern standards, of course, there inevitably remain large gaps and neglected areas. Biographical coverage is strongly affected by the class and gender biases general in the period. Persons in upper and middle classes are much more fully represented than those of lower classes, and males much more fully than females.

The gender imbalance is typified by Roger North, who at the end of the century wrote full lives of three of his brothers but rarely mentioned his four sisters in his biographical writings, although he provided a little intriguing information about one of them, Mary, Lady Spring, who 'had a superior wit, prodigious memory, and was most agreeable in conversation,' and who 'instituted a sort of order of the wits of her time and acquaintance' before dying at an early age following the birth of a child.[26] Earlier in the century Thomas Heywood attempted to remedy the imbalance with volumes of the lives of women in 1624 and 1640, one of which was reprinted in 1657 with the title *The General History of Women*, but these are slight and superficial works mainly concerned with mythological figures.[27] Edward Phillips relegated his brief accounts of women who were poets to a supplementary section of his *Theatrum Poetarum* in 1675.

More noteworthy are some of the exemplary biographies of pious and saintly women. For these the biographers were able to cite not only biblical precedents but numerous patristic models acceptable to Protestants, including writings by Augustine on his mother Monica, by Gregory of Nazianzus on his sister Gorgonia, and by Jerome on Marcella, Paula, and Fabiola. Philip Stubbes's life of his wife, *A Christal Glasse for Christian Women. Contayning An Excellent Discourse, of the Godly Life and Christian Death of Mistresse Katherine Stubbes*, first published in 1591, proved popular enough to go through a series of editions in the earlier seventeenth century and was still being reprinted as late as 1646. A particularly fine later biography of the same type is Richard Baxter's admirable and moving account of his wife, *A Breviate of the Life of Margaret, the Daughter of Francis Charlton ... and Wife of Richard Baxter* (1681). Samuel Clarke's *Lives of Sundry Eminent Persons in this Later Age* (1683) includes a section titled 'The Lives of Several Ladies and Gentlewomen in this

Later Age,' which contains some valuable biographies by various authors of women commemorated as religious figures.

One of the biographical types of the lives of women which would repay further examination is that generally neglected form, the funeral sermon. Many funeral sermons on women which include significant biographical elements were published. A number of them provide eloquent representations of the beauty of holiness that deserve to rank with Jeremy Taylor's famous eulogy for Lady Carbery, for example Thomas Ken's sermon in 1682 on the death of Margaret, Lady Maynard, who lived for years at the court of Charles II, where her husband held an official position, and yet remained unspotted of the world, exemplary both for her religious devotion and her serenity of spirit.[28] But more than this, many of the sermons give historically and socially interesting details, not only about religious practices and about domestic life, but about the broader roles and cultural activities of their subjects.

Sermons about women of the upper classes often provide information about the ways in which they carried out the traditional roles of the lady of the manor in providing hospitality for country neighbours and dependants, and in administering various forms of welfare to the inhabitants of family estates and adjacent villages. At a time when many of the gentry were being seduced away from their responsibilities in the rural world, John Dobson in 1670 commends Mary, Lady Farmor, for upholding the old tradition of 'great housekeeping' at her country estate: although she was a native of London, 'yet she would not sneak thither to avoid the charge of *house-keeping*,' and the great hall of her country house remained hospitably open rather than being divided in the new manner into private rooms. The preachers praise their subjects for dispensing medicines as well as hospitality. William Fuller in 1628 states that Lady Frances Clifton's house was 'an Apothecaries shop open to all commers, without money, or exchange,' and later in the century Ken tells us that Lady Maynard was 'a common Physician to her sick Neighbours, and would often with her own hands, dress their most loathsome soars.'[29]

The funeral sermons are of course inevitably shaped by male perspectives and generally by quite traditional viewpoints, but they serve to reveal a number of women of remarkable character and accomplishments among both the aristocracy and the middle classes. The sermons on aristocratic ladies include Edward Rainbowe's on Susanna Howard, Countess of Suffolk (1649), which gives an extensive and exceptionally interesting account of her knowledge and critical appreciation of poetry, especially that of George Herbert, and Rainbowe's sermon on

Anne Clifford, Countess of Dorset, Pembroke, and Montgomery (1677), which describes such aspects of her life as her great building projects for castles, country houses, almshouses, and churches, and refers to her friendship with John Donne.[30] Among the sermons on middle-class women is John Prude's on the 'Learned and Ingenious' Mrs Ann Bayard (1697), which praises not only her piety and charity but also her knowledge of languages, her mastery of Greek, and the beauty not only of her countenance but also of her Latin compositions.[31] It provides an impressive account of her precocious learning and ability in philosophy, informing us that when young she had already attained the knowledge of a bearded philosopher and that she was a skilled disputant.

Biographical coverage of professions and vocations during the period is extensive in range but quite uneven. Apart from prominent public figures, clergy and scholars are best represented. There are many distinguished lives of intellectual figures, including such secular examples as Thomas Stanley's fine biographies of great classical thinkers in his *History of Philosophy*, Rawley's life of Bacon, Toland's life of Harrington, and Aubrey's life of Hobbes, the fullest and most ambitious of his *Brief Lives*. On the other hand, as Fuller pointed out in his *Worthies*, relatively few adequate lives were written of lawyers and judges. As late as 1747 the compilers of *Biographica Britannica* complained that few lives existed of physicians. There are few seventeenth-century biographies of merchants that deal with their business careers, although many funeral sermons testify to their piety and list their charitable benefactions. Yet even in these neglected areas some notable works were produced by the end of the century. Aubrey's life of the great physician William Harvey is one of the finest of his *Brief Lives*. Roger North, who criticized the lack of legal knowledge apparent in Gilbert Burnet's life of Sir Matthew Hale, provided a full account of the legal career of his brother Francis, Lord Guilford, the Lord Keeper, and did his best to describe and analyse the mercantile career of a second brother, Sir Dudley North.[32]

Writers are better represented in the biographical literature than other categories of artists, partly because of the practice of publishing prefatory lives and because of the appearance of such works as Wood's *Athenæ Oxonienses*. Wood took special pains to collect biographical information about musicians as well as writers, but painters remained quite neglected by biographers until the end of the century.[33] Richard Graham deplored this neglect, declaring he was 'asham'd to acknowledge how difficult a matter' he had found it to uncover even 'the least Information' about English painters; and, following such Continental precedents as Giorgio Vasari's *Lives of the Artists*, he made the first move to fill this gap in his 'A Short Account of the most Eminent Painters Both Ancient and Modern,' appended to John Dryden's translation of C.A. Du Fresnoy's *De Arte Graphica* in 1695.[34] Many types of scientists and mathematicians also remained relatively neglected, as they have been even in much later times, but Aubrey, with his special interest in 'ingeniose' innovators, did pioneering work in these areas.

Although biographical coverage was biased and uneven in terms of class, gender, and profession, there were a number of tendencies that caused seventeenth-century life-writers to give increasing attention to those of relatively humble and obscure status. While the Protestant emphasis on the equality of all believers and view of sainthood as embracing all the saved justified the extension of religious biography far beyond traditional areas, on the secular side the desire of antiquaries like Wood for completeness in coverage of their fields led to the inclusion of great numbers of obscure figures in such a work as *Athenæ Oxonienses*. John Prince in his *Worthies of Devon* defended himself for having included 'mean and obscure Persons, memorable for little else but the Scribbling of a Book, or so' by the precedent of Wood.[35]

Most significant perhaps is the fact that brief biographers such as Fuller and Aubrey included many relatively obscure figures as a result primarily or simply because of their interest in the variety of human characters and accomplishments. That such interest was widespread is shown by the publication of many journalistic biographies as pamphlets from at least the 1630s onward, not only sensational lives of criminals but accounts of otherwise obscure persons notable merely for the display of some striking individuality or eccentricity. These are often slight productions but sometimes substantial. Examples from the 1630s include two works by one of the most popular journalistic writers of the period, John Taylor, the Water Poet: *The Great Eater of Kent* (1630), about a figure whose sole claim to fame was, as the title suggests, his enormous appetite and capacity for eating, and *The Olde, Old, Very Olde Man: Or, the Age and Long Life of Thomas Par* (two editions in 1635), a digressive but lively account in verse incorporating considerable biographical information about a man famous for longevity, reputed to have reached the age of a hundred and fifty-two. The single and singular claim to fame of another figure of the period is advertised in the title of a pamphlet by Thomas Heywood published in two editions in 1637: *The Phoenix of these late times: Or the life of Mr. Henry Welby, Esq; who lived at his house in Grubstreet forty-foure yeares, and in that space was never seene by any*.[36]

The ultimate example of seventeenth-century lives of the obscure is provided at the end of the century by Richard Gough's *Antiquities and Memoirs of the Parish of Myddle*.[37] Gough gives accounts of the inhabitants of a Shropshire parish, from the reign of Elizabeth onward, organized according to the seating plan of the parish church. These are only short character sketches with a little biographical information, but they display an unprecedented degree of inclusiveness, reaching down to the lowest social levels.

At the upper levels the social range of *Myddle* includes Daniel 'Wicherley' (i.e., Wycherley), steward to the Marquis of Winchester, described as a shrewd, probably unscrupulous man, who has risen to the position of squire and who has a son, William, 'excellently skilled in dramatic poetry,' and also prosperous tenant farmers, one of whom is depicted as a cheerful hospitable figure reminiscent of Chaucer's Franklin. At the opposite, particularly interesting, lower extreme, those Gough describes at the bottom of the social and economic scale include farm labourers ruined by drink and improvident ways, persons who are 'night walkers' and thieves, a man with a wooden leg who brought down a woman from London he says is his wife, by whom he has three children, and who 'lives in the cave in Haremeare Hill' and has maintenance out of the parish, and David Higley, upon whom Gough comments: 'What hee gott with hard labor hee spent idely in the Alehouse. A rude person and fitt company for Bearewards and such like persons.' Rudimentary though these lives and characters are, they represent a radical advance in biographical coverage. The principle of inclusiveness could scarcely be carried further.[38]

CHAPTER 2

Lives of the Protestant Saints

I

The foundation for Protestant religious biography, the most widely practised of all forms of life-writing in seventeenth-century England, was firmly laid in the previous century by John Foxe. In the constantly expanding editions of his enormously popular *Actes and Monuments* or 'Book of Martyrs,' published between 1563 and 1583, Foxe provided Protestant England with its own vivid and memorable martyrology: accounts of the lives and especially the deaths of Cranmer, Latimer, Ridley, and the other Anglican martyrs of the reign of Mary. He sought to show that the Church of England in his own time had produced martyrs comparable with the authentic martyrs of the early Christian era: he declared, 'if Martyrs are to be compared with Martyrs, I see no cause why the Martyrs of our time deserve not as great commendation as the other in the primitive church, which assuredly are inferiour to them in no point of praise.'[1]

With this declaration Foxe initiated a program for providing Protestant adaptations or replacements of the ancient form, the saint's life. The most popular type of medieval biography, the saint's life culminated in such great collections as the *Legenda Aurea*, translated and published by Caxton in England in 1483 as *The Golden Legend*. But in the sixteenth century the cult of the saints came under attack by such humanist reformers as Erasmus, and it was decisively repudiated as idolatry by the Protestant reformers. In England official homilies issued during the reigns of Edward VI and Elizabeth attacked the veneration of saints, most of the saints' days were eliminated from the calendar in the Prayer Book of Edward VI, and images of saints were removed from churches. In the new circumstances, Protestant religious biography in later sixteenth-century and seventeenth-century England developed partly from the older traditions of the saint's life and partly in reaction against them.

The highly sceptical Protestant attitude toward medieval hagiography was plainly set out by the Anglican bishop, historian, and biographer Gilbert Burnet, in the later seventeenth century. Burnet commented in the preface to his life of Sir Matthew Hale (1682) that for many ages no lives were written but by monks, 'through whose writings there runs such an incurable humour, of telling incredible and inimitable passages, that little in them can be believed or proposed as a pattern.' He considered that, as a result of rivalry between Benedictines, Dominicans, Franciscans, and others in making claims for founders and other saints of their orders, the hagiographers carried 'that art of making Romances, instead of writing Lives, to that pitch, that the World became generally much scandalized with them.' He referred unfavourably to the work of the Jesuits of Antwerp currently engaged in publishing 'a vast and voluminous Collection of all those Lives,' which he regarded as neither believable nor imitable, and therefore without exemplary value.[2]

As the great pioneer of Protestant religious biography, John Foxe intended his work to replace hagiographical collections like *The Golden Legend*, and he was concerned to distinguish it from superstitious and idolatrous compilations of the kind Burnet condemned. He considered himself the modern counterpart not of the medieval hagiographers but of the more authentic Christian historians and biographers of the primitive era. He saw himself as a modern Eusebius, writing of later-day martyrs as Eusebius had written of the early martyrs in his *Ecclesiastical History*. He not only provided a martyrology but set out a Protestant version of history. He held that the church had become corrupted about the year 1000, and he looked for his doctrines and models to the first thousand years of the Christian era, particularly the period to about 440.

Although Foxe provided accounts of martyrdom rather than full lives, he was the first notable English writer to face many of the problems of Protestant religious biography. Certain special features of Protestant biography emerge clearly in his 'Book of Martyrs.' As his work demonstrates, for the Protestant biographer the category of the saint was not so clearly defined or limited as for the medieval hagiographer, since there was no institutional recognition to correspond with Roman Catholic canonization. The very essence of the medieval saint's life was the miracle, but Foxe rejects claims of medieval and later-day miracles as false and superstitious, although he admits prophecy, prophetic dreams, and portents, and sometimes gives them special prominence.

The conspicuous place Foxe gives to dreams and prophecies illustrates the part played by the 'Book of Martyrs' in establishing conventions that run through Protestant biography in the late sixteenth and seventeenth century. Foxe showed that, like his prototype Eusebius, he took seriously the fulfilment of prophetic dreams and visions, in his accounts of such figures as William Hunter, Robert Samuel, and Cuthbert Simpson, and his example influenced later biographers. Thus Daniel Featley in his life of John Jewel (1609) refers to Foxe for precedents when he credits his subject with special powers of divination.[3] Continuing this tradition, other seventeenth-century biographers attribute prophetic powers to the most diverse religious figures: Archbishop Laud, George Herbert, Nicholas Ferrar, and James Ussher, among many others. Whole collections of prophecies ascribed to Ussher were published in the later seventeenth century, for example, *Strange and Remarkable Prophecies* (1678). In Protestant biography the practice of establishing the saintliness of the subjects not only by showing the exemplary holiness of their lives but also by attributing prophetic power as a mark of special divine favour became so firmly established that Walton, who had omitted this element in earlier versions, felt impelled to add a prophetic dream to a late edition of his life of Donne.

Following the same pattern as Foxe, the later Protestant biographers of the sixteenth and seventeenth centuries turned away from the hagiographical traditions of the medieval period when they considered the Roman Catholic Church to have become corrupted by superstition and idolatry. As models for their biographies they commonly cited both biblical examples and patristic works of the early centuries of Christianity. They naturally viewed Scripture as providing the ultimate exemplar and authority, for they held that, as an anonymous biographer of Thomas Wadsworth declared in 1680: 'the Historical parts of the Scriptures are little other than Annals and Descriptions of the Lives of the Patriarchs, Judges, Kings, Prophets, &c.' Henry Newcome in his life of John Machin in 1671 is typical in his citation of biblical precedents for the writing of Christian biography: 'God himself eminently commends to us this way of improving the World, by proposing the best Patterns, since so considerable a Part of the Bible, is a Sacred Register of Holy Mens Lives, and one whole Book, that of the Acts of the Apostles, seems chiefly designed, to conveigh to us the History of St. Pauls life after his Conversion.' As well as such biblical exemplars, the Protestant biographers frequently cited such patristic models as the funeral orations of Gregory of Nazianzus and Gregory of Nyssa and Possidius's life of St Augustine.[4]

By the late sixteenth and early seventeenth century, in addition to Foxe's work, a number of other modern biographies of Continental and English reformers also became available as models. Edward Bagshaw in his life of Robert Bolton in 1635 provides a typical list of the range of models favoured by Protestant English biographers of the earlier seventeenth century. He declares: 'It hath beene the pious custome of ancient and later times, to commend to posterity the eminent graces of the Saints departed. Famous are those Panegyricke Orations made at the Tombes of the Martyrs in the Primitive times.'

> Memorable also are the Funerall Orations of the two *Gregories*, *Nyssen* and *Nazianzen* on *Basill* the great: And in later times, to give a few instances, (for the number in this kinde is infinite) *Melancthon* and *Camerarius* wrote the life of *Martin Luther*; *Junius* the life of *Ursine*; *Beza* the life of *Calvin*; *Antonius Faius* the life of *Beza*; *Josias Simler* the life of *Peter Martyr*; and D[r]. *Humphrey* the life of our most renowned *Jewell*.
>
> This manner of honouring the Saints is warranted by GODS owne example; who (for ought is revealed to us) took order for *Moses* buriall, digged his grave, covered him with molds, and made for him that excellent Funerall Sermon expressed in the first Chapter of *Joshuah*.[5]

Among the biographies of Continental reformers Baghshaw cites, Théodore de Bèze's life of Calvin was published in an English translation in 1564. He mentions only one English precedent, Laurence Humphrey's Latin life of John Jewel, published in 1573, but other English models for the Protestant religious biographer appeared in increasing numbers from the early years of the seventeenth century.[6]

While such pioneering works as Foxe's 'Book of Martyrs' and Humphrey's life of Jewel provided important sixteenth-century precedents, it was not until the seventeenth century that the great expansion of Protestant English biography took place. Apart from the lives of the Marian martyrs and other early Reformation figures, there was a necessary time lag, since biographies were not normally written until after the deaths of the subjects. In the early years of the seventeenth century a much broader field opened. The figures who had led the Church of England during the reign of Elizabeth gradually became eligible for biographical treatment, and the number of subjects increased rapidly from year to year. Stimulated by the continuous religious debates and conflicts of the period, the increase in the writing of Protestant religious lives was so great that if one judges by numbers this became the dominant form of biography in seventeenth-century England.

II

When the Puritan sects grew in strength and gained power many nonconformist lives were written, but Anglican biography emerged first and had the most steadily sustained development through the seventeenth century. The Anglican biographers had the support of the official establishment, including the universities, except during the period of Puritan rule in the 1640s and 1650s, and they had much more continuous access to the press than nonconformists. Most Anglican biographies were written by clergymen and academics with some degree of official support, and even the biographies written by laymen were often prompted by the ecclesiastical establishment. Daniel Featley, the clergyman who was one of the great pioneer figures of seventeenth-century Anglican biography, wrote his life of Jewel (1609) with the encouragement of Archbishop Bancroft and Dean (later Bishop) Morton as part of an official plan for the defence of Anglicanism in the battle with Roman Catholicism. His work was given special status, for it was published as a preface to an edition of Jewel that was ordered placed in all parish churches, just as Foxe's 'Book of Martyrs' had earlier been placed in many churches. Later in the century the Anglican layman Izaak Walton likewise wrote his lives of Hooker and other divines partly at the prompting of his friend Bishop Morley, in order to defend the Church of England against Puritan attack.

As the cases of Featley and Walton illustrate, during the course of the seventeenth century Anglican biography moved through a series of distinct phases, conditioned by the changing historical circumstances of the church. While Anglican biographers commonly professed the aim of defending the *via media* of the Church of England against the false extremes of Roman Catholicism and Puritanism, Featley is characteristic of the phase in the later sixteenth and earlier seventeenth century when the main thrust was defence against the Roman Catholic threat. Walton is typical in the same way of the later phase after the Puritan sects acquired power and the emphasis shifted to defence of the Church of England against the Puritans. Anglican biography was constantly shaped by such political and polemical purposes.

In many of its successive phases of development, Anglican biography recapitulates to a striking degree the development of religious biography in the early centuries of the Christian era, the period to which the writers frequently turned for their models. As Christian biography begins with the celebration of the early martyrs and confessors, so Anglican biography begins with the celebration of Anglican martyrs in response to the Roman Catholic persecution of the reign of Mary. This phase was so effectively handled by Foxe that there was little need for later Anglican biographers to return to it. In the mid-seventeenth century Foxe's status became somewhat controversial, as the Laudian party tended to view him as Puritanical. Thomas Fuller, who had been brought up to admire the martyrs celebrated by Foxe, comments wryly in his *Holy State* (1642) that he has seen the ashes of martyrs rise and fall in the market place.[7] But in the earlier period, when the Church of Rome was viewed as the chief threat to the Church of England, Foxe was generally seen as speaking with the voice of the Church of England, and his work had the status of the definite record and celebration of the Anglican martyrs, as its placing in parish churches demonstrates.

From the celebration of martyrs and confessors early Christian biography moved to a series of related types: apostles and missionary priests, doctrinal fathers and combatters of heresies, and institutional leaders, and a corresponding movement took place in Anglican biography. This second phase began in the sixteenth century with Laurence Humphrey's life of John Jewel (1573), commemorating the first great doctrinal father of the Church of England, but the main development occurred in the early years of the seventeenth century. Daniel Featley then led the way with his English life of Jewel, prefaced to Jewel's *Works* in 1609, which was based on Humphrey's Latin life but was a skilful reshaping, designed to correct what Featley and others regarded as Humphrey's excessively Calvinistic bias. In form and style it is so superior to Humphrey that it qualifies as an original work.[8]

In 1612 a second great pioneering work of seventeenth-century Anglican biography appeared: Sir George Paule's life of Archbishop Whitgift, the Elizabethan administrative leader of the Church of England.[9] Paule, who had been Whitgift's secretary, had an excellent knowledge of his subject, and he produced an admirable political biography, emphasizing Whitgift's combination of firmness and moderation in his handling of those opponents intent on carrying the religious reformation to further lengths than the archbishop and queen desired. The appearance of Paule's life of Whitgift in close succession to Featley's life of Jewel did much to complete the foundations of seventeenth-century Anglican biography, and both works became influential.

To the biographies of martyrs, doctrinal fathers, and administrative leaders, lives were soon added of missionary priests, those who struggled heroically in the face of real danger to bring truth as defined by the Church of England to every corner of the land. The most distinguished early work in this category is George Carleton's life of Bernard Gilpin, published in Latin in 1628 and in an English translation in 1629. This is the stirringly written account of a man who devoted his life to missionary work in a wild and barbaric region of the Bishopric of Durham, combatting both paganism and the Roman Catholicism that continued to have a strong hold in the north of England. In addition to this biographical type, numerous lives appeared of those who fought the religious battles on a more intellectual level, the controversialists and combatters of heresies, who might be seen as modern equivalents of such a figure as St Augustine. Featley's life of Jewel belongs partly in this category, and his equally fine later life of John Reynolds (or Rainolds) is primarily concerned with the career of a controversialist dedicated to the defence of the Church of England against false Roman Catholic doctrine.[10]

In earlier Christian biography once Christianity had become firmly established much of the emphasis shifted to the combatting of corruption and worldliness. A similar emphasis developed in the Anglican biography of the mid-seventeenth century under the special stimulus of Puritan attacks on the worldliness of the established Church of England, which included Milton's tremendous indictment in *Lycidas* of 'such as for their bellies sake / Creep and intrude, and climb into the fold!' To counter Puritan attacks on the episcopacy, Anglican biographers provided lives of ideal bishops, emphasizing their asceticism and unworldliness. One of the pioneering biographies of this type is John Harris's life of Arthur Lake, a Bishop of Bath and Wells notable for both sanctity and austerity, published in 1629. Similar biographies continued to appear after the overthrow of the episcopacy, as part of the defence of the Church of England during its period of affliction. Henry Isaacson in his life of Bishop Lancelot Andrewes published in 1650 places special emphasis on Andrewes's asceticism and disregard for worldly wealth, in combination with his exceptional learning, and Izaak Walton places similar emphasis in his biographies of the holders of high Anglican office, Donne and Sanderson.[11]

As well as in lives of bishops, the Anglican defence against Puritan attack was conducted in biographies of ideal parish priests. As was natural in an England that was still largely rural, special prominence was given to the ideal country clergyman. Barnabas Oley provided a short but influential example in his life of George Herbert prefixed to *The Country Parson* in Herbert's posthumously published *Remains* in 1652. Walton carried this type into the Restoration and produced its masterpiece in his life of Herbert published in 1670. It is to be noted, however, that such biographies of ideal priests and bishops written in defence of the Church of England sometimes proved double-edged instruments, since it was difficult to write these lives without implying that the truly exemplary figures were exceptional rather than typical.[12]

Another clearly identifiable type, which may be termed the man of peace, becomes prominent in Anglican biography in the mid and later seventeenth century. It is at the opposite pole to the earlier type of the fierce controversialist. It emerges partly as a result of the sense that the bitter controversies of the earlier part of the century had led to the catastrophe of the Civil War, and it is associated with a reaction against controversy in favour of practical divinity, charity, and compromise, fostered specially by moderate Anglicans intent on reasserting the concept of a comprehensive Church of England with latitude for much divergence of view. A fine example of biography in this category is Edmund Vaughan's life of Thomas Jackson published in 1653. Vaughan demonstrates Jackson's love of peace, moderation, and charity, as manifested in his writings, where he shunned controversy, in the government of his college, where he established remarkable harmony as President of Corpus Christi, Oxford, and in public affairs, where he lamented growing divisions, prayed for peace, and could not be comforted on the outbreak of the Civil War. Similar themes are prominent in the biographies of Walton, who praises Jackson in his life of Hooker, and in an anonymous life of that notable moderate Thomas Fuller published in 1661.[13]

While this type of Anglican biography continued to appear in the Restoration, another type in partial contrast to it then came to the forefront: the life that celebrated the heroes of the Church of England in its period of affliction during the Puritan ascendancy. Among the most distinguished examples are John Fell's lives of Henry Hammond (1661) and Richard Allestree (1684).[14] These are biographies of men notable not only for sanctity and learning but also for loyalty. Hammond suffered ejection from his clerical charge and academic posts at the hands of the Puritans, but continued to exercise his ministry and work for the Royal and Anglican cause. Allestree, who was a student at Oxford when the Civil War broke out, joined the Royal army, and after being ordained as an Anglican priest engaged in important secret work for his cause during the Cromwellian period. Walton's life of Robert Sanderson (1678) can be placed in the same category, and many less notable biographies appeared of loyal Anglican clergy who suffered ejection by the Puritans, such as Peter Barwick's life of his brother, John Barwick, as well as voluminous compilations on the suffering of these clergy by David Lloyd and others.[15] These lives can be seen as a partial revival of the earliest Anglican type, the celebration of martyrs for the faith. There were in truth fewer claimants to the full status of martyrdom in the later period than in the earlier one, but that made the writing of lives of those Anglicans who displayed heroism in their resistance to the Puritan powers all the more necessary.

Another type of biography that came into special prominence in Anglican circles in the later seventeenth century is that of the lay figure notable either for saintly life or for the repentance and reformation of sin. This type developed particularly after the Restoration in the attempt to counter the growing scepticism and licentiousness of the era. Fell expressed an awareness that while in 1660 Hammond's church was restored his ideals were not.[16] Many Anglican biographers recognized that lay figures were more effective than clerical as subjects for lives written to defend church and religion against their new enemies. Notable examples are Gilbert Burnet's biographical accounts of the Earl of Rochester (1680) and Sir Matthew Hale (1682), the one describing the deathbed repentance of a brilliant and notorious aristocratic rake and sceptic, and the other giving the life of a judge eminent for learning and probity, piety and asceticism. Burnet's funeral sermon for Robert Boyle in 1692 has as its subject the man of advanced learning in the new sciences who remained strong in religious faith, one whose 'peculiar and favourite Study' was 'Chymistry' and whose life and character furnished a lesson to 'the whole Tribe of *Libertines*.' John Evelyn, who summarized and commented approvingly on this sermon in his diary, wrote for private circulation a life of Mrs Godolphin, a maid of honour at the court of Charles II, which gave a picture of saintliness in a corrupt environment. Anthony Walker developed a similar theme of piety in a licentious age in the funeral sermon he expanded into a biography of Robert Boyle's sister, Mary Rich, Countess of Warwick.[17]

In Puritan biography as distinct from Anglican a number of historical phases can also be traced, but the development began later and was less continuous. Puritan biography separated only gradually from the Anglican during the earlier seventeenth century, and it was handicapped by restrictions on publication. Biographies of Puritan nonconformists who suffered Anglican persecution could not be published free of censorship before 1640 or for much of the period after 1660. The fragmented nature of seventeenth-century Puritanism, comprising extremely varied groups ranging from Presbyterians and Independents to Quakers and Socinians, and the absence of institutional resources equivalent to those of the Church of England provided further difficulties and limitations. But the great efforts made to collect and publish Puritan biographies by one man, Samuel Clarke, partly compensate for such disadvantages, since between the 1650s and 1680s he gathered together and brought out in a series of collected volumes a large number of these lives by many authors from many sources.[18]

Among the Puritan biographies are to be found versions of many of the same types as appear among the Anglican biographies, although one leading Anglican type is naturally lacking: there are no lives of ideal bishops by anti-episcopal Puritans. The closest equivalents are biographies of Puritan ecclesiastical statesmen, such as Thomas Ball's life of John Preston, published by Clarke. But there are many lives of exemplary clergy, including Puritan versions of the ideal country parson, such as John Carter's biography of his father of the same name published in 1653, that may be set beside Anglican examples like Oley's and Walton's lives of George Herbert. There are Puritan lives of controversialists, for example John Lightfoot's biography of Hugh Broughton published in 1662, comparable with Featley's life of Reynolds, and Puritan lives of missionary priests, for example Stanly Gower's life of Richard Rothwell, another of those published by Clarke, comparable with Carleton's life of Gilpin. And there are notable Puritan as well as Anglican lives of lay figures, for example Richard Baxter's biography of his wife, Margaret Baxter.[19]

The most striking and characteristic difference between Puritan and Anglican biographies is the greater prominence given in the Puritan lives to inner religious experience and conversion than is common in Anglican biography. The Puritan emphasis on inward religion and the importance of conversion created special problems for the biographer. Only in unusual circumstances could the biographer gain the knowledge of his subject's inner life to deal adequately with it, although he was often aided by spiritual diaries and testimonies left by the subject. But the great Puritan forms of life-writing were the autobiography and the diary, rather than biography. There are few if any Puritan biographies as vital and impressive as the great Puritan spiritual autobiographies and journals: John Bunyan's *Grace Abounding to the Chief of Sinners*, Richard Baxter's *Reliquiæ Baxterianæ*, and George Fox's *Journal*.

III

While the Protestant religious biographies of the seventeenth century exhibit a wide range of developments, they nevertheless possess a high degree of homogeneity. The biographers develop many versions of Protestant lives, both Anglican and Puritan, but their work exhibits common qualities arising from its exemplary nature and purposes. The biographers of all religious groups share the view that the purpose of biography is not so much to explore individuality as to provide ideal models of life and character for instruction and imitation. They seek to show the ways in which their subjects embody their conception of the ideal pattern for the Christian, the Protestant, the Anglican, the Presbyterian, or the Independent, rather than to differentiate them from all others. Many of the religious biographers share the view of the great Puritan divine Richard Baxter, who declined in his autobiography to provide individual detail about his own spiritual life, 'seeing God's Dealings are much what the same with all his Servants in the main, and the Points wherein he varieth are usually so small,' and stated in his preface to Samuel Clarke's *The Lives of Sundry Eminent Persons in this Later Age*, 'Gods Graces are much the same in all his holy ones.'[20] The biographers tend to concentrate on the common ground between their subjects and the ideal models rather than upon qualities that are peculiar to the subjects: they are characteristically more concerned with similarities than with differences.

In practice, as the various phases and developments of Anglican and Puritan biography demonstrate, this does not mean the reduction of all individuals of a particular religious group to a single type or pattern, for the Bible and tradition provided a number of approved types or patterns. But it means the association of the subject with an established type or combination of types and the development of parallels with those types, often at the expense of the subject's complexity and individuality. In the religious biographies the individual is frequently subordinated to the typical, and emphasis is often placed on what marks the subject as belonging to a group more than on what marks him or her as unusual or unique. Once the ideal model has been determined the biographer then tends to work from it by a deductive method rather than inductively from his subject.

The biographers were well aware that they were following long-established tradition when they worked in this way from biblical types. They often cited such patristic precedents as St Gregory of Nyssa's encomium on his brother St Basil, which is full of extended comparisons with Moses, Samuel, John the Baptist, Paul, and other biblical figures. Their practice of developing comparisons with biblical figures was specially stimulated in the seventeenth century by the popularity of the funeral sermon. The funeral sermon, like other sermons, was always preached on a particular biblical text, and when it incorporated a biography or character of the person commemorated the preacher naturally tended to link the two aspects. He frequently chose a text he could use to associate the person with a biblical figure, and then employed all the ingenuity at his command to showing the ways in which the person resembled the biblical figure.

This practice carried over into longer biographies, which in some cases were expanded from the biographical sections of funeral sermons. An example is Nicholas Bernard's life of James Ussher (1656), which grew out of a funeral sermon.[21] Bernard took his text in the sermon from Samuel, and he devoted much of the subsequent biography to developing parallels between Ussher and Samuel. Like other religious biographers he added patristic to biblical parallels and compared Ussher also to St Augustine as represented in Possidius's life. From such comparisons with biblical and patristic figures, many biographers moved to comparisons with the great Protestant reformers like Luther and Calvin, as Edward Bagshaw does in his life of Robert Bolton in 1635.

The characteristic method of the seventeenth-century religious biographer is revealed very clearly in Barnabas Oley's brief life of George Herbert prefaced to Herbert's *Remains* (1652). Oley divides his biography into two parts. His purpose in the first part is not to show what is peculiar to Herbert but what Herbert has in common with two other exemplars of Anglican holiness, Thomas Jackson and Nicholas Ferrar: 'First, I will give thee a briefe of some confrontments common to them all.' In the second part Oley is concerned with the difference between Herbert and the two others, but he conceives of this difference not in terms of a complex individuality but in terms of traditionally established biblical and patristic types: 'In summ, To distinguish them by better Resemblances out of the Old and New Testament, and antiquity: Me thinks, Doctor J. has somewhat like the spirit of Jeremy, Saint James, and Salvian. Master Herbert, like David, and other Psalm-men, Saint John and Prudentius. Master F. like Esay, Saint Luke, and Saint Chrysostome.'[22]

The biographers often search out precedents in biblical and other holy models for nearly every aspect and happening of their subjects' lives. Their main purpose in writing frequently appears to be to demonstrate that their subjects correspond in every way, in small as well as great things, with such models. Thus, to give just a few examples, William Hinde makes a point of telling us that John Bruen came to Oxford, which was then somewhat 'Popish,' at about the same age, sixteen, as Augustine was sent to Carthage. Increase Mather informs us that Richard Mather when chosen moderator of an assembly of New England churches suffered the same fate as Luther, 'who in a Synod was surprised with a violent Fit of the Stone.' John Gauden compares Hooker's being slandered by a loose woman to the similar experience of Athanasius. According to William Dillingham, Laurence Chaderton wept in saying farewell when he resigned as master of Emmanuel College, Cambridge, like Paul saying farewell to the elders of Ephesus, and Richard Mayo makes the same comparison in describing Edmund Staunton's ejection as President of Corpus Christi, Oxford. Such examples could be endlessly multiplied.[23]

While engaging in this constant search for comparisons with holy exemplars, which undercuts concern with individuality, the biographers often display an ingenuity in forcing their subjects to fit the approved patterns which is worthy of a period that admired the ingenuity of wit in metaphysical poetry. They had good patristic precedent for their ingenuity in works like Gregory of Nyssa's encomium on Basil, which includes such strained biblical parallels as comparison of the circumstance that Basil was buried without material lavishness with the fact that Moses left no tomb that has been found.[24] How far a seventeenth-century biographer was prepared to go in such ingenuity even when it ran contrary to plain evidence is illustrated by John Whitefoote's funeral sermon for Bishop Hall (1656). Whitefoote treats Hall as comparable with the patriarch Israel (or Jacob). As Genesis 27:11 states that Israel was a smooth man and Esau a hairy man, so Whitefoote declares that Hall was a smooth man because he possessed a smooth terse wit.[25] The engraved frontispiece published with the sermon shows that on the more literal level Hall was in reality a hairy man with a large spade beard.

As another example to show how far biographers and preachers were prepared to go in developing strained biblical comparisons, one may take an extract from Bishop (later Archbishop) John Williams's funeral sermon for King James I, published with the title *Great Britains Salomon* (1625). Williams builds most of the sermon around comparisons between James and King Solomon, and attempts, while passing over the faults or sins of both figures, to demonstrate that the English king parallels the biblical monarch in an almost endless number of aspects of his life and character:

> For the *bulke*, or the *mould*, I dare præsume to say, you never read in your lives, of two Kings more fully *parallel'd* amongst themselves, and better distinguished from all other *Kings* besides themselves. King *Salomon* is said to be *Vnigenitus coram Matre sua*, the onely sonne of his Mother, *Proverbs* 4.3. so was King *James*. *Salomon* was of complexion white, and ruddie, *Canticles* 5.10. *verse*. so was King *James*. *Salomon* was an infant King, *Puer paruulus* a little childe, I *Chron.* 22.5. *verse*. so was King *James* a King at the Age of thirteene *moneths*. *Salomon* began his raigne in the life of his *Prædecessor*, I *Kings* 1.32. So, by the force, and compulsion of that *state*, did our late Soveraigne King *James*. *Salomon* was *twice crown'd*, and anoynted a King, I *Chron.* 29.22. So was King *James*. *Salomons* minority was rough through the quarrells of the former Soveraigne; So was that of King *James*. *Salomon* was learned above all the Princes of the East, I *Kings* 4.30. So was King *James* above all *Princes* in the universall world. *Salomon* was a Writer in *Prose*, and *Verse*, I *Kings* 4.32. So in a very pure and exquisite manner was our sweet Soveraigne King *James*. *Salomon* was the greatest *Patron* we ever read of to *Church*, and *Churchmen*; and yet no greater (*let the house of Aaron now confesse*) then King *James*. *Salomon* was honoured with *Embassadors* from all the *Kings of the Earth*, I *Kings* 4. last *verse*; and so you know, was King *James*. *Salomon* was a maine Improver of his *home* commodities, as you may see in his *Trading* with *Hiram*, I *Kings* 5.9. *verse*; and, God knowes, it was the daily study of King *James*. *Salomon* was a great maintainer of *shipping*, and *Navigation*, I *Kings* 10.14. A most proper Attribute to King *James*. *Salomon* beautified very much his *Capitall Citie* with *Buildings*, and *Water-workes*, I *Kings* 9.15. So did King *James*. Every man liv'd in peace under his *vine*, and his *Figge-Tree* in the daies of *Salomon*, I *Kings* 4.25. And so they did in the blessed daies of King *James*. And yet towards his End, K. *Salomon* had secret *Enemies*, *Razan*, *Hadad*, and *Jeroboam*, and prepared for a *Warre* upon his going to his *Grave*, as you may see in the *verse*, before my *Text*. So had, and so did King *James*. Lastly, before any *Hostile Act* we reade of in the *History*, King *Salomon* died in peace, when he had lived about 60. *Yeares*, as *Lyra* and *Tostatus* are of opinion. And so you know did King *James*. You see therefore a Mould fitted for another *Salomon* in the *Bulke*, and *Generall*.

After asking his auditors and readers to consider more fully such similarities as the improvements made to the water systems of Jerusalem and London during the reigns of the two monarchs, Williams introduces a final set of parallels from Scripture and ecclesiastical history for the manner of James's death, to demonstrate that 'as he lived like a *King*, so he died like a *Saint.*'[26]

Williams's funeral sermon on James became notorious for flattery, but this did not deter later biographers, whether Anglican or Puritan, from similar excesses. The biographies of later rulers provide examples of equally strained comparisons with biblical figures, for example *The Life and Death of King Charles the Martyr, Parallel'd with our Saviour in all his Sufferings*, published anonymously in 1649. Ten years later after the death of Oliver Cromwell, the great opponent of the royal martyr, Henry Dawbeny cited some of the precedents for elaborate and ingenious biblical comparisons, and asked: 'Have we not seen a compleate Parallel, between Elias and Dr. Luther, even to the Chariots of Israel, and the Horsemen thereof? and another between his Successor Elisha, and Mr. Calvin, to the double portion of his spirit, and many of our Modern Doctors, put in scale with some of the Apostles themselves?'[27] Supported by such precedents, Dawbeny proceeded to develop an extended comparison between Cromwell and Moses, elaborating thirty parallels at great length.

The religious biographer's determination to link his subject with ideal, often biblical, types and demonstrate conformity with those types inevitably makes for the simplification of character. It produces biographies that are more notable for unity than complexity. The biographies are most successful when the subject is or can be represented as a man or woman of strong simple faith, as in Carleton's life of the heroic missionary priest Gilpin, but they are less adequate in the case of more complicated characters, for then the unity is often achieved at the expense of avoiding recognition and exploration of any ambiguities or tensions. The result furthermore is biographies in which different types may be clearly enough distinguished from each other but persons assigned to the same type or category are often much less clearly differentiated, particularly when emphasis on similarities is intensified by special polemical purposes.

The tendency of the biographers to make their individual subjects fit standard patterns can be illustrated by examining seventeenth-century lives of Anglican bishops by various authors. The biographers of the bishops commonly take the view that Paul in 1 Timothy 3 and Titus 1 set out the ideal prescription for the bishop, and they constantly work to demonstrate that their subjects correspond in every way with this ideal. Following a pattern already established by such patristic writers as

Gregory of Nazianzus in his panegyric on Athanasius, Foxe in the sixteenth century endeavoured to show that Cranmer fully exemplified the Pauline ideal. With the seventeenth-century Puritan attack on the episcopacy this matter assumed special polemical significance. Opponents like William Prynne denied scriptural sanction for the episcopacy in such tracts as *The Unbishoping of Timothy and Titus. Or a Briefe Elaborate Discourse, Prooving Timothy to be no Bishop (Much Lesse any Sole, or Diocæsan Bishop) of Ephesus, nor Titus of Crete* (1636). The Anglican supporters of the episcopacy on the contrary appealed to the Pauline passages as scriptural authority for the order of bishops, and the special polemical pressures ensured that the biographers adhered closely to the same pattern.

One may take as an example John Harris's life of Arthur Lake, Bishop of Bath and Wells (1629). Nearly the whole life is developed in terms of Paul's description of the ideal bishop, supplemented by reference to models provided by church fathers and bishops of the early church. Harris tells his reader: 'thou mayest easily perceive what an eminent patterne of all vertue as well personall as pastorall God hath bestowed upon our Church in the person of this one man, whom as oft as I reflect on ... me thinkes I may well ballance him with any of those whom the Church of Rome boasteth of, and whom she daily canonizeth among the Saints.' Harris's starting point is always the abstract virtue, and Lake is presented only as he exemplifies these virtues. The biography is skilled in its own terms, accomplished in style, and it was justly admired by Walton. But it is marked by a thoroughly deductive method and by the exclusion of all that does not fit the exemplary scheme, the aim of setting forth the ideal model for the Anglican priest and prelate. Even in the sections on private virtues anything very intimate or individual is excluded as irrelevant.[28]

Harris's life of Lake represents in extreme form the pattern that appears again and again in seventeenth-century Anglican lives of bishops, which were written, as John Whitefoote declared after the abolition of the episcopacy in his funeral sermon for Bishop Hall in 1656, to demonstrate that prelacy and piety are not such inconsistent things as some would make them. The concern of the biographers is much less with revealing their subjects' individuality than with showing their common adherence to the same Pauline ideal. Quoting patristic authority, Richard Baddeley and Joseph Naylor go so far as to write in their biography of Bishop Morton (1669): 'Now as (never too often quoted) *Gregory Nazianzen* saith, in his Oration of that renound *Athanasius* ... Why should I *either trouble you, or my self, to super-rogate unto you the dilineation or description of a man, whom Saint* Paul *hath before-hand so compleatly deciphered.*' As this statement implies, if the principle on which such biographies are built is carried to its logical conclusion, all that is individual is eliminated, and biography in fact becomes altogether superfluous. The comment at the end of the century by Philip Stubbs on the way in which individuality is extinguished in eulogistic funeral sermons might well be applied to many of the exemplary lives of the period written under the influence of principles of this kind: he observed that while 'they are made for every body,' they 'do indeed fit no body.'[29]

IV

As many of the developments that have been outlined and examples that have been considered suggest, seventeenth-century religious biography is often both shaped and limited by political and polemical purposes as much as by its exemplary nature. Whatever disagreement may exist among biographers of the various religious parties about doctrines and observances, they generally agree in conceiving and developing biography as a highly political form, following the precedent of Foxe's fiercely polemical 'Book of Martyrs.' Their choice and development of exemplary models are almost invariably conditioned by their political circumstances and aims.

In this era of heated religious disputes even the best of the biographers like Featley in the early part of the century and Fell and Burnet in the later part practise biography very much as a form of controversial writing. No one indeed exemplifies the seventeenth-century love of religious controversy more fully than Featley, who declared even in his popular manual of private devotion, *Ancilla Pietatis* (1626), that the study of controversies is 'not only most needfull, but delightfull also to them that are therin exercised.' He constantly engaged in anti–Roman Catholic polemics, with such works as his attack on the Jesuit John Fisher, *The Romish Fisher Caught and Held in his own Net* (1624). As Anthony Wood states, he made his reputation as 'one of the most resolute and victorious Champions of the reformed Protestant Religion in his time' and 'a most smart scourge of the Church of *Rome*'; and his lives of Jewel and Reynolds, although distinguished and historically important works of religious biography, are no more than minor offshoots of his career as a controversialist.[30]

In the later years of the century the controversial note is equally strong in Fell's lives of Hammond and Allestree, except that the focus has shifted from anti-Catholic to anti-Puritan propaganda. These lives of men notable for loyalty to the Church of England during its period of oppression include fierce attacks on the Puritans and Cromwell. While some biographers like Peter Heylyn wrote with the special purpose of upholding the Laudian or 'High Church' party, other biographers of the period such as Burnet wrote with just as strong contrary purposes and biases to uphold the 'Broad' or 'Low Church' parties.

A partial exception to the highly polemical tradition of religious biography emerged in the middle years of the seventeenth century, as has already been noted. In reaction against the harm done by the controversies and divisions that led to the Civil War, biographies were written of the type of figure who may be termed the man of peace, such as Vaughan's life of Thomas Jackson. But as analysis of Walton's lives will show, even this kind of biography was in practice given a controversial slant. Far from treating Anglicans and Puritans even-handedly, Walton constantly seeks to represent the Anglicans as the party of peace and moderation as opposed to the belligerent, angry, extreme, and unreasonable Puritans.

The work of such biographers as Walton and Fell reveals clearly the ways the acute conflicts of the period which stimulated the production of religious biography at the same time limited its development. The degree to which concern with individuality was reduced if not overwhelmed by polemical purposes and pressures appears when one compares Fell's lives of Hammond and Allestree. One can discern some essential differences between the two figures: Hammond emerges as the more contemplative character and Allestree more as the man of action; but since Fell designs both as ideal Anglican exemplars of loyalism as opposed to Puritans and rebels, his emphasis falls more upon similarities than differences. Rather than freely revealing and exploring individuality, the polemical biographer was bound to demonstrate his subject's orthodoxy as defined by the party to which he adhered, and to employ all the means at his disposal in support of that party. Anthony Wood's criticism of Peter Heylyn's life of Laud could be applied to many of the polemical biographies. Wood shared many of Heylyn's High Anglican and anti-Puritan prejudices but he commented that Heylyn was in some things 'too much a Party to be an Historian.'[31] The biographies are commonly so affected by ulterior political motives as to lack balance and objectivity. They frequently suffer from suppression and distortion.

Biographies that came closest to rising above the limitations of party bias and polemics ran the risk of remaining unpublished. Among the lives that have survived in manuscript, one that suggests by contrast how much many of the published biographies are weakened by their partisan narrowness and bitterness is that of Bishop William Bedell written by his son, the younger William, which has been printed only in modern times. The elder Bedell went to Ireland as a bishop of the established Protestant Church of Ireland; after the outbreak of the Irish rebellion in the early 1640s he was imprisoned by the rebels, and he died of fever soon after being released. His remarkable character is indicated by the fact that three biographies were written of him, lives by Gilbert Burnet and Alexander Clogie in addition to that by the son, as well as shorter character sketches by Nicholas Bernard and by Walton in his life of Sir Henry Wotton.[32] The biographies by Burnet and Clogie are the fullest, but the masterpiece is the briefer but more intimate life by the son. It stands in relation to the others rather like Roper's life of More in relation to Harpsfield's fuller and more formal but less intimate biography. But more than this, the life of Bedell by the son is superior also in its greater freedom from party bias and ulterior motives.

The son gives a picture of Bedell as one who opposed what he saw as Roman Catholic corruption but followed a policy of friendship with Catholics in Ireland, including priests and the titular Catholic bishop of his area. After the outbreak of the rebellion when property was plundered he turned over the plate of his church to the Catholic bishop rather than allow it to fall into secular hands. He fostered the Irish language, and his yeoman ancestry gave him a sense of closeness and sympathy with the Irish peasantry. The son records that his father was long left undisturbed during the rebellion and told he should be the last Englishman to leave Ireland, and that when he died his burial was honoured by the Irish rebels.

This is an outcome not really explained by Burnet or Clogie because they are too hostile to Catholics and Irish. Their purpose is the definition of the ideal bishop in specifically left-wing Anglican terms, as an 'apostolic' prelate who represents a strongly Protestant version of 'primitive' Christianity: Clogie titles his biography *Speculum Episcoporum; Or, The Apostolick Bishop*. They are drawn to Bedell as a heroic figure of the Broad and Low Church groups, a Calvinist, whose promotion had been inhibited by Laud. Their bias is so strongly anti-Catholic that they are much less successful than the son in conveying the tolerance and charity that really made Bedell remarkable. Ironically, in fact, Burnet's prejudice against the Irish Catholics actually causes him to diminish the figure he is attempting to celebrate. He describes the rebels as cannibals or wild beasts, wolves or bears or worse, and he concludes that their favoured treatment of Bedell therefore should probably be attributed to Providence rather than to 'any impressions that his worth made on those Barbarians.'[33]

The son brings out the father's individuality more fully than the other biographers, and at the same time he realizes better than the others the ultimate aim of the seventeenth-century religious biographer to depict the figure of exceptional holiness. His life is convincing as the portrait of a man who loved his enemies and was loved by them, while Burnet and Clogie in their more narrowly partisan biographies really obscure rather than bring into prominence the most authentically saintly qualities of Bedell's character. In this era of fierce conflict and controversy the son's life of Bedell stands out as a remarkable exception which reveals by its difference the limitations of the more typical polemical religious biographies.

V

Protestant religious biography remains in the later years of the seventeenth century in many respects a conservative and backward-looking form, as the biographers' frequent appeals to the authority of established models suggest. In contrast to the more radical developments taking place in some of the secular branches of biography, this well-established type, while constantly adapting in various ways to changing historical circumstances, does not alter greatly in its fundamental nature: it is really more notable for continuity than for change. In the Restoration period the biographers were sometimes affected by advances in scholarship and historical study, and some reaction occurred against the excesses of the exemplary tradition, which resulted in modifications, but there were no radical innovations.[34]

After the Restoration a number of the biographers criticized and turned away from the strained biblical parallels that had been common in earlier lives of religious figures. Thus John Barnard in his biography of Peter Heylyn censured George Vernon's previous life of Heylyn for high-flown comparisons with Moses and Joseph where there was inadequate similarity.[35] But it remained rare to write the life of a bishop without reference to the Pauline model, and the highly schematic approach apparent in Harris's life of Lake continued to be common even in the most distinguished religious biographies.

Fell declares in his biography of Hammond in 1661 that he writes the life of 'this Saint' as one sent that we might believe history regarding the 'Excellency of primitive Christians.' His phrasing is reminiscent of that employed by Foxe a hundred years earlier, and his biographical principles are not fundamentally very different from Foxe's, even though his life is much fuller and larger in scale than any of Foxe's, and his political thrust is quite different. At the opening of his life he refers to the growing reaction against the faults of the exemplary tradition, but half his biography is organized in abstract terms as an ideal 'character,' and he follows a similar pattern in his life of Allestree (1684). Burnet employs the same procedure in his life of Sir Matthew Hale (1682), where he states: 'I am now to present the Reader with such a Character of Him, as the laying his several Virtues together will amount to.' The concern to demonstrate the subject's conformity with ideal models and to provide a pattern of sanctity and virtue for emulation remains dominant.[36]

Burnet's life of the great lawyer and judge Hale represents Restoration religious biography at its best. The author's consciousness of the growing reaction against the faults of the exemplary tradition is shown by a defensive tone, his fear that the biography will be regarded as a mere panegyric. But he is determined to continue that tradition, and to present Hale as a pattern of religion and virtue in order to combat the fashionable licentiousness and scepticism of the age. He declares, 'my Design in Writing is to propose a Pattern of Heroick Virtue to the World.'[37]

In many ways this is a highly impressive biography. Burnet conveys well Hale's religious faith and practice, and his remarkable integrity, compassion, and charity. He gives a memorable picture of the austerity of Hale's life, and provides a good account of his wide-ranging learning, both in traditional areas and in the 'curious Experiments, and rare Discoveries of this Age.'[38] But for all its merits, the biography suffers from severe limitations in the handling both of Hale's professional and private life.

Burnet fails to give an adequate account of the great legal ability which is really Hale's chief claim to distinction. He attempts to compensate for his own lack of legal knowledge by introducing expert testimony from other sources, but this provides no more than a partial solution. Nor does he deal at all fully with Hale's private life. In stating his principles Burnet advocates describing the subject's private life when this serves an exemplary purpose but criticizes those who write lives 'too jejunely, swelling them up with trifling accounts of the Childhood and

Education, and the domestick or private affairs of those persons of whom they Write, in which the World is little concerned.' He provides little information about Hale's sometimes troubled domestic life, his two marriages and his children. He declares that he draws a veil over these matters because it signifies little to the world to know the exercise of Hale's patience.[39]

Burnet's life of Hale came under strong attack for its defects and limitations in the writings of Roger North at the end of the seventeenth and beginning of the eighteenth century. In his autobiography North declares that Burnet 'wanted both information, and understanding' for his undertaking in this life. He states that Burnet was not even fit for his chief purpose of panegyric because he did not truly know the virtues Hale had fit to be praised. In his life of his brother Francis, Lord Guilford, North renders high tribute to Hale's legal powers and integrity but criticizes him for personal prejudices and vanities. North depicts Hale as a man who surrounded himself with flatterers and who misguidedly professed great abilities in philosophy, science, and divinity while underrating his real legal abilities. North furthermore gives an account of Hale's unhappy domestic life, which Burnet had suppressed: he declares that Hale said 'there was no wisdom below the girdle,' that he married as his second wife a servant maid, and that all his sons were debauched.[40]

In his criticism of Burnet's life of Hale, Roger North's own biases need to be taken into account. North belonged to political and religious parties, 'Tory' and 'High Church,' opposite to those supported by Burnet and Hale, and Hale had been an opponent of his brother, Lord Guilford. But North's criticisms gain some support from other sources. Aubrey displays a candour about Hale's domestic life that contrasts strikingly with Burnet's evasions: he comments on Hale's first marriage, 'He was a great cuckold,' and states that his second marriage was 'to his servant mayd, Mary.' Even Richard Baxter, who was highly sympathetic to Hale and freer of class bias than North, mentions contemporary criticism of Hale for marrying beneath himself in his second marriage.[41] Such sources make it clear that, even when North's biases are taken into account in his judgment that Hale was an extraordinary combination of learning and wisdom joined with ignorance and folly, he was right to maintain that Hale was a much more complex character than he was represented as being by Burnet.

What makes North's criticism of Burnet's life of Hale specially interesting is that it reflects a great divide in biographical writing: it is a case of an older type of biography being judged by newer standards. While

Burnet's life represents the type of exemplary religious biography that had been the dominant tradition in life-writing during the seventeenth century, North judges it by the more secular standards that gradually emerged into increasing prominence in the second half of the century. Burnet's lives of Hale and the Earl of Rochester are exceptionally fine examples of the traditional type. Yet North's indictment of these lives, in a 'General Preface' to his own biographical writing, is withering: he terms them 'mere froth whipped up to serve a turn.'[42]

CHAPTER 3

Patterns in Religious Biography

The aims of the seventeenth-century religious biographer clearly differ in the most fundamental ways from the business of the biographer as set out in Samuel Johnson's classic definition: 'to give a complete account of the person whose life he is writing, and to discriminate him from all other persons by any peculiarities of character or sentiment he may happen to have.'[1] The religious biographer is moved by purposes antithetical to Johnson's two principles. He seeks not to display the individuality of his subject by discriminating him from all other persons but to show his conformity to ideal models and patterns, and not to give 'a complete account of the person' but an account of religious aspects worthy of imitation. Such aspects can never be the whole of the person's life, even if they may be close to that perhaps in the case of the authentic saint.

Some of the more secular seventeenth-century biographers anticipate Johnson's views, as will be seen, but the religious biographers follow very different principles of selection and emphasis than would arise from his definition of biography. What this means in practice may be considered here in relation to a number of aspects of the religious biography of the period: the handling of time, the treatment of private and professional life, the representation of the body, views of faults and weaknesses, and areas of suppression or silence, as well as some of the implications for artistry and style.

I Time: Chronology and Dates

One of the most distinctive features of seventeenth-century religious biography is the handling of time. The writers commonly show much less concern for dating and chronology than secular or modern biographers, and the proportions and emphasis they give to the various stages of life are also very different. They tend to view biography as an iconic more than a narrative form. They often provide only a brief narrative of the life, followed by a much more extensive 'character,' an analysis of moral and religious qualities organized schematically rather than chronologically. And the biographers attach little importance to dates because, following such patristic models altogether lacking dates as Possidius's life of St Augustine, they consider them insignificant *sub specie aeternitatis.*

Among the seventeenth-century English biographers, John Harris in his life of Arthur Lake represents the same extreme case of the biography without a single date as Possidius's life of Augustine. Edmund Vaughan in his life of Thomas Jackson gives just one date, in connection with a prophecy, but none for either birth or death. A more common case is the biography where the only date given is that of the subject's death. This of course was often the date most easily learned. As Thomas Fuller expresses the matter in his life of Henry Smith through the image of the river Nile, the source is obscure but the place of influx into the sea is eminently known.[2] But the primary reason for giving the date of death is that it was considered most significant in religious terms. In this as in other things John Foxe helped to establish the precedent. He gave the dates for death and martyrdom in his 'Book of Martyrs' but not for birth, even in the case of major figures like Cranmer.

Daniel Featley is characteristic of the practice of religious biographers in the earlier seventeenth century. In his life of Reynolds he gives no date for birth but the exact hour for the death. In his life of Jewel he gives the date of Jewel's birth in the margin but provides few other dates, none until the 1560s, even though others were readily available to him in his source, Humphrey's earlier Latin life of Jewel. Such examples make it plain that the neglect of dating in many of the religious lives arises not so much from lack of information as from the writers' differences in values and purposes from secular and later biographers.

An interesting case is that of Henry Isaacson. He published an elaborate work on chronology, *Saturni Ephemerides* (1633), which contained an eloquent statement of the importance of this subject: 'The chiefe light and Eye of *History* is *Chronology*,' and he quoted an unnamed authority as declaring that without chronology history would be but a confused heap. But when he turned to the writing of biography he gave only two dates in his otherwise fine life of Lancelot Andrewes, including date of death but not of birth; so it is impossible to tell from this work how long various phases of Andrewes's career lasted or how old Andrewes was during particular episodes.[3]

There are, however, some exceptions to the common neglect of dating among religious biographers in the earlier part of the seventeenth century, and the biographers later in the century tended to show an increased concern with chronology. From the beginning some biographers of figures prominent in public affairs, like Paule in his life of Whitgift, recognized the need to provide a reasonable number of dates; and later biographers, particularly after the Restoration, were often affected by newer antiquarian and historiographical movements. It is significant that Walton gave scarcely any dates, not even the year of birth, in the first version of his life of Donne in 1640 but showed an increased awareness of their importance in subsequent versions and in lives written later, although as Anthony Wood discerned he still often remained vague and misleading.[4] Fell, who is representative of Restoration practice, provided enough dates in his life of Hammond to give some sense of chronology, and an adequate, although still rather sparse, number in his life of Allestree.

For fuller appreciation of the importance of dating and chronology, however, one must turn from religious to more secular types of seventeenth-century biography. The relative neglect of the dimension of time by the religious biographers is all the more striking in view of the fact that Wood and a number of other secular writers, who regarded biography as a branch of history and were strongly influenced not only by older traditions of chronicles and annals but by newer antiquarian movements, developed an obsessive interest in dating and chronology. This is indeed the manifestation of a distinctively new Renaissance attitude toward the past. It is one of the areas in which religious biography never breaks entirely free of its generic limitations and a wide divide opens between it and secular biography.

II Time: Early Years and Final Hours

As well as in their attitudes to dating and chronology, the special values and purposes of the seventeenth-century religious biographers affect their handling of time in a second way, that is in the relative proportions they give to the different periods of life, especially in the disproportion between the treatment of the early and final parts of life. Characteristically the biographers move very rapidly over the early years but concentrate much attention on the last days, even on the final hours, of the earthly life.

To modern readers conditioned by Romantic and Freudian revolutions, the brevity of the treatment of childhood and youth is striking. Daniel Featley's statement in his life of Jewel is characteristic of the religious biographers of the early seventeenth century: 'I willinglie passe in silence those yeares which harmelesse simplicitie doth best commend.'[5] The biographers later in the century rarely advance much beyond Featley's position. Even the best of the Restoration biographers commonly devote no more than a sentence or two to the childhood of their subjects. Burnet takes Hale from birth to the age of seventeen in a single sentence, and Fell passes almost as quickly over Allestree's youth.

Sometimes the reason given by the biographers for lack of treatment of childhood and youth is simply lack of information, but they also justify the omission by biblical precedent. Ferdinando Nicolls points out biblical parallels for the slightness of the information he provides about the youth of his subject, the merchant Ignatius Jurdain (or Jourdain). He comments: 'Few things are recorded of John the Baptist untill the day of his shewing unto Israel,' and observes that little is recorded of Christ himself before his public ministry. Such precedents reinforced the view common among both religious and secular biographers that childhood is relatively unimportant and that young children differ little from each other. David Lloyd in his *Memoires* writes of the Earl of Bristol that he passes by the earl's infancy, for 'all children are alike in their Long-coats.'[6]

While information about childhood and youth is sparse in most religious biographies, the little that is given tends to follow quite conventional patterns. There is often a tribute to pious parents or an influential schoolmaster. With the exception of some lives of clergymen, few of the biographies provide much fuller accounts of grammar school and university education. The writers often supply evidence of early religious devotion, most fully in the special cases of biographies of children and youths notable for precocious piety who died young. In keeping with long-established hagiographical traditions, the biographers commonly give one or two anecdotes from the early years to show the subject's promise of future distinction. Just as Roper in his life of More included Morton's prophecy of More's future greatness, Featley shows in his life of Jewel that Jewel's Oxford tutor Parkhurst recognized his pupil's exceptional qualities. The biographers also like to give an anecdote to demonstrate that their subject was specially preserved in youth by divine power from danger or death: thus Vaughan records that Jackson while a student at Oxford was saved on one occasion from great danger of drowning, so that 'All men concluded him to be reserved for High and Admirable Purposes.'[7]

Conversion narratives, which were developed especially by Puritan biographers, of course follow a pattern of their own, but they too tend to be conventional more than individual. Apart from some indication of early sinfulness or worldliness, they rarely provide much information about life before the beginning of conversion. In the view of Puritan biographers, conversion is the true birth, where real life begins. Again and again they give very similar details concerning the process of conversion, the development of the conviction of sin, and the receiving of a call on hearing the sermon of a powerful preacher, quite often at Cambridge, or upon reading the Bible or some devotional work. Generally the biographers are either unable or unwilling to provide the kind of vivid detail about unregenerate youth and inner spiritual conflicts that appears in such great Puritan autobiographies as John Bunyan's *Grace Abounding to the Chief of Sinners*.

Apart from the special concern of the Puritan writers with conversion, the religious biographers concentrate their interest not on the beginning but on the end of earthly life. From the modern viewpoint perhaps the most striking of all aspects of the seventeenth-century exemplary life is the great prominence given to the subject's death. The biographies are often titled 'The Life and Death,' and the death is frequently given as much space as all the years of the earlier life. A famous example is Gilbert Burnet's life of the Earl of Rochester, which is almost confined to the last few weeks of its subject's mortal existence, while the earlier dissipated and profane years are brought in only for contrast. When James Boswell asked Samuel Johnson whether Burnet 'had not given a good life of Rochester,' Johnson replied: 'We have a good *Death*: there is not much *Life*.'[8]

As social and cultural historians, who have in recent years been much interested in attitudes toward death, have shown, the special prominence given to deathbed scenes in this period follows naturally from the Protestant shift in emphasis from sacraments to inward faith.[9] Both in the Anglican and Puritan ways of death great importance was attached to manifestations of faith in the final days and hours of the individual's life. Hence the seventeenth-century biographies are shaped by the viewpoint John King had expressed in his funeral sermon for Archbishop

Piers in 1594: 'Lastly ... One day is as much as all the rest, for it is ... the birth day of eternity: and as the tree falleth, so it lyeth.' Like Jeremy Taylor in his funeral sermon for Archbishop Bramhall (1663), the biographers held: 'The last dayes are the best witnesses of a Man.'[10] They and their informants closely scrutinized the words and attitudes of the dying man or woman for evidence of the condition of the soul, for the proof of salvation they saw as the great purpose of earthly life, upon which the person's eternal condition would depend.

In their representation of the deaths of their subjects, the biographers' concern with demonstrating parallels with biblical, patristic, and other holy figures appears in its most fully developed form. They make every effort not only to show that their subjects followed an approved pattern in their final hours, but often to suggest also that in the end they received marks of special divine favour. Thus Increase Mather tells us that Richard Mather had a prophetic presentiment of his death, like Ambrose and Gorgonia of old and Gesner, Melanchthon, and Sanford among modern divines. The biographers find special significance even in what might seem accidental or unimportant coincidences. Edward Bagshaw considers it noteworthy that Robert Bolton's final sickness was the quartan ague, the disease that brought Calvin to his end. Thomas Plume tells us not only that John Hacket died without fear, like Basil in Gregory of Nazianzus's account, but that at the time of his death he was seventy-eight, the same age as Athanasius and Jerome at their deaths. An anonymous biographer comments that Joseph Mead in dying before the outbreak of the Civil War was taken away from evils to come as God took away Josiah and as St Augustine according to Possidius was carried away when the Goths and Vandals descended on Hippo.[11]

This concentration upon similarities with approved models rather than individual differences appears markedly in the representation of deathbed scenes. The last words of the dying persons are frequently cast in a conventional form. The biographers and their subjects follow the pattern set out in Revelation 22:20: 'He which testifieth these things saith, Surely I come quickly; Amen. Even so, come, Lord Jesus.' Again and again the biographers tell us that the last words of the dying man echoed this biblical text. In James Janeway's biography of his brother, John Janeway asks at the end: 'Now come dear Lord Jesus, come quickly,' and this appeal is recorded in much the same words in numerous biographies from the late sixteenth throughout the seventeenth century.[12]

Some special patterns appear in the representation of the final days of clergymen. For example, there is the recurring figure of the preacher who desires to die in the pulpit. John King in his funeral sermon for Archbishop Piers in 1594 quotes the saying of Sydus that just as a general should die in the field, 'where should a preacher die but in the pulpit?' These words are often repeated by seventeenth-century biographers as they demonstrate the ways in which their subjects endeavoured to follow this ideal pattern. William Jenkyn tells us that William Gouge continued to preach despite great infirmities in his later years, having at times to be carried into the pulpit, and that he would have accounted it a mercy 'if he who Preacht so much in his life, might also have dyed Preaching.' Bedell in his last sermon, according to Clogie, spoke as one who already saw heaven; his hearers wept and thought it a presage of his death, which occurred a week later. In his funeral sermon on Baxter, William Bates writes: 'He continued to preach so long notwithstanding his wasted languishing Body, that the last time, he almost died in the Pulpit. It would have been his joy to have been *transfigured in the Mount.*' Walton's well-known picture of Donne preaching his own funeral sermon takes its place as one of the high points of this tradition.[13]

While the biographers in writing of the deaths of their subjects work within well-established patterns, they display nowhere more than here all their eloquence and artistic skills. Daniel Featley provides memorable accounts of the deaths of both Jewel and Reynolds. He describes how Reynolds, the great controversialist, on his deathbed called at first for books of controversy but finally only the Bible: he continued to engage in conferences for preparation of the King James version, 'and in a manner in the *very translation of the booke of life was translated to a better life.*' Bishop Hacket, in Thomas Plume's biography, died hearing the bells he had put in place in his restored cathedral of Lichfield after the devastation of the Civil War. Walton appears again as part of a great tradition in having Herbert on his deathbed call for musical instruments as emblematic of his joining in a divine harmony.[14]

Jeremy Taylor's eloquent tribute in his funeral sermon on Lady Carbery is among the famous passages of seventeenth-century prose: 'She liv'd as we all should live, and she died as I fain would die.' Even the slighter accounts of the deaths of the less notable in this period can be very moving. Roger Fenton writes of John Newman, citizen and grocer, that he died peaceably on the sabbath, 'even as if hee had stolne a nap: wee that were present with him could not tell when he went.' In phrases that have affinity with the opening of Donne's 'A Valediction: Forbidding Mourning,' Thomas Pierce tells us in his funeral sermon on Edward Peyto (1659): 'That knot of union betwixt his body and his soul, was not violently *broken*, but very leisurely *untyed*; they having parted like *two friends*, not by a rude *falling-out*, but a loving *farewell*.' It is not surprising that the modern biographers of such figures as Jewel and Donne have often chosen simply to reproduce the accounts of the deaths provided by the early biographers. In doing this they have shown their awareness that the modern biographer could scarcely match either the authenticity or the artistry of the seventeenth-century accounts.[15]

III Professions: Clerical and Lay

There is a marked contrast between the religious biographers' treatment of lay and clerical figures as members of professions. The biographers rarely provide much information about secular occupations but they often give very full accounts of the clerical vocation and life. This emphasis arises naturally, since the clerical biographies were usually written by clergymen and directed at least in part to clergy. For the clerical readers information about the exercise of the ministry had special use for instruction and emulation, and in a profoundly religious period the authors could rely upon a high degree of interest also in lay readers.

In contrast to the common neglect of childhood and youth in religious biography, Anglican and many nonconformist authors of lives of clergy recognized the importance of providing information about their subjects' education. They usually gave at least the name of the subject's grammar school and often the name of an influential early schoolmaster, as well as some information about college tutors and academic careers for the university educated. The importance attached to the school is shown by John Lightfoot in his life of the belligerent nonconformist controversialist Hugh Broughton, as he expresses his regret about his lack of information: ''tis pity the Schole and Master should lose the Honour of the Education of such a Scholar.'[16] While the beneficial influence of early schoolmasters is commemorated in many biographies, for example that of Ward and Mulcaster in Isaacson's life of Lancelot Andrewes, in some other cases such as the son's life of Bedell exceptional suffering is recorded at the hands of harsh and cruel schoolmasters. When they move from grammar school to university, in lives of those for whom the universities were open, the biographies often become more detailed and interesting, as in Ball's life of Preston and Hill's life of Barrow, which are considered in later chapters.

The biographies of clergy are rich in information about their subjects' habits of study as well as about their devotional practices. The clergy in these lives often seem to compete with each other in the attempt to spend the greatest number of hours each day in study. They compete also in their feats of memory, with the aid sometimes of the artificial systems of memory popular during the period. Fuller according to his anonymous biographer had so remarkable a memory that he could list every shop-sign from Temple Bar to Cheapside. John Howes tells us that Thomas Ball when he was still an undergraduate could repeat from memory all the New Testament, and provide book, chapter, and number of any verse of the Old or New Testament given to him. One biographer, however, is candid enough to record the opposite extreme: William Durham states that Robert Harris's memory was so bad he feared he would forget his own name.[17]

Some Restoration biographers, such as Fell in his life of Hammond, provide full and fine analyses of the learning and contemplative, inward mental and spiritual qualities of their clerical subjects, but generally the writers give most attention to the more active aspects of the clerical profession, especially to preaching. In his funeral sermon for the Presbyterian Thomas Manton, William Bates expresses the view that prevailed among Protestants of all denominations: 'the Preaching of the Word is the principal part of the Minister's Duty, most essential to his Calling, and most necessary to the Church.' Interest was naturally strong in this subject among both men and women in a great sermon-going age. Stephen Denison records of Elizabeth Juxton in his sermon for her funeral that when living in London she generally heard nine or ten sermons a week, 'whereof foure of them constantly upon the Sabbath day,' and John Ferrar in his biography of Nicholas Ferrar states that Nicholas's mother heard twelve thousand sermons during her life. The biographers were conscious therefore of writing for an audience of experienced and discriminating connoisseurs of sermons and preaching.[18]

Accounts of preaching and the ministry include strongly conventional elements, designed to demonstrate that the clerical subjects followed the proper Scriptural injunctions and approved models. Thus the biographers tell us again and again in almost identical words that the preachers combined the qualities of Boanerges, the son of thunder, and Barnabas, the son of consolation, and praise their subjects as Apollos mighty in Scripture. They repeatedly develop variations on certain images, for example the comparison of the preacher to an angel. Walton introduces this image in his life of Donne, influenced perhaps by

Donne's own use of it in his poem 'To Mr. Tilman After he had Taken Orders.' Isaacson describes Andrewes as 'An Angell in the Pulpit.' According to an anonymous life printed by Samuel Clarke, it was said of Samuel Fairclough 'That if *Angels* were to Preach, they would do it in Mr. *Fairclough*'s Stile.' The image receives its most memorable development in George Rust's description in his funeral sermon of Jeremy Taylor as a handsome and eloquent young preacher at St Paul's, like 'some young Angel, newly descended from the Visions of Glory.'[19]

While the biographers build their accounts of preaching partly around conventional elements, they provide more individual detail in this area than in most others. They not only discriminate between various schools of preaching but give good descriptions of the personal styles of sermon writing and delivery of many preachers. In the case of Hooker, for example, John Gauden provides a fine contrast between his and Walter Travers's style of preaching, while Walton gives a memorable picture of his bashfulness in preaching with his eyes fixed in one place, accounts derived in both cases from Fuller's *Church-History*. Gilbert Burnet gives an equally good description of the late seventeenth-century decorum and effective simplicity of John Tillotson's sermons: 'No affectations of Learning, no squeezing of texts, no superficial Strains, no false Thoughts nor bold Flights, all was solid and yet lively, and grave as well as Fine.'[20]

Many of the most individual elements appear in accounts of strongly evangelical Anglican and nonconformist preachers. These preachers and their biographers were less bound by conventional decorum than more conservative types of Anglican. Oliver Heywood writes of John Angier: his 'taking hold with both hands at one time of the supporters of the Canopy over the Pulpit, and roaring hideously, to represent the torments of the damned, had an awakening force attending it.' The biographer defends Angier for using expressions and gestures which by the time this life appeared in 1685 would seem indecent. Sir Henry Ashurst tells us that Nathaniel Heywood preached sometimes three hours and would have preached and prayed even four or five hours, forgetting in his zeal his own strength and his hearers' patience, and straining his voice with ultimately fatal result; and he observes: 'In his best health he was an extraordinary Sweater, especially in his preaching; his sweat hath dropt at his Hair-ends, wet his Band all over; Letters wet in his Pocket through Linings, as if put in water.' The biographers provide vivid accounts too of the effect the preachers had on their audiences, ranging from the rapt response of the huge audience Fuller drew as a young preacher at the Savoy in London, in the anonymous biography, to Fuller's own memorable report of the way in which the doleful 'damn' of the evangelical William Perkins sounded in the ears of his Cambridge audience.[21]

Such fine and detailed accounts of clerical careers bring out all the more strongly by contrast the relative neglect of the lay professions by the religious biographers. The majority of these biographers of lay as well as clerical figures were themselves clergymen, and inevitably they lacked the degree of interest and special knowledge of the professional lives of lay persons that they possessed for their own calling. The eminent Puritan divine Richard Baxter states in his sermon for the funeral of Henry Ashurst that he will say little of his subject as a merchant because others can better do this.[22] Moreover, the preachers of funeral sermons were often inclined to consider the lay professions to be not greatly relevant to their purposes, and this neglect was carried over from the sermons into other biographical writings. Thus, as has already been observed, the funeral sermons and biographies of merchants and other prosperous business people often emphasize their generosity and charity but tell us very little about their business activities.

John Donne in his sermon for the funeral of Sir William Cokayne, a rich City merchant and alderman, makes only general mention of his subject's skill and prosperity in business and never states what his business actually was. George Thomason, the great seventeenth-century collector of pamphlets and sermons, made a note on his copy of Edward Reynolds's funeral sermon for Peter Whalley that Whalley was (like Thomason himself) a stationer, but one could not learn this from the sermon itself. Nor do poets necessarily fare better than merchants or stationers. Henry Bagshaw in his funeral sermon for Sir Richard Fanshawe does not mention that his subject was a poet and translator, and Nicholas Brady in his sermon for Thomas Shadwell, Poet Laureate, tells us nothing of him as poet or dramatist.[23]

Even Gilbert Burnet's life of Matthew Hale, perhaps the finest of primarily religious seventeenth-century biographies of a layman, illustrates the characteristic limitation. This is a life of Hale as an exemplary figure of religion and virtue, rather than as a lawyer or judge, the fields where his chief eminence from a more worldly viewpoint really lay. Burnet is quite conscious of the limitation, and he brings in some legal authorities to testify, in order to make up for his own lack of expertise, but this is not central to his purpose, and as Roger North emphasized it was not an adequate solution.[24]

IV Private Life

If the authors of seventeenth-century religious biographies provide little information about their subjects as members of professions except in the case of clergy, neither do they often tell us much about their subjects' private lives that is not closely and narrowly related to their exemplary purposes. Evidence to support Philippe Ariès's thesis that increasing prominence is given in this period to private life as a separate sphere may be found in the work of such secular biographers as Aubrey but rarely in the religious biographies.[25] The representation of private life in these biographies usually extends little beyond devotional practices and habits of study. Such information as the biographers provide commonly falls into established patterns traceable to biblical and patristic models, which allow little individual variation.

Even when the authors of exemplary lives had a long and close knowledge of their subjects, they usually preferred to adopt a decorum of dignified impersonality rather than venture on intimate biography, as examples from all parts of this period demonstrate. Early in the century Paule feels it necessary to apologize in his life of Whitgift: 'I feare least I have held the Reader too long in these private matters,' when he has been writing of Whitgift's love of his house at Croydon and his bounty to the poor, scarcely very intimate matters. In the middle years of the century Vaughan's life of Jackson is typical: despite his close association with Jackson, Vaughan tells us nothing of the private side of his life, nothing of his habits, manners, appearance, or health. Later in the century, as has been seen, Burnet in his life of Hale criticizes those who swell lives with accounts of domestic and private matters 'in which the World is little concerned,' and he constructs a biography notable for exclusions in these areas.[26]

The information the typical religious biographer provides about the way of life and habits of his subject, even in such matters as dress and diet, is designed primarily to show how completely the man or woman is absorbed in the Christian. The emphasis is frequently influenced by special polemical motives. Thus the biographers of Anglican clergy, concerned to defend their subjects against Puritan charges that the clergy of the established church were worldly and self-interested, often place special emphasis upon their subjects' renunciation of worldly ambition and material rewards, upon the austerity of their lives, and upon their charitable benefactions. The Anglican biographers, however, reject what they consider the false extremes of Roman Catholic and monastic asceticism, and in this as in other matters uphold the principle of the *via media*. John Ferrar, for example, while describing Nicholas Ferrar's austere life, makes it clear that this devout figure, who was sometimes charged by Puritans with adopting Roman Catholic practices, disapproved of asceticism that weakens health as a kind of suicide.[27]

In describing their subjects' ways of life, habits, and attitudes toward worldly goods, the biographers who seek to demonstrate adherence to approved scriptural and patristic patterns, rather than to bring out individual differences, take as one of their most influential models Possidius's life of St Augustine. Just as Possidius states that Augustine made no will, for as a poor man of God he had nothing to leave, so Harris tells us that there were no legacies to recount in Lake's will because he had already given away all he possessed, and Vaughan makes the same point about Jackson, as do Baddeley and Naylor about Morton. The biblical precedents, however, provide a range of possibilities, and sometimes biographers take the view that worldly prosperity may be a mark of divine favour. Fell shows an ability to bend poverty and prosperity equally to his purposes: he takes the facts that Hammond died wealthy and Allestree died poor to be evidence of their sanctity in both cases.

Biographers of both clerical and lay figures attempt to surpass each other in their accounts of the greatness of their subjects' charities. Often they provide mere listings of types or amounts of benefactions, but this is one area in which they sometimes give more individual detail. Burnet provides some of the finest examples in his life of Hale. He describes how in the country Hale made able beggars gather stones for roads but in the city gave to rogues rather than neglect the deserving, and tells us not only that he treated servants as friends but that his mercifulness extended even to animals: he kept old horses and dogs and showed anger at a person who caused the death of a bird. William Hinde advocates a similarly humane attitude to animals in his life of John Bruen, a country gentleman who abandoned blood sports. An anonymous life printed by Samuel Clarke tells us of the nonconformist clergyman Richard Blackerby: 'He was exceedingly careful to have none of Gods creatures lost; he would always have a Fowl or two allowed to come familiarly into his Eating Room, to pick up the lesser Crumbs that would fall from the Table.' Simeon Ashe records a striking example of charity differently directed in his sermon for the funeral of Essex, Countess of Manchester: he states that this aristocratic lady would give her breasts to suck to the children of the poor.[28]

In keeping with their aim of showing the man or woman to be completely absorbed in the Christian, the biographers rarely provide any accounts of their subjects' recreations. They seldom follow the precedent of Melchior Adamus, who had described Luther's fondness for chess, wood-turning, music, shooting, and gardening.[29] Featley tells us of Jewel: 'His onely recreations from studies were studious,' and Thomas Gouge states that William Gouge spent no time in recreation. Occasionally, however, the English biographers record their subjects' enjoyment of conversation, walking, riding, gardening, or contemplating the creation, the world of nature. Love of music, which figures prominently in Walton's life of Herbert, is sometimes mentioned by such other biographers as Peter Barwick in his life of John Barwick.[30]

From the modern viewpoint the most striking gap in the seventeenth-century religious biographers' treatment of private life is in the domestic area, the lack of information about family relations, marriage, and children. This neglect may arise partly from the facts that ancient hagiographical models had often been developed around monastic ideals of celibacy, and that the institution of a married clergy was still relatively new in England. In the light of the biblical injunction to the Christian to put aside all things of the world, the religious biographers often appear to regard wives and children as irrelevant to the main business of life, just as Bunyan in *The Pilgrim's Progress* included wives and children among the vanities of his Vanity Fair.

In the biographies of male figures information about marriage and family life often does not extend beyond the name of the wife or wives, and in many cases not even this much is provided. This neglect is common throughout the whole century in both Anglican and nonconformist lives. Lightfoot in his life of Broughton makes only a passing reference to his subject's marriage, incidental to another point. John Howes in his life of Thomas Ball tells us that his subject was blessed in marriages with three religious and virtuous gentlewomen, and blessed also with 'a hopeful posterity,' but he gives no names or other details.[31] Plume mentions Hacket's two marriages without giving the name of either wife. Sometimes the number of children is given, if at all, only in the margin, as in Bagshaw's life of Bolton. Nicholas Bernard tells us nothing of Ussher's marriage until late in the work we find this prelate visiting a married daughter in Wales. In other cases we learn of the subject's marriage only in deathbed scenes, where a previously unmentioned wife and children appear to ask the blessing of the dying man.

One biography that is highly unusual for the candour with which it describes sexual relations between husband and wife is Arnold Boate's life in 1651 of his wife Margaret (née Dungan), who died at the age of twenty-five. He writes of her with great affection but states 'the verie temper of her bodie made her so absolute a stranger to all sinfull lusts, as she never knew what it was to take anie the least pleasure in our conjugall imbraces' and informs us that in all eight years of their marriage she never submitted to those embraces without reluctance, although this physical coldness did not prevent her from loving him greatly. Boate's candour may be connected with the fact that although he shapes his life as a religious biography he was not a clergyman but a medical man — and he published the biography not in England but in Paris, where he and his wife lived in the later years of their marriage.[32]

There are a few other notable exceptions to the common neglect of domestic life in religious biography, although they lack Boate's candour about sexual relations. Some nonconformist biographies embody the Puritan idealization of marriage that is symbolized in Milton's representation of the relations between Adam and Eve before the Fall in *Paradise Lost*. The finest and most loving accounts of marriage appear in Puritan lives of wives by widowed husbands, for example Richard Baxter's *Breviate* of the life of Margaret Baxter, and in the biographies of husbands by widows, such as Lucy Hutchinson's life of Colonel John Hutchinson.

Baxter's *Breviate* is one of the few biographies that includes intimate personal letters. Richard Parr appended a large collection of letters to his life of Ussher, but these are not of a very private nature. Fell states that he has omitted Hammond's correspondence as Hammond himself would have wished.[33] In keeping with such omissions, the biographers rarely tell us more about their subjects' friendships than about their domestic lives, although Walton, as will be seen, is exceptional in the emphasis he places on friendship.

V Appearance and Physical Attributes

As some of the omissions in the treatment of private life suggest, seventeenth-century religious biographers, primarily concerned with the spiritual life, give little attention to the body. The human as animal is excluded as far as possible, and the life of the senses is scarcely represented. Information about health is sometimes given, but sexual life is practically omitted, apart from some references to youthful sin in conversion narratives and occasional mention of false slander of sexual laxity. The biographers usually tell us little about the size or shape of the body, and little about appearance or features, important though these may be as a mark of the subject's individuality. Their importance was pointed out by John Evelyn, who in his *Numismata* (1697) praised Providence for ordaining such a variety of looks and countenances among humans, and observed that there would otherwise have been great confusion in the world and even in marriages.[34] Their importance was recognized too by some of the more secular biographers, notably John Aubrey, and certain authors of lives of public figures, but the religious biographers tended to represent their subjects in almost disembodied or abstract forms.

In their neglect of the body and appearance, the authors of seventeenth-century lives were influenced by long-established traditions of Christian biography. Praise of the body was part of the classical *laudatio funebris*, but Gregory of Nazianzus declined to deal with the topic because his concern was with inner qualities, and patristic funeral orations and biographies provided little physical description. Other reasons for the neglect are indicated by Fell in his life of Allestree: 'As to his bodily appearance and outward features, as they are of less importance, so are they in recent memory, and by sculpture and other delineations are so generally known, that there will be no need they should be exprest by words.'[35] Not only does Fell regard outward appearance as relatively insignificant but he overlooks the fact that writers may tell us much about their subjects' physical characteristics that even painters and sculptors cannot very well represent, and he lacks the kind of historical imagination needed to recognize that what is not recorded in the present will be lost to the future.

This failure in historical imagination is common among both religious and secular biographers in the period. With the notable exception of John Aubrey, biographers were more inclined to recognize the value of providing information about such matters as appearance for those from the distant past than for contemporaries. Thus Bedell's early biographers provided no systematic description of his body or features, and it was apparently only many years after his death that Burnet made inquiries about his appearance.[36] Walton took pains to provide a more vivid description of the long-dead Hooker than of a contemporary like George Herbert whom he had seen with his own eyes.

Some of Sir Thomas More's early biographers adapted Erasmus's fine description of More's appearance, but the Protestant biographers of the seventeenth century rarely emulated this model. Many even of the most distinguished of these biographers throughout the century provided no information at all about the bodily appearance or characteristics of their subjects. None appears in Featley's life of Jewel (1609), Isaacson's life of Andrewes (1650), Bernard's life of Ussher (1656), or Fell's life of Allestree (1684). Even where some information is given about appearance in religious biographies it is seldom detailed or precise, sharp or individual. The anonymous life of Henry Wharton prefixed to Wharton's *Sermons* (1697) is typical: 'As to his Person, He was of a middle Stature, of a brown Complexion, and of a grave and comely Countenance.' This could scarcely be less individual. As will be observed in the discussion of Walton, Anglican biographers tended to represent their subjects as physical embodiments of the *via media*, free of anything extreme or peculiar. Thus Fell tells us of Henry Hammond: 'His *Stature* was of just height and all proportionate dimensions, avoiding the extremes of gross and meager.'[37]

When the biographers mention the face their motive is often to relate their subjects to sacred types or holy figures, rather than to give information for its own sake or to establish individuality. Thus Thomas Gouge in his life of William Gouge tells us that some have observed his father's face resembled that which usually passes as Moses'. Clarke describes Richard Vines as looking like a portrait of Luther, and Baddeley and Naylor state that Morton was similar in appearance to a printed description of Beza.[38] More precise and individual detail about facial and bodily appearance, however, begins to appear in biographies of clergy influenced by newer scientific or antiquarian movements in the later part of the century, as will be seen in subsequent discussion of the anonymous life of Thomas Fuller and Abraham Hill's life of Isaac Barrow.

The biographers of Fuller and Barrow both reveal the unworldly nature of their scholarly subjects partly by describing their unusual carelessness about dress, but few of the religious biographers make much reference to clothing as a means of establishing their subjects' characters, unless it is to demonstrate special humility and religious vocation, in accordance with long-established hagiographical tradition. Thus John Ferrar tells us that Nicholas Ferrar as a child would wear no lace because he was resolved to become a clergyman. Some Anglican biographers advocate a moderate plainness rather than an ascetic extreme in dress as in other things. Donne tells us in his commemoration sermon on Lady Danvers that in dress 'Her *rule* was *mediocrity*' and warns that 'to weare worse things, then others doe' may be a form of pride.[39] But other biographers, both Anglican and Puritan, represent their subjects as remarkable not merely for scholarly carelessness like Fuller and Barrow but for the holy simplicity and humility of their clothing. Among clerical figures already considered, Bedell according to his son's account appeared as a bishop in brogues, and among the laymen Hale is described by Burnet as dressing so humbly that he was once seized by a press gang. Walton, however, as will be seen especially in his life of Herbert, is the seventeenth-century biographer who provides the most masterly development of the hagiographical tradition of the symbolic use of clothing that had earlier been embodied in such sixteenth-century works as Cavendish's life of Wolsey and Roper's life of More.

While the religious biographers usually gave little place to description of the body or appearance of their subjects, they frequently recognized that one physical attribute was too important to be ignored in lives of clergy: the voice. In accordance with biblical and patristic precedents, they often represented preachers as essentially being voices. An anonymous biographer of Samuel Bolton states that this nonconformist clergyman was 'All Voice,' '*Tota Vox*,' as Gregory of Nazianzus had said of John the Baptist, that is one who spoke through his whole life as well as in the pulpit. Some biographers attach such importance to the actual physical voice that they seem to come close to equating success in the ministry with strength of lungs. They show that the careers of clergy, Anglican as well as Presbyterian, were much affected by the quality of their voices. Bedell, according to his son's life, decided to leave the great church of Bury St Edmunds because of the weakness of his voice, and Edward Rainbowe, according to an anonymous biographer, was rejected as a preacher at Lincoln's Inn for one who had a louder voice. But some biographers give cases of ministers who succeeded despite weakness of voice or impediments in speech by virtue of their other qualities.[40]

VI Faults and Suppressions

In cases where seventeenth-century religious biographers admit faults or weaknesses in their subjects, they tend to follow established patterns, often derived from biblical and patristic models, just as they do in setting out the virtues, so that there usually appears to be little more variety or individuality in the faults than in the virtues. One of the patterns that displays strongly conventional elements even in the representation of experiential religion is the conversion narrative, based on the models of Paul and Augustine, in which youthful sinfulness is recognized and indeed often emphasized in order to demonstrate the greatness of the transformation that comes with conversion. Following the precedent of St Augustine, the biographers like to refer to early episodes of stealing fruit. Thus in one of the biographies printed by Samuel Clarke we are told that Samuel Fairclough stole pears from an orchard when a child. According to Anthony Walker, Elizabeth Walker as a child once took an apple from her mother's stores but, displaying a fine moral sense, then put it back. Thomas Wadsworth, as his biographer informs us, was a little more original: as a boy he stole a tulip, but afterwards like Augustine confessed his sin.[41]

Some other biographies provide more historically interesting details than the stories of stealing fruit. Cockfighting and gambling enter into various accounts of youthful sin, but the hazards of light and profane literature and the drama are more emphasized in biographies shaped by seventeenth-century Puritanism. Bagshaw tells us that Bolton at Cambridge loved stage plays, cards, and dice and was a horrible swearer, sabbath breaker, 'and was ever glad (as I have heard him say) of *Christmas-holy-dayes*, and marvellous melancholie when they were ended.' Burnet informs us that Hale had a youthful period of vanity at Oxford, caused by seeing stage plays, and that on coming to London he resolved never to see another. Joan Drake's biographer in 1647 shows the bad consequences of play-going in London, describing how in her thoughts she likened the Puritan divine John Dod 'unto *Ananias*, one whom at a play in the Black-Friers shee saw scoft at, for a holy brother of *Amsterdam*.' Margaret Duck, according to a biography appended to her funeral sermon in the same period, avoided such dangers, for she refused to go to playhouses though she lived near Blackfriars. Later in the century Anthony Horneck provides another example of temptation nobly resisted, for his biographer tells us in 1697: 'You would not find him perusing *Lucretius, Spinosa, Machiavel,* or *Hobbs,* nor sporting with *Ovid, Virgil, Catullus, Tasso,* or *Cowleys Mistress* or our modern Plays.'[42]

Apart from the accounts of youthful frivolity and sinfulness in conversion narratives, there is just one fault that the seventeenth-century religious biographers frequently admit in their subjects, and that is the passion of anger. The list of divines and other exemplary religious figures of the period who possessed an angry temperament is an extraordinarily long one. The biographers leave us with the sense that this era of fierce controversy and civil war was indeed an angry century. They often justify or excuse their subjects' tendency to anger by citing precedents in the Bible and among church fathers and leaders of the Reformation. William Hinde in his life of John Bruen states that this pious country gentleman was by nature passionate, angry, and hasty, but cites Paul as a parallel, and observes: 'Many of the ancient Fathers were of violent and fierce spirits, savouring much of pride and passion, as they were men.' His examples include Jerome, whose angry spirit evident in his writings was indeed notorious, Augustine, Chrysostom, and Ambrose, and Calvin among modern divines.[43]

Some biographers evidently regard anger not only as normal but even as commendable. Anthony Walker in his life of the Countess of Warwick feels obliged to defend her against the charge of 'Defect of Anger,' which might imply 'want of zeal against sin, and sinners.' Other biographers, however, including Burnet in his life of Hale and Fell in his life of Allestree, commend their subjects for managing to conceal or overcome their naturally passionate and choleric natures. The clergy who reacted against religious controversy like Thomas Jackson in Vaughan's life are among the exceptions to those with angry temperaments, as are William Gouge, who according to the biography by his son Thomas was never known to be angry in twenty years, and Bedell, whom Burnet contrasts in his good temper with such figures as Luther and Calvin. But Walton, as will be seen, is the biographer most concerned to represent his subjects as notable for meekness and mildness.[44]

In a few cases biographers move beyond the conventional and deal with graver faults than anger in their subjects. Fuller in *Abel Redevivus* tells us that Francis Junius in his youth turned atheist. He asks himself whether he should remain silent about this and follow the injunction 'Tell it not in Gath,' but he concludes that the error must not be concealed and that others may learn from it (although in his *Worthies* he states that from charity he sometimes avoids complete candour). Featley in his life of Jewel handles well his subject's temporary apostasy, when on the accession of Queen Mary he signed a document seeming to renounce Protestantism. Featley expresses his sorrow: 'I would most willingly have layd my finger upon this foule scarre, but the truth of love must not prejudice love of truth.' Recognizing no doubt that any attempt at concealment would be futile, he concedes that Jewel did not have the stuff of martyrs but employs his rhetorical skills to put the apostasy in perspective, showing that Jewel immediately repented and referring to other great figures of the church who denied faith only to become stronger subsequently.[45]

In some other cases, however, biographers admit suppression of episodes or aspects of their subjects' lives. Richard Mayo writes regarding Edmund Staunton's patience in affliction that this clergyman had a great trial which 'for some reasons' he conceals. John Barnard in his life of Peter Heylyn explicitly advocates the suppression of things that might be seen as discreditable in his subject's career, and criticizes another biographer, George Vernon, for mentioning old charges relating to Heylyn's journalistic activities and to a clandestine marriage; he holds that, true or false, these should have been omitted. Many of the religious biographers of the period follow the policy Barnard advocates, and silently pass over problematical aspects of their subjects' lives or deal with them in evasive ways.[46]

A common area of suppression is in family background and connections. Sometimes the biographers justify omission of information about family by patristic precedent. St Basil in his homily on the martyr Gordius declared that concern with family was one of the aspects of profane panegyric to be rejected by the sacred encomiast.[47] But the seventeenth-century biographers are specially inclined to suppress any information about family that would not be in accord with the elevation and decorum, harmony and unity, that they seek to establish for their subjects' lives. They often prefer to be evasive even when the suppressed information need not be seen as really discreditable to their subjects.

John Featley tells us that Daniel Featley's father had 'an employment in *Oxford*,' rather than revealing that he was actually a college cook, just as Cavendish in his life of Wolsey had withheld the report that Wolsey's father was a butcher. Fell in his concern to emphasize Hammond's loyal Royalism during the Civil War and Interregnum refrains from mentioning that Hammond's close relations included prominent rebels. One must turn from Fell's biography to Anthony Wood's much more candid *Athenæ Oxonienses* to discover that Hammond's brother Thomas was a Parliamentary general who acted as one of the judges at the trial of Charles I and 'escaped the halter, or at least perpetual imprisonment' only because he died before the Restoration, and that his nephew Colonel Robert Hammond served as the king's jailer on the Isle of Wight. A more serious omission occurs in John Harris's life of the Anglican bishop Arthur Lake. In emphasizing his subject's unworldliness Harris never mentions that Bishop Lake's brother was a powerful (and corrupt) officer of state, whose advancements at every stage preceded the bishop's progressive ecclesiastical preferments. This circumstance does not necessarily bring Arthur Lake's integrity into question, but it is a matter a biographer should not entirely evade.[48]

The tendency of authors of exemplary biographies to omit aspects and problems in their subjects' lives that might complicate the picture they seek to present may be illustrated by the mid-seventeenth-century biographies of two Anglican prelates, respectively from the right and left wings of the church, Lancelot Andrewes and James Ussher. In his *An Exact Narration of the Life and Death* of Andrewes (1650), Henry Isaacson represents Andrewes as an ideal figure of sanctity, unworldliness, and learning. In many ways later biographers confirm this picture, but they point to a few questionable aspects left unmentioned by Isaacson: nepotism in the case of an unworthy brother, and servility to state and monarch regarding the Essex divorce. More fundamentally, Isaacson fails to examine the coexistence of the unworldly scholar with the powerful prelate, and never considers such questions as whether Andrewes's scholarly interests caused him to neglect his public responsibilities.

Nicholas Bernard's *The Life & Death of the Most Reverend and Learned Father of our Church Dr. James Usher, Late Arch-Bishop of Armagh* (1656) is a similar case. Like Andrewes, Ussher was a dedicated scholar, eminent for learning, who held high ecclesiastical office. As Andrewes became Bishop of Winchester, Ussher became Archbishop of Armagh. Nothing in Bernard's life suggests any tension between different roles, except that he records Ussher's deathbed prayer for forgiveness of omissions. Bernard does not choose to tell us of any of Ussher's omissions, but the biographers of Bedell do. Clogie states and Burnet emphasizes that Bedell suffered from lack of support from the archbishop who was his superior, because Ussher was so absorbed in scholarship that he neglected the administration of his archdiocese.[49]

Roger North's withering criticism of Burnet's life of Hale for its suppressions and distortions has already been mentioned. According to North the suppressions include Hale's vanity about his learning and his susceptibility to flattery, as well as such aspects of his domestic life as his unworthy second marriage and his dissolute sons.[50] The pattern of suppressions detectable in such biographies is part of the context that needs to be considered for Walton's lives, where questions about omissions and evasions frequently arise.

VII Style

The exemplary religious biographies of the seventeenth century exhibit a wide range of prose styles, as the biographers come under the influence of the numerous shifts and movements in literary fashion and art during the period. They display all the rich variety of a century remarkable for the diversity and splendour of its prose styles. The range includes the elaborate rhetorical Ciceronian style of Featley's life of Jewel early in the century, and in the middle decades both the complex style, rich in imagery and allusion, of Hacket's life of Williams and the polished strong simplicity of Harris's life of Lake and Vaughan's life of Jackson. The Restoration era brings both the magisterial grandeur of Fell's lives of Hammond and Allestree and the plain style of Burnet's life of Hale, which accords both with Hale's love of antique simplicity and with Burnet's own ideal, defined in his praise of the prose of Hale's *Contemplations* as 'clear and Masculine, in a due temper between flatness and affectation.' Walton's intimacy of voice and cultivated appearance of artlessness provide still another variety, in the lives Wordsworth declared were written with a pen shaped from a feather 'Dropped from an Angel's wing.'[51]

An indication of the literary distinction of some of the earlier seventeenth-century lives is the fact that the authors include translators who provided the King James Version of the Bible. Modern biographers of figures such as Jewel, Andrewes, and Donne, however much they may expand and correct, usually fall back upon the seventeenth-century biographies for the great moments of their subjects' lives, because of the stylistic excellence and power as much as the evidential value of the early accounts. Judged in terms of prose style, many of these lives have good claims to be considered among the most impressive of all English biographies.

For all the variety and excellence of the prose, however, certain stylistic limitations are common in these biographies. By its very nature, exemplary biography tends toward abstraction, since the writers are more intent on deriving principles for the instruction of the reader than providing individual detail. The biographers tend to adopt a stylistic decorum of dignified impersonality and generality, lacking precision and, with some exceptions such as Walton, displaying little intimacy. Because of their persuasive and polemical purposes, furthermore, the biographers often develop styles that are more rhetorical than factual. These qualities are apparent in biographies both early and late in the century, as may be illustrated by Featley's life of Jewel and by Fell's lives of Hammond and Allestree.

Featley's life of Jewel, based on Humphrey's earlier Latin biography, is designed to lessen the Calvinistic bias but not otherwise to alter the substance of the original so much as to improve on the artistry and style. Featley, who was a disciple of the great rhetorician Reynolds, employs all the devices of classical rhetoric. His grand Ciceronian style is rich in imagery and rhythm, with elements both of 'metaphysical' and Euphuistic wit, including much play upon the word 'jewel.' The result is a masterpiece of rhetorical elaboration, patterning of word and sound, so accomplished that Jewel's nineteenth-century biographer felt he could do no better than to begin and end with Featley's first and last paragraphs.[52] But the work is open to the Baconian criticism that the concern is with words more than with things, and the style, as far from transparent as could be, often comes between the reader and the subject.

Fell's lives of Hammond and Allestree belong to a period of neoclassical reaction against the 'false wit' of such an earlier style as Featley's. They are accomplished specimens of the 'Augustan' style that emerged in the Restoration. At best Fell achieves a grandeur of generalization that anticipates such later masters as Samuel Johnson. He writes about Hammond's scholarly learning that he was 'one whose knowledge seem'd rather infus'd then acquir'd' and 'in whom the learned Languages might be thought to be the Mother-Tongue.' He describes memorably Hammond's unworldliness: 'the World and its appendages hanging so loose about him, that he never took notice when any part dropt off.' Sometimes, however, the stylistic elevation takes the form of a stilted Latinism ludicrously out of keeping with the subject, as when he writes of Hammond: 'Sauces he scarce ever tasted of.'[53]

Fell's style is marked by formality and impersonality. Although he had a long and close acquaintance with Allestree, in his biography he refers to himself as 'Mr. Fell' and avoids intimacy of tone and detail. His dignity of style is often achieved at the cost of vagueness. His most serious limitation is a lack of concreteness. While he achieves a degree of precision in some matters closely related to his exemplary purposes, he often prefers general to specific statements. He adheres in fact to the same principles of decorum as predominate in the funeral sermons of the period. For example, Lewis Southcomb tells us in his sermon for the funeral of John Culme (1690) that his subject was 'for a considerable number of years' at 'one of the Fountains of Learning' without giving either the number of years or the name of the university. Similarly, when Fell comments on Hammond's valuing of friendship, rather than identifying the friends by name he refers to them only as 'one eminently near to him,' 'that Friend of his with whom he had then the nearest opportunity of commerce,' 'that excellent person,' 'the good *Lady*,' and 'the Family where he was.' He informs us that Hammond at Oxford became a fellow of his college 'by a very unusuall concurrence of providential

Events' but he gives no indication of what those events were. In a description of his subject's bodily appearance, he tells us that Hammond had a clear and florid complexion, 'so that (especially in his youth) he had the esteem of a very beauteous person; which was lessen'd onely by the colour of his Hair'; but he does not say what that colour was.[54]

Fell represents the exemplary religious biography of the Restoration at its most distinguished, and his practices compare favourably with those of many of his contemporaries. On one occasion John Aubrey even cited his work as precedent for his own recording of seemingly trivial biographical detail. But it is significant that Aubrey and his friend Anthony Wood at other times viewed Dr Fell, Dean of Christ Church and Bishop of Oxford, as an enemy, leader of a conservative Oxford establishment opposed to their own principles and practices.[55] An examination of Fell's style helps one to understand why Aubrey insisted so much on the value of 'minuteness' of detail, and why he then sometimes encountered criticism as a radical innovator.

CHAPTER 4

Izaak Walton's Lives

I

Among Anglican exemplary biographers Izaak Walton is unique for his long and sustained work and for his apparently wide scope. His labours as a biographer extended over more than forty years. Becoming a biographer almost by accident in order to provide a prefatory life for John Donne's collected *Sermons* in 1640 on the death of Sir Henry Wotton, who was originally to have supplied the life, he went on to write biographies of Wotton (1651), Richard Hooker (1665), George Herbert (1670), and Robert Sanderson (1678). In later years he made large additions to the earlier lives, and he continued with his revisions until 1681.[1]

On the surface Walton's lives give the appearance of wide scope and great variety, since his subjects include in Donne and Herbert two great Anglican poets, in Donne a famous preacher and Dean of St Paul's, in Herbert a saintly country clergyman, in Hooker a great theologian and doctrinal father of the Church of England, in Wotton an exemplary Anglican layman, who took deacon's orders on his retirement at Eton College after a distinguished diplomatic career, and in Sanderson a figure who exemplified the suffering and loyalty of the Anglican clergy during the period of Puritan rule and became an influential prelate on the Restoration. Walton extended his scope even further by inserting in the five biographies brief sketches of other notable Anglican figures: John Whitgift in the life of Hooker, William Bedell in the life of Wotton, and Nicholas Ferrar in the life of Herbert. Taken together his biographies appear to comprise the Compleat Anglican.

This appearance of wide range and variety, however, is deceptive. The life of Donne, the only one written in its first version before the Civil War, stands in many ways apart from the others and needs to be given separate consideration, but the other four biographical subjects, despite the surface appearance of variety, are shaped by Walton into the same basic type, the figure who is the man of peace and the practical Christian rather than the holy warrior or the fierce controversialist. While Walton writes with the polemical purpose of defending the Church of England against its Puritan opponents, he is in strong reaction against the disputes about theology and church government that led to the tragic divisions of the Civil War. His ideal Anglican as represented in Wotton, Herbert, Hooker, and Sanderson is a figure of charity, peaceableness, and moderation, exemplifying the Church of England as a *via media*, seeking conciliation and harmony, avoiding disputes and divisions in favour of practical Christianity. Walton makes the four men, superficially different though they are, variations on this single type.

Walton established his predominant pattern in 1651 in the life of Sir Henry Wotton, the first of the fuller biographies to follow the short and hastily written 1640 version of the life of Donne. He introduces the emphasis upon peaceableness and moderation immediately in the opening picture of his subject's family background. He tells us that Wotton's father was 'averse to all Contentations,' and he develops the theme fully in his account of Wotton's diplomatic career as English ambassador in Venice, giving many instances to show his charitable and conciliatory approach, his moderate and ecumenical spirit in his relations with the Roman Catholic clergy. Walton represents Wotton throughout his life as the great enemy to all disputes in religion, even to his epitaph at the end, rendered in English as 'The itch of disputation will prove the scab of the church.'[2]

This pattern established in the life of Wotton also dominates the biographies of Hooker, Herbert, and Sanderson. While Walton writes in the life of Hooker with special purposes of claiming the doctrinal support of this great Anglican figure for the official Restoration establishment of the church, his emphasis falls on Hooker's peaceableness and moderation in every phase of his career. At Oxford, Walton tells us, Hooker was 'never known to be angry, or passionate, or extream'; in London at the Temple he was reluctantly drawn into controversy with the Calvinist Walter Travers but he conducted this not as a war against an enemy but 'with the spirit of meekness and reason,' showing a 'Dove-like temper,' and he displayed the same qualities in his treatment of dissenters both in his great *Of the Laws of Ecclesiastical Polity* and in his work as a country clergyman. Likewise, in his life of Herbert Walton links his subject with Ferrar at Little Gidding and 'many of the Clergy that were more inclin'd to *practical piety*, and *devotion*, then to doubtful and needless Disputations.' The same theme shapes the life of Sanderson. Walton represents him as even from youth 'mild, and averse to oppositions,' and emphasizes that during the Civil War and Interregnum his loyalty was combined with moderation, that he worked to compromise with opponents, and that after the Restoration he presided over the Savoy Conference with 'much mildness, patience, and reason,' seeking compromise with dissenters.[3]

Combined with the theme of ideal Anglican harmony, peaceableness, and moderation is a second theme that runs through all four of these lives and that has the effect of further demonstrating the similarity rather than the difference or individuality of Wotton, Hooker, Herbert, and Sanderson: the theme of pastoral retreat. While Walton's special purpose here is to repudiate the charge of worldliness and self-seeking so often brought against the Anglican clergy by their opponents, the theme embodies values specially dear to him: it is at the centre of *The Compleat Angler* (1653), which is full of allusions to biblical and classical pastoral. In that work, as has often been noted, angling and Anglicanism are closely linked: piscatory pastoral is combined with defence of Anglican values. Anglers are seen as representing primitive Christian virtues, in the context of a simple, tranquil life close to nature, as repudiating worldly ambition and money-getting, and as standing for a way of life in many ways antithetical to that of the Puritans. The biography of Wotton was published just two years before *The Compleat Angler*, and both it and the three later lives could almost be read as extensions of that work: they are four variations on its central theme.

In these biographies Walton locates his subjects in a pastoral setting as quickly as possible, even when doing so involves great distortion of chronology, and he keeps reminding us of that setting. In the life of Wotton he begins by emphasizing that the members of his subject's family, although notable for their public service, preferred modesty and retirement, and declined various high offices. He passes rapidly over Wotton's long and important career as a diplomat, while stressing his disregard for money and worldly goods, and brings him as soon as he can to the final phase of his life, his retirement to a peaceable life of study and religious contemplation at Eton College. This striking imbalance and shifting of emphasis away from Wotton's public role is caused partly by Walton's lack of information about the diplomatic career, but it is prompted just as much by his desire to develop the pastoral theme and move into an idyllic picture of Wotton's life at Eton, where the retired diplomat takes up both angling and Anglican orders as a deacon.

The same theme of pastoral retreat is extensively developed in the lives of Hooker, Herbert, and Sanderson. Walton represents Hooker as one who preferred the quietness of life in a college or in a country parish to the prominence of involvement in controversy at the Temple in London, and describes him as resigning his position in London for the more obscure and peaceable life of a country clergyman at Boscombe and Bishopsbourne, where he could work on his *Ecclesiastical Polity* with fewer distractions. Walton emphasizes his primitive Christian life in the country, his humility, and his poor clothing, and moves so literally into the pastoral mode that he represents Hooker as once being found by his friends tending sheep.[4]

The biography of Herbert is built around the subject's turning away from his early ambition for a career in court and public life, dictated by his aristocratic family background, to dedicate himself humbly to the service of God as a country parson at Bemerton. Walton informs us that Herbert when University Public Orator 'seldom look'd towards *Cambridge*, unless the King were there, but then he never fail'd'; but he moves rapidly over the earlier phases of the life and devotes most of the biography to the brief final period of two or three years at Bemerton, '*an almost incredible story, of the great sanctity of the short remainder of his holy life,*' with many anecdotes to show Herbert's piety and humility as a country parson and his total renunciation of worldly ambition. Walton comments at the end: 'Thus he liv'd, and thus he dy'd like a Saint, unspotted of the World.'[5]

In the case of Sanderson it would not suit Walton's pastoral theme to emphasize in the same way the short final period when at the end of his life his subject became Bishop of Lincoln. Hence Walton gives more space to Sanderson's earlier time as country parson for many years at Boothby Pagnell. Since Sanderson was the only one of Walton's subjects to live through the period of the Civil War, the biography develops the special theme of the way in which the pastoral idyll, the ideally humble, simple, practical Christianity of his life in the country, was shattered by the war, and seeks to demonstrate his exemplary loyalty during the period of affliction. On the Restoration Walton emphasizes that Sanderson reluctantly accepted episcopal rank, and retained his former simplicity and humility, spending his income upon repair of his cathedral and episcopal residence rather than for the enrichment of his family.[6]

II

Walton's development of the same basic themes in all four lives of Wotton, Hooker, Herbert, and Sanderson certainly does not lead to the extinction of all differences between his subjects. He recognizes that the external circumstances and histories of the four men differ in many ways, but he is frequently more concerned to bring out the similarities than the differences. It is difficult in his biographies to distinguish clearly or sharply between Hooker at Bishopsbourne, Herbert at Bemerton, Sanderson at Boothby, or even Wotton at Eton (although he does not have the clerical charge of the other three). The similarity between the four figures is shown by the vocabulary Walton applies to them: he describes them all as meek, humble, peaceable, representing a primitive Christian ideal, as he sees it, while he terms their opponents, like the Puritans in *The Compleat Angler*, restless, busy, and angry.

Rather than revealing the complex individuality of his characters, Walton drastically oversimplifies them to make them conform to his primitive Christian ideal. His subjects were in reality men of unusual complexity and sophistication. He no more conveys the wide-ranging culture, polished urbanity, and fine wit of Wotton, who has been termed 'the most widely cultivated Englishman of his time,'[7] than he deals adequately with his diplomatic career. While he praises the learning of his subjects, he does little to show the power of Hooker's intellect or the nature of Sanderson's scholarship. He takes literally the surface simplicity of Herbert's later life and writing, almost as if he were a naive rather than a highly cultured figure. This persistent simplification is of course perfectly in keeping with the pastoral mode of Walton's biographies: William Empson defined the pastoral process as 'putting the complex into the simple.'[8]

Nowhere does Walton's oversimplification and reduction of the individuality of his characters appear more than in his handling of their speech and writing. He follows the ancient practice among historians of inventing speeches for his subjects, even though it was under strong criticism in his time. This type of historical falsification had been decisively repudiated by William Camden in his annals of Queen Elizabeth (1615), and such Restoration biographers as an anonymous author of the life of Joseph Mead (1664) and Thomas Gumble in his life of General Monck (1671) made a point of emphasizing that they did not follow this discredited practice. It was termed by John Milton in his *History of Britain* (1670) 'an abuse of posteritie.'[9] In the preface to his life of Sanderson in 1678 Walton shows some awareness of such criticism but nonetheless informs his readers that he has 'been so bold, as to paraphrase and say what I think he (whom I had the happiness to know well) would have said upon the same occasions.'[10] The problem here is not only the 'abuse of posteritie' but the diminution of individuality. In putting his own words into the mouths of his subjects, Walton makes them all speak in much the same way, in the same simple style. As the passages of dialogue in *The Compleat Angler* demonstrate, he had little dramatic capacity for the development of individual style in speech; in his revisions of that work he sometimes shifted speeches from one character to another.

For Walton to have given much attention to the writings of his subjects would have complicated his picture of ideal primitive Christianity and rural pastoral simplicity. Accordingly he offers relatively little consideration of the writings, and he very much oversimplifies their nature when he does refer to them. He creates the impression, for example, that the style of Hooker's *Ecclesiastical Polity*, which he may not actually have read, is a simple one, and has James I praise Hooker for his unaffected style.[11] Hooker's Ciceronian elaboration and grandeur are characterized much more accurately by other contemporary biographers and historians, including John Gauden, who describes the style as 'a majestick kinde of *ampleness*, and stately luxuriancy,' and Thomas Fuller, who develops a memorable image of Hooker 'driving on a whole flock of severall *Clauses* before he came to the *close* of a sentence,' and notes that his periodic constructions and copious manner caused those of inadequate capacities to censure his style 'for perplext, tedious, and obscure.'[12] In the case of Herbert's poetry, Walton contributed to the misleading impression of its simplicity that long concealed its real complexity and subtlety, the art hidden by art that critics have gradually discovered in it.

As modern scholarship has shown, especially that which has been brought to bear on the biographies by the students of Hooker, Donne, and Herbert, Walton achieved his results by highly deductive methods, by much selection and invention, suppression and manipulation of his materials.[13] Modern scholars have recoiled from Walton again and again in frustration, since he had access to much information not available to later biographers but has often proved quite unreliable. His picture of Hooker seeking rural retreat at Boscombe for his work on the *Ecclesiastical Polity*, for example, runs counter to the evidence: Hooker actually carried out his great work in the centre of London, where he could consult the necessary sources and maintain contact with other scholars; and he probably never resided at Boscombe at all. Moreover, the story of Hooker's being found in a rural parish tending sheep, although it may not be entirely Walton's own invention, is quite false. To demonstrate Hooker's unworldliness, Walton states that his excellent library was his only treasure, although he knew Hooker left a large fortune at his death, over a thousand pounds, an embarrassing fact Walton attempts to pass off by suggesting this accumulation was the work of a servant rather than of Hooker himself.[14]

Similar suppressions and distortions occur in the biographies of Wotton, Herbert, and Sanderson. In his desire to represent Wotton as a conciliatory ecumenical figure, Walton conceals the militantly Protestant nature of this diplomat's policy in Venice.[15] In the case of Sanderson, on the other hand, he conceals the fact that by some standards his subject was altogether too conciliatory to be regarded as a suffering Anglican loyalist during the Interregnum: he actually compromised with Cromwell's regime rather than be deprived of his benefice, and an anecdote Walton gives of his being wounded by a Puritan soldier in order to make him appear a martyr is an invention without actual foundation.[16] In his desire to represent Herbert as renouncing things of the world in favour of life as a humble country parson he avoids revealing that the poet's rural living of Bemerton was actually a valuable one.[17]

The opening of the life of Herbert provides a good illustration of Walton's methods of selection and suppression. His description of Herbert's family background is designed not only to show the poet's aristocratic origins but to be in harmony with his loyal Anglicanism and his devout and saintly nature. When the real facts are considered, however, it is evident that Walton is picking his way here through a minefield. One could never guess from his account the bloody history of the Herbert family, and there is nothing in his picture of Herbert's saintly mother to show how her second marriage to Sir John Danvers, a very handsome man half her age, was resented by his family, even though Donne had recognized in his sermon commemorating her the need to justify the apparent incongruity of this marriage.[18] There is no reference to the fact that Danvers became one of the regicides, signing the death warrant of Charles I. Nor is there any suggestion that the poet's brother, Edward, Lord Herbert of Cherbury, was notable for duelling and dissipation (as he made no attempt to conceal in his autobiography) and that he compromised with the Parliamentary party in the Civil War, or any allusion to the fact that as author of *De Veritate* he became the 'father of deism.' All such information would be quite out of harmony with the portrait of Herbert Walton seeks to construct.

Among the contradictory evidence Walton suppresses in order to make his subjects conform to his ideal is any indication of a tendency to anger or bad temper. While anger is one of the few potential faults allowed their subjects by many other exemplary religious biographers of the period, it is antithetical to the pastoral world of his lives. His scheme requires that the angry figures should be the disruptive Puritans, such as Herbert's opponent, Andrew Melville. He never suggests any possibility of anger in Herbert himself, although the poet's brother, Lord Herbert of Cherbury, states that he was subject to anger, and an understanding of some of his poems, such as 'The Collar,' with its play upon 'choler,' depends partly upon recognition of this fact. In the life of Sanderson, Walton in order to emphasize the bishop's charity and conciliation toward the nonconformists at the Savoy Conference passes silently over what Richard Baxter refers to as his 'aged Peevishness.' Hence it is not surprising that Walton did not undertake a biography of the most conspicuous of the Anglican martyrs of the 1640s, the notably choleric Archbishop Laud, whose rigorous policies represented the antithesis of Walton's motto, 'Study to be quiet,' and that he actually makes little allusion to Laud, even though he is paradoxically linked in many respects with the Laudian party of the Restoration Church of England.[19]

III

Walton writes of his work in the preface to his life of Donne: 'he that wants skill to deceive, may be safely trusted,' but the appearance of naive, artless simplicity he cultivates is highly deceptive.[20] His biographies are in reality impressive for their fine artistry and careful patterning, and for the skilful development of 'fictional' methods, scenes, and anecdotes. They sometimes appear loosely organized and digressive, but apparent digressions such as the insertion of lives of Whitgift, Bedell, and Ferrar in the biographies of Hooker, Wotton, and Herbert are not really digressions at all when Walton's purposes are understood but serve to reinforce his principal themes. Except in the case of the last biography, the life of Sanderson, where his digressiveness does perhaps get out of hand, his lives are marked by the fine, even relentless, unity that is so characteristic of exemplary religious biographies of the period.

As an example of the careful patterning that marks Walton's artistry, one might take the references to clothing in the life of Herbert. There are two mentions of the young Herbert's liking for fine clothing in the earlier part of the life, symbolizing his youthful ambition for a courtly career. Then when Herbert decides to take Holy Orders, Walton tells us, he sends for the tailor and exchanges the silk clothes and sword of the courtier for canonicals. Finally, as a result of a Good Samaritan episode in which he assist a carter whose horse has bogged down, he meets his musical friends in Salisbury wearing muddy clothing, which with the ensuing dialogue with the friends illustrates how completely the courtier has been replaced by the humble, unworldly country clergyman. The reference here to Herbert's love of music is part of a pattern developed with similar artistry to symbolize the divine harmony of the poet's life of religious dedication.[21]

Walton's skilful development of 'fictional' or 'novelistic' methods is specially apparent in the life of Donne, which is full of memorable scenes and anecdotes. This life is a partial exception to the patterns that shape the other four. It was written in its first version in 1640 before Walton had fully established the favourite patterns that emerged in the life of Wotton and *The Compleat Angler*. He made large additions to it, including most of the well-known anecdotes, in later editions in 1658, 1670, and 1675, but he was obliged to recognize that Donne was too powerfully individual and the shape of his life too unusual to be made to fit the patterns he had established in the other lives. He expresses consciousness of this difference by describing Donne's life more than once as 'various.' His biography of Donne shares with that of Herbert the themes of overcoming early worldly and courtly ambition and finding a clerical vocation, but in Donne there is the element lacking in Herbert and the others of the 'irregularity' of the early years. Not only was Donne's complexity much too great to allow representation of him as fitting the simple primitive Christian mould, but there was no opportunity to develop the theme of rural pastoral retreat as in the other lives, for it was well known that Donne was entirely urban in his tastes and had refused rural preferments when they were offered him.

Walton is very conscious that he has in Donne a most remarkable figure and a highly dramatic life, and in many ways he effectively exploits these advantages in his biography; yet even in this case he very much oversimplifies various aspects of his subject's character and career. As Donne in later years liked to compare himself to Paul and Augustine, Walton builds his life on the conversion pattern, and establishes a strong, simple contrast between the worldly and 'irregular' youth and the saintly later years, between Jack Donne and Dean Donne. But he really tells us very little about the nature of Donne's early sins, a subject that still remains obscure today, and focuses rather upon the overcoming of worldly ambition in favour of religious dedication. This biography, like that of Herbert, is imbalanced strongly in favour of the later years, being titled in its first version 'The Life and Death.' The imbalance is inevitable, since Walton had first-hand knowledge of Donne only in Donne's later years, when Walton was one of his parishioners, and it suits the thematic emphasis he desires, but it is regrettable, since it leaves unknown so much of Donne's earlier years, the period of the great poetry.

Walton provides a fine authentic picture of many aspects of the later Donne as saintly dean and great preacher but he gives no adequate sense of the complexity and brilliance either of Donne's intellect or of his poetry. He conveys neither the sensuality nor the scepticism of the early verse. He introduces several of the spiritual and religious poems but only to give simple and misleading autobiographical readings of them. Nor does he represent adequately the complications and conflicts of Donne's religious development, or the fact that the sins that most troubled him were not the sins of a dissolute youth in the past but the sins of the present: pride, egotism, unevenness of temperament. He displays little either of Donne's baroque theatricality or of his wit, the quality many of his contemporaries most admired. This life of Donne will always be memorable for its finely told anecdotes, but modern scholarship has shown that many of these anecdotes are false or of dubious reliability; and much modern scholarship has been devoted to the attempt to get behind Walton's simple dramatic contrast between Jack Donne and Dean Donne.

While the life of Donne stands as a partial exception to the pattern of the other four biographies, Walton works in a number of ways to reduce the difference between Donne and his other subjects, thus from time to time diminishing rather than emphasizing his individuality. He creates the sense that Donne's life and character have much in common with those of his other subjects by introducing into the biography episodes which are close counterparts to those in the other lives, for example, anecdotes showing the rejection of opportunities for worldly wealth, even when this means the impoverishment of the subject's family, and anecdotes involving prophetic dreams, to suggest a figure specially favoured by God. As well as inserting such conventional elements into the life of Donne in the same way as in the other lives, he makes the pattern of the deathbed speeches of Donne and Herbert, which are partly at least his own invention, similar to each other. He further increases the sense of similarity between Donne and his other subjects by significant omission. In addition to his relative neglect of the early life and early poems, he avoids much mention of Donne's activities as a controversialist, in order to make him appear, like the others, a figure of peaceableness and moderation.

Among the common themes Walton develops in all five lives is that of friendship. Inspired by such biblical texts as John 15:12-15, he makes friendship an integral part of his central concern with charity and harmony. His emphasis upon the importance of friendship in the lives of his subjects grows with revisions. A list of Donne's friends not found in the 1640 life is added in 1658; in the life of Wotton sections on friendship with Bedell and Morton not found in 1651 are added in 1654. He sometimes carries this emphasis further than evidence appears to warrant. While Gauden writes of Hooker: 'His Friends or *Confidents* were few, but choise,' Walton gives the impression that friendship played a much larger part in Hooker's life, and introduces here as in the other lives and *The Compleat Angler* prose hymns in celebration of friendship. He gives such prominence to the theme that Charles Cotton in commendatory verses included in the collected edition of the *Lives* in 1675 saw friendship as Walton's main motive in writing the lives. This special emphasis is closely linked with the sense of intimacy that gives Walton's style much of its often celebrated 'charm,' which wins over readers even in an era of deconstruction. He states that he writes as 'the poorest, the meanest' of Donne's friends, and he draws the reader into the same circle of friendship. But the prominence he gives friendship in all five lives serves not to differentiate but to reinforce the sense of similarity between his subjects.[22]

Even in the matter of bodily appearance Walton, in contrast to such a biographer as John Aubrey, generally prefers to emphasize what his subjects have in common rather than what differentiates them. He implies that in their height most of the figures exemplify the same Anglican *via media*. He uses virtually the same words to describe both Donne and Sanderson, telling us that the former was 'of Stature moderately tall' and that the latter was 'moderately tall,' and states similarly that Herbert was 'of a stature inclining towards Tallness' and that Wotton was 'tall of stature.' He represents only Hooker as a definite exception to this pattern, a man 'of mean stature,' in keeping with his humility. The physical description of Hooker with 'his Face full of Heat-pimples' is the most individual that occurs in the lives. Walton, again in contrast to Aubrey, seems to recognize the interest of such details only in the case of a subject who has long been dead. It is regrettable that he did not record such information about Herbert, for example, since only a single sketch is known to exist by way of an authentic portrait.[23]

IV

Walton's lives belong to a borderland between devotional writing and true biography. The balance between the actual and the ideal is like that in *The Compleat Angler*, where there is a selection of details from real landscape and actual rural life and an admixture of scientific natural history, but the details are selected to give an idyllic picture, and unpleasant or inharmonious aspects of country life are omitted. In the biographies, although he can never admit any good of the Puritans, when Walton encounters a figure he disapproves of, like John Wall in the life of Sanderson, he tends simply to turn away and refuse to go into detail; so also with aspects of the lives and characters of his biographical subjects that would not suit his ideal picture. He seeks to follow the principle he attributes to Hooker: 'Love thinks not evil, but covers a multitude of Infirmities.' It is significant that when he wrote to a publisher to recommend a prospective biographer of John Hales he gave the opinion that this biographer was likely to carry out the work very well, 'because I think he will doe it affectionately.'[24]

Walton's biographies are so much more notable for their artistry than their accuracy that when they are judged by modern standards they are open to such harsh verdicts as Leslie Stephen's condemnation. Stephen, who possessed a concern for accuracy appropriate to his position as the editor of the great British *Dictionary of National Biography*, commented on Walton's biography of Donne: 'There are two objections to the life if taken as a record of facts. The first is that the facts are all wrong; and the second is that the portraiture is palpably false.'[25] The modern biographers of Donne, Herbert, Hooker, and Wotton have repeatedly shown that Stephen's judgment is essentially right: not only are many of Walton's details wrong or dubious but his central theses and interpretations are often mistaken and misleading.

The practices of Walton that are dubious by later standards are sometimes excused as general in his period but, as will be seen in discussion of Anthony Wood's reactions to his work, criticism of his inaccuracy had already begun in his own time. In truth he could no more resist manipulating his material to construct ideal images of his subjects than Lytton Strachey could resist manipulation with the opposite purposes, and his lives prompt questions about the validity of mixing fact and fiction in biography similar to those raised about Strachey's biographies by Leslie Stephen's daughter Virginia Woolf. Walton's faults are more amiable than Strachey's, in keeping with his valuing of charity, and no one could accuse him of want of generosity to his subjects (leaving the Puritans aside) as Virginia Woolf criticized Strachey; but it cannot be overlooked that his sacrifice of facts to higher truth as he conceived it is the common justification of propaganda.[26]

Walton sees his subjects as much superior to himself in both saintliness and learning but he shapes them so far in terms of his own ideals that one might almost say of his biographies as he declares of *The Compleat Angler*: 'the whole Discourse is, or rather was, a picture of my own disposition.'[27] The life of Donne, more individualized than the others, stands out as a partial exception. But the criticism of Sir Peter Lely's portraits recorded by Dryden might well be applied to the other four biographies: 'he drew many graceful Pictures, but few of them were like. And this happen'd to him, because he always studied himself more than those who sate to him.'[28]

CHAPTER 5

Lives of Public Figures

I

Lives of contemporary public figures written in the seventeenth century provide abundant evidence of the ways in which eras of disruption may both stimulate and impede the development of biographical literature. The great conflicts and crises of the period prompted the production of far larger numbers of political and military biographies than had appeared during any earlier period in England, and these include works of enduring interest and value. But the biographers writing in response to the wars and controversies faced special problems and limitations, and many of the lives of political and military leaders are defective and disappointing, not only by later standards but by those of the time.

Gilbert Burnet complained regarding the biographies of great public figures in his *Memoires of the Lives and Actions of James and William Dukes of Hamilton and Castleherald* (1677) that in spite of the example of Plutarch, 'there is no sort of History worse done.'[1] His complaint raises the question why so much of the achievement in this field is so disappointing during a time of great public events, an era whose striking, varied, and contrasting personalities have long continued to fascinate posterity. As Burnet pointed out, the primary problem was not lack of models, for finer models existed in this field than in any other area of biography. Among classical models there was Suetonius as well as Plutarch; and the most distinguished sixteenth-century achievements in English biography, Cavendish's life of Wolsey and Roper's life of More, both fell partly at least in this category.

Yet explanations for the relative lack of success and distinction in many seventeenth-century biographies of public figures are not difficult to find. The biographers were faced with two major problems. The first was the confusion between biography and history. In a period when biography was commonly seen as a branch of history, the lines were often not drawn clearly enough between the life of the individual and more general history, and in the biographies public events tended to overwhelm or displace the personal and private. The second great problem was the limitation arising from censorship and bias. Candour and freedom of expression had always been severely restricted in writings relating to political matters and public affairs, and the conflicts, great oppositions, which make the seventeenth century historically so interesting very much made against impartiality and detachment in the biographies of public persons, as has been apparent in many of the lives of prominent religious figures already considered.

Some of the initial problems that faced the seventeenth-century biographer who sought to deal with great public figures are illustrated in an anecdote in Fulke Greville's life of Sir Philip Sidney, which was written in a peaceful period long before the Civil War although not published until 1652. Greville tells us that he once planned to write a history or biography of Queen Elizabeth, and after her death approached the Secretary of State, Sir Robert Cecil, asking to peruse obsolete records in the royal council chest. In response to the secretary's questioning, Greville replied he conceived that a historian was bound to tell nothing but the truth, but that to tell all truths would be to wrong and offend princes and states and to stir up not only particular men but families against himself. Nevertheless the request was refused. The secretary told Greville he dared not let any man living see the contents of the council chest without the king's approval.[2]

After the breakdown of the old royal and ecclesiastical systems of censorship in the 1640s some very candid 'secret histories' and scandalous biographies were published, but this relative freedom did not extend far or last long. Fuller in his *Holy State* (1642) comments that as governments changed while he was engaged on that work so did what was allowable to print. Later in the century Thomas Gumble in his biography of General Monck (1671) echoes Sir Walter Ralegh's rueful comment in his *History of the World* that he who follows truth too near the heels may be kicked in the teeth. Gumble had been Monck's chaplain, and his biography, although not totally uncritical, is discreet and respectful, but even so it ran into trouble with the official censors of the Restoration government which caused publication to be delayed. Some of Anthony Wood's problems with censorship will be noted below: in

1693 pages of his collection of biographies, *Athenæ Oxonienses*, in which he was held to have libelled the great Earl of Clarendon were ordered to be publicly burned by the hangman.[3]

Even more than from restrictions of censorship, the biographies of contemporary public figures throughout the century suffered from the biased and partisan approaches their authors commonly brought to their subjects. Many of the biographies were designed primarily as political propaganda. Those of the Civil War period were often shaped as part of the pamphlet warfare between the Anglican and Royalist presses of Oxford and the Puritan and Parliamentary presses of London. Later in the century John Dryden provided some definitive commentary on the partisan biographers of his time, in his preface to translations of Plutarch's lives (1683): 'They are not Historians of an Action, but Lawyers of a party ... and in front of their Histories, there ought to be written the Prologue of a pleading, *I am for the Plaintiff,* or *I am for the Defendant.*'[4] Such bias is the primary reason why there are no satisfactory contemporary biographies of the central figures of the great seventeenth-century conflict, Charles I and Oliver Cromwell: with some partial exceptions the early biographies or professed biographies are works of hagiography or vilification.[5]

The difficulty of making and maintaining the proper distinction between biography and history often proved as great a problem for the biographers of public figures as the limitations arising from bias and censorship. The biographers rarely heeded Montaigne's declaration that he would rather have Brutus's private conversations than his public speeches, and 'rather know what he did in his study and in his chamber than what he did in the Forum and before the Senate.' They seldom adopted principles of the kind Samuel Johnson was to set out in his classic statement in the *Rambler* in 1750, when he emphasized that the biography of the public figure must deal with the private life rather than being a mere record of public activities and affairs: 'the business of the biographer is often to pass slightly over those performances and incidents, which produce vulgar greatness, to lead the thoughts into domestic privacies, and display the minute details of daily life.'[6]

To some degree the essential principles for the proper distinction between biography and history were recognized in the sixteenth century by Cavendish, who was careful not to allow public events to overwhelm his life of Wolsey. He commented, for example, on Henry VIII's coronation: 'I Omyt and leave the circumstaunce therof to historygraffers of Cronycles of pryncs / the w^{che} is no part of myn entendement.'

Some English writers of the later seventeenth century anticipated Johnson in emphasizing the ways in which biography differs from more general history. Dryden in his life of Plutarch declared that in history and annals one is led only into rooms of state but in biography into private apartments where one sees the hero in undress. Roger North understood well the proper distinctions and strongly asserted them, as will be seen. But most seventeenth-century biographers of public figures failed to appreciate sufficiently the importance of representing the private lives of their subjects and of analysing the relations between the public and private lives. They generally followed the same practice as David Lloyd, who declared in his *State-Worthies* (1670) that he set down 'rather the remarkes of mens publick capacities, than the minute passages of their private lives.'[7]

The fact that the term 'history' was used both for biography and general history sometimes makes it difficult to judge the intention of an author or to be sure what the proper criteria are for assessing a work. On examination it becomes evident that many seventeenth-century works that at first sight have the appearance of biographies are really intended by their authors as general histories. This is often the case with works concerned with monarchs and their reigns. William Camden's *The Historie of the Most Renowned and Victorious Princesse Elizabeth, late Queene of England* (1630) is really a history of the queen's reign in annal form, with little aspect of intimate biography.[8] Bacon's *Historie of the Raigne of King Henry the Seventh* (1622) is likewise more history than biography, although it concludes with a fine character analysis. There is nothing about Henry before his accession to the throne, and little about his private life. Edward Herbert's huge folio, *The Life and Raigne of King Henry the Eighth* (1649), has a misleading title. It is really about the reign rather than the life: only one paragraph in the 575 pages is given to the king's life before he succeeded to the throne.

Even in works more clearly intended as biographies the writers often give scarcely any attention to the private lives of their subjects, as may be illustrated by biographies of the two most influential royal counsellors of Charles I, the first Duke of Buckingham and Archbishop Laud. Sir Henry Wotton's *A Short View of the Life and Death of George Villiers, Duke of Buckingham*, written during his retirement at Eton and published in 1642, has some notable merits. It is polished, weighty, and dignified in style. Wotton develops both a reflective philosophical strain and a fine tragic sense as he depicts the duke's rapid rise to eminence and the sudden catastrophe of his assassination. His biography is remarkable for objectivity and detachment in the treatment of a highly controversial royal favourite.

This detachment is the special strength of the biography but also its weakness. Wotton comments: 'I observe it not usuall amongst the best patterns, to stuffe the report of particular lives, with matters of publike record, but rather to dive (as I shall endeavour, before I wipe my pen) into secret and proper afflictions,'[9] but he provides little of the intimate and personal, even though he had extensive first-hand contact with the duke. He omits most matters not directly connected with Buckingham's public role. He does not even mention the duke's interest in art, though his own surviving letters show that he collected paintings for Buckingham while English ambassador at Venice. This biography is the work of a diplomat who has the advantage of much experience in public affairs but who has learned all too well the dangers of indiscretion. It is impressive as an essay concerned with political principles but too impersonal to be notable as a biography. Wotton died before he could write his intended life of his friend John Donne: one wonders whether he would have tried to maintain so impersonal a tone in it.

Peter Heylyn's life of William Laud, titled *Cyprianus Anglicus* (1668), is an example of biography as a branch of history in which the biography is overwhelmed by the history.[10] It is essentially a political work concerned with Laud's role as Charles I's chief minister in affairs of both church and state after the death of Buckingham. In contrast to Wotton's detachment and objectivity, this is a fiercely polemical defence and justification of the martyred archbishop and his policies from the attacks made at his trial and by writers such as William Prynne in *Canterburies Doome*. Heylyn displays here the kind of extreme partisanship that prompted even Anthony Wood, who shared his High Anglican prejudices, to judge 'in some things he was too much a Party to be an Historian'; and S.T. Coleridge annotated his copy of the life with indignant objections to Heylyn's distortions.[11] But the biography is as much limited by the failure to maintain the distinction between biography and history as by the excessive partisanship.

The heart of any reader approaching the work as biography must sink when he encounters the statement in the dedicatory epistle by Heylyn's son, Henry: '*Together with the Story of this* Great Man, *you have likewise that of the Age he lived in.*' The heart sinks further with the author's statement in his introduction: 'Before we come unto the History of this Famous Prelate, it will not be amiss to see upon what *Principles* and *Positions*, the *Reformation* of this Church did first proceed.'[12] This signals a movement not into biography but into ecclesiastical history designed to support High Anglican principles and refute Calvinists and Puritans.

In dealing with Laud's career Heylyn follows the method of chronicle history and almost entirely excludes any intimately personal element. A rare exception is an anecdote in which he describes the beginning of his own acquaintance with Laud, but he feels it necessary to justify its inclusion by the example of a French historian, and makes this apology: 'A passage, I confess, not pertinent to my present Story, but such as I have a good precedent for from *Philip de Comines.*' He then passes quickly on to tell us: 'It is now time to look into the following Parliament.'[13] He makes little use of the first-hand knowledge he had gained as one of Laud's chaplains and makes little reference to the great amount of personal detail that had emerged during the archbishop's trial, when all aspects of Laud's life had been examined at the insistence of his enemies. In more than five hundred folio pages he tells us hardly so much about Laud's personal life as would fill a paragraph or two. Nor does he develop the dramatic aspects of the trial but interrupts his account of it with military history presented in chronicle fashion.

The result is a work that is a double failure. It fails as a defence of Laud because it is so uncritical as to be convincing only to the converted. Heylyn never faces the question of the degree to which Laud was the architect of his own disasters and those of his church and king but just blames the Puritans. And it fails as a biography because Laud is presented not so much as a human as an impersonal set of policies and a vigorous driving force for their implementation. Heylyn carries the avoidance of personal information so far that some episodes he describes are almost incomprehensible, at least on a first reading. It is not until a brief character sketch at the end that he tells us that Laud was very short of stature, even though he has previously mentioned libels of the archbishop as 'the great little man,' 'Little Vermin,' and 'Urchin.' His biography entirely lacks the kind of personal detail that interested Aubrey, who thinks it worth mentioning that Laud was 'a great lover of Catts.' Heylyn's limitation is shown even by comparison with the Earl of Clarendon's *History of the Rebellion*, for Clarendon describes significant aspects of Laud's personality suppressed by Heylyn: he refers to the archbishop's 'natural infirmities,' including his choleric disposition, his 'uncourtly quickness, if not sharpness' of temper. Fuller likewise writes more candidly of Laud: 'Amongst his humane frailties, *choler* and *passion* most discovered it self.'[14]

Gilbert Burnet's *Memoires of the Lives and Actions of James and William*

Dukes of Hamilton and Castleherald (1677), concerned with two brothers who were at the centre of Scottish affairs during the Civil War period, is another case of biography overwhelmed by history. While Burnet is critical of the flattery and partiality that have frequently characterized the biographies of great persons, he is scornful also of lives 'swelled with trifling and impertinent things,' and he tends to view the private aspects of life as too trivial properly to receive much attention from the biographer. His standpoint is indicated in a statement at the opening of his life of James, Marquis and later Duke of Hamilton: 'But since the following Narration is to be filled with great and considerable Transactions, wherein this Marquis was so eminently engaged, I shall dismiss such Particulars as were of less concernment, and therefore at one step shall leap over the whole tract of his Youth; neither shall I interrupt my Narration of Publick Matters with Accounts of his Personal and Domestick Affairs, which shall be referred to one place, in which, as I give his Character, such of those as are fit to be made publick shall be mentioned.' Burnet segregates the private and domestic aspects of life, and provides little space or detail for them. The *Memoires* is a large folio volume, but biography is difficult to find among the general history and documents. The true nature of the work is indicated by the later part of the long title: *In which an Account is given of the Rise and Progress of the Civil Wars of Scotland With other great Transactions both in England and Germany, from the Year 1625, to the Year 1652. Together with many Letters, Instructions, and other Papers Written by King Charles the I.* The degree to which history outweighs biography in Burnet's *Memoires of the Lives and Actions* of the Dukes of Hamilton is indicated by the fact that the volume was actually published as the second part of a history of Scotland.[15]

II

In a period when secular and religious politics were inseparable, a high proportion of the political biographies had churchmen, ecclesiastical statesmen, as their subjects. Two such biographies written in the middle of the seventeenth century that present more interesting features than Heylyn's life of Laud are Thomas Ball's life of the Puritan leader John Preston and John Hacket's life of the Anglican Archbishop John Williams. These are two instructive cases because both possess a potential for distinction that is realized only in part. Although they have a number of merits, they demonstrate strikingly the problems and confusions afflicting political biography in the period.

Thomas Ball's *The Life of the Renowned Doctor Preston* is a substantial and detailed biography of John Preston (1587–1628), who achieved academic distinction at Cambridge, became Master of Emmanuel College and chaplain to Charles as Prince of Wales, and involved himself in ecclesiastical politics at a high level as leader of a Puritan party still working within the Church of England. The earlier part of the biography is primarily concerned with Preston's academic career at Cambridge, while the later part deals with his political career as a central figure in the power struggle for control of the established church between Puritans and the emerging Laudian party.[16]

Ball, who had once been Preston's pupil, writes with close knowledge of his subject's Cambridge career. He describes how young Preston at Queen's College first devoted himself to natural philosophy, adoring Aristotle 'as his tutelary saint,' and then, after conversion by a sermon of John Cotton's, studied with equal zeal the Bible and works of divinity, including the schoolmen, whom he delighted to read in the oldest editions. Ball provides a vivid picture of Preston's youthful dedication to study. He tells us that Preston studied even between the ringing and tolling of bells for meals, that when he retired at night he would let the bedclothes hang down so that he might be awakened by cold when they fell off and then resume his studies, and that he would sometimes read Aquinas even as the barber cut his hair, blowing off any hair that fell on the book. This account of Preston's academic life at Cambridge has a fullness, concreteness of detail, and intimacy that have few parallels in the period.[17]

Ball makes it clear, however, that Preston from the beginning had ambitions extending beyond the academic sphere. Under Cotton's influence he decided to become a Puritan minister but at the same time to seek high position and power. He attracted King James's attention at a famous disputation for the entertainment of this hunt-loving monarch on the question whether dogs could make syllogisms; and he sought and gained the powerful patronage of Fulke Greville and the Duke of Buckingham. But, as Ball shows, his political career was troubled and ultimately tragic. His relations with Buckingham were extremely perplexed and tortuous, and eventually he realized that the duke, rather than being a real friend of the Puritan party, was trying to gain its support only for his own purposes, and that he was secretly wooing the rising Laudian party. Exhausted from these political strains and from overwork, and prey to psychological obsessions, Preston died in 1628, not quite forty-one years old.

Ball is less successful in dealing with Preston's later political career than he is in handling the earlier academic phases. His analysis of the relations between Preston, Buckingham, and James I, who were all playing different games, has much of interest but also a number of limitations. This is the case of a biographer who, like Cavendish in his life of Wolsey, has imperfect understanding of the intrigues in which his subject was engaged, as Preston worked, for example, to oppose the schemes for a Spanish and later a French marriage for Prince Charles.

More than this, Ball's biography suffers from a lack of critical detachment. Ball writes as a wholehearted admirer of Preston and constantly insists on his sanctity and probity, but he often reveals him as a rather Machiavellian figure, irresistibly drawn to the intrigues of the royal court, and even praises him for his Machiavellian political skills. He shows that although Preston's anti-episcopal principles forbade his accepting a bishopric he was relentless in his search for position and power. He reveals that Preston was in fact, like Buckingham, one who loved to temporize and wait on events, possessing an almost fanatical love of secrecy and indirection, but while he criticizes duplicity in Buckingham he justifies Preston's dubious ways as being in a good cause, even when the good cause is difficult to separate from self-interest.

While it is full of interesting detail, this is a naive rather than a fully controlled biography. Ball writes without consciousness of the degree to which he provides ammunition for charges of Puritan hypocrisy. Although he makes occasional defensive comments, on the whole his work is not merely, like Heylyn's life of Laud, an uncritical biography but it is an unconsciously subversive one, full of ironies of which the author seems unaware. E.W. Harcourt, when he brought out an edition of this life in 1885, saw Ball's Preston as one who remained 'unspotted from the world,' but the biography really provides more support for Fuller's view of Preston in the *Worthies* as the 'perfect politician,' like the lapwing fluttering on the place furthest from its eggs, the embodiment of 'that *simulation*, which some make to lye in the *Marches* of things lawful and unlawful.' Ball's life of Preston might be read as a detailed elaboration on this description, but one written in a spirit of uncritical admiration, showing less insight into the essential issues than Fuller displays in a few words.[18]

John Hacket's life of John Williams, titled *Scrinia Reserata*, which was completed in 1657 close to the date of Ball's life of Preston although not published until 1693, is in some ways an Anglican counterpart of the Puritan biography, written like it in defence of a churchman whose career had ended in defeat. Hacket was a deprived Anglican clergyman who turned to writing this biography during the period of Puritan rule in an attempt to justify a highly controversial prelate of his church. On a larger scale than the life of Preston, his work occupies 450 folio pages, perhaps the longest biography that had been written of an Englishman, if one excludes such primarily historical narratives as Edward Herbert's *King Henry the Eighth*. While it is more sophisticated than the life of Preston, it is in its combination of strengths and weaknesses like that biography both a fascinating and a frustrating work.[19]

This life has many of the potentialities of a great biography, including a remarkable subject. The pattern of Williams's life was a very dramatic one. He rose with striking suddenness from obscure origins to be Bishop of Lincoln, Lord Keeper of the Great Seal, and an important political figure, then abruptly fell from power and suffered impeachment and a long imprisonment in the Tower of London, but was subsequently elevated as Archbishop of York before suffering a final decline to a lowly position in his last years. Moreover, Hacket possessed many of the qualifications of an ideal biographer: he was learned, widely read in literature and history in many languages, and familiar with new movements in historiography, numbering among his friends not only Thomas Fuller but John Selden, whom he terms 'my great Friend while he lived.' He was ideally placed for information about his subject, with a long and close knowledge of nearly the whole of Williams's career, gained partly as a confidential member of the prelate's own household. As he states: 'I spend all my little Skill upon this Subject; for I can draw no Picture so like, because I knew none so well.'[20]

Hacket is fully conscious of the special interest his subject has from the extraordinary vicissitudes of his life: he comments, 'Few men ever lived whose lives had more Paradoxes in them.' He manages, despite all the complications, to give his biography a basically strong and dramatic two-part structure, with a central turning point, which he states is modelled on Camerarius's life of Melanchthon but which really seems to have more in common with Cavendish's life of Wolsey.[21] As he recognizes, it has much of the dramatic potentiality of traditional tragic structure, with symmetrical rising and falling actions. The first part deals with Williams's spectacular rise to high place. The central point comes with the death of James I, which occurs at the peak of Williams's power and prosperity. The second part from the accession of Charles I is the narrative of Williams's fall and the prolonged afflictions and adversities of his later years. Despite the apparent temporary recovery when he becomes

Archbishop of York, the real turning point is marked, as in Cavendish's life of Wolsey, with his deprivation of the Great Seal, which follows on the death of King James.

There is drama too in the way Hacket develops and analyses Williams's relations with the four figures who dominated and to a large extent determined his destiny: James I and the Duke of Buckingham, Charles I and Archbishop Laud. He shows how Buckingham, the all-powerful royal favourite, first raised Williams and then turned against him, and how James retained trust in him but Charles, moved by Buckingham and Laud, rejected him. He describes with much vivid detail how Laud, whom Williams had raised to a bishopric, became his mortal enemy and persecuted him relentlessly for fifteen years. As well as these major figures, Hacket introduces a fascinating variety of other characters, including Francis Bacon, William Hakluyt, Lancelot Andrewes, William Harvey, George Herbert, the Ferrars of Little Gidding, and John Milton. While he vilifies such figures as Cromwell and Milton, his purpose of defending Williams causes him to avoid many of the usual Anglican and Royalist stereotypes and write of the two great martyrs, Charles and Laud, in a relatively complex and ambiguous way.

This life of Williams is primarily a political biography. While Hacket credits his subject with all proper piety and religious devotion, he recognizes that he was above all 'a great Statist,' a statesman in both ecclesiastical and secular affairs.[22] He shows Williams as from his early years a highly political animal, and sets out to defend his behaviour and policies from the criticism he had drawn from both the opposed parties of Puritans and Laudians. He pictures Williams as essentially in an earlier Elizabethan tradition, attempting to apply principles of compromise to the great seventeenth-century conflict. He demonstrates that in ecclesiastical matters Williams was the antithesis of Laud, opposing Laud's 'innovations' and favouring a conciliatory approach to the Puritans, and that he worked for reconciliation in the disputes between king and Parliament. He holds that the key to Williams's policies was in the balance between conservative principles and pragmatic recognition of current realities.

Hacket's defence of Williams's policies must no doubt remain as controversial as those policies themselves, but it is carefully argued and deserving of respect. Since he wrote in the 1650s when the failure of Laud's policies had become a bitter living reality, he had of course the advantage of hindsight, but he makes a strong case that Williams's policies were not only consistent but offered more promise than those of his opponents. On this political level Hacket is more successful in defending Williams than Heylyn is in defending Williams's great opponent, Laud. That his case should be taken seriously was confirmed by the great nineteenth-century historian of the Civil War, S.R. Gardiner, who held that if Williams instead of Laud had been trusted by Charles, 'there would have been no civil war and no dethronement.'[23]

Hacket is not so successful, however, in defending Williams's character as in defending his policies. He is not entirely uncritical. He refers to a fault Williams himself admitted, a tendency to immoderate anger, and notes his bad judgment in remaining loyal to subordinates even when they no longer deserved loyalty. He deals repeatedly with a more serious charge, that Williams displayed overweening pride and ambition, but on this subject the biographer's position is an ambiguous one, not unlike that of Cavendish in the life of Wolsey. He recognizes that Williams possessed 'a lofty Spirit, whose motion tended upward, restless to climb to Power and Honour,' and that his pride contributed to his downfall, but he admires the prelate for his sense of grandeur. He seems little troubled by Williams's worldliness or his notorious pluralism and amassing of benefices. Nor does he display much concern about the questionable aspects of Williams's political methods, his employment of outrageous flattery in courting James I and Buckingham, and his secret use of such 'Machiavellian' devices as spies and bribery. Hacket indeed is an evident admirer of Machiavelli, whom he frequently cites in the biography. Like Ball in the life of Preston, he tends to employ a double standard, criticizing Williams's opponents for their dubious methods while justifying Williams's own use of them. In the annotations he wrote in a copy of this work, Coleridge commented ironically on the 'fine india-rubber Conscience' sometimes manifested by Hacket as well as by Williams.[24]

Despite Hacket's close personal knowledge of Williams, his biography lacks much intimacy, although he does not carry impersonality so far as Heylyn does in his life of Laud. While he tells us little of Williams's early years, he suggests some of the significance of his subject's Welsh origins, and he gives one piece of surprisingly candid information, prompted by his desire to defend Williams against slanders that he was either a eunuch *ab utero* or sexually unchaste. The truth, Hacket states, is that Williams was injured at the age of seven in jumping from the walls of Conway in a way that left him sexually incapable.[25] Hacket goes on to provide some interesting details about Williams's studies at Cambridge, about his courtly dress and manners in youth, and about his later habits and tastes: his large hospitality as Bishop of Lincoln, his great love of music, and his way of life at his palace of Buckden, where he drew criticism by having comedies performed. While Hacket emphasizes Williams's cheerfulness and wit, he gives no examples of his informal conversation or private letters, although providing many letters and documents about state business. His picture of Williams the man is much less complete than his picture of Williams the politician and statesman.

The biography suffers above all from a lack of sufficient focus on Williams. Like so many seventeenth-century lives of public figures, it frequently moves away from its subject into general history, and it digresses into many topics only loosely connected with Williams. Hacket tells us that one of Williams's great problems as Lord Keeper was to hold pleaders to their subjects and prevent digression and irrelevance, but he has not learned this lesson himself. The result is a great compendium of information about seventeenth-century politics and ecclesiastical affairs, society, and personalities. This gives the work its own kind of fascination. Coleridge in his *Table Talk* declared it 'delightful and instructive,' and said one gains more insight from it about the times before the Civil War 'than from all the ponderous histories and memoirs now composed about that period,' but it is significant that he did not praise it primarily for its value as a biography of Williams.[26]

Hacket justifies numerous digressions by his exemplary purposes. He declares that he has the intention of showing in one life the rule for any life, and he takes aspects and episodes of Williams's life as the basis for moving into essays or sermons on subjects such as anger, slander, and immoderate feasting. He carries further than any other biographer the seventeenth-century fondness for citing parallels and analogues. At his conclusion he makes a statement that explains much of the nature of his work: 'my Scope is not so much to insist upon the memorable things of one Man's Life; as to furnish them with reading out of my small store, that are well wishers to Learning, in Theological, Political and Moral Knowledge.'[27]

Hacket's style is rich and complex, heavily laden with imagery and allusion, often drawn from such sources as Pliny's *Natural History*. His range of literary reference is extraordinarily wide, and he inserts quotations from many authors, often in Latin and Greek. English poets, especially Spenser and Jonson, are well represented. His development of imagery has witty 'metaphysical' aspects and is sometimes memorable and effective, as when he represents Williams's conflict with Laud and two of the latter's followers as a game of chess with a black bishop and two rooks against a white bishop. But the elaboration of style often distracts attention from the biographical subject. Ambrose Philips, who in 1700 published his own life of Williams, taking his material from Hacket, commented on the latter: 'I can liken the Lord Keeper, as represented by him, to nothing so properly as to the statue of some Ancient Hero, so beset with Trophies and Ornaments, that the Comliness and just Proportion of the Image underneath is scarce discernable at first sight.'[28]

Hacket's life of Williams shows strikingly the way in which an intelligent and learned seventeenth-century biographer was handicapped by the lack of a firmly established tradition in the genre. Even though Hacket possessed far greater sophistication than Ball displayed in the life of Preston, and knew leading examples of classical and Renaissance biography, he failed to learn the necessary lessons and lacked the proper instincts. The result is that a potentially great biography suffers from confusion of purpose and an inappropriate style. If one judges it as a grand eccentric seventeenth-century work like Robert Burton's *Anatomy of Melancholy* or Sir Thomas Browne's *Pseudodoxia Epidemica*, one may appreciate it as Coleridge did. But if one judges it more narrowly as biography, the severe criticism of Samuel Johnson is justified. Johnson commented that Hacket's life of Williams is written 'with such depravity of genius, such mixture of the fop and pedant, as has not often appeared.'[29]

III

While many seventeenth-century lives of public figures are by modern standards defective and disappointing, this is nonetheless a field of biography that is far from barren. It shows a remarkable advance over the previous century. In the sixteenth century political biography of contemporary and near-contemporary public figures was virtually unpublishable unless it was officially approved eulogy or propaganda, and no more than a handful of works have survived that hold much interest. In contrast, despite all the problems of continued and renewed censorship, the field of political biography suddenly opened in the seventeenth century, and a rich variety of lives of public figures was produced. Many of those not immediately publishable were preserved in manuscript and brought into print in later times. If there are no major masterpieces on a large scale, there are numerous biographies that possess value, many that are successful in part at least, and even a few lives of public figures that might be termed minor masterpieces.

In the category of the partly successful biography, a not uncommon case is the one that has already been illustrated to some extent in Ball's life of Preston, that is the work that in its opening pages and intermittently thereafter provides memorable accounts of its subject's life and character, but then in the middle and later part ceases to be so much a biography as a more general history, a chronicle of *res gestae* or a political or ecclesiastical tract. An interesting earlier example of a biography that becomes merged in history in this way is an anonymous life written about 1600 although not published until 1728, *The History of that Most Eminent Statesman, Sir John Perrott*.[30]

Perrot was an Elizabethan soldier and administrator, Lord Deputy of Ireland, reputed to be an illegitimate son of Henry VIII, whose career ended tragically with his execution for treason in 1592. The biography is written as a portrait of 'heroical virtue' and defence of Perrot's conduct in Ireland, a dangerous subject, which the author even in a manuscript that long remained unpublished treats with considerable caution although with sympathy for his subject. In its opening pages this biography provides a vivid and detailed picture of Perrot's character – both inner and outer qualities, his great physical stature and strength, and his magnanimity of mind – and offers a balanced, candid revelation of his defects as a man who was choleric, lecherous, and prodigal in youth. It develops the portrait of this Tudor aristocrat partly through good anecdotes complete with dialogue: episodes such as Perrot's quarrel at the age of eighteen with the young Lord Abergavenny, and a fight in a brothel with a royal yeoman in which his spirit pleased Henry VIII. It provides much information about Perrot's role in Ireland before it becomes in the later part more a history of Irish affairs than a biography, and then breaks off to avoid the sad and perilous subject of the catastrophe.

Although the anonymous biographer does not sustain in the later part the promise of his opening, the life of Perrot illustrates some of the ways in which biographies of eminent secular figures at their best represent an advance beyond the usual limitations of exemplary religious biography. Not only are the secular biographers in some cases more ready to admit faults and imperfections in their subjects than religious biographers but they also display greater recognition of the importance of their subjects' outward attributes, including appearance, clothing, and manner. While Heylyn, for example, makes little reference to

Laud's smallness of stature, even though Laud's enemies exploited his littleness in their satiric attacks on him, secular biographers of public figures could draw on traditions and models extending as far back as Suetonius's lives of the Roman emperors, which attached importance to appearance, including 'majesty' or the lack of it.

The anonymous biographer shows that appearance and manner were significant factors in Perrot's career. He gives this description of his subject: 'His Countenance full of Majestie, his Eye marvellous percing, and carrying a commaunding Aspect, insomuch that when he was angrie, he had a very terrible Visage or Looke,' and he compares Perrot's 'percing' eyes to those of Augustus Caesar. He demonstrates that Perrot's majestic appearance gave him an advantage. When the Lord Deputy attended the Irish parliament he was the most eminent man there 'both in Goodlines of Stature, Majestie of Countenance, and in all Things else.' Eyewitnesses declared they had never beheld a man so impressive as Perrot was in his parliament robes, and this grandeur of appearance and dress helped him to maintain his hold over the people.[31]

Another fine although short biography of an aristocrat, Sir Edward Walker's life of Thomas Howard, second Earl of Arundel, written in 1651 five years after the earl's death, shows that aristocratic pride could be revealed through plain as well as splendid dress. As Walker emphasizes, Arundel possessed not only the refined tastes that made him a great patron and collector of art but also the haughtiness of the Howards, carried so far that he disdained to compete in show with other aristocrats. He was the greatest asserter of 'the ancient Honour of the Nobility and Gentry that lived in his time,' and 'was not popular at all, nor cared for it.' When he went to Scotland for the coronation of Charles I in Edinburgh in 1633, while all others vied in display he wore plain clothing, exhibiting his aristocracy simply through his stateliness of manner, 'so that it was a common Saying of the late Earl of *Carlisle*, Here comes the Earl of *Arundel* in his plain Stuff and trunk Hose, and his Beard in his Teeth, that looks more like a Noble Man than any of us.' As Cromwell is supposed to have instructed Lely to paint him complete with warts, so Walker, although highly respectful of his subject, gives a picture of Arundel that includes even the 'Warts or Moles on his Cheeks.'[32]

While Walker wrote his life of Arundel at the request of the earl's widow, several of the best-known lives of men involved in military action and public affairs during the Civil War were the work of the subjects' wives or widows themselves. The life of William Cavendish, Duke of

Newcastle, was written by his wife while he was still alive, and lives of Colonel John Hutchinson and Sir Richard Fanshawe were written by their widows. These three biographies, composed within a few years of each other after the Restoration, share some of the same limitations. They are eulogistic and relatively uncritical in the manner that eventually became notorious in biographies written by wives and widows, and they all suffer from incompleteness. None provides as much intimate detail as one might have hoped in view of the writers' closeness to their subjects. Yet they all have interesting and appealing aspects.

Lucy Hutchinson's *Memoirs of the Life of Colonel Hutchinson*, written not long after her husband's death in 1664, although not published until much later, is the biography of a notable Puritan figure, which provides fine personal detail at the opening and intermittently in later passages. It reveals an attractive character, moderate, humane, and highly cultured. It is memorable for such parts as the picture of Hutchinson's admirable cheerfulness when imprisoned on the Restoration in a damp Kentish castle, where he diverted himself by sorting cockle-shells his wife and daughter gathered for him, with as much delight as he had previously taken in the richest agates and finest engravings. But in other matters Lucy is more reticent. She passes by the 'little amorous relations' of their courtship and love, telling us that they would exceed the finest romances but are not worthy of mention among the greater transactions of her husband's life. Much of the biography is concerned with Colonel Hutchinson's military and political affairs, including his difficulties and disputes with members of his own party, and his life frequently tends to become submerged in more general history.[33]

While Hutchinson suffered in the Puritan and Parliamentary cause, Sir Richard Fanshawe and the Duke of Newcastle both suffered in the Royalist cause. Ann Fanshawe completed her *Memoirs*, which incorporate the life of her husband, about 1676.[34] In the earlier part she provides a fine picture of his character and a good narrative of his services during the Civil War, with well-told anecdotes. The later part, which is evidently based partly on his diaries, deals with Fanshawe's career after the Restoration as English ambassador in Spain and Portugal. Following a pattern similar to Lucy Hutchinson's biography, it then moves away from the more personal level into diplomatic history. There is only an incidental reference to the achievement for which Sir Richard Fanshawe is best remembered today, his translation of Camoens.

Margaret Cavendish's life of her husband, the Duke of Newcastle, published in 1667, was written to demonstrate his services and sufferings in the Royalist cause and to establish his claims to recognition and reward in the Restoration period.³⁵ Original and indeed notoriously eccentric in many things, the duchess employed an unusual scheme of organization, giving first the duke's military history, as recorded by his secretary, second her account of his life in exile on the Continent during the Puritan regime, third her picture of his character, and fourth a selection of his writings, 'Essays and Discourses.' She provides abundant evidence to show that the duke's financial and property losses were greater than those suffered by any other subject in England during the Civil War but does not attempt completeness in other areas. She tells us little about the duke's earlier life and provides little description either of his outward appearance or of his intimate relations. The biography is absurdly uncritical, as appears especially in her account of the duke's literary activities. She considers that he is the finest poet and dramatist of the age, an opinion by no means supported by the specimens of his writing she prints. Although it is the work of an aristocrat, this is in many ways a naive biography, not unjustly described by Samuel Pepys as 'the ridiculous history of my Lord Newcastle wrote by his wife.'³⁶

Yet Margaret Cavendish's life of her husband has qualities that later won the admiration of Charles Lamb.³⁷ While it is uncritical, it is written with touching affection, and despite its limitations it provides in the two middle parts a memorable portrait of a great aristocrat. It gives a fine picture of the magnificence of his way of life, even in exile in Rubens's house in Antwerp. Not only does it convey well such aspects of his character as his love of horses, and their love of him, but it impresses upon us his magnanimity and the lack of bitterness with which he viewed his enormous losses and the devastation of his estates in England.

Most of the large body of lives celebrating Royalist heroes of the Civil War falls into unproductive categories of eulogy, propaganda, and *res gestae*, but three short biographies by Edward Walsingham are an exception: lives of Sir John Smith and Sir Henry Gage, published in Oxford in 1644 and 1645, and of Sir John Digby, written about 1645 although not published until 1910.³⁸ Walsingham quotes Bacon's *Advancement of Learning* on the need for biographies that are more than barren elegies.³⁹ His lives have much of the elegy about them but they are not barren, and while his motive is commemoration and support of the Royal cause, they are freer of the excesses of propaganda than most works of the kind. Unlike many propagandists he recognizes the valour of opponents, thereby adding to the stature of his heroes. He also has the rare virtue of keeping his eye on his subjects rather than straying into general history. He has a good narrative style in dealing with action, a good eye for detail, and a restraint in developing imagery that brings him close to the ideal Robert Southey was later to develop in his life of Nelson for the naval or military biographer where the emphasis must be upon action without falling into biographically sterile *res gestae*.

The three biographies all follow the same pattern. A narrative of the life, consisting largely of military action, is followed by a character analysing the outer and inward man. The similarity is increased by the fact that the three lives intrinsically have much in common. All three figures were educated on the Continent, in at least the case of Digby because of Roman Catholic faith. All three fought in the Low Countries and returned to England on the outbreak of the Scots War and the Civil War. All rose rapidly in the Royal service in the Civil War, and all were killed relatively young in the period 1644–5.

These similarities might lead to lack of differentiation, but Walsingham succeeds quite well in bringing out the differences between the three men both in characters and military careers. The simplest and most straightforward in character and life is Sir John Smith. The pattern of his life seems determined by the fact that he was descended from Richard I's standard bearer. In the biography his recapture of the royal standard during the Battle of Edgehill at the opening of the Civil War is the centre of a finely unified narrative. His character as Walsingham presents it is completely that of the soldier, one who cared little for dress, appearance, or refinement of manner, and was a man of few words, stern and awful in aspect, the commander of armies not of ladies.[40]

Walsingham represents both Gage and Digby as more complex, or at least more rounded and varied in interests and accomplishments, than Smith. He shows that both were remarkable for versatility. Gage was a notable linguist, who translated French and Latin works, and loved study when he had time for it, in contrast to Smith, who left off his youthful studies as soon as he could, and Gage was more subtle and intellectual than Smith as a military commander. He had more concern with outward appearances and refinements in living. He was a born politician, possessed administrative abilities as well as a skilled pen, and was an accomplished courtier, becoming Royalist governor of Oxford. In contrast to Smith, who was shy of women and died unmarried, he had an ideally happy marriage.

The life of Digby, perhaps the finest of the three, is the biography of a man even more notable than Gage for his versatility and accomplishments, as gentleman, soldier, commander, scholar, and traveller. Embodying the Castiglione ideal, he spent four years abroad perfecting himself in liberal arts, languages, and music. His remarkable character was shown when he was captured in youth by bandits in Italy. In an episode that might have come from the *Arcadia* or *The Faerie Queene*, the bandits gave up their intention of robbing and killing him, and asked him to become their leader; and he similarly impressed his captors during the Civil War. Walsingham's emphasis is not merely on his accomplishments but on the sheer power of character that caused even his enemies to admire him, and that appeared also in his patience in enduring suffering in imprisonment. Walsingham shows him as pious and chivalrous, one who fought under the cross, so modest he blushed when praised, and free from the lust, swearing, and drinking common among soldiers.

In their representation of heroic virtue these three biographies are prose equivalents of idealistic Cavalier lyrics. They are celebrations of aristocratic order and values, loyalty, chivalry, and courage, written in a spirit like that of Lovelace's poems. Although the characters are idealized, each is represented with a degree of individuality and realism. While they possess some of the inevitable limitations of biographies in a celebratory and elegiac mode, Walsingham's lives deserve to be regarded as minor classics. More than narrowly upholding a partisan cause, they worthily fulfil the wish the anonymous biographer of Sir John Perrot expressed at the beginning of the century that lives might be written of England's 'heroicall Spirites' comparable to those of Plutarch and other biographers of ancient times and foreign countries: 'I see no Reason but that our Countriemen of this our English Nation, might reap much Benefit by one another's Examples, as well as the Grecians and other Nations did gayne Knowledge and Honor by reading, and carrying in Remembrance the Histories and Narrations of one another's Lives, Deedes, and Sayinges.'[41]

IV

Although seventeenth-century biographies of public figures like Heylyn's life of Laud and Hacket's life of Williams frequently suffer from confusions caused by the common view of biography as a branch of history, in another way life-writing gains from this view. While the biographers often fail to distinguish clearly between the spheres proper to biography and those proper to history, so that biographical subjects become submerged in general history, on the other hand the finest contemporary histories of seventeenth-century events are rich in biographical elements, in portraits and analyses of individuals. The most memorable and best-known parts of the great histories by Edward Hyde, Earl of Clarendon, and by Gilbert Burnet are the biographies and character sketches they embody. If biography during this period is often diluted by history, history is much enriched by biography in Clarendon's *History of the Rebellion and Civil Wars* and his autobiographical *Life* and in Burnet's *History of his Own Time.*

Clarendon's biographical portraits range from his famous and moving elegy for his friend, Lucius Cary, Viscount Falkland, killed in battle at the opening of the Civil War, to his equally memorable critical characterization of the leader of the opposed party in the war, Oliver Cromwell. He laments the death of Falkland as 'a losse, which noe tyme will suffer to be forgotten, and no successe or good fortune could repayre,' and describes his 'prodigious partes of learninge and knowledge,' his 'inimitable sweetnesse and delight in conversation,' his great humanity, integrity, and courage, and his grief at the division and bloodshed of war. In contrast, he pictures Cromwell as a person of remarkable but perverted abilities, possessing exceptional courage, judgment, and understanding of men, 'a great spiritt, an admirable circumspection and sagacity, and a most magnanimous resolution,' dedicated to the wrong ends, 'a brave, badd man.'[42]

Burnet's character sketches differ from Clarendon's not only in embodying a 'Whig' rather than a 'Tory' view of the seventeenth-century conflict but in other respects as well. The differences between them have been well analysed by the later historian, C.H. Firth. He points out that Clarendon's characters tend toward the general and typical. They often lack specific detail: Clarendon tells us that Sir Harry Vane had 'an unusual aspect' but does not tell us what it was. But he possesses high literary skills, and his portraits are finely polished and unified works of art. Burnet's characters, on the other hand, are less finished but display excellent powers of observation and are often more individual, with more vivid detail, even if sometimes presented in unfinished catalogues.[43]

Burnet's eye for individual detail is immediately apparent in his portrait of one of Charles II's dominant ministers in English and Scottish affairs, John Maitland, Duke of Lauderdale: 'He made a very ill appearance: He was very big: His hair red, hanging odly about him: His tongue was too big for his mouth, which made him bedew all that he talked to:

And his whole manner was rough and boisterous, and very unfit for a Court.'[44] Burnet has some of the same instinct as Aubrey for fixing on those qualities that most mark one person as different from all others. Paradoxically, he often provides more vivid characterization in the brief sketches in his *History* than in his fuller biographies.

Many of the finest analyses and most memorable portrayals of the great seventeenth-century political figures by their contemporaries are embodied in briefer memoirs than the full-scale histories of Burnet and Clarendon. No one provides us with a more vivid glimpse of Cromwell than the Royalist Sir Philip Warwick in his *Memoires of the Reigne of King Charles I*, as he describes his first view of him as a still obscure Member addressing the House of Commons at the opening of the Long Parliament in November 1640: 'I came one morning into the House well clad, and perceived a Gentleman speaking (whom I knew not) very ordinarily apparelled; for it was a plain cloth-suit, which seemed to have bin made by an ill country-taylor; his linen was plain, and not very clean; and I remember a speck or two of blood upon his little band, which was not much larger than his collar; his hatt was without a hatt-band: his stature was of a good size, his sword stuck close to his side, his countenance swoln and reddish, his voice sharp and untunable, and his eloquence full of fervor.' This description of Cromwell is sharpened by Warwick's sense of contrast both with his own fashionable dress as a courtier in 1640 and with the Lord Protector's 'great and majestick deportment and comely presence' when Warwick years later was brought before him as a prisoner at the palace of Whitehall.[45]

The portraits of public figures in the shorter memoirs of the period are sometimes remarkable for candour. Some of the writers allowed themselves unusual freedom because they intended their work to remain in manuscript rather than to be publicly circulated, and some took advantage of the opportunities provided by the conflicts of the Civil War and the breakdown of the old system of censorship during the 1640s and 1650s. Sir Anthony Weldon's description of James I, which was published posthumously in his *The Court and Character of King James* in 1650, illustrates the candour of the 'secret histories' that came into print at that time:

> He was of a middle stature, more corpulent through his cloathes then in his body, yet fat enough, his cloathes ever being made large and easie, the Doublets quilted for steletto proofe, his Breeches in great pleits and full stuffed: Hee was naturally of a timorous disposition, which was the reason

of his quilted Doublets: His eyes large, ever rowling after any stranger came in his presence, insomuch, as many for shame have left the roome, as being out of countenance: His Beard was very thin: His Tongue too large for his mouth, which ever made him speak full in the mouth, and made him drink very uncomely, as if eating his drink, which came out into the cup of each side of his mouth: His skin was as soft as Taffeta Sarsnet, which felt so, because hee never washt his hands, onely rubb'd his fingers ends slightly with the wet end of a Napkin: His Legs were very weake, having had (as was thought) some foul play in his youth, or rather before he was born, that he was not able to stand at seven years of age, that weaknesse made him ever leaning on other mens shoulders, his walke was ever circular, his fingers ever in that walke fidling about his Cod-piece.[46]

Weldon develops his picture of James as the antithesis of the 'majesty' traditionally attributed to monarchs in official portraits and biographies, and his representation provides a striking contrast to eulogies like John Williams's in his funeral sermon for the king. Weldon had been expelled from the royal court and was no doubt prejudiced, but he displays a power of observation and provides a concreteness of detail that give his portrait more authenticity than merely satirical biography and bring the subject vividly before our eyes.

The finest in many ways, fullest and most elaborate analysis of the character of King James's grandson, Charles II, was written in a very different spirit from both Weldon's and Williams's pictures of the earlier monarch. George Savile, Marquis of Halifax, achieved a remarkable degree of detachment in his *A Character of King Charles the Second*, composed in the late seventeenth century and first published in 1750. Equally careful to do justice to the king's merits and open in revealing his faults, he provided a splendidly judicious assessment. Halifax, the great 'trimmer,' famous in his own political career for his moderation and abhorrence of extremes, showed in his character of Charles II, as in his other writings, the possibility of rising above the bitter conflicts and partisan biases that had characterized his century, often with damaging effect on historical and biographical writing as well as upon the nation at large.

CHAPTER 6

Lives of Writers: Scientists and Antiquaries

I

From the mid-seventeenth century an increasing number of substantial and interesting lives were published of intellectual and literary figures notable at least in part for secular achievements. Often of medium length, these biographies frequently appeared as prefaces to editions of their subjects' writings. The subjects included scientists and philosophers, antiquaries and other scholars, and poets. These lives are generally freer from traditional conventions and limitations than the exemplary religious lives and lives of public figures in the period. The authors usually moved beyond the celebration of their subjects' piety and virtue in order to present their secular achievements, and the biographies naturally ran less risk of becoming submerged in general history than the lives of great public figures. The emergence of these lives from the 1650s onward contributes to the sense that the middle of the century is an important turning point in the history of English biography.

The writers of these lives necessarily turned to different precedents and models, more relevant to their purposes than those cited by the authors of exemplary religious lives and lives of public figures. Edward Phillips in his prefatory life of John Milton (1694) provides a long list of precedents. Among classical writers he includes not only Plutarch, who wrote lives of 'the most Renowned Heroes and Warriours of the *Greeks* and *Romans*,' but more significantly Diogenes Laertius, who wrote 'the Lives of the Ancient *Greek* Philosophers.' Among contemporaries he mentions not only Walton but also 'Mr. *Thomas Stanly* of *Cumberlo-Green*, who made a most Elaborate improvement to the foresaid *Laertius*, by adding to what he found in him, what by diligent search and enquiry he

Collected from other Authors of best Authority.' Among recent Continental writers he praises 'the Great *Gassendus* of *France*' for his biographies of Epicurus and of 'the most politely Learned Virtuoso of his Age, his Country-man, Monsieur *Periesk*.'[1] These three figures, Diogenes Laertius, his modern counterpart Thomas Stanley, and Gassendus (Pierre Gassendi), are the models most often cited by the biographers of the writers and scholars to be considered here.

Diogenes Laertius in his loosely ordered but entertaining lives written in the third century AD provided many anecdotes and sayings of the Greek philosophers, as well as vivid details about their characters and ways of life. His work served as a starting point for Thomas Stanley, but the latter's *The History of Philosophy* (1655, 1656, 1660, 1662) is much more than merely an improvement on Diogenes Laertius. Taking the form of a series of lives principally of the ancient Greek philosophers, it is in its own right a major publication of the new seventeenth-century biography, as well as a notable work in the history of English classical scholarship.

Stanley was not only a fine classical scholar and a poet, a Fellow of the Royal Society, esteemed by John Evelyn and Sir Thomas Browne, but also a gifted biographer. He possessed a strong sense for individuality of character. His biographies commonly include a section titled 'How he lived,' and they are rich in personal detail, such as information about his subjects' physical appearance, family and domestic life, friends and disciples, with many sayings and anecdotes gathered from various classical sources. In the case of Socrates, for example, he provides specific details about the philosopher's appearance, as an unhandsome bald man with a flat nose, about his dress, limited to a single garment a year, about his manner of speaking, his recreations, his dancing and playing with children, and about his relations with his wives, notably the scolding Xantipe, as well as giving an extended account of the trial and death.[2] Stanley's eyes are attracted to the same kinds of vivid individual detail in his written sources about the classical philosophers as John Aubrey seized upon from his personal observation and gossip for his contemporaries.

Stanley conceived his work as carrying out a program for the history of philosophy advocated both by Montaigne in his *Essaies* and by Bacon in *The Advancement of Learning*, but he declared also: 'The learned *Gassendus* was my precedent.'[3] For many seventeenth-century English biographers of intellectuals and scholars the most influential of Continental models was Pierre Gassendi's life of the French polymath Nicolas-

Claude Fabri de Peiresc (1580–1637), published in Paris in 1641 and brought out in London in 1657 in an English translation by W. Rand, dedicated to John Evelyn, with the title *The Mirrour of True Nobility & Gentility*.[4] This biography provides an extensive narrative and analysis of Peiresc's life, which conveys well not only his love of learning but his individuality of character and life-style.

Gassendi shows the completeness of Peiresc's absorption in the world of books partly by describing the setting of his chamber: 'His Bed was exceeding plain, and his Table continually loaded and covered with Papers, Books, Letters, and other things; as also all the Seats round about, and the greatest part of the floore'; and he gives us a picture of the way in which the books spread out from the scholar's study even to the porch of his house. As well as describing Peiresc's methods of study, he provides a full account of his personal habits and tastes, ranging from a fondness for 'Musk-Millions' to a love both for birds, for which he had corn scattered in the winter, and for cats: 'he procured out of the East, Ash-coloured, Dun, and speckled Cats beautiful to behold.' Gassendi records such individual aspects of character as Peiresc's special sensitivity to sun and wind: 'he had a Servant with him, that waited upon him with an hand-Canopy, to keep off the Sun-beams, if need were, & the wind.' Through such detail Gassendi creates a memorable picture of a wide-ranging scholar whose character and habits were as original as his researches and studies. It is not surprising that seventeenth-century English biographers of men of learning turned to this work as a model.[5]

While the biographies of writers and scholars were influenced by precedents ranging from Diogenes Laertius to Gassendi, many of them were shaped also by their nature as prefatory lives. Since the majority of the biographies to be considered in this and the next chapter were written as prefaces to editions of their subjects' writings, both length and treatment were affected by their prefatory form. Depending partly on the format of the publication to which the prefatory lives were attached, considerable variation was possible in size, but usually they were intermediate in length, falling somewhere between the typical 'brief life' of the period and the book-length biography. Normally they were considerably shorter than Gassendi's full-length life of Peiresc, and therefore could incorporate only a moderate amount of the kind of detail he included.

Their nature as prefatory biographies gives these lives certain characteristic strengths and limitations. The fact that they were generally intended for publication with posthumous editions of their subjects' writings, and prepared sometimes at the behest of publishers and booksellers with the purpose of recommending those writings, meant that they ran almost the same risk as funeral sermons of being excessively eulogistic. Samuel Johnson complained that the life Thomas Sprat attached to his posthumous collected edition of Abraham Cowley's works in 1668 was 'a funeral oration rather than a history.'[6] On the other hand, the biographies have special value in the concern they typically display with the relation between the writer and the work: they commonly provide analysis of the writing, including literary style, describe circumstances of composition and the impact and reception of publications, and give extensive accounts of creative and scholarly accomplishments and of the patterns of writers' careers, although they vary in the degree to which they move beyond aspects related to the work to a more fully rounded kind of biography.

To illustrate the range and development of predominantly secular seventeenth-century English biographies of intellectual, scholarly, and literary figures, we may take examples from three fields in which achievement was specially distinguished during the period: science and mathematics, historical and antiquarian study, and poetry. The lives of scientists and antiquaries will be considered in the present chapter, while the lives of poets will be reserved for separate treatment in the next chapter.

II

It is appropriate that Francis Bacon, who in *The Advancement of Learning* made an eloquent appeal for the improvement and increase of biographical writing, should be the subject of one of the finest of the secular seventeenth-century prefatory lives, written by William Rawley and published with a posthumous collection of Bacon's works, *Resuscitatio*, in 1657.[7] Rawley had long served Bacon as chaplain and amanuensis, assisting in the preparation of his works for publication. After Bacon's death he served in a rural parish as an Anglican clergyman, but he acted also in effect as Bacon's literary executor and made the dissemination of Bacon's works the main business of his life. His biography of Bacon demonstrates the special strengths as well as some of the defects characteristic of the prefatory life.

Rawley's narrative of the phases of Bacon's life is brief, but it establishes the pattern that has been followed by all Bacon's later biographers, emphasizing the contrast between Elizabeth's reluctance to give him preferment and his rapid rise under James I. In keeping with the nature of a prefatory biography, however, Rawley is much less concerned with Bacon's career as a lawyer and statesman than with his work as a writer and philosopher. He displays a number of the limitations inherent in the life written by the dedicated and admiring servant, anxious to represent his subject in the best possible light. He refers only obliquely to Bacon's fall from high place on charges of corruption, suggesting that his fault was really only that he placed too much trust in unworthy servants. He passes silently over other controversial aspects of Bacon's character, apart from defending him against charges of indifference or unorthodoxy in religion. Nor despite his intimate knowledge of his subject does he provide very much of the kind of personal detail Gassendi gives in his life of Peiresc, published in an English translation in the same year as Rawley's biography. For this kind of detail we have to await Aubrey's notes on Bacon prepared for Anthony Wood.[8]

Rawley's approach to Bacon is natural and appropriate, however, in a biography published as a preface to a collection of the writings, and it has the merit of placing the emphasis where it most belongs. Bacon as philosopher and writer is more important than Bacon as public figure, and Rawley is right to concern himself primarily with his powers of mind, his originality as a thinker. He records that Bacon at Cambridge, aged about sixteen, fell into dislike of the prevailing Aristotelian philosophy, not from lack of respect for Aristotle but because he considered the way unprofitable, leading to disputation rather than to useful works. Rawley then proceeds to draw on his knowledge of Bacon's writings, both published and manuscript. He does not attempt a detailed analysis of individual writings or of Bacon's system of thought but in general terms conveys well his sense of Bacon's great mental powers and originality.

Rawley frequently provides first-hand information of value which otherwise might have been lost. He tells us much about Bacon's habits of work which no one else perhaps was so well qualified to provide. He states that others can judge the completed works, 'But with what Celerity he wrote them, I can best testifie.' He tells us that Bacon's major work, *Instauratio Magna*, was 'no Slight Imagination, or Fancy, of his Brain; But a Setled, and Concocted, Notion; The Production, of many years, Labour, and Travell.' 'I my Self, have seen, at the least, Twelve Coppies, of the Instauration; Revised, year by year, one after another; And every year altred, and amended in the Frame thereof; Till, at last, it came to that Modell, in which it was committed to the Presse.' He gives a fine account of the way in which Bacon put even meals to profit for serious conversation, not dominating but drawing out men to speak of things about which they were expert, so that he learned much from others: he 'would light his Torch, at every Mans Candle.'[9]

Rawley also provides a good analysis of Bacon's style as a writer, his striving for masculine clear expression rather than flights of eloquence or affectation of phrase, which was joined paradoxically with real literary artifice and polish. He comments: 'And if his Stile were Polite, it was because he could do no otherwise.' He observes that while Bacon sought to emphasize matter rather than manner, yet his innate gifts for expression were such that if he had occasion to repeat another man's words he would improve upon them, 'As if, it had been Naturall to him, to use good Forms.'[10]

Rawley no doubt learned much himself about the arts of writing from Bacon, so that although his biography is brief it is weighty and concentrated; while valuable for the specific information and concrete evidence it provides, it is also eloquent and memorable in its generalizations and magisterial in its conclusions. In emphasizing that although Bacon was a great reader of books he had his knowledge not from books but from within himself, Rawley writes: 'if there were, a Beame of Knowledge, derived from God, upon any Man, in these Modern Times, it was upon Him.' He provides confirmation of the greatness of Bacon's originality by demonstrating the fame and influence he achieved, one of the most interesting sections of the biography. He tells us that Dr Samuel Collins, Provost of King's College, Cambridge, declared when he read *The Advancement of Learning* that he found himself in a case to begin his studies anew, having lost all the time of his previous studying. Rawley specially impresses upon his reader the international stature of Bacon's reputation, which he perceives as not only great but growing: 'This Lord is, more and more, known.'[11]

Rawley's relative neglect of Bacon's public career on the one hand and of the more intimate aspects of his private life on the other hand prevents his account of Bacon from being a full and rounded biography. If the central problem of literary biography is to relate the life and the work, Rawley's concern is more with the work than with the life, but he provides an admirable account of aspects of the life that are most closely related to the work. His achievement was such that two hundred years after the appearance of his biography James Spedding, the greatest of all Bacon scholars, whose monumental edition of the works has never been entirely superseded, declared that Rawley's life 'is still (next to Bacon's own writings) the most important and authentic evidence we possess concerning him.'[12]

Few biographies were written in the later seventeenth century of the scientists and mathematicians who attempted to carry forward Bacon's program for the advancement of learning, apart from the brief lives of John Aubrey, but one of some distinction is Abraham Hill's life of Isaac Barrow, prefaced to John Tillotson's edition of Barrow's English works in 1683 (and republished in an expanded version in 1716), which takes the form of a letter to Tillotson.[13] Barrow was an Anglican clergyman, and Hill duly commends his religious dedication, but appropriately gives special emphasis to his important work in mathematics and other secular fields. His is in many ways a more comprehensive and fully rounded biography than Rawley's life of Bacon.

Hill does not offer technical analysis of Barrow's work in mathematics but he provides an excellent general account of his studies and career, and the pattern of his life. He traces Barrow from a very unscholarly boyhood to the great and varied scholarly accomplishments of his maturity. He tells us that as a boy Barrow was much more given to fighting than to studying, so that his father 'often solemnly wisht, that if it pleased God to take away any of his Children, it might be his Son *Isaac.*' The advance Barrow made from this unpromising beginning is measured by the words of Charles II, who when he appointed him Master of Trinity College, Cambridge, said '*he had given it to the best Scholar in England.*'[14]

In contrast to Rawley's relative neglect of Bacon's part in public life, Hill brings out well the way in which Barrow's career was affected by public events, including the unsettled conditions of the Civil War and Interregnum. He tells us that as a Royalist student at Cambridge in the 1640s Barrow was denied advancement, and so spent a period of travel and study in Italy and Turkey. Since the times were unfavourable for Anglicans to study divinity, he turned to secular fields, especially mathematics, and in geometry produced a Euclid superior to any previous one. In the improved circumstances after the Restoration, Barrow was appointed to mathematics lectureships in London and Cambridge, but Hill shows us that he was eventually deterred from mathematical studies partly by lack of appreciation, since his *Lectiones Geometricæ* was thoroughly read and understood by only two persons, and describes finally how he resigned the Cambridge lectureship in favour of Isaac Newton, returned to the study of divinity, and became an academic administrator in his later years as Master of Trinity College, where his achievements included the building of the new library designed by Sir Christopher Wren.

Hill cites Barrow's observation that the unsettled times caused him to enter upon several studies rather than dedicating himself to a single one, but he brings out well the underlying unity as well as the variety of his works. He shows that Barrow was moved throughout his career by the newer scientific and rationalistic spirit. As a student at Cambridge he became discontented with the shallow physiology then taught in the universities, and read the works of Bacon, Descartes, Galileo, 'and other the great Wits of the last Age, who seemed to offer something more solid and substantial.' He displayed this rationalistic spirit even in reading and writing poetry: he valued the part that consisted in description, 'but the Hyperboles of some modern Poets he as much slighted.' Likewise in the sermons of his later years, 'he having apply'd himself much to Mathematicks, had acquir'd a Habit to write with Exactness, to proceed directly toward his Scope, and to make use of Solid Proofs rather than Figures of Rhetorick.'[15]

Hill provides excellent analysis of Barrow's character as well as of his studies and career. While he shows Barrow as the complete scholar, whose only estate at his death was his books, he depicts him also as possessing qualities not always associated with scholars, including both moral and physical courage, urbanity and knowledge of the world, as well as a remarkable serenity and cheerfulness of temperament. He tells us that Barrow could learn to play all games, and that he could talk easily with those in all walks of life and accommodate his discourse to all capacities, as shown when in his early travels he contracted friendships with merchants and diplomats in Turkey, and manifested later by his success with financial appeals for the new Trinity College library. Hill's representation of Barrow's character is the more effective in that it is integrated with the life rather than segregated as a separate 'character' in the manner of much seventeenth-century exemplary biography.

Something of Hill's special merit as a biographer is indicated by the way in which he brings out the coherence underlying the apparent contradictions of Barrow's character in the following passage: 'His first Schooling was at the *Charterhouse* for two or three Years, when his greatest Recreation was in such Sports as brought on fighting among the Boys; in his after-time a very great Courage remained, whereof very many Instances might be set down, yet he had perfectly subdued all Inclination to quarrelling, but a Negligence of his Cloaths did always continue with him.' Hill provides various illustrations to show courage as a constant element in Barrow, in the form of moral courage when he proclaimed rather than concealed his Royalism as a student at Cambridge, and in the form of physical courage in an episode when he tackled and restrained a fierce mastiff that attacked him and when *en route* to Turkey he manned a cannon against pirates attacking the ship. At the same time Hill demonstrates how pacific Barrow's temperament had become in his maturity, as appeared even in his poetry: 'for Satyrs he writ none; his Wit was pure and peaceable.'[16]

More than many seventeenth-century biographers Hill gives us some sense of his subject's physical qualities, his bodily characteristics and appetites. Less bound than many of his contemporaries by the decorum of dignity (although more reticent in some matters than Aubrey), he tells us that Barrow 'seem'd intemperate in the Love of Fruit' and 'he was very free too in the Use of Tobacco, believing it did help to regulate his thinking.' Since, as Hill states, Barrow's portrait was never made from life and the effigy of his monument little resembled him, he provides a quite detailed verbal picture, describing him as small, lean, and very strong, with fair and clear complexion, thin skin (which made him sensitive to cold), and light auburn hair, very fine and curling.[17]

Hill's inclusion of such physical description demonstrates one of the ways in which his life of Barrow is an advance over Rawley's life of Bacon. Rawley provided no indication at all of Bacon's appearance or bodily characteristics. While Rawley was primarily concerned with Bacon's intellect and writings, and gave little attention to aspects of his life and character not directly related to these, Hill provides a relatively complete picture of Barrow the man as well as the scholar. He writes deprecatingly that his work is 'but a Sceleton, till some other Hand lay on the Flesh and Sinews,' but in fact he gives a real sense of life and fullness to his representation of Barrow.[18]

III

While there are few seventeenth-century lives of scientists and mathematicians comparable to Hill's life of Barrow, another field of energetic inquiry and great scholarly activity during the period is much more fully covered by the biographers: historical and antiquarian learning.[19] The advances in historical studies were in fact closely linked to the advances in the sciences: rather than being simply backward looking, many of the antiquaries saw themselves as followers of Bacon, attempting to apply newer scientific methods to the investigation of the past. They succeeded during this period in laying the foundation for the study of prehistoric and Roman Britain, Anglo-Saxon language and literature, and a great range of medieval institutions: monasteries, feudalism, parliament, courts, and legal systems. Since there are clear affinities between various aspects of antiquarian and biographical research, it is natural that biographies were produced of the leading seventeenth-century antiquaries. Anthony Wood and John Aubrey, who were themselves important antiquaries, gave special attention to figures in this field, and such scholars as the Elizabethan pioneer William Camden and his successors in the new century, William Somner and Sir Henry Spelman, were the subjects of biographies attached to editions of their works, while a life of Sir Robert Cotton was prefaced to a catalogue of his library.[20]

These lives of seventeenth-century antiquaries often suffer from a common limitation: even more than Rawley's biography of Bacon, they tend to be accounts of the works rather than fuller lives of the persons. This is not surprising in view of the intense absorption in studies that characterized the antiquaries of the period. An example is Edmund Gibson's life of Sir Henry Spelman, published anonymously with his edition, *Reliquiæ Spelmannianæ*, in 1698. After describing how Spelman, a landed gentleman, at the age of fifty left his country estates and settled in London to dedicate himself fully to medieval studies, especially feudal law and ecclesiastical history, Gibson gives a good account of the scholarly problems he faced and solved, and of the making of his great, though unfinished, *Glossary*. But the biographer tells us relatively little about the man as distinct from the work, little about his family and domestic life, or about his friendships, except with other antiquaries, and nothing about his habits and recreations. Nor does Gibson really do enough to explain the origins of Spelman's antiquarian interests or to convey adequately the pleasure he found in his studies.

White Kennett in his biography of William Somner, prefaced to Somner's *A Treatise of the Roman Ports and Forts in Kent* in 1693, is more successful than Gibson in giving us an account not merely of the work but of the man who was intensely absorbed in the work.[21] Explaining what is unexplained in the life of Spelman, he shows how Somner's early environment in Canterbury fostered his development of antiquarian interests, so that he devoted much of his life to the study of this ancient city and its great cathedral, and moved from this into related fields, especially Anglo-Saxon studies.

The most memorable section of Kennett's life is his picture of Somner's love of the antiquities of Canterbury and dedication to their study:

> He lov'd much, and much frequented the *Cathedral* service; where after his devotions were paid, he had a new zeal for the honour of the *House*, walking often in the *Nave*, and in the more recluse parts ... with a curious and observant eye, to distinguish the age of the buildings, to sift the ashes of the dead; and, in a word, to eternize the memory of things and Men. His visits within the City were to find out the Ancestors, rather than the present inhabitants; and to know the genealogie of houses, and walls, and dust. When he had leisure to refresh himself in the Suburbs and the fields, it was not meerly for digestion, and for air, but to survey the *British bricks*, the *Roman ways*, the *Danish hills* and *works*, the *Saxon Monasteries* and the *Norman Churches.*

Kennett describes how Somner watched over such excavations as the digging of foundations, and bought coins and other relics that were turned up by the workmen. He conveys Somner's delight in the study of the written records, 'in *classic Historians*, in old *Manuscripts, Leiger-books, Rolls* and *Records*,' which made him such an authority on historical and legal matters that 'he was consulted as a *Druid* or *Bard*.' With such detail Kennett creates an attractive and convincing picture of a man who was wholly dedicated to antiquarian study, a concrete embodiment of the character of a complete antiquary. As he tells us, even Somner's recreations had an antiquarian flavour, such as shooting with the long-bow, 'which no doubt he lov'd as much for the antiquity, as for the health and pleasure of that manly sport.'[22]

Kennett provides a fine analysis of the originality and pioneering nature of Somner's *The Antiquities of Canterbury*, which was the culmination of his early work. Kennett declares: 'This accurate performance is the more laudable, because he could find no way, but what he made,' and commends Somner for achieving the reward of the true antiquary, treading in unknown steps and bringing to light 'the hidden things of past ages.'[23] He shows how Somner's early achievements led to desire for new conquests, further enlargement of knowledge. As with so many lives of antiquaries, however, eventually Kennett's account of the work tends to displace the biography of the man. When he comes to Somner's important Anglo-Saxon studies he moves away from Somner himself to give a history of Anglo-Saxon scholarship in England.

Perhaps the finest of all seventeenth-century lives of antiquaries is an anonymous biography, *The Life of that Reverend Divine, and Learned Historian, Dr. Thomas Fuller*, published in 1661.[24] The author deals with a number of aspects of Fuller's wide-ranging works, but he gives special attention to the antiquarian studies embodied in *The History of the Worthies of England*, and so the life is appropriately considered here with the biographies of antiquaries. It was separately published but it may have been conceived as a prefatory life for the *Worthies*. It displays some marks of haste and incompleteness but it was obviously written with close personal knowledge. It provides an intimate portrait of Fuller as seen by a contemporary, a vivid and memorable picture of his character, and an excellent account of the various phases of his career.

The biography has three leading themes: Fuller's relation to public affairs during the Civil War, his methods and career as a preacher, and his learning and scholarly work. The biographer brings out very well the exceptional moderation Fuller displayed during the Civil War and Interregnum even while he remained a loyal Anglican and Royalist. He shows how Fuller's tolerant spirit and abhorrence of controversy and bloodshed caused him to be misunderstood and criticized by both parties during the war, while he responded with friendship even to those who attacked him. The biographer provides an excellent account too of Fuller's practices as a preacher, his eloquence and his popularity, which was so great that throngs gathered around his chapel in London: 'the Sextonry so crowded, as if Bees had swarmed to his mellifluous discourse.'[25] But above all the anonymous writer excels in depicting Fuller as a scholar.

The biographer is exceptionally good on the research for and composition of the *Worthies*. He describes how Fuller began the work when he marched with the Royal armies as chaplain during the Civil War, and praises him for not allowing himself to be overcome by the 'stupidity' that overcame many learned men at that time but pursuing his studies in any quiet interval. He states that wherever Fuller came he spent most time in viewing church monuments and other antiquities: 'He would endure contentedly an hours or more impertinence from any aged Church-officer, or other superannuated people for the gleaning of two lines to his purpose.'[26] The biographer goes on to tell us how Fuller digested his notes at Basing House when it was under siege, how he later went to London as the best place to finish the *Worthies* with the aid of books and learned men, and how, after temporarily abandoning the work when stunned by the news of the king's execution, he took it up again and finished it before his death in 1661. The anonymous writer gives little attention to Fuller's other scholarly works such as *The Church-History of Britain*, but his account of the prolonged composition of the *Worthies* is remarkably full, in many ways surpassing such precedents as Rawley's account of Bacon's methods of work.

The biographer depicts Fuller as someone who almost matched Somner in his dedication to scholarly studies, even though he was more versatile in character and had a far more varied career. He tells us that Fuller from student days at Cambridge onward scarcely allowed himself any recreation or exercise, except for marches of war and later attendance at the press during the printing of his books, 'when it was a question, which went the fastest, his Head or his Feet.' He describes how even in his final sickness Fuller's thoughts dwelled on 'his beloved Book,' and in his bed he called to his attendant for pen and ink to make improvements in it, until at last as death approached he thought only of heaven. The writer suggests that Fuller's death was brought about by his scholarly dedication, telling us that after he died an influx of blood burst from his temples, which was thought to have been caused by too much study in methodizing and completing the *Worthies*.[27]

After demonstrating Fuller's devotion to study and writing, the biographer comments: 'So that if there were any Felicity or Delight, which he can be truly said to have had: it was either in his Relations or in his Works.' He does not, however, write as fully about the 'Relations' as about the works. Apart from informing us that Fuller married twice, that both marriages were happy, and that he took great care in the education of his children, the writer tells us relatively little about his subject's domestic life. He states that when Fuller was unfixed from study 'no Man could be more agreeable to Civil and Serious mirth,' and that he was cheerful and helpful to friends and neighbours, but he does not provide much detail about these aspects of character.[28]

On the other hand, like Hill in his life of Barrow, the anonymous author is much superior to most seventeenth-century biographers in describing his subject's appearance and mannerisms. In contrast to the neglect of the body and outward aspects of the person that is common in exemplary religious lives, this biographer sets out to 'Enliven' an engraved portrait of Fuller 'with some of those natural Graces which were unexpressible in him by the Pencill; withall to shew what a convenient Habitation learning and vertue had chosen.' He tells us that Fuller was rather tall, large but not corpulent, sanguine with a pleasant ruddiness of face, and provides such detail as a description of his light-coloured, naturally curled hair. One of the few biographers before

Aubrey to describe his subject's manner of walking, he even comments on Fuller's 'Majesticall' gait. He informs us that Fuller was negligent in dress and careless even 'to seeming inurbanity' in manners, preferring an old English simplicity and ease, and that, no doubt through absorption in study, he often passed familiar acquaintances without noticing them. Such individual details give solidity and life to this memorable portrait of a scholar who was more than a scholar, a great preacher and a notable advocate and exemplar of moderation in an era of bitter conflict.[29]

Rawley's life of Bacon, Hill's life of Barrow, Kennett's life of Somner, and the anonymous life of Fuller have not been given the attention they deserve, if literature is broadly conceived, in the histories of English literary biography. These biographers of scientists and scholars were among the pioneers in facing basic problems of literary biography, in attempting to determine, with varying degrees of success, how best to analyse the relation between the writer and the writing and how best to maintain the balance between the two. Viewed as literary biographies their works are not unworthy companion pieces to the lives of the poets to be considered in the next chapter.

CHAPTER 7

Lives of the Poets

I

Lives of poets, dramatists, and other writers of imaginative literature are rarer in the seventeenth century than lives of divines, scholars, and public figures. Although before the end of the sixteenth century Thomas Speght published a brief prefatory biography of Chaucer, no biographies appeared in the Shakespeare first folio in 1623 or with Donne's *Poems* in 1633. The first life of Donne, by Walton, did not appear until the folio edition of Donne's *Sermons* in 1640, and in it Donne was viewed as a religious more than as a literary figure. Similarly Fulke Greville in his life of Sir Philip Sidney, published belatedly in 1652, presented Sidney as a Protestant hero rather than as a poet.[1] But literary biography is one of the fields in which significant advances took place in the second half of the century, both in the number and quality of the lives. During this period valuable accounts of poets were included among the brief lives of Aubrey and Wood, and a number of the biographies of poets that were published then in the form of prefaces are innovative and substantial. The achievements in this area were much greater than one would suspect from the slight attention given to the seventeenth century in standard histories of English literary biography.[2]

We may take as examples of developments in literary biography during the period the lives of three seventeenth-century poets who had very different careers: John Davies' life of John Hall, a remarkable prodigy who died young without fulfilling his early promise, Thomas Sprat's life of Abraham Cowley, another precocious poet, whose mature achievements caused him to be generally regarded by contemporaries as the greatest poet of the era, and finally a group of five lives of the figure who in the eyes of posterity emerged as the giant among the seventeenth-century poets, John Milton. These represent a good variety of biographical types and approaches. Davies' life of Hall and Sprat's life of Cowley are prefatory lives as different as their subjects: the former is short but fascinating, relatively intimate and candid, the second is much longer, more elevated and formal. The five early lives of Milton include other diverse examples of prefatory lives as well as brief biographies by John Aubrey and Anthony Wood, and they display a wide range of approaches to their subject.

The life of John Hall of Durham, who died in 1656 at the age of not quite twenty-nine, by John Davies of Kidwelly, who had been his contemporary and friend at Cambridge, was prefixed to Hall's translation, *Hierocles Upon the Golden Verses of Pythagoras* (1657).[3] Its theme is the tragic pattern of a life in which brilliant youthful promise and remarkable early achievements were followed by various misfortunes and an early death, leaving strongly the sense of waste, failure to achieve a great potential. Davies, who was a prolific author and translator, writes in a plain but effective style and handles the narrative skilfully. He begins with the event that brought instant fame to Hall when he had been only a few months as a student at Cambridge, the publication of his *Horæ Vacivæ or Essays*, a 'sudden breaking forth' which amazed not only the whole university but 'the more serious part of men in the three Nations' and even won recognition abroad. Then Davies moves back to explain the circumstances of Hall's earlier years that prepared for this astonishing emergence, before going on to his later career. He shows that Hall's early fame was quickly consolidated by his *Poems*, but that after he moved to London much of his energy was exhausted by political writing and journalism on behalf of the Commonwealth. His troubles included financial struggles and an ill-fated marriage, and he fell into dissipated ways before he was overtaken by the sickness that caused his premature death. Davies quotes Thomas Hobbes's elegiac comment on him: '*Had not his debauches & intemperance diverted him from the more serious studies, he had made an extraordinary person; for no man had ever done so great things at his age.*'[4]

The excellence of the biography lies not only in Davies' handling of this tragic pattern but in the fine detail about Hall's practices and achievements as a writer and the relatively intimate account of other aspects of his life. Thus Davies convinces us of Hall's remarkable facility as a writer by his first-hand reports. He tells us that at Cambridge acting as amanuensis he wrote out most of Hall's *Divine Poems*, 'which I took from his mouth, extreamly surprized at the inexpressible facility of his vein,' and informs us of Hall's translation of a Latin treatise of Michael Maierus: 'Almost one half of it was done in one afternoon, over a glasse of wine in a Tavern.' He demonstrates that Hall had an exceptionally good memory, and states that after preparation by mental organization, 'he would dictate four or five hours together, beyond the speed of the readiest *Amanuensis*, and that with so much choice & certainty that he seldom altered a word in anything he writ, so that most of his works were in print before ever he saw them.'[5]

Davies makes it clear, however, that Hall's great facility was matched by his carelessness about his writings, so that some were lost and others were imperfectly published. He tells us that Hall began a remarkable work of fiction titled 'Leucenia' while he was at Cambridge and added to it in London but that it was lost when he lent the manuscript to a friend, and that most of the numerous poems he wrote after the publication of his *Poems* were likewise lost. Davies comments on his lack of care about revising and proof reading: 'Mr. *Hall* was much guilty of what the greatest Authors are, viz. an impatience to overlook what haply they had taken an abundance of pains withall.' He tells us that Hall left various writings at his death in disordered manuscripts, including the results of his studies in chemistry: 'two Books in *Spencer's* Stanza ... which I have by me confusedly shuffled together in broken papers.'[6]

Davies is as good on other aspects of Hall's nature and personality as on his character as a writer. As far as brevity and a certain reticence on some subjects allow, he gives a quite rounded view. He does not neglect Hall's physical characteristics, describing him as somewhat above average stature but not proportionately strong, and telling us that he had broken a leg in youth which made him averse to walking and exercise: 'insomuch, that in the yeers 1650, and 1651, being enclined to pursinesse and fatnesse, rather than he would use any great motion, he thought fitter to prevent it by frequent swallowing down of pebble-stones, which proved effectuall.' Davies informs us too that Hall's unconventionality showed in his carelessness about appearance, and his 'looking on a Barber as a tedious Torment.'[7]

Davies provides analyses of Hall's temperament, manners, and habits, which reveal both his subject's strengths and his weaknesses. He tells us that Hall was choleric but soon appeased, and that he had a severe and melancholy look but when wakened in discourse 'he put on much facetiousnesse and affability.' His friends included persons of note: at Cambridge he was intimate with Samuel Hartlib and Henry More, but his dislike of solitude and his habit of conversing affably with all 'made him guilty of a familiarity many times with persons much below him.' Davies does not conceal that Hall's disregard for conventions extended to financial matters: he was careless about money, 'seldom receiving or paying any himself; whence haply it comes, that he is not unjustly taxed with a neglect and forgetfulnesse of his engagements.'[8]

In contrast to the neglect of domestic life and marital relations by many seventeenth-century biographers, Davies gives an interesting although brief account of Hall's marriage. He tells us that in 1647 Hall married hastily a beautiful and talented gentlewoman: 'But the influences of this Conjunction of Wits proved very fatall.' The marriage was opposed by both families, partly because of the couple's lack of fortune, and a family feud led to their separation, but they continued to correspond. Davies states that the wife's letters were 'so excellently well penn'd, and with so much passion, that had they been preserved, and but a little refined, they might have been owned by Monsieur *de Balzac*, or *de Volture*.' He leaves the impression that the marriage might have been greatly happy if it had not been for family opposition and lack of financial means.[9]

The biography is notable finally for its unusual balance of moral judgment. Charges including dissipation, love of wine and women, had been brought against Hall by Royalist pamphleteers and other political opponents. Davies does not seek to deny Hall's 'irregularities and excesses,' which arose partly from reaction against early self-denials and austerities and partly in response to later disappointments, but he asks tolerance for human frailty, criticizing those who harshly censure openly admitted faults resulting more from weakness than from secret and calculated depravity. He is specially concerned to defend Hall, a Baconian rationalist and sometime associate of Hobbes, against one reproach 'heavier than all the rest': 'That he was guilty of a certain neglect and dis-care of things sacred, which some ignorantly, some enviously, stretch to a kinde of *Atheisme*.' Writing at the height of the Puritan regime, Davies defends Hall against those who 'measure all others by their own fantasticall apprehensions.'[10]

Altogether Davies' life of Hall is a biography worthy of its remarkable subject. While consistently sympathetic to Hall, Davies breaks much freer of the limitations of conventional exemplary biography and of the type of barren elegy or eulogy condemned by Bacon than do most biographers of his period. His biography has few precedents for its combination of individual detail, intimacy and candour of portraiture, recognition of complexity, and fine balance, and its accuracy has been confirmed by modern research on Hall's life and career.[11]

II

Like Davies' life of Hall, Thomas Sprat's life of Abraham Cowley is the biography of a poet remarkable for precocity written soon after the subject's death by one who had close knowledge based on intimate friendship, but otherwise there is little similarity between the two works or the careers they record. In contrast to Hall's disappointments in maturity, Cowley achieved such literary fame in his later years that on his death in 1667 he was buried in Westminster Abbey beside Chaucer and Spenser. Sprat's life, in its English version, was prefixed to his great folio collected edition of Cowley's works published in 1668 and frequently reprinted, and appeared also in a Latin version.[12] Sprat, who was appointed literary executor by Cowley, saw himself as official biographer, and in keeping with his subject's exalted status he produced a life that was not only much longer than Davies' life of Hall but more elaborate and monumental in every way. An Anglican clergyman, later dean and bishop, he was much more strongly influenced than Davies by the traditions of exemplary biography, and he justified the life of Cowley as providing profitable moral instruction.

The biography is cast in the form of an epistle to Cowley's friend Martin Clifford. As the title, 'An Account of the Life and Writings,' indicates, it has two main parts: a narrative of the life and a consideration of the works. In the first part Sprat traces Cowley's life through three clearly defined phases: the precocious youth and early writings before the Civil War; the poet's service in the Royalist cause during the war and his subsequent exile in France; and finally his return to private life and literary activity in England during the later 1650s and the Restoration period. Sprat then moves in his second section into an extensive critical discussion of the writings, and concludes with two shorter final parts: a character analysis of Cowley and an account of his last days and death.

The biography has qualities Sprat's contemporaries admired. It is written in a polished and dignified style, and it provides an attractive picture of Cowley, his poetic genius and learning, his dedication at great personal cost to the Royal service, and his modesty and other private virtues. But it suffers from the imbalance and limitations of the idealized life; it lacks concreteness of detail; and it does not provide so intimate an account as one might have hoped from Sprat's close acquaintance with Cowley and his use of the epistle form.

These limitations produced a later reaction against Sprat's biography. Just as Cowley's own literary reputation suffered a decline in the generations following his death, so the contemporary admiration for the biography was replaced by a more critical and negative view. This life came under strong attack in the later eighteenth century from Samuel Johnson in his own biography of Cowley in his *Lives of the Poets*. He commented that Sprat was 'an author whose pregnancy of imagination and elegance of language have deservedly set him high in the ranks of literature; but his zeal of friendship, or ambition of eloquence, has produced a funeral oration rather than a history: he has given the character, not the life of Cowley; for he writes with so little detail, that scarcely any thing is distinctly known, but all is shown confused and enlarged through the mist of panegyrick.'[13]

Johnson's strictures are quite understandable. In keeping with his desire to present an ideal portrait of Cowley, Sprat made suppressions which affect both his edition of the writings and his biography. In the edition he suppressed a passage in Cowley's preface of 1656 to his *Poems* that had given rise to a charge of disloyalty to the Royal cause. He declared that he would have suppressed passages in Cowley's youthful series of love poems, *The Mistress*, which might cause moral offence, if the suppression had not been forbidden by the holder of the copyright. In Sprat's defence, however, it should be noted that he was endeavouring to carry out Cowley's wishes in these matters. The poet had asked him to suppress the offending passage in the 1656 preface, and in his will he had directed him to refrain from publishing anything that might give offence to religion or good manners.[14]

Such evasions and suppressions might not in themselves have seriously damaged the biography. Sprat is probably right in the impression he gives that there was really little discreditable to be hidden in Cowley's life. The more serious weaknesses in the biography are the lack of concreteness that Johnson criticized and the omission of nearly all intimate detail. Sprat constantly prefers dignified generalization to the specific. Thus he writes that Cowley's parents were 'Citizens of a virtuous life and sufficient Estate,' in order, Johnson suggested, to avoid the vulgar detail that the poet's father was a grocer. Sprat's vagueness about dating has been the despair of Cowley's later biographers when they attempt to establish the time of such events as the poet's residence in Royalist Oxford and the beginning of his exile in France. Sprat is no more specific about places than dates. He states that Cowley on his return to England from exile studied botany and botanized in 'a fruitful part of *Kent*': the place is still unknown.[15]

Sprat's account of Cowley's character and habits suffers from the same vagueness and lack of the specific. Rather than seeking to bring out Cowley's individuality, he declares: 'There was nothing affected or singular in his habit, or person, or gesture.'[16] He provides no description of Cowley's appearance or physical characteristics, and the poet remains in his biography a rather abstract and disembodied figure. Sprat comments on Cowley's talent for friendship but gives few names, and little specific information even about his own and Clifford's friendship with the poet or about Cowley's relations with such influential patrons as the second Duke of Buckingham.

The biography contains a passage regarding Sprat's decision not to publish Cowley's letters that has become notorious. He praises the excellence of Cowley's private letters, and states he believes that he and Clifford have the largest collections of them. Then he writes, addressing Clifford, 'But I know you agree with me, that nothing of this Nature should be publish'd.' He argues: 'The truth is, the Letters that pass between particular Friends, if they are written as they ought to be, can scarce ever be fit to see the light ... In such Letters the Souls of Men should appear undress'd: And in that negligent habit, they may be fit to be seen by one or two in a Chamber, but not to go abroad into the Streets.' In accordance with this principle, Sprat may have gathered in most of Cowley's letters and destroyed them, for few survive. The loss has been lamented by S.T. Coleridge among others. In this matter, as in his other suppressions, Sprat was probably doing what Cowley would have wished, and even today the extent to which it is proper to publish personal letters can be debated, but Sprat's principles and methods are scarcely compatible with good biography, and they have deprived us of much of value he might have given us.[17]

Sprat's idealization of Cowley, his suppressions and lack of concreteness, have made him a much-criticized figure in the history of English biography. It would be a mistake, however, to suppose that in these things he was a malign innovator. In truth he was essentially a traditionalist in biography, despite the interest in newer ways of thought he displayed in the *History of the Royal Society* for which he is now best remembered, and he followed the conventions firmly established in seventeenth-century moral and religious biography. Odium has been attached specially to him, not only because of Johnson's attack but because his biography as that of a historically important literary figure has received more attention than many similar lives of primarily religious figures. His life of Cowley displays most of the same characteristics as the contemporary biographies by another Anglican clergyman who rose like Sprat to become successively dean and bishop, John Fell's lives of Henry Hammond and Richard Allestree. Sprat's dignified decorum, preference for abstract generalizations rather than specific detail, for formality rather than intimacy, and even the explicitly considered decision to omit correspondence are exactly the features one finds in Fell's biographies, and they have parallels in many lives in the exemplary tradition.[18]

Sprat makes it plain at the opening of his biography that he follows Cowley himself in esteeming the poet's virtues above his literary talent and works. His highest praise is reserved for Cowley's moral character, and he quotes as the finest eulogy on his death Charles II's comment: '*That Mr. Cowley had not left a better Man behind him in England.*'[19] As Johnson suggested in comparing the life of Cowley to a funeral oration, this biography has all the marks of the practised writer and preacher of sermons. Yet despite his adherence to the moralistic conventions of the exemplary life, Sprat is to be credited with one innovation in literary biography that was not only important but influential, since the life of Cowley was frequently reprinted and became very well known: the prominence he gives to examination of the poet's writings.

Sprat is a pioneer in providing extensive critical discussion in the biography of an English poet, although there were precedents enough for the comprehensive treatment of writings in the lives of divines and scholars familiar to him. Even though he insists that Cowley's virtue counts for more than his work, he gives almost as much space to his account of the writings as to his narrative of the life. He makes a grand survey of Cowley's works, with some critical analysis of the main areas, and attempts defence against some negative criticisms. He displays the range and variety of Cowley's literary achievements, and conveys well his great stature as it was then conceived.

Sprat's critical analysis is valuable primarily as a contemporary estimate, rather than as an assessment of more enduring worth. He states that the *Davideis* was the finest divine poem he had seen,[20] but he was writing just at the time of the appearance of *Paradise Lost*, and much both in Cowley's work and in Sprat's analysis of it subsequently fell victim to changing taste. Like other parts of the biography, Sprat's critical discussion suffers from his tendency to make large, vague generalizations, in contrast to Samuel Johnson's later examination of particular passages of the poems, which he used as the basis for his famous or notorious attack on the metaphysical style of poetry. But Sprat's structure, the main two-part division with the narrative of the life followed by critical discussion of the work, may have influenced later biographers including Johnson. Johnson's life of Cowley was the first of his *Lives of the Poets*, and he adopted a similar clearly marked two-part division in it and in subsequent lives of Milton and other poets.

III

How different John Milton's position was from Cowley's after the Restoration is illustrated by the contrast in Sprat's attitudes to the two poets. While he commemorated Cowley not only as a great literary figure but as a moral exemplar and loyal defender of the Royalist and Anglican causes whose death was mourned by the king himself, he took a far more negative view of Milton. He concluded his biography of Cowley with an account of that poet's burial in Westminster Abbey in a ceremony attended by 'a great many Persons of the most eminent quality' followed by the placing in the Abbey of a memorial designed by the Duke of Buckingham, but he is reported as Dean of Westminster to have refused to allow a memorial tablet for one of Milton's nephews which mentioned the uncle to be placed in the Abbey, 'because the name of Milton was, in his opinion, too detestable to be read on the wall of a building dedicated to devotion.'[21]

Sprat's view of Milton shows the degree of hostility with which the blind poet was frequently regarded following the Restoration because of his association with a defeated and reviled cause, as a Puritan attacker of the Anglican episcopate, a defender of the regicides, and an official of Oliver Cromwell's government. Nevertheless Milton's stature as a poet was sufficiently recognized that in the later years of the seventeenth century biographers gave more attention to him than to any other literary figure, although open publication of their work was sometimes inhibited by the poet's dangerous political status. Milton was in the quarter-century following his death in 1674 the subject of five important biographies.

John Aubrey included a biography of Milton in the manuscript of his *Brief Lives* in the 1680s, and Anthony Wood incorporated a life of the poet in his *Athenæ Oxonienses*, published in 1691–2. In addition Wood preserved among his manuscripts an anonymous life of Milton, acquired from an unknown source. When with the lapse of censorship after the 'Glorious Revolution' it became possible to bring out sympathetic accounts of the poet, two prefatory biographies were published, although the authors took precautions about revealing their identities. Milton's nephew Edward Phillips published anonymously a prefatory life with an edition of Milton's *Letters of State* in 1694, and John Toland published a life, signed only with initials, in the first collection of Milton's prose writings, *A Complete Collection of the Historical, Political and Miscellaneous Works of John Milton*, which appeared in 1698 with an Amsterdam imprint although it was actually printed in London.[22]

The biographical writings of Aubrey and Wood will be considered more fully in later chapters, but it may be noted here that their lives of Milton display merits and faults very characteristic of the two authors. Aubrey's account of Milton shows his typical diligence as a collector, for it reveals that he gathered information from Milton's widow, from his brother Christopher, from his nephew Edward Phillips, and from John Dryden. Characteristically too his life of Milton is fragmented and unfinished but provides vivid and fascinating personal detail.

As well as information about Milton's family and parentage, education, travels, three marriages, blindness, and literary work, Aubrey gives descriptions of Milton's appearance, manner of life, and habits that are memorable both for substance and phrasing. He tells us: 'His harmonicall and ingeniose soul did lodge in a beautifull and well-proportioned body,' and describes the poet as 'a spare man,' 'scarce so tall as I am,' so fair in his complexion that 'they called him the *lady of Christ's College.*' He specifies the shape of Milton's face, the colour of his hair and eyes, and even describes his voice, informing us that it was 'delicate tuneable' and that (as Dryden told him) the poet pronounced the letter R very hard. In providing such details he excels the other early biographers, and he gives fuller information than the others also about Milton's daily habits. His account of Milton is notable, furthermore, for its freedom from political and religious prejudice. He declares that whatever Milton wrote against the monarchy was not prompted by animosity or party feeling but written 'out of a pure zeale to the liberty of mankind,' and states that he has been trying for two years to obtain from Milton's nephew copies of the 'two admirable panegyricks, as to sublimitie of witt' the poet wrote on the rebel leaders, Cromwell and Lord Fairfax.[23]

Wood's inclusion of a biography of Milton in his *Fasti Oxonienses* attached to *Athenæ Oxonienses* is an indication of his desire to make the latter work as comprehensive as possible, since Milton was a Cambridge man, not one of the Oxford men who were ostensibly Wood's primary subjects. His life of Milton is more finished than Aubrey's but dryer and more pedestrian; and, in striking contrast, it is violently hostile because of his strong Royalist and High Anglican prejudices. It is based partly on notes Aubrey collected for him and partly on the anonymous biography in his possession, but it displays none of the sympathy for Milton that appears in these two sources. Wood recognizes that Milton was 'a person of wonderful parts' but considers that his great abilities were directed to bad political and religious ends.[24] Wood's hostile comments on Milton, which appear not only in the biography in the *Fasti* but scattered elsewhere in the *Athenæ*, have indeed become notorious. He terms the poet 'that villanous leading Incendiary' and calls him an 'impudent lyer.' He could in fact never resist any opportunity for having a fling at Milton. In his copy of Edward Phillips's *Theatrum Poetarum* (1675), preserved among his books in the Bodleian Library, where Phillips alluded to his family connection with an unnamed famous late author, Wood annotated: 'John Milton / a rogue.'[25] But he made in the *Athenæ* a valuable bibliographical contribution. He provided a fuller list of Milton's writings than the other early biographers, basing it on his own first-hand examination of the publications.

In contrast to Wood's biography, the anonymous life preserved among his manuscripts (which has sometimes been inconclusively attributed to the poet's nephew John Phillips or to Cyriack Skinner) gives a highly sympathetic view of Milton, presenting him as an exemplary moral and religious figure.[26] It is not an especially distinguished work but quite competent, reasonably detailed and concrete. It provides a well-ordered account of Milton's career, which includes many of the essentials in brief form. But the anonymous biographer gives most prominence to the controversial prose writings and makes surprisingly slight mention of the poetry, only the briefest of references to *Paradise Lost*.

The narrative of the life is followed in the traditional manner of exemplary biography by a 'character,' which contains the most valuable information. The biographer defends Milton's virtue, integrity, and dedication to the service of God, and presents him as a champion of liberty who never supported the 'corrupt designs of his Masters.' He provides an attractive picture of Milton's personality, emphasizing his gentleness and humanity, his sweet and affable nature. He gives some detail about Milton's physical appearance, his tastes including his love of music, and his habits, telling us, for example, as an indication of the poet's courage:

'hee wore a Sword while hee had his Sight, and was skill'd in using it.' Among the most interesting information is the statement that when Milton awakened in the morning he 'had commonly a good Stock of Verses ready against his Amanuensis came' and if the latter's arrival was later than usual 'hee would complain, Saying *hee wanted to bee milkd.*' A few such intimate glimpses of the poet as this give the anonymous life special value and leave one wishing for more.[27]

Edward Phillips's biography is longer and both more detailed and more formal than the anonymous life. Phillips states of his life of his uncle that he has 'reduced into form and order what ever I have been able to rally up, either from the recollection of my own memory, of things transacted while I was with him, or the Information of others equally conversant afterwards, or from his own mouth by frequent visits to the last.'[28] His life of the poet is ably composed, polished and dignified in style, written not only with close knowledge of Milton but with extensive knowledge of biographical tradition. As has already been noted, he displays a range of reading befitting one educated by Milton, which extends from Plutarch and Diogenes Laertius to Fulke Greville, Walton, and Gassendi; and his special interest in literary biography is shown in other publications such as his *Theatrum Poetarum.*

Phillips provides a skilfully organized narrative of Milton's life, following a pattern similar to that of the anonymous biographer but giving more detail at nearly every point, for example, about the character and influence of the father, about early studies and education, about the Italian journey and those who welcomed and entertained Milton on the Continent, about the first marriage, and about the difficulties and great achievements of the later years. Phillips is weak on dates: he gives slightly mistaken dates both for Milton's birth and death, while the anonymous biographer gives the correct ones. But he displays remarkable precision in other matters, such as information about Milton's various places of residence. He specifies the successive London dwellings, sometimes with descriptions like this one that reveal Milton's character and tastes: 'a pretty Garden-House he took in *Aldersgate*-Street, at the end of an Entry; and therefore the fitter for his turn, by reason of the Privacy, besides that there are few Streets in *London* more free from Noise than that.'[29]

In contrast to both Aubrey and the anonymous biographer, Phillips provides no description of Milton's appearance, but he gives interesting information about the poet's habits and way of life, and about his friendships as well as about his marriages. He states that although Milton's manner of life was austere when he lived in his uncle's household after the latter's return from Italy, 'once in three Weeks or a Month, he would drop into the Society of some Young Sparks of his Acquaintance, the chief whereof were Mr. *Alphry*, and Mr. *Miller*, two Gentlemen of *Gray*'s-Inn, the *Beau*'s of those Times, but nothing near so bad as those now-a-days; with these Gentlemen he would so far make bold with his Body, as now and then to keep a Gawdy-day.'[30] Phillips makes good use of his special personal knowledge to provide fuller information than the other biographers about the poet's family life, including an account of the way in which the blind Milton used his daughters as readers, often of works in languages they did not know. He does not tell this to Milton's discredit but makes it clear that the practice was irksome to the daughters, and Milton's reputation in later times was to be much damaged by this account or by distorted readings of it.

Phillips's biography is much more truly the life of a poet than the anonymous biography. In contrast to the anonymous biographer's emphasis on Milton as an exemplary figure and as a controversial writer, Phillips leaves no doubt that his reason for writing is Milton's greatness as a poet. He does not incorporate into the life an extended literary discussion or critical essay as Sprat does in the life of Cowley, but he praises Milton's achievements as a poet in the highest possible terms. He describes Milton as one 'scarce to be parallel'd by any the best of Writers our Nation hath in any Age brought forth' and as 'the Ornament and Glory of his Countrey.' He declares that Milton's juvenile poems 'contain a Poetical Genius scarce to be parallel'd by any *English* Writer,' and he singles out *Lycidas* for praise among the early poems. He states that *Paradise Lost* is the noblest heroic poem 'in the general Esteem of Learned and Judicious Persons, of any yet written by any either Ancient or Modern.'[31]

While the anonymous biographer does no more than mention *Paradise Lost*, Phillips provides valuable information about the composition of the epic. We owe to him the information that Milton first planned to write his work on the Fall in the dramatic form of a tragedy, and that the verses of Satan's address to the Sun in Book 4 of *Paradise Lost* 'several years before the Poem was begun, were shewn to me, and some others, as designed for the very beginning of the said Tragedy.' Phillips also tells us how for a period of some years when he visited his uncle Milton would show him 'a Parcel of Ten, Twenty, or Thirty Verses at a Time' for correction of faults of the amanuensis in spelling and punctuation. He has preserved for us such remarks as Milton's statement 'That his Vein never happily flow'd, but from the *Autumnal Equinoctial* to the *Vernal*.'

He tells us as well of Milton's unhappiness when *Paradise Regained* was generally regarded as inferior to *Paradise Lost*.[32]

In style Phillips's life is often closer to the dignified formality of Sprat's biography of Cowley than to the lively informality of Aubrey's life of Milton. Phillips in fact did not choose to include in his own biography all the vivid personal detail about the poet he provided for Aubrey. He preferred to present Milton as a quite elevated figure. In his life a picture of Milton as the sublime poet begins to emerge. This will be carried further by eighteenth-century biographers such as Jonathan Richardson, who make a transfer from the poetry to the poet, and endeavour to create a poet worthy of the noble heroic poetry. Yet Phillips is still close enough to Milton to give us the reality rather than the myth. As Helen Darbishire has observed, the living Milton is to be found in the early lives rather than the later monuments.[33]

John Toland, who wrote the last and longest of the seventeenth-century lives of Milton, drew much of his material from Phillips's published biography but supplemented it with additional information from the poet's widow, daughter, and other sources. His most significant innovation was to make extensive use of the poet's own writings as biographical sources. He states: 'The amplest part of my Materials I had from his own Books, where, constrain'd by the Diffamations of his Enemys, he often gives an account of himself.'[34] As the first to draw extensively upon the great autobiographical passages in Milton's writings, Toland deserves a place as a pioneer not only in the biography of Milton but in English literary biography more generally: his use of his subject's writings is much fuller and sounder than that made by such an earlier biographer of poets as Izaak Walton.

Toland, however, was not concerned primarily with Milton as a poet to nearly the same extent as Phillips. His interest was rather in Milton as the advocate and defender of liberty, and his biography is shaped by its nature as a preface to an edition of Milton's prose writings. Toland was a republican, an admirer of James Harrington, whose work he edited and whose life he wrote. He included in his biography of Milton a eulogy of the executed republican Algernon Sidney, and he linked Milton with John Locke as an advocate of toleration.[35] If Phillips initiates the representation of Milton as the sublime poet, Toland stands, much more clearly even than the anonymous biographer, at the beginning of the long 'Whig' tradition of depicting Milton as the liberal, the great champion of liberty, which extends through the eighteenth and nineteenth centuries into the twentieth century.

Toland moves quickly through Milton's life to his political writings and activities. Following the pattern set out in Milton's own statements, he traces the poet's work as defender of liberty through its various phases: religious, civil, and domestic. He approves Milton's attacks on the bishops and his arguments in favour of divorce, and he is bold enough to quote Milton's defence of the regicides and advocacy of a republic, although he regards the poet's model commonwealth as inferior to Harrington's. He displays the greatest enthusiasm for Milton's defence of liberty of the press in *Areopagitica*. He states that in controversial matters he gives Milton's own words to avoid distortion, and this is indeed the special merit of his biography.[36]

For Toland even *Paradise Lost* is significant primarily as a political work. He declares that Milton's design in it was to display the various aspects of liberty and tyranny. He does not undertake much literary analysis of the poem, although he cites the praise of Dryden and others. His limitations in critical judgment are shown in such remarks as his comment on Milton's early plan for an Arthurian epic: 'But this particular Subject was reserv'd for the celebrated Pen of Sir *Richard Blackmore*.' His biography, however, marks one real advance in the literary study of Milton: in keeping with his policy of drawing as fully as possible on the poet's own writings, he uses Milton's statements of his literary principles and programs to give an account of his gradual development of his plans for *Paradise Lost* that extends far beyond Phillips's account. He can be credited too as the first to develop the theme of the writing of *Paradise Lost* as a magnificent triumph over the obstacles of long interruption, blindness, and political defeat.[37]

Toland's biographical principles are more conservative than his political views. Although his interests are primarily secular rather than religious, he adheres to the principles traditional in exemplary biography, and provides little that is intimately personal but deliberately excludes detailed consideration of the poet's private life. However, if his biography generally emphasizes the political at the expense both of the private and of the literary, it has the advantage of bringing into prominence the areas of Milton's work that had been most neglected by earlier biographers such as Phillips because of their sensitive and dangerous nature: even at the end of the century Toland's publisher had good reason to employ a false Amsterdam imprint.

Toland's biography and the other early lives of Milton complement each other very well in the variety of their perspectives and emphases.

Aubrey's special interest in the intimate personal aspects of Milton's life is balanced by the anonymous biographer's concern with the moral and religious dimensions, just as Phillips's emphasis on the centrality of the poetry is balanced by Toland's interest in the political writings and activities. In contrast to the strongly sympathetic views of these four biographers, Wood's life serves to embody the hostile view of Milton that was widespread after the Restoration, as well as to lay the foundations of the poet's bibliography. Taken together the five early lives provide a much fuller biographical account of Milton than had been provided for any earlier English poet.

When Samuel Johnson wrote his biography of Milton, published early in his series of *Lives of the Poets* in 1779, he was able to draw on three of the five seventeenth-century lives. Those by Aubrey and the anonymous biographer were unknown to him, since they were still unpublished, but he made extensive use of Edward Phillips's life and some use of Wood's and Toland's: his view of the politics of the poet, whom he termed 'an acrimonious and surly republican,' was indeed not very different from Wood's. Johnson's remark to Boswell in 1773 that 'he did not think that the life of any literary man in England had been well written' is frequently quoted, but it is not so often remembered that after the reading he subsequently undertook for his life of Milton he stated that this poet's life 'has already been written in so many forms, with such minute enquiry' that he would not have prepared a new biography if it had not been required by the series of prefatory lives upon which he was engaged. He had partly in mind earlier eighteenth-century biographies by Elijah Fenton (1725) and Jonathan Richardson (1734), but the terms in which he refers to Fenton's 'elegant Abridgement' of Milton's life suggest a biographical tradition that was long established, and in truth its foundations were well laid before the end of the seventeenth century.[38]

The early lives of Milton demonstrate strikingly the great advance that took place in literary biography during the seventeenth century if one compares the biographical treatment of Milton with that of Shakespeare. Shakespeare died less than sixty years before Milton. No biography of any substance was written in the decades following his death, and the biographical record that remains is very sparse: a quite limited number of facts and documents and a scattering of anecdotes of uncertain reliability. In contrast, Milton's life was quickly recorded in remarkable detail within a few years of his death. This comparison of course has to take into account Milton's role in public life and the autobiographical passages in his writings, which give his biographers an advantage over Shakespeare's. Even so, when one considers the series of early lives of Milton in relation to the neglect of Shakespeare's life, it is clear that in the course of the seventeenth century a revolution occurred in the biography of literary figures.

CHAPTER 8

Brief Lives: Thomas Fuller and Anthony Wood

I

No type of biographical writing is more characteristic of seventeenth-century England than the brief life. It has such ancient antecedents as the collections of short lives by Diogenes Laertius, Suetonius, and Cornelius Nepos, and character studies in classical histories, and such sixteenth-century precedents as the work of John Leland and John Bale, but in the seventeenth century it achieves an unprecedented popularity and vitality. It becomes omnipresent and appears in a remarkable variety of forms, ranging from short prefatory lives to biographical sketches in funeral sermons, and lives and characters incorporated in histories such as those of Clarendon and Burnet. Brief lives are gathered together in many of the biographical collections that appeared in the later part of the century, defined and organized on many different principles: by county in Thomas Fuller's *Worthies*, by institution in Anthony Wood's *Athenæ Oxonienses*, by religious denomination and political party in David Lloyd's *Memoires* of Anglicans and Royalists, and by profession or calling in William Winstanley's *Lives of the English Poets*.

Such works reflect and sometimes combine many different aims, from the propagandist's polemical defence of a party to the antiquarian's attempt to provide pioneer reference works, and they have many different kinds of value. Most obviously, as discussion in the first chapter has already indicated, they provide an enormous expansion of biography into new areas beyond the traditional categories of saints and great public persons to figures of a great many ranks and types.[1] They have inescapable limitations arising from their brevity, but at best their smallness in scale is compensated for by the special powers of concentrated analysis and expression that give distinction to a number of branches of seventeenth-century literature. The popularity of the brief life is an aspect of the fashion for compressed expression reflected in the vogue during this period for the essay and the Theophrastian character, as is apparent in Fuller's *The Holy State* and *The Profane State*, where essays, characters, and brief lives appear side by side.

The principles that lie behind seventeenth-century brief biography at its best are expressed by Leopold Finch in the dedication of translations by various hands of Cornelius Nepos, *The Lives of Illustrious Men*, in 1684: 'It often happens, that a Prince is better represented by his Coyns, then by his Statues; so without detracting from the just praise of others, *Nepos* may possibly give as lively an Idea of an *Alcibiades* or *Themistocles*, as those who have drawn out their Descriptions to a greater length; For as in Mens Faces, so in their Actions, there are certain peculiar Airs that distinguish one from another; if you hit these, you give the Character as effectually, as if your Canvass was as large as the Object, and you took in every Hair.'[2] This is an ideal that is most fully achieved by John Aubrey, the undoubted master of the seventeenth-century English brief life, whose work will be examined in the next chapter.

Two figures who are best considered before Aubrey deserve attention as representing two antithetical possibilities for the brief life, Thomas Fuller and Anthony Wood. Fuller and Wood share a double aim, to extend the range of biography by carrying coverage into new areas, and to bring to bear on biography the new antiquarian spirit and expertise that developed during the seventeenth century, but in most respects they are strongly contrasting figures. Fuller's achievement is most notable in the first of the two areas. In his *Worthies* he provides a remarkable breadth of biographical coverage, a grand representation of the variety of human character and life-patterns, and goes further than any biographer before Aubrey in attempting to display the full range of human individuality. Wood's achievement is most notable in the second area, recognition of the importance for biography of scholarly research, appreciation of the importance of factual detail and accuracy. He does not have Fuller's degree of fascination with individuality but carries much further the application to biography of the advanced and scrupulous kind of scholarship that figures like Camden, Somner, Dugdale, and Spelman displayed in their studies of such historical fields as Roman Britain, Anglo-Saxon England, medieval feudalism, the legal system, and parliament.

II

Thomas Fuller, whose distinction as an Anglican clergyman and historical writer caused him to be commemorated in the fine anonymous biography that has already been considered,[3] included brief lives in many of his publications. Some are incorporated in *The Holy State, The Church-History of Britain,* and *The History of the University of Cambridge,* and others are collected in *Abel Redevivus,* but his biographical work culminated in *The History of the Worthies of England.*[4] Like so many other notable works of seventeenth-century English biography, the *Worthies* is a product of the disruption of the Civil War and its aftermath, which cut Fuller off from the exercise of his Anglican ministry and caused him to find other occupations. He worked on it for at least seventeen years. It was ready for publication in 1660 but was revised in the light of an attack on his work by Peter Heylyn and appeared posthumously in 1662.

A special feature of the *Worthies* is the organization by counties: this is biography in a local context, reflecting the strongly provincial nature of seventeenth-century England, an era when the terms 'county' and 'country' were often used interchangeably. Motivated by a strong, although not blatant, patriotism, the *Worthies* is in the tradition of the great celebrations of England and its shires by Camden, Speed, and Drayton. Fuller places his brief lives in a context that includes descriptions of local monuments and buildings, medicinal waters and herbs, commodities, wonders, and proverbs, among other things, so that notable persons appear as having grown from the local soil and environment.

Fuller's comprehensiveness in the *Worthies* is unprecedented. He attempts to provide brief biographies of notable persons of the whole of England and Wales from the beginning of records to his own time, excluding only the living (with occasional exceptions). In aim and principle the *Worthies* is the largest in scope of all seventeenth-century biographical works. Fuller makes his way through a series of categories of persons in each county. His first categories are princes, saints, martyrs, and confessors, while others incorporate prelates, judges, statesmen, soldiers, seamen, writers (including scholars and scientists), benefactors, and lord mayors of London.

Fuller's final category is a general class of 'Memorable Persons,' which allows his most radical extension of biographical coverage beyond conventional areas. He declares that he includes persons here regardless of rank, even the humble, vulgar, and 'mechanicks,' although aware that some may object to such disregard for social class, when he places a blacksmith beside the great Lord Burghley among the notable natives of Lincolnshire. This category, which he compares to 'a publick *Inn*, admitting all Comers and Goers, having any *extraordinary* (not vitious) *Remark* upon them,' adds much to the splendid variety of the *Worthies*.[5] William Adams is included because he was the first Englishman in Japan, Leonard Mascall because he was the first to introduce carp into England, Thomas Parr because he lived to be over a hundred and fifty years old, and Hester Temple because she survived to see seven hundred descendants. Jeffrey, the court dwarf, is included because of his small size, while Walter Parsons and William Evans, royal porters, are included because of their large stature: in an antimasque, Evans drew Jeffrey out of his pocket. John Lepton is included because he rode from London to York in six days; mysteriously Mr Kidson is included even though Fuller has been able to discover nothing about him. Subjects range from Robin Hood to Thomas Tarlton, jester to Queen Elizabeth, and James Yorke, a blacksmith so skilled he could shoe Pegasus.

Fuller brings in whole categories of people previously neglected by biographers. With the aid of Elias Ashmole, for example, he includes a large number of alchemists, such as George Ripley, Thomas Charnock, and Edward Kelley. He gives some prominence to musicians, for example William and Henry Lawes and John Dowland. Notable schoolmasters, such as Richard Mulcaster and Thomas Robertson, are included. Writers gain a large representation: not only divines and scholars but poets and dramatists in substantial numbers. Fuller is the author of the first biography, however brief, of many of the great Elizabethan and Jacobean writers, such poets as Daniel and Drayton, and figures as diverse as Shakespeare and Robert Burton.

In many respects the biographies of the *Worthies*, like the *Church-History*, grew out of the antiquarian interests Fuller shared with Wood. Great labours of research went into the making of the lives in the *Worthies*, as the anonymous biographer suggests with his vivid picture of Fuller's zeal in consulting church monuments and learned men of many localities even in the midst of the Civil War. Fuller drew on church registers and unprinted records in the Tower and elsewhere. His use of printed sources, including funeral sermons and prefatory lives, was both extensive and discriminating. He is careful to specify his sources, and his work provides in effect a critical survey of published biographical literature. He displays proper scepticism regarding both medieval lives of saints and Foxe's Protestant hagiography. While he makes good use of church monuments he also provides witty comments on their unreliability; he declares in the *Holy State* that in some monuments the red veins of marble seem to blush at the falsehoods written on them.[6] In many cases where he was opening new biographical subjects and had little to aid him either in monuments or written sources, he sought information from surviving relatives, friends, and associates, for example about Samuel Daniel from the poet's acquaintances and about Lord Herbert of Cherbury from his brother, Sir Henry Herbert.

The antiquarian aspect of the *Worthies* is shown not only in Fuller's wide-ranging research, his careful acknowledgment and critical use of sources, but also in such matters as his concern for dating. In 'The General Artist' in his *Holy State* he emphasizes the importance of chronology, 'without which History is but an heap of tales.' In the *Worthies* he criticizes the neglect of dates by earlier biographers: he states for example that in the otherwise commendable life of Thomas Jackson by Edmund Vaughan nothing is lacking except the dates of birth and death. In his own practice in the *Worthies* he attempts, as he declares, to provide some dates for each of his subjects when they can be determined: at least birth and death or *floruit*. Elementary though this may seem, it is a real advance over the work of many earlier seventeenth-century biographers.[7]

Working single-handed in troubled times on a project of such enormous scope as the *Worthies*, which was published as a folio volume of over a thousand pages, Fuller of course could not achieve complete accuracy. He was led into mistakes sometimes by errors in his sources, despite his critical spirit. Posthumous publication probably accounts for certain obvious errors remaining uncorrected, for example the date of the assassination of the first Duke of Buckingham being given as 1620 rather than 1628. This circumstance probably also explains the lack of an index, which is ironical since the *Worthies* contains an eloquent statement of the need for indexes in such works.[8] It is to be noted, however, that Fuller's scholarship both in the *Worthies* and in the *Church-History* came under some attack in his own period. In truth the *Worthies*, despite the antiquarian merits it possesses, is more notable for range, breadth, and liveliness than scholarly depth.

The *Worthies* is an uneven work, and the lives it incorporates vary widely in quality. Many are fragmentary, not only brief but slight in every way. For example, the life of Shakespeare, which has attracted special attention because of the importance of its subject, offers a memorable nautical image contrasting Shakespeare as like 'an *English man of War*' with Jonson as 'a *Spanish great Gallion*,' but it does not provide much more. In spite of the diligence he often displayed in examining church monuments, Fuller fails to furnish dates for Shakespeare's birth and death, even though these appear on the Stratford monument. He attempts little account of Shakespeare's dramatic career, although he took an interest in the stage that is shown in many anecdotes about the theatre scattered throughout the *Worthies*.[9]

Fuller certainly did not lack the ability to write more substantial biographies than those that appear in the *Worthies*. His skills are impressively demonstrated in memorable longer biographies that he included in *The Holy State* and *Abel Redevivus*, for example the lives of William Perkins in both volumes. But the vast scope of the *Worthies* did not permit such relatively extensive treatment of his subjects there. In the *Worthies*, rather than developing any single biography fully, he develops the special potentiality of the large collection of brief lives to exhibit the great diversity of human character and patterns of life, as in a grand survey or panorama. This sense of variety is built up through the rapid movement from one subject to another. The comparisons are most often left for the reader to make, but the *Worthies* depends implicitly upon a comparative method possible only in such a collection of brief lives. While the authors of exemplary religious biographies insistently use comparisons to demonstrate their subjects' similarities with ideal models, Fuller and Aubrey implicitly use the comparative method in the opposite way to reveal the differences between their subjects. Their interest in individuality, their eye for distinctively personal features, appears cumulatively as they move from one biography to another and then to another.

Fuller records a great variety of individual details of all kinds about his subjects. He describes their temperaments, telling us that William Gilbert (famous for the magnet) was cheerful, although this is uncommon in a retired scholar, while Richard Holdsworth 'had the infirmity of ingenious Persons to be Cholerick.' He describes their habits not only when awake but even when asleep, for example the sleepwalking of John Poultney. He mentions special features of their speech, informing us that Joseph Mead could pronounce the letter R only with difficulty, that Dean Overall was so used to Latin that he found it difficult to discourse in English, and that Sir John Harington's wit was so sharp that an attendant feared he would make an epigram on her. He describes their unusual accomplishments and innovations, recording that John, Lord Harington, was one of the first to keep a religious diary. And he tells us of their recreations: how Alexander Nowell loved fishing (and accidentally invented bottled ale). In his revelation of individuality through the accumulation of such detail, Fuller is unexcelled, at least until the emergence of Aubrey.[10]

Two other aspects of the *Worthies* that give special distinction to Fuller among seventeenth-century biographers are natural corollaries of this fascination with the variety of human nature: remarkable charity and freedom from prejudice, and recognition of the value of biography as entertainment. Fuller's attraction to diversity, his charitable outlook that allows appreciation of a wide variety of characters and systems of belief, frees his work from the highly partisan political and religious propaganda that limited so much seventeenth-century biographical writing. His admission of entertainment as a proper aim for biography implies a belief in the worth of reading and writing lives that extends beyond the merely didactic and makes much of his work relatively free of the narrowly exemplary traditions that had dominated biography in the period.

Fuller's biographical writing is marked by a degree of moderation and impartiality that has few parallels in this era of bitter conflict, apart from the exceptional figure of Aubrey. If in other respects his scholarship falls short of Wood's, in this respect he is far superior to his fiercely partisan and prejudiced contemporary. He carried his moderation so far as to offend both the Puritans and his own Royalist and Anglican party, when during the Civil War he called for peace in similar sermons in Puritan London and Royalist Oxford. In his *Church-History* his impartiality is shown by the fact that he offended the supporters of Archbishop Williams by praising him too little and his opponents by praising him too much. Coleridge concluded that he was freest of prejudice of any of the great figures of his time.[11]

In the *Worthies* Fuller's moderation appears in his impartial criticism of the opposite Protestant and Roman Catholic biases of such writers as Bale and Pits, in his sympathetic biographies both of Puritan nonconformists and Roman Catholics, and in his fair handling of such controversial subjects as Archbishop Laud. He is fair even in his treatment of those who had attacked him, such as John Saltmarsh. In some lives, for example that of Cardinal Allen, he employs the device of two parallel columns to show differences of opinion regarding his subject, thus anticipating the modern casebook method. In the life of Henry VIII he uses *three* columns to make it clear that he rejects both extremes in views of this monarch.

In the seventeenth-century context Fuller's emphasis on the value of biography as entertainment is as unusual as his moderation and impartiality. He states in his preface that merely to tell the time and place of men's births and deaths and the names of their books would make a dull subject, and that therefore he has interlaced, not as meat but as condiment, many delightful stories. His statement is unsophisticated but he establishes the important principle, little acknowledged by many previous biographers, that entertainment is one of the proper aims of biography, that biography like poetry should combine pleasure with instruction. This is one of the important ways in which he seems to anticipate Aubrey, who developed the same principle so fully that in modern times popular dramatic entertainments have been based on his *Brief Lives*.[12]

Fuller sought to amuse the reader not only by inserting many entertaining anecdotes like the famous one of Sir Walter Ralegh and the cloak but also by developing a witty style. He is sometimes quite facetious, as when he describes the founder of Brasenose College in Oxford as dying 'before he had finished one *Nostrill* thereof' or tells us that Queen Matilda was not a nun but a 'Virgin at large.' Such a style may tend to deprive his subjects of dignity but it is a healthy antidote to the over-solemn, reverential attitude of much seventeenth-century biography in the exemplary tradition. And Fuller is not lacking in dignity when this is appropriate, for example in the imagery he uses to convey the admirable unworldliness of the Reverend William Brightman: 'Walking thorough the *vineyard of this world*, he pluckt and eat a few grapes, but put up none in his Vessel, using wealth as if he us'd it not.'[13]

The special importance Fuller attached to entertaining the reader in his scholarly works was so unorthodox as to result in unfavourable criticism. Kennett in his life of Somner criticized him for mixing puns and tales with his scholarship. Peter Heylyn attacked the *Church-History* for its '*Merry Tales*,' declaring that it should be called '*Fullers Miscellanies*.' He accused Fuller of providing a jest book mixed with ecclesiastical history, and of converting church history into romance and fables, as well as of displaying doctrinal unorthodoxy. Fuller replied, but characteristically insisted on making his peace with Heylyn.[14] His liking for wit and entertainment does not really undermine the serious aspects of the *Worthies*, except in so far as it may lead him to be uncritical in including good anecdotes. His concern with entertaining the reader means more than the introduction of interesting anecdotes and the development of a witty style. It grows most basically from his fascination with the varieties of character and the ways in which they exhibit the human comedy.

How successful he was in making the work entertaining is shown by Samuel Pepys's response: he records in his diary on 10 February 1662 that the night after he bought the *Worthies* he stayed up reading it until two o'clock in the morning, losing sight of the time.[15]

III

It is indicative of the contrast between Fuller and Wood that no one would be likely to be kept from bed at night by the pleasure of reading Wood's major biographical work, *Athenæ Oxonienses*. While Fuller's *Worthies* survives by virtue of its range and variety, its liveliness, its values as literature and entertainment, Wood's *Athenæ Oxonienses* represents the collection of brief biographies shaped as the reference work. It belongs as much to the history of scholarship as to that of biography, and is one of the few seventeenth-century works that retains its place on the shelves of a well-stocked reference room.

Wood is in many ways a less appealing character than Fuller. In contrast to the remarkably charitable Fuller, he was crabbed, quarrelsome, and highly prejudiced. While Fuller made peace even with those who set out to be his enemies such as Heylyn, Wood quarrelled even with friends and benefactors such as Aubrey. While Fuller was an urbane figure with experience of life in many spheres, familiar with courtiers and generals as well as with clergy and scholars, and travelled widely throughout England while working on the *Worthies*, Wood was much more reclusive, and his life was virtually confined to Oxford, spent there on the fringes of academic circles, largely in libraries and archives. But while his life and the focus of his work were narrower than Fuller's, his scholarly achievement was in many ways more impressive.

Wood's biographical labours, centred upon figures connected with Oxford University, extended over the quarter-century from 1670 to 1695. His *Historia et Antiquitates Universitatis Oxoniensis*, published in a Latin version in 1674, included brief biographies of university figures. The first edition of his chief biographical work, on the bishops and writers of Oxford, *Athenæ Oxonienses*, which in an epistle 'To the Reader' he justifiably termed 'this Herculean labour,' was published in English in two large folio volumes in 1691 and 1692. He continued further work on it until his death in 1695, and a second edition incorporating his additions was published in 1721, again in two folio volumes. In the first edition the living were excluded, with some exceptions in the appended *Fasti*, but they were included in the second, so that the chronological range ultimately extended from medieval writers like John Skelton to newly emerging figures like Joseph Addison.[16]

Since the ostensible subject of the *Athenæ* is Oxford men, its scheme is less inclusive than that of Fuller's *Worthies*, but its scope is still very large. As there were only two English universities, Wood's categories of bishops and writers includes approximately half the university-educated Englishmen in these two classes. Furthermore, Wood interprets the category of writer broadly, so that any Oxford-educated clergyman, for example, who had written a tract or published a sermon gained admission to his work.

Moreover, Wood did his best to make the *Athenæ* a real dictionary of national biography for England by including many figures who were not eligible according to any strict interpretation of his scheme for the work. He employed a series of pretexts to introduce the lives of persons unconnected with Oxford, often digressively inserting them within the biographies of Oxford men with whom they had some link or with whom they shared a surname. He used such means to bring into his work many Cambridge men. For example, he added a biography of the poet Thomas Randolph to an account of an Oxford man of the same name, and he inserted the life of Christopher Marlowe in that of Thomas Newton, to whom *Tamberlaine* was once attributed. He introduced the life of Andrew Marvell in the biography of Marvell's opponent, Samuel Parker, stating: 'for here I think it very proper to be brought in and no where else.' By these methods Wood so expanded the scope of *Athenæ Oxonienses* that in an introduction to the second volume in 1692 his friend James Harrington (a lawyer and poet not to be confused with the author of *Oceana*) commented that, although 'by its Title confin'd to one University only,' 'The Work, in its several commendable Digressions, seems almost to contain an exact and full History of Learning, and of the Learned Men in England.'[17]

By freely introducing long digressions Wood indeed brought into the *Athenæ* not only numerous Cambridge men but many persons who belonged to spheres far removed from both the universities. He attached the life of Izaak Walton to that of Walton's biographical subject, Hooker. He included a life of William Lilly, the popular astrologer, with that of the quite unrelated scholar and humanist of the same name. He inserted the life of the plebeian John Taylor, the Water Poet, within the bibliography of the writings of Taylor's opponent, George Wither. He even provided a note on John Bunyan, in his life of Edward Fowler, who wrote an attack on Bunyan.

The *Fasti* appended to the *Athenæ*, which was designed to provide a chronology of Oxford University events, was also exploited by Wood as a means of inserting the biographies of many figures who were neither Oxford bishops nor Oxford writers. Thus he introduced into the *Fasti* Cambridge men believed to have earned or been honoured by a second Oxford degree, including the poets Milton and Cowley. He brought in also officials of state who were given honorary degrees in the Interregnum, among others Oliver Cromwell, who is rarely thought of as an Oxford man. When after the Restoration the Duke of Monmouth was honoured in the same way, this gave Wood the pretext for introducing brief biographies of all Charles II's illegitimate children he had been able to identify.

Wood could not of course ever break entirely free of the limitations of coverage imposed by the basic scheme of the *Athenæ*. Cambridge men and non-university men inevitably remain less represented than Oxford men, even though he stretched his scheme to the breaking point to bring in as many as possible. There is severe limitation in terms of gender, since the universities were open only to males, although Wood occasionally found means of introducing lives of women: for example he inserted the life of Anne Killigrew in the biography of her father, Henry Killigrew, and the life of Katherine Philips in the biography of her friend Jeremy Taylor.

Wood's biographical coverage is naturally influenced too by his personal range of knowledge and interests. He does not display so much interest in new areas of learning, science, and invention as his friend Aubrey, although he gives scientists increasing prominence in the last lives he wrote. As one might expect, he is at his best on scholars in traditional fields, such as antiquaries and historians. He gives considerable attention to poets and other literary figures: for many of them he provides not only the first life but a life that remained the best until at least the appearance of the *Dictionary of National Biography* two centuries later.[18] He shows a special interest in musicians, and includes many figures like Orlando Gibbons and John Bull, especially in the *Fasti*.

IV

Even more than for its wide range, the *Athenæ* is notable for the solidity and accuracy of the biographies it contains. Wood was justifiably very conscious of his position as an innovator in biographical scholarship, the first to apply to biographical writing on a large scale the resources and methods of the advanced antiquarian movement of his period. His pioneer status is shown by the ridicule he sometimes encountered, by the lack of cooperation he often suffered, and by the fact that his work long remained without real counterpart. Aubrey noted that Cambridge men showed no inclination to carry out any such work for their university,[19] and it is thanks largely to Wood that we are today so much better informed about the lives of many sixteenth-century and seventeenth-century Oxford men than we are about their Cambridge counterparts.

Wood's sense that the scholarship of the *Athenæ* marked a great advance over the work of other biographers is shown in his frequent criticisms of the shortcomings of his predecessors and contemporaries. His comments on the biographical and historical writings of such predecessors as Bale and Foxe sometimes reveal the asperity of his nature but they often demonstrate a healthily sceptical attitude. He frequently comments on Bale's bitterly anti-Roman Catholic prejudices with such phrases as '*foule-mouthed Bale.*' He is more respectful of Foxe but notes the presence of many errors arising from dependence on unreliable witnesses. Showing his own anti-Puritan prejudices, he terms Samuel Clarke 'a scribling Plagiary,' and with more justification he attacks David Lloyd as a 'most impudent Plagiary.' Only a few scholars such as William Camden, Brian Twyne, whose collections on Oxford history marked him as a kindred spirit, and Andrew Allam, who rendered valuable assistance with the *Athenæ*, entirely escape his criticism.[20]

Among the earlier biographers and historians who come in for criticism in the *Athenæ* is Fuller. In his biography of William Camden in the first volume in 1691, Wood criticized Fuller as 'credulous' in his *Church-History*, and Harrington in his introduction to the second volume in the next year, praising Wood as an innovator, declared that he was anticipated by none but such 'mean and fanciful Authors' as Lloyd and Fuller.[21] Because of his High Church sympathies, Wood was inclined to be prejudiced against such latitudinarian Anglicans as Fuller, but in truth if we compare Wood with Fuller and other earlier biographers we sense that we have in Wood for almost the first time modern standards of scholarship. Wood's scholarship is so much more substantial than Fuller's as to make Fuller appear a gentleman amateur in comparison.

The degree to which Wood was consumed by antiquarian zeal is strikingly shown by an episode in his autobiography, *Life and Times*. Writing of himself in the third person, he describes his reaction when in working on his history of the University of Oxford he managed in 1660 to obtain the keys to the room in the Schools tower containing the university registers and other archives:

> He was so exceedingly delighted with the place and the choice records therein, and did take so much paynes for carrying on the work least the keys should be taken away from him, that a great alteration was made in him. About 2 months after his entrance into the said tower, his acquaintance took notice of the falling away of his body, the fading of his cheeks, the chang[e] of the redness in them to white, &c. Yet he was very cheerfull, contended [contented] and healthfull, and nothing troubled him more than the intermission of his labours by eating, drinking, sleeping, and somtimes by company which he could not avoid.

Wood's dedication to scholarship is evident not only throughout his own work but in the assistance he gave to others. Although by modern standards he can be criticized for failing to acknowledge the debt he owed to such assistants as Aubrey, he was himself generous in giving help to other scholars.[22]

In the *Athenæ* Wood made extensive use not only of Oxford University records such as matriculation registers but of many other sources. In a preface to the first volume in 1691 his friend Harrington lists a wide range of the sources, including manuscripts in the Bodleian and Cotton libraries, records at the Tower and Heralds' Office in London, wills at the Prerogative Office, cathedral archives, church registers, and monuments and windows in churches. Volumes of Wood's transcriptions and notes from many of these sources survive among his manuscripts in the Bodleian Library. As well as employing all the resources one might expect of a good seventeenth-century antiquary, Wood was a pioneer in turning to sources few if any scholars had previously thought of exploiting: for example, he used Bodleian readers' records in his life of John Price, and he sometimes consulted book auction records for bibliographical information.

Since the majority of Wood's subjects were writers, he was able to draw much of his information from printed sources. He scrutinized his subjects' writings, and examined printed funeral sermons and biographical prefaces wherever these existed. He acknowledged many such sources explicitly, providing in effect bibliographies of existing biographical writings, much more extensive than Fuller's, as well as frequently commenting on their value or lack of value. Since he was familiar with the resources of the Bodleian Library and Oxford college libraries, and had extensive collections of books and pamphlets of his own, as well as access to other private libraries, very little that was in print escaped him.

Wood supplemented such sources with many letters of inquiry. During the years he was engaged in biographical work between 1670 and 1695 he addressed numerous letters to persons who were his subjects or potential subjects, and to surviving relatives, friends, and associates of those no longer alive, with requests for information, sometimes under such headings as parentage, time and place of birth, grammar school, university, preferments, employments and places, writings, date and place of death, and burial. In addition he used various of his acquaintances and regular correspondents in gathering such information. Large numbers of the letters he received in response to his inquiries survive among his papers in the Bodleian Library.[23]

These manuscripts have received little attention from scholars, but they are interesting for the light they shed on the problems faced by the seventeenth-century biographer. Wood's first problem was to determine which figures were eligible for inclusion in his biographical works centred on Oxford University, since the records to which he had access provided no complete registers of persons who had studied or held positions in the university. As part of his preparation he drew up a list of writers educated at Cambridge from Fuller's history of that university, so that he might omit them 'because my work should not be endless,' even though he later found pretexts for including many of them. Among the advice he received was a letter from Henry Wilkinson, 19 December 1671, urging him not to include any of unsound opinion, and to omit altogether the Unitarian John Biddle, the Roman Catholic Sancta Clara (otherwise known as Francis or Christopher Davenport), and Thomas Hobbes. This advice came rather strangely from Wilkinson, since on the Restoration he had been ejected as principal of Magdalen Hall for nonconformity, and he had more recently been excommunicated by the established church, and fortunately Wood ignored it.[24]

Once he had decided which persons to include, Wood often then had much difficulty in obtaining even the most basic information about them, such as the dates of birth and death. Those to whom he directed inquiries often proved to have no exact or reliable information about the time of birth of near relatives, or sometimes even about the date of their own birth. Furthermore, he and Aubrey, when working to assist him, both at times detected informants apparently pretending to be younger than they actually were. Aubrey complained to Wood in a letter of 1 February 1671: 'Dr Chr: Wren hath putt a trick on us as it seemes, for he hath made himselfe a yeare younger then indeed he is,' although in this case he was actually misled by another informant, and his doubt about Wren's accuracy was unjustified.[25]

Dates of death were usually much easier to determine than dates of birth, but they sometimes posed special problems. In 1692 Wood sought information about Richard Cromwell, who had been his father's reluctant successor as Lord Protector, from Jeremiah White, who had served as Oliver Cromwell's domestic chaplain and remained close to his family. In his first letter of reply White evaded Wood's question about the date of Richard Cromwell's death, and when Wood complained about this White made an unexpected reply: 'It is the strangest thing to me in Nature, that you should be displeas'd I have not acquainted you with the time of Mr Richard Cromwell's death; and the place of his burial; when my selfe and all his ffreinds doe hope, & believe he is yet living. That Worthy, (however unfortunate) Gentleman has as yet gone throw no death, but a political one.' White made it clear that members of the Cromwell family in the later seventeenth century wished to avoid all publicity. He informed Wood that 'Persons of Honour' related to Richard Cromwell desired him 'to mention onely the place of his birth.' The persons of honour no doubt included Richard's sister Mary, Lady Fauconberg, who through her marriage had entered circles of the royal court.[26]

The Cromwells were by no means the only persons reluctant for Wood to include them in his biographical works. In the same month of April 1692 that Wood corresponded with White about the Cromwells he received an impassioned plea from one W. Thornton: 'I humbly and earnestly request you to say nothing of me in your Historie.' He assured Wood, 'upon ye faith of a Christian,' he had written nothing for the press and had no intention of ever writing anything. The reason he gave for wishing to avoid notice was simply his liking for a quiet life out of the public eye: 'I make it my businesse to passe through ye World wth as little noise as I can.' But many of those who declined to cooperate in the inquiries of Wood and Aubrey had good reasons like the Cromwells for shunning publicity, because of their association with defeated and reviled causes in the aftermath of the Interregnum and Restoration. Since Wood's hostility to nonconformists became well known, he was partly to blame himself for such lack of cooperation. Aubrey reported to Wood on 8 September 1680 that when he inquired about William Prynne, the prolific Puritan pamphleteer, he found that Prynne's nephew was 'afrayd of my Queres, as many people are, and also of AW.'[27]

Among Wood's friends and regular correspondents John Aubrey was specially useful. Generally resident in London, he was able and willing to carry out various kinds of research there for Wood, and he was particularly valuable as a source of informal information. Wood described himself in his epistle 'To the Reader' in the *Athenæ* as 'a Person who delights to Converse more with the Dead, than with the Living,' one so given to a solitary and retired life as to be 'as 'twere Dead to the World,' and contrasts himself with those who frequented common rooms, coffee houses, and clubs.[28] Aubrey, on the other hand, was gregarious, with a wide range of interests and acquaintances, and he ideally supplemented Wood's limitations by providing information and reports of a kind that could be gained only through informal contact and conversation.

While he used Aubrey for information from informal sources, Wood's primary concern in his research was with the collection of factual material and establishment of its accuracy, in such matters as dates, degrees, offices, preferments, and publications. He states indeed that names and times are the things chiefly required in history, which for him includes biography. The importance he attached to dating and chronology is specially striking in contrast to the neglect of these matters by many previous seventeenth-century biographers. It is shown in his criticism of other writers, for example his comment that Henry Savage, historian and Master of Balliol, lacked 'a timing head.' The 'Vindication' of his work against criticism it had received from Bishop Burnet, which is included in the second edition, rightly claims that the *Athenæ* is 'most exactly written according to time,' and states that Wood has given 'the very Day, and sometimes the Hour of a thing done.'[29]

It is significant that Wood was evidently the first to spot factual errors, particularly regarding dates, in the biographies of Izaak Walton. Among the books from Wood's collections preserved in the Bodleian Library is a copy of Walton's *Lives* in the 1670 edition, inscribed by its author: 'ffor Mr Wood.' Wood has marked it with annotations to correct some of Walton's errors. While in his account of Hooker in the *Athenæ Oxonienses* Wood praised Walton's lives as 'well done, considering the education of the author,' and in his biography of Donne he quoted Hales's praise of Walton, later when he examined the Oxford records for his life of Wotton he discovered and pointed out Walton's errors especially in chronology. Likewise he appears to have been the first to detect the errors and fabrications, including false dates, in James Howell's *Epistolæ Ho-Elianæ*.[30]

A special strength of Wood's biographies is his concern with his subjects' writings. He is a great pioneer in the field of bibliography. He makes it clear that his purpose is to deal even with figures like Sir Philip Sidney and George Calvert, Lord Baltimore, primarily as authors: he leaves it to other historians to describe Calvert's colonizing activities. As a bibliographer he not only made full use of the Bodleian Library's collections and catalogues, but his manuscripts record his searches over many years in private collections for the works of poets and dramatists not well represented in university or college libraries.[31] He examined at first hand a high proportion of the works he listed, and while he did not attempt, or profess much capacity for, detailed or subtle literary criticism, he provided some description and characterization of many of them. He faced and solved many bibliographical problems. He established the canon of authors' works, identified many authors of anonymous and pseudonymous publications, noted the distinctions between different editions of the same work, and incorporated in his biographies a vast amount of information about sixteenth- and seventeenth-century conditions of authorship, censorship, and publication.

In the cases of prolific seventeenth-century authors like William Prynne and George Wither, Wood's bibliographical labours were on a heroic scale. He lists forty-two works by John Davies of Kidwelly, and over a hundred including some unpublished by George Wither, a high proportion of which he had, as he states, 'seen and perused.'[32] As has already been noted, one of his special contributions to Milton biography is bibliographical: he provided the fullest list of Milton's writings, based on examination of the publications, that appears in the early lives of the poet. This is characteristic. Wood's bibliographies of the writings of many English authors remained virtually the fullest and best to be published until the appearance of the Short-Title Catalogues in the twentieth century.

V

Wood not only provided much more substantial factual information about such matters as dates and publications than Fuller and other predecessors but he carried candour much further than most of the earlier biographers. Fuller stated in the *Worthies* that, while he omitted the living to avoid flattery, for reasons of charity he did not claim to tell the whole truth about his subjects: he concealed faults and mentioned only the virtues of many persons, especially those of recent times. In contrast,

Wood's candour in revealing or alleging faults in his subjects was so great as to draw much criticism upon him and get him into serious trouble. In his preface to the first volume of the *Athenæ* Harrington observed that the work contained 'some harsh Expressions' that might better have been softened and some severely critical passages that might best have been omitted, and in his introduction to the second volume a year later he felt it necessary to make apology for Wood's 'disadvantageous Representations' and 'disobliging expressions.' The problems caused by Wood's candour when carried to the point of reckless indiscretion culminated in his prosecution and conviction for libellously alleging corruption against the late Earl of Clarendon, with the result that the offending pages of the *Athenæ* were publicly burned and Wood was formally expelled from the University of Oxford.[33]

The eminent figures Wood portrays critically in the *Athenæ* include other statesmen and peers as well as Clarendon. He represents the Earl of Shaftesbury as a time-server, and pushes his account of him so far in the direction of satiric biography as to quote Dryden's satire upon him in *Absolom and Achitophel* in place of an epitaph. He describes Philip, late Earl of Pembroke and Montgomery, as so illiterate that he could scarcely write his name, and the current earl as so choleric that he has broken many heads wiser than his own. He is as candid in his treatment of the ecclesiastical and academic hierarchies as the peerage. He declares that Ralph Brideoake became a bishop through the influence of the Duchess of Portsmouth, a royal mistress who was always ready to accept a bribe, and states that Robert South, the prominent Anglican divine, obtained at Westminster School 'a considerable Stock of Grammar and Philological Learning, but more of Impudence and Sauciness.' He describes Dr John Wallis, the mathematician, who held a series of high positions in Oxford University, as one 'who, at any time, can make black white, and white black, for his own ends.' His biographies of both the prominent and the obscure, both the living and the dead, contain many such highly critical and disparaging remarks.[34]

Although Wood's strongly critical treatment of many of his subjects drew attack upon him from various quarters, his candour provides a healthy antidote to the reverential approach and suppressions that marked the long-dominant exemplary religious tradition in biography. Wood seems to go out of his way to avoid the kind of moralizing characteristic of that tradition. In remarkable contrast to the elaborate religious and moral commentaries of Burnet and others, he describes the life of the famous and notorious Earl of Rochester as 'short, but pleasant,' a viewpoint that appears astonishing in the seventeenth-century context.[35] But while Wood can be praised for his frankness and honesty and his relative freedom from conventional moralizing, he leaves no doubt that much of his criticism of his subjects is prompted by his political and religious prejudices.

Wood's prejudices are indeed conspicuous and notorious. The 'Vindication' of the *Athenæ* against Burnet's criticisms describes the way in which Wood used the work to fight again the battles of the Civil War that had taken place in his formative years: 'In it you'll find a great deal of the Mystery of Iniquity acted in that dismal Rebellion which was commenced by the Puritans, and other Factious People, *Anno* 1642, opened and displayed.' As this statement suggests, Wood was fiercely Royalist and Anglican, Anglo-Catholic and Laudian in his sympathies. He was viewed by Burnet and other contemporaries as having Roman Catholic sympathies.[36] In the *Athenæ* when he deals with the sixteenth-century religious Reformation, his portraits of Roman Catholics are often more favourable than those of Calvinists, and he strongly defends even such controversial figures as Cardinal Wolsey. When he comes to the Civil War and Restoration, he has high praise for Anglo-Catholics, including Laud, and in contrast he provides many bitter and vitriolic portraits of Puritans.

Like aspects of his life of Lord Shaftesbury, Wood's accounts of such Puritan religious figures as Calybute Downing, Thomas Manton, and Vavasor Powell are so strongly critical as to amount to satiric biography. He is equally harsh in his judgments of leading secular figures of the Puritan and Parliamentary causes. He describes John Bradshaw as 'the monster of Men'; his characterization of John Milton as 'impudent lyer' and 'that villanous leading Incendiary' has already been noted. His hostile prejudice appears even in cases where he provides favourable characterizations of Puritans. He tells us that Henry Wilkinson was public-spirited, 'a rare thing in a Presbyterian,' and that John Howe was a 'Person of neat and polite Parts, and not of that sour and unpleasant converse as most of his persuasion are.' In such cases he represents the exceptions as proving the rule. It is not surprising that Wood found nonconformists inclined to be uncooperative when he approached them with biographical inquiries.[37]

One of the nonconformists who did prove helpful was Increase Mather, the President of Harvard College, when Wood addressed inquiries to him about New England figures while he was on a mission in England. The tone of Mather's letters suggests that Wood's religious prejudices may not yet have been known by New Englanders. He reported to Wood on 8 October 1691 that his negotiations on behalf of New England were now finished, and that the king 'has graciously restored many priviledges to ye Country: And in particular o^r Colledge is Confirmed to us.' He told Wood that he expected his ship to sail back to New England in a fortnight, and 'I would faign carry wth me the 2^d part of y^r Athenæ Oxonienses.' He can scarcely have suspected how hostile Wood would prove to be to those of his religious beliefs in that volume. It was not published in time for him to take it back with him to Boston, but in July 1692 William Whiting wrote to Wood that a copy would be sent to Mather there by 'the first ship that goes.'[38]

Strong though his prejudices were, Wood did not allow them entirely to overwhelm his scholarly objectivity. He was willing to recognize merit, especially in learning, even among Puritans. Perhaps influenced by Edward Bagshaw's biography, he comments respectfully on Robert Bolton: 'a most religious and learned Puritan.' He praises John Wilkins for his abilities and achievements even while condemning his inconstancy in religion, and shows respect for the scholarship of John Tombes, in spite of his dislike of Tombes's anabaptism. He is very critical of Henry Marten, the regicide and republican, but recognizes his talents. Although radical in his own views, John Toland was sufficiently impressed by Wood's fair-mindedness to declare, in the preface to his life of Harrington, that while Wood was much prejudiced in favour of Royalists and 'mortally hated all Republicans' he 'never deny'd justice to either side.' In Wood's favour it can at least be argued that his prejudices are always so open that no one could be misled about them.[39]

Wood's biases are not confined to religious and political matters. They appear in his lives of poets as well as in his lives of Puritans. His attitude toward poets as a class is ambiguous. He takes considerable interest in them, but he regards them as rather frivolous and vain, a bohemian crew with unsettled heads, given to indulgence in drink, unreliable, improvident, and impoverished. He writes of George Gascoigne's 'rambling and unfixed head.' He tells us that Thomas Randolph 'by indulging himself too much with the liberal conversation of his admirers (a thing incident to Poets) brought him untimely to his end.' He states that Robert Hayman was 'phantastical, (as most Poets are)' and that Payne Fisher was 'a true time-server, (incident to most Poets).' He considers that musicians display similar characteristics to the poets. He describes John Bull as a superb organist 'posses'd with crotchets, as many Musicians are.' He complains that the unsettled ways of musicians and poets make it difficult for the biographer to gain reliable information about them, but he is not without sympathy for them, partly because he recognizes that scholars like himself share some of their unworldly characteristics. He describes Henry Jacob, for example, as 'a shiftless Person, as most meer Scholars are.'[40]

VI

It is significant of Wood's austere conception of biography that one of the writers he specially criticizes for frivolity is Walter Pope, who was not only a distinguished astronomer but the author of what Wood terms in the first edition of the *Athenæ* 'vain and trivial things,' most notably a very popular life of a highwayman, *The Memoires of Monsieur Du Vall* (1670). Wood expanded his criticism in a fuller account of Pope and his works ultimately included in the second edition. He did not live long enough to read Pope's highly unorthodox and entertaining biography of Seth Ward, Bishop of Salisbury, published in 1697, but his nephew and champion Thomas Wood then immediately issued a pamphlet defending Wood's type of biography as opposed to Pope's. In phrases sometimes reminiscent of Heylyn's attack on Fuller's witty style, Thomas criticized Pope for his 'Comical and Bantering Stile,' his frequent anecdotes and jests, his playful and facetious violation of narrative conventions, and in particular for writing biography under the influence of 'the ridiculing History of *Don Quixote*.' Pope had published a translation of Cervantes, and his life of Seth Ward provides what is perhaps the first clearly recorded instance of the influence on English biography of the novel, as opposed to romance. Thomas Wood emphasized that in contrast to Pope's work the *Athenæ* was designed to be useful rather than entertaining.[41]

In contrasting his uncle's work with Pope's, Thomas Wood goes so far as to state that the *Athenæ* was intended 'for nothing else but a *Record* or *Registry*,' but in truth Wood's biographies are often much less objective and sometimes much more vital than this description would suggest.[42] The *Athenæ* is far from being an impersonal reference work. Wood stamps his personality upon it not only through the frank expression of his prejudices, all his likes and dislikes, but also through structure and style that are personal to the point of eccentricity. In organization many of the lives of the *Athenæ* are so digressive that Burnet criticized the work as 'a Tumultuary mixture of Stuff and Tattle' thrown together.[43] Wood indeed often appears to proceed almost by a method of free association.

Prompted by his desire to extend the scope of the *Athenæ* as far as possible, he employs any pretext to digress from the life of one subject to that of another.

As a result of such practices, Wood's biographies often begin with the life of one figure but conclude with the life of another or incorporate several others along the way. His life of Richard Corbet is mainly concerned with Matthew Wren, and that of Cuthbert Sydenham mainly with John Lilburne, from which it moves to Lilburne's brother. Wood sometimes introduces the biography of a second figure even within his bibliography of his primary subject's writings. He incorporates the life of Sir John Gell, the Parliamentary general, in his bibliography of Peter Heylyn's writings, and also brings in William Sanderson. In his bibliography of Thomas Vaughan he inserts first the life of Henry More, then the life of Sir Robert Moray, the Scottish Secretary of State, and finally the life of another, apparently quite unrelated, Robert Moray (or Murray). Wood's biographies often resemble a Chinese box which contains another box, and then another inside that one. He complained about works that lacked indexes or were badly indexed, and fortunately he partially compensated for his digressive ways by providing an extensive index for the *Athenæ*.[44]

Just as Wood's organization is remarkably loose and digressive, his style is often careless and clumsy. One early reader of *Athenæ Oxonienses*, an antiquary with literary tastes named James Wright, complained that Wood's nonsensical periods and ungrammatical and absurd expressions were 'so frequent that some are apt to think, how learned so ever he may be in other Languages, he hardly understands his mother-tongue.'[45] While, in contrast to Fuller and Aubrey, he is generally lacking in a comic sense, his style is so little controlled that one scarcely knows whether he intends a humorous effect when he writes that Thomas Sternhold made his metrical versions of the Psalms 'thinking thereby that the Courtiers would sing them instead of their sonnets, but did not, only some few excepted,' or tells us that Thomas Chaloner when shipwrecked 'did catch hold of a Cable with his teeth, and so escaped, but not without the loss of some of them.'[46]

Wood's style is often most lively and vital in his critical attacks, but he is carried away by such anger against Puritan leaders like William Fiennes, Lord Saye and Sele, that his sentences become incoherent with rage. His general carelessness about style is significant of the completeness of his break with the rhetorical tradition that dominated so much seventeenth-century biography in the exemplary tradition, and indicative of the extent to which his concern is with matter rather than manner. Although he is fond of some wordy circumlocutions such as 'entered upon the stage of this vain world' for 'was born,' he generally achieves at least a compression and a concreteness that contrast favourably with the copious grandeur and elevated vagueness of the more carefully wrought rhetorical styles of many biographers of the period.

The idiosyncrasies of Wood's style and structure contribute to the sense that the lives of the *Athenæ* often serve to reveal his own personality more fully than the characters of his biographical subjects. Placing his emphasis upon such factual information as dates and lists of publications, he is less concerned than Fuller or Aubrey with revelation of his subjects' personal characteristics. He does not share Fuller's purpose of entertaining the reader with interesting human detail, and he lacks the awareness that both Fuller and Aubrey possess of the biographical value of the anecdote. Nor does he have Aubrey's interest in such aspects as the appearance, manners, habits, and personal relations of his subjects. In his correspondence with Aubrey he criticized him for providing too much trivial detail about such things, and he chose to include in his own biographies only a limited amount of the often vivid and interesting personal information Aubrey sent him about many of his subjects.

Wood has so little capacity for appreciating good anecdotes that on occasions when he includes those supplied him by Aubrey he tends to spoil them in the retelling. For example, Aubrey writes that Sir Kenelm Digby was so impressive in appearance, manner, and speech 'that had he been drop't out of the clowdes in any part of the world, he would have made himselfe respected. But the Jesuites spake spitefully, and sayd 'twas true, but then he must not stay there above six weekes.' Wood follows Aubrey closely, without acknowledgment, but so changes the conclusion as to deprive the anecdote of its point. He writes: 'the Jesuits, who cared not for him, spoke spitefully, and said *'twas true, but then he must have stayed there above six weeks.*' Here of course the omission of the crucial 'not' may simply be accidental, but it is not uncharacteristic of Wood's ineptness in handling anecdotes.[47]

Although not only less skilled in handling anecdotes than Aubrey but less interested in many kinds of personal information, Wood nevertheless did incorporate in his lives enough personal detail drawn from Aubrey and other sources that Harrington in his preface to the first volume of the *Athenæ* in 1691 felt it necessary to defend his inclusion of the apparently 'trivial and immaterial' and the 'little accidents' of life, on the grounds that these may be significant. In his introduction to the second volume a year later Harrington notes that some have criticized Wood for preserving 'the little particulars' about his subjects, but observes that much has been lost through failure of such timely observation: 'For while no Man writes what every Man knows, at last none know, what none have ever written.'[48] In the *Athenæ* Wood has in fact preserved much interesting information about the varied characters and practices of sixteenth- and seventeenth-century scholars and writers, and he displays much of the rich field of well-cultivated self-expression, eccentricity, and obsession that flourished among the academics, clergy, and poets who were his subjects.

While by virtue of Wood's 'Herculean labour' of scholarly research the *Athenæ* remains even today an indispensable reference work, it would be a mistake to think of his biographies as merely dry factual chronicles. Wood not infrequently moves beyond such chronicles to give, for example, a picture of Joseph Glanvill and Thomas Hobbes quarrelling like youths when they met late in life, or an account of Bishop Thomas Couper's troubled domestic relations. He informs us about the dietary habits of Bishop George Morley, who ate only once in twenty-four hours, and of Samuel Aneley, who 'seldom or never drank any Beer, only Water,' when a student at Oxford. His records of the achievements of his subjects are not limited to their academic or public activities and writings but he tells us that Nathaniel Conopius was the first to drink coffee in Oxford, and that Heirome Zanchy, the proctor, was lusty at cudgelling and football. Wood's *Athenæ Oxonienses* includes enough such 'little particulars' that it deserves to stand with Fuller's *Worthies* and Aubrey's *Brief Lives* as a work often exhibiting the seventeenth-century interest in the range and variety of human individuality.[49]

Although it lacks the wit of Fuller and the special genius of Aubrey, *Athenæ Oxonienses* has proved to be a work of remarkably enduring value. Generations of later biographers have been greatly indebted to it. The editors of the large-scale biographical dictionary of the eighteenth century, *Biographia Britannica*, commented on the *Athenæ* in the preface to their first volume in 1747 that, while Wood's style was 'by no means elegant' and his biases and spleen were frequently evident, 'Yet with all these defects, it is out of comparison more useful and instructive than anything than had appeared before.'[50] Samuel Johnson acknowledged his use of it in his biographies of Cowley and Milton in 1779. He may well have been familiar with it from an early age, for the name of his father, '*Mr.* Michael Johnson, *Bookseller in* Litchfield,' appears in the list of subscribers printed with the second edition in 1721.[51] It provided one of the main foundations for a high proportion of the lives of sixteenth- and seventeenth-century figures in the great *Dictionary of National Biography* of the 1880s and 1890s, as it will no doubt prove to have done again in that work's successor, published since the completion of this study, the *Oxford Dictionary of National Biography*.

CHAPTER 9

Brief Lives: John Aubrey

I

Among the greatest of Wood's services to biography was his encouragement of John Aubrey's biographical activities. Aubrey (1626–97), a member of the Wiltshire gentry educated at Oxford, inherited an estate but lost it after becoming involved in law suits. He declared in a letter: 'but the trueth is, I was never made to manage an estate, & was predestinated to be cosind & cheated.' He then lived an unsettled life, largely in London. He became a founding member of the Royal Society, cultivated acquaintance with such advanced intellectuals as Thomas Hobbes, James Harrington, and William Harvey, and pursued a wide range of interests in diverse fields, including topography, archaeology, natural history, folklore, education, mathematics, and painting. His interest in biography began early. At the age of twenty-five in 1652 he was already planning to write the life of Francis Potter and not long afterwards he began to plan a life of Bacon. But Wood provided the impetus that turned biography from a minor to a major interest of Aubrey.[1]

At an early stage of his biographical studies, in the later 1660s, Wood asked Aubrey's assistance in gathering material on Oxford writers.[2] Aubrey then began to make notes for Wood's use. He states that he commenced the project 'playingly,'[3] but he soon became absorbed in it, and even though Wood quarrelled with him, as Wood did with many others, Aubrey continued to gather and send him information he had collected. To stimulate Aubrey in this work that was useful to him, Wood encouraged him to think of preparing his lives for separate publication. Aubrey then composed drafts of many of his biographies in the period 1679–80, and gave his chief manuscript the title 'Brief Lives,' probably the title he would have chosen for publication if he had completed the work.

Aubrey had great, indeed notorious, difficulty in organizing and bringing his work to a finished state. He published only one work, his *Miscellanies*, during his lifetime, and at his death left numerous others including the biographies in unfinished manuscript form. In the case of the biographies he recognized that much of what he had written was too candid for publication during his lifetime. But fortunately he took good care for the preservation of his manuscripts, depositing them in the Ashmolean Museum, newly founded in Oxford by his friend Elias Ashmole, and although they suffered some losses most of the manuscripts of the lives have survived.[4] Except for their use in the *Athenæ* by Wood, who omitted much of the personal detail that was their special excellence, they remained unprinted for more than a century. Finally they were published partially in the late eighteenth and early nineteenth centuries and more fully in an admirable scholarly edition in 1898 by Andrew Clark. In the twentieth century the more popular and less scholarly editions by John Collier and Oliver Lawson Dick added some expurgated passages previously considered unpublishable.[5]

While Aubrey's achievements in archaeology and a number of other fields have been increasingly appreciated in recent years,[6] his work as a biographer has not often been taken as seriously as it deserves to be. His reputation has suffered because of the uncompleted and fragmented condition in which he left his biographical writings. This has led to a view of him as a mere collector. Even his admirer and editor O. Lawson Dick states that his genius was for collection rather than selection. James Sutherland in his *Oxford History of English Literature* volume, *English Literature of the Late Seventeenth Century*, writes that Aubrey had 'endless curiosity and enthusiasm, but little judgement; his mind was a piece of flypaper that trapped whatever happened to be floating by at the time.' Donald Stauffer in his long-established standard survey, *English Biography before 1700*, states: 'because Aubrey's writings are unfinished notes and to a large extent formless, they are not of major importance in a study of the art of English biography.'[7] Such judgments, however, ignore the highly original nature of what Aubrey collected, and they do no justice to his principles and methods. His constitutional inability to complete his work was indeed a real and serious defect, but it was a defect arising in part from his radically empirical approach to biography.

Aubrey has suffered the fate of the successful revolutionary in that many of his innovations have come to be taken for granted, and he is not given so much credit as he deserves because he is not often enough read in the context of the biographical writing of his own century. At the same time his reputation still suffers because of the radical nature of his departure from established biographical tradition. He carried his concern for individuality so far that he is often regarded as one who has an eye only for the odd and eccentric, and he gave such a prominent place to the intimate and personal that he is often viewed as primarily a retailer of scandalous gossip, as entertaining but trivial. One of his modern editors, John Collier, titled his selection from the lives in 1931 *The Scandals and Credulities of John Aubrey*.

II

Even though he left his work in unfinished form, Aubrey deserves to be considered the most original figure among the English biographers of the seventeenth century. When one comes upon Aubrey after reading the earlier biographers of the century one has almost the same sense of encountering something totally new as one has when one comes upon John Donne's *Songs and Sonnets* after reading the Spenserian and Petrarchan love poets of the 1590s. One may find in earlier English biographies aspects that anticipate Aubrey, just as one may find in Wyatt and Sidney aspects that anticipate Donne, but he has no close precedent for his most distinctive and valuable qualities.

In the field of biography Aubrey breaks as decisively with the past as do his friends Hobbes, Harrington, and Harvey in the fields of political thought, economics, and medicine. He is the first notable English biographer to make a complete break with long-established exemplary traditions and conventions. He works by an empirical method, abandoning the deductive principles that had to a large extent prevailed in biography. His interest is not in relating the individual to any type or pattern but in individuality itself, what differentiates one individual from another. He perceives that individuality may be manifested through minute particulars of appearance, dress, speech, manners, and habits. He records many kinds of information, particularly vivid and precise personal detail, that earlier biographers had not thought worth providing, and he has good claims to be considered the first to bring private life fully into English biography. He is extraordinarily candid and includes much in his lives that earlier biographers had not thought fit to be recorded, and at the same time remarkably objective and tolerant, free from the biases, prejudices, and ulterior motives that had usually shaped and distorted biography. He develops the confined form of the brief life in ways that paradoxically so enlarge the scope of biography as to make most earlier portraits appear incomplete and flat in comparison.

Some of Aubrey's apparently casual remarks in a letter to Wood on 14 May 1673 suggest how decisive his break is with established traditions in biography as well as in other fields. He writes that he would like to sell his finely bound set of the works of St John Chrysostom, for he wishes to devote himself to studies in such areas as mathematics and 'the new discoverys of ye Virtuosi,' as well as English antiquities. He declares: 'I shall be well enough contented to let the Fathers be thumbed by the Divines.'[8] His proposal to sell the works of Chrysostom and turn away from the church fathers has the force of a symbolic gesture, which has among its implications his rejection of the exemplary religious tradition in biography as he moves to apply to biography the same sort of empirical principles many of his fellow members of the Royal Society were applying to the world of nature.[9]

As this letter implies, Aubrey's methods are in striking contrast with those of a biographer with such exemplary religious purposes as Walton.[10] Walton began with or early developed an image of his subject, and he selected, shaped, and sometimes distorted the evidence to support that image. Much of his emphasis was upon what the person had in common with other holy men as representative of an ideal pattern. Aubrey, on the other hand, begins with the collection of facts, observations, and ideas, selecting especially those that are most highly individual, that show the difference of his subject from all other persons or the majority of them, and he is unwilling to select or suppress or shape his evidence in order to develop any simple or single image. His defect is indeed the opposite of Walton's. Walton writes well-shaped lives but he oversimplifies his subjects, and he does not fully distinguish one subject from another. Aubrey, in contrast, fails to give complete shape to his lives or to reach a final synthesis, but at his best in his fullest lives he produces many-sided views of his subjects. His lives are lacking in finish but there is never any danger that one of his subjects could be mistaken for another.

Aubrey's break with the kind of exemplary tradition represented by Walton is so complete that when any material belonging to that tradition is printed among his biographies it stands out as strangely atypical. In the edition of the *Brief Lives* most widely circulated and read in modern times, O. Lawson Dick included some such passages: high-flown panegyrics on the Earl of Cork and the Countess of Warwick and a comparison of Charles Cavendish with the biblical figure Abner. But reference to the earlier and more scholarly edition of the *Brief Lives* by Andrew Clark reveals that these passages are not by Aubrey but copies among his papers from funeral and commemoration sermons by Anthony Walker and William Nailour.[11] In fact they are just the kind of conventional and empty elegies condemned by Aubrey in critical remarks directed against the 'high style' and lack of 'minuteness' of Dr Richard Blackburne's version of the life of Hobbes: 'Now I say the Offices of a Panegyrist, & Historian, are much different. ... I never yet knew a Witt (unles he were a piece of an Antiquary) write a proper Epitaph, but leave the reader ignorant, what countryman &c: only tickles his eares with Elogies.'[12] Such panegyrics and comparisons with biblical types, characteristic of the exemplary tradition, have no place in Aubrey's own work.

The originality of Aubrey appears strikingly not only when his work is compared with typical exemplary biographies but even when it is compared with the best and most innovative of earlier and contemporary lives, such highly competent biographies written from close personal knowledge as Rawley's life of Bacon and Hill's life of Barrow. These lives have a merit that Aubrey's lack: they are fully organized and coherent, finished according to their author's intentions, in contrast to Aubrey's incomplete drafts. But if one reads Aubrey's lives after Rawley's and Hill's one is immediately impressed by how much Aubrey includes that they leave out, particularly in the way of personal detail.

While Rawley provides no physical description of Bacon, Aubrey gives such detail as the report (from Harvey) that Bacon had an eye like a viper. In a brief space Aubrey gives much information about Bacon's habits, interests, and way of life that has no counterpart in Rawley. He includes a lengthy account of the houses and gardens at Gorhambury designed or remodelled by Bacon that, as Wood observed in a note to Aubrey, is entirely lacking in Rawley.[13] Rawley gives a general account of Bacon's conversation but only Aubrey gives specific examples. Rawley gives no more than a hint of Bacon's carelessness with money and the way his servants took advantage of this but Aubrey provides such details as the fact that one of Bacon's servants kept three coaches. While Rawley chooses to leave the impression that Bacon's marriage was a happy one, Aubrey comments candidly on its unhappiness and records the suggestion that Bacon was homosexual. Although Aubrey does not provide so full an account of various aspects of Bacon's intellect and writings as Rawley, he gives in spite of his greater distance from his subject a vivid and rounded picture of Bacon as an individual that makes Rawley's more finished portrait appear flat and abstract in comparison.

Hill's life of Barrow may actually owe some of its excellence to Aubrey, for Hill sufficiently appreciated Aubrey's merits to request a copy of the latter's manuscript life of Barrow as part of his preparations for his biography,[14] but Aubrey's short sketch remains superior to Hill's work in its vividness and fine personal detail. Hill gives a good systematic account of Barrow's career and achievements, but his picture of Barrow's character is colourless in comparison with Aubrey's, and Aubrey manages to give more specific information at a number of points despite the relative brevity of his account, for example the names of Barrow's early schoolmasters and even the sums of money paid to them. While Hill writes of Barrow's youthful fondness for fighting in general terms, Aubrey states that as a schoolboy he fought the butchers' boys of St Nicholas Shambles. Hill mentions Barrow's carelessness in dress, but Aubrey gives an anecdote that reveals it concretely and vividly: 'As he was walking one day in St. James's parke, looking ... his hatt up, his cloake halfe on and halfe off, a gent. came behind him and clapt him on the shoulder and sayd "Well, goe thy wayes for the veriest scholar that ever I^d mett with."'[15]

Hill is among the limited number of seventeenth-century biographers who provides information about his subject's bodily appearance, but it is Aubrey who leaves us with the most memorable image: 'He was a strong man but pale as the candle he studyed by.' While Hill gives no detail about Barrow's death, except to say that the sickness was a fever, Aubrey gives a more candid account, stating that he died of an overdose of an opiate pill, which he had acquired the habit of taking when he was in Turkey. It is Aubrey alone who gives the superbly Shakespearian detail (learned from Mr Wilson, at whose house Barrow died): 'As he lay expiring in the agonie of death, the standers-by could hear him say softly, "I have seen the glories of the world."'[16]

The result is similar if one compares Aubrey's biography of Milton with the other early lives of the poet. The anonymous life and the life by Milton's nephew Edward Phillips are highly competent biographies, superior to the average in precision and concreteness, but Aubrey, without the advantage of special closeness to the subject, provides the most vivid personal detail. So it is in case after case. Some earlier and contemporary biographies provide partial anticipations and parallels for Aubrey's special qualities, but only as tendencies that are so much more fully developed in Aubrey as to become a difference in kind, and one finds nowhere else in the biographies of the century the full range of Aubrey's interests and talents. To find close parallels for Aubrey's vivid and candid recording of personal detail, one has to go outside the field of biography, to Erasmus and Montaigne among earlier writers, and to Pepys among English contemporaries. Like Montaigne and Pepys, Aubrey represents the coincidence of new sensibilities with unique talents.

III

In his extensive surviving correspondence with Wood and elsewhere, Aubrey provides many statements of his purposes and principles which show his consciousness of the originality and special merits as well as limitations of his lives. The best starting point for an examination of the lives is a letter to Wood, 15 June 1680. Aubrey begins: 'I have, according to your desire, putt in writing these minutes of lives tumultuarily, as they occur'd to my thoughts or as occasionally I had information of them.' He emphasizes his great candour, and observes that Wood will need to exercise censorship because his unexpurgated lives are not fit to be published for about thirty years. He laments the loss of much of interest from the past because it remained unrecorded, and continues: 'I doe not here repeat any thing already published (to the best of my remembrance) and I fancy my selfe all along discourseing with you, alledgeing those of my relations and acquaintance ... so that you make me to renew my acquaintance with my old and deceased friends.'[17]

In this letter Aubrey is over-optimistic in telling Wood that his manuscript lives 'may easily be reduced into order,' but he reveals the advantages he gains from the fact that his lives originated as notes for Wood. There is great gain in liveliness, informality, and candour, a freedom from the crippling traditions of biographical dignity and discretion, possible only in writing addressed to a friend in whom Aubrey could have confidence. The fact that he did not need to include all that was already in print was liberating too. To have done so would have been superfluous because Wood already had unrivalled mastery of the printed sources. This circumstance freed Aubrey to concentrate on the more personal and informal aspects in which he excels. It is here that he takes biography into new areas – sometimes too far indeed for Wood's liking. While his biographies are inevitably incomplete, he has the special merit of focusing on the private aspects most neglected by previous biographers, and upon matters that would quickly have been lost and forgotten if he had not recorded them.

In the letter of 15 June 1680, Aubrey recalls Wood's special reason for enlisting his assistance:

> 'Tis a taske that I never thought to have undertaken till you imposed it upon me, sayeing that I was fitt for it by reason of my generall acquaintance, haveing now not only lived above halfe a centurie of yeares in the world, but have also been much tumbled up and downe in it which hath made me much knowne, besides the moderne advantage of coffee-howses in this great citie before which men knew not how to be acquainted, but with their owne relations or societies. I might add that I come of a longaevous race, by which meanes I have imped some feathers of the wings of time, for severall generations; which does reach high. When I first began I did not thinke I could have drawne it out to so long a thread.[18]

Presumably Wood initially asked Aubrey's assistance as one who shared his own antiquarian interests, and, having leisure and London residence, could search London records not accessible to Wood in Oxford. But as this letter shows, Wood soon recognized Aubrey's special value to be his informal access to personal information because of his gregarious habits and wide acquaintance, as compensation for Wood's own limitations as an antisocial character, one who preferred conversing with the dead to conversing with the living.

Aubrey's correspondence with Wood shows that he undertook at his friend's request many conventional antiquarian researches in London, such as examination of funeral monuments and church registers. He displays much concern, for example, with establishing precise dates for births and deaths of his subjects, intensified by the astrological interests he shared with many of his contemporaries.[19] But despite his fascination with antiquities he complains that he found such research tedious, and he undertook it reluctantly.[20] His correspondence and the biographies themselves confirm his statement in his letter of 15 June 1680 that his purpose was not on the other hand to repeat what was already in print. For example, in his life of Cowley he refers the reader to Sprat's biography without duplicating it but supplements it where it is incomplete, listing the poet's charitable bequests in his will, which Sprat omitted, and most significantly adding information and precision where Sprat had been silent or vague for reasons of dignity and decorum: while Sprat stated that Cowley's father was a virtuous citizen, Aubrey states he was a grocer, and he mentions such faults or limitations as the fact that Cowley 'discoursed very ill and with hesitation,' which Sprat evaded or passed over.[21]

Studies of Aubrey's achievements as an antiquary have shown that his real distinction lies in his movement beyond conventional textual sources to engage in fieldwork. Similarly as a biographer it is not so much in his use of the written records of the dead as in his observation and gathering of information from the living that Aubrey showed his special skill and originality. As a researcher among written records he did only what many antiquaries of the period could do equally well, but as an observer and collector from informal sources he went far beyond his contemporaries. He took full advantage of the fact that he belonged to a great complex of interrelated families, so that many of his biographical subjects were actually relatives, and he made extensive use of the large circle of acquaintances he had developed after his youth in Wiltshire during his residence in Oxford and London. He became so zealous and persistent in his inquiries for biographical information that he became something of a joke and sometimes made himself a nuisance. Even Wood made fun of this zeal, remarking on one occasion that Aubrey would break his neck running down stairs rather than miss a person 'who can tell such and such stories.'[22]

Aubrey was extraordinarily energetic in his search for information from his subjects themselves when they were still alive and from all who knew or had known them, from their relatives, friends, and associates, their servants, and even the tradesmen who served them. He sought information about Shakespeare from his Stratford neighbours, about John Ogilby from the player John Lacy, who had been his apprentice, about Katherine Philips from her cousin, and about Milton not only from the poet's widow, brother, and nephew but even from his apothecary, as well as from Andrew Marvell, who promised but failed to provide minutes of Milton's life. Samuel Johnson, writing at a time Aubrey's lives were still unpublished and unknown, complained that English biographers often told one less about their subjects than one might have learned from their servants,[23] but Aubrey nowhere showed his zeal and lack of conventional decorum more than in the persistent inquiries he made of his subjects' servants and tradesmen. He gained information about Archbishop Abbot from the prelate's old servant Nightingale, who wept when he spoke of him, information about John Fletcher from Fletcher's tailor, and about John Selden from Selden's saddler, and he even made a note to himself to ask Hobbes's apothecary, Mr Shelbrooke at the Black Spread-eagle in the Strand, about the 'physique' Hobbes took on the rare occasions he took any.[24]

Aubrey's use of informal and oral sources was so unorthodox and carried so far as to prompt warnings in his own lifetime of the dangers of unreliability. He records that the great antiquary Sir William Dugdale told him he must not put in writing '*Hear-sayes*,' and in a letter the naturalist John Ray warned him against undue credulity.[25] The criticism that he was credulous developed especially in the eighteenth century because of the superstitious beliefs he recorded (without endorsing) in his entertaining compilation of marvels, *Miscellanies*, but similar criticism of the lives was occasionally made in his own time by Wood. While Wood was glad to make much use of Aubrey's material, when his own indiscretions got him into trouble he attempted to shift the blame, and characteristically he sometimes grumbled about Aubrey's unreliable and erratic nature and complained that he stuffed his letters with fooleries and misinformations.[26]

The charge that Aubrey displays undue credulity in his biographies arises precisely from the fact that he did include in the lives many of the '*Hear-sayes*' of the kind that were regarded suspiciously by more conventional seventeenth-century antiquaries like Dugdale and Wood but would be viewed by many modern historians as representing valuable and often essential resources of oral history. He adopted the principle of recording much of dubious accuracy but giving the sources so that others might evaluate it accordingly. Naturally these sources varied widely in reliability, and sometimes ones that should have been trustworthy provided highly dubious information. For example, the story that Arthur, son of John Dee, as a boy played with plates of alchemical gold is given as told by Arthur himself to Ralph Bathurst. The story that Sir Thomas More displayed his daughter naked to his prospective son-in-law William Roper is presumably a fabrication based on More's description of a custom in his *Utopia*, but it is told as coming from one who had known the Roper family.[27]

When Aubrey tells an anecdote he frequently cites the name of a witness. He gives the story of Sir John Denham's mischievously painting out London shop signs with a brush and a pot of ink as told him by 'R. Estcott, Esq., that carried the inke-pott,' a witness who could hardly be improved upon. He allowed himself some freedom in speculation but he usually labelled his speculations as such. His comment that, since Ben Jonson had one eye larger and lower than the other like the actor Clun, 'perhaps he begott Clun' has often been cited as an example of Aubrey's penchant for scandalous invention but it is significant that he places 'perhaps' even in his manuscript notes.[28]

Aubrey made high claims for his accuracy in the lives, writing of them in a letter to Wood: 'I beleeve never any in England were delivered so faithfully and with such good authority.'[29] He was in reality of course far from infallible. He desired to achieve a scientific level of accuracy but he lacked the rigour necessary always to attain it even to the degree his material might have admitted. Yet his scrupulousness is shown by his leaving many blanks where he lacked exact information, and he often displays an extraordinary concern for precision: he writes of Sir William Petty's poverty in his youth that he has heard Petty say 'that he lived a weeke on two peniworth (or 3, I have forgott which, but I thinke the former) of walnutts.'[30] While he received some contemporary criticism he also earned early praise for his accuracy. John Toland, the deist, considered him superstitious but praised him as honest and 'most accurate in his accounts of matters of fact.'[31] When the fullest and most finished of his lives, such as those of Hobbes, Harvey, and Milton, have been subjected to close examination in modern times, this verdict has been confirmed.

Even more fundamentally than in his use of informal sources, Aubrey's break with the prevailing biographical practice of his time appears in his concern for the preservation of minute, apparently trivial, personal detail. He was well aware that he was an innovator in this matter. Like Montaigne in sixteenth-century France, who wrote about himself in unprecedented detail and suffered attack on that account, Aubrey violated traditional decorum in the minuteness of the information he provided about his biographical subjects, as he indicates in his complaint about the elevated vagueness customary in epitaphs. In a letter to Wood in May 1680, referring to Richard Blackburne's criticism of his work on his life of Hobbes, he writes: 'Pox take your Orators & piets, they spoile lives & histories. The D^r says that I am too minute; but a hundred yeare hence that minutenesse will be gratefull.' He adds: 'Sir Wm Petty ordered me to be so.'[32] This statement suggests Aubrey's affinity with the empirical methods of the new science and mathematics: Petty was 'the father of statistics.' It suggests his affinity too with the movement toward realism in literature based on the accumulation of precise, minute detail that was shortly to emerge in other genres such as the novels of Defoe.

Aubrey's concern with minute personal detail is linked with a special and novel quality of historical imagination. The fact that his activities in collecting information invited ridicule by others points to the radical nature of this vision. He goes beyond his contemporaries in recognizing the claims of posterity. He is the first English biographer to recognize so fully that future generations may be interested in minute and even apparently trivial information about remarkable persons of his own time. This type of historical imagination is often thought of as not developing until the eighteenth century in such figures as Boswell and Horace Walpole. Cyril Connolly has commented on the double vision of Walpole, his concern with posterity as well as the present, his desire to communicate with the unborn.[33] Such a double vision is already remarkably developed in Aubrey, well in advance of his contemporaries.

This novel kind of historical imagination arises from Aubrey's combination of strong interest in the past with fascinated examination of contemporary life. His historical interests developed in early childhood. He states: 'I was inclined by my Genius from my childhood to the love of antiquities,' and tells us that as a boy he 'did ever love to commune with old men as living histories' and that he was always inquiring of his grandfather about the old times, about the rood loft and the ceremonies of the priory.[34] These interests issued in a variety of antiquarian studies: as a student at Oxford he sketched the ruins of Osney Abbey, he later worked on county histories of Wiltshire and Surrey, as well as recording rural customs and superstitions in other writings, and he discovered and did enduringly important work on the prehistoric monument of Avebury. He has indeed sometimes been termed the father of English archaeology.

In his historical studies Aubrey was inspired by the motive of preserving records and memories of the past from oblivion. In a favourite image he compares remains of the past to fragments of shipwrecks escaped the storms of time, and he declares that retrieving knowledge of earlier times resembles the art of the conjurer, making those in their graves walk again.[35] His sense of the importance of rescuing remains of the past from oblivion was first stimulated by the fact that his native area of Wiltshire was rich in monastic ruins, and it was later intensified by the Civil War, which swept away the world of his youth. It has often been noted how frequently the phrase 'when I was a little Boy (before the Civill Warres)' occurs in his writings. His symbol for the fragility and vulnerability of the relics of the past is the stained glass of the church windows destroyed by the Puritans.[36]

Aubrey's awareness of how much that we might like to possess from the past has vanished without trace leads him to perceive the importance of preserving a wide range of information from the present for the future. This historical vision is shown in a remark in his draft of a preface to his life of Hobbes: 'Men thinke, because every body remembers a memorable accident shortly after 'tis donne, 'twill never be forgotten, which for want of registring, at last is drowned in oblivion.' He comments on his lives in his letter to Wood of 15 June 1680: "'Tis pitty that such minutes had not been taken 100 yeares since or more: for want wherof many worthy men's names and notions are swallowd-up in oblivion; as much of these also would [have been]....'[37]

Many of the leading antiquaries of the period were Aubrey's friends, including Dugdale and Ralph Sheldon as well as Wood, but he went beyond them in applying an antiquarian perspective to the more private and intimate, most highly individual, aspects of the lives of his contemporaries and those of the recent past. While others either confined themselves to the more distant past or recorded the more public activities and events of the present, Aubrey was almost alone in perceiving that personal information of many kinds about notable contemporaries would soon be forgotten if not written down, and that it might be as worth recording as the appearance of the ruins of Osney Abbey. In much of Aubrey's antiquarian work his historical imagination looks backward. In his 'Description of the North Division of Wiltshire' he begins, 'Let us imagine then what kind of a countrie this was in the time of the ancient Britons,' and he develops a remarkable picture.[38] But even more remarkable for the period is the forward-looking nature of his vision, the way in which with his eye on the future he examines his contemporaries as closely as he and other antiquaries examined church monuments and prehistoric or medieval remains.

IV

Aubrey's distinction lies not only in his diligence as a collector and his special kind of historical imagination but also in his acuteness of observation, his eye for the individual in all areas of life, and his literary ability. Those who have seen him merely as a collector have underestimated not only the originality of what he collected but also his artistic powers, and his ability to give life to his subjects, which is suggested by his image of the magic arts of the conjurer. Together with the scientist's concern for minuteness and precision, he possesses the visual sense of the painter, and he is as much an artist as an antiquary.

None of Aubrey's talents as a biographer is more remarkable than his visual powers. When he reviewed his life in later years he declared: 'If ever I had been good for anything, 'twould have been a painter, I could fancy a thing so strongly and had so cleare an idaea of it.' As a child he practised painting by copying pictures, and in mature years he took lessons from a professional painter, Jacob de Valke. He was a friend and admirer of a number of artists, including the miniaturist he termed 'the prince of limners of this age,' Samuel Cooper, whose highly realistic and individual portraits have often been recognized to provide a visual counterpart to his own verbal portraits. A number of Aubrey's sketches and paintings survive. They are attractive and accomplished enough, but his visual skill finds its most effective expression in his representation of his subjects in his biographical writings.[39]

Aubrey recognized that bodily appearance and attributes are important aspects of individuality. His visual sense made him highly aware of the almost infinite variety of looks and countenances among humans on which John Evelyn commented in his *Numismata*.[40] In the vivid realism of his bodily portraiture he far excels most of the biographers not only of his own period but of the next century, including Samuel Johnson. He remains virtually unmatched in this aspect of biography in England prior to Boswell's fine representation of Johnson's appearance, dress, and manner, and for portraits in miniature, like his friend Samuel Cooper, he has never been excelled.

Aubrey sets out the types of information he seeks to provide about his subjects' physical appearance in a note of instructions to himself about his life of Hobbes: 'Describe face, eyes, forehead, nose, mouth, eyebrows, figure of the face, complexion; stature of body; shape (slender, large, neat, or otherwise); figure of head and magnitude of head; shoulders (large, round, etc.); arms, legs, how? –'[41] His descriptions are based on direct observation of a high proportion of his living subjects. When the subjects were unknown to him or already dead he sought descriptions from those who had known them, and examined portraits and monumental effigies.

Aubrey often begins his descriptions by recording the first impression the eye would naturally register about the size, shape, and general aspect of the subject. Thus he tells us that Robert Boyle and Sir William Petty were both very tall, six feet high, while Lord Falkland at the opposite extreme was unusually short. He informs us that Edmund Waller had a thin, weak body, that Robert Hooke was fairly short and somewhat crooked, and that Sir John Popham, to judge by his portrait, was a 'huge, heavie, ugly man.'[42] Then Aubrey gives special attention, as any portrait painter would, to the face, especially the eyes.

Aubrey attaches the same importance to the eyes as the Elizabethan miniaturist Nicholas Hilliard, who wrote: 'chiefly the drawer should observe the eys in his pictures, making them so like one to another as nature doeth, giving life to his worke, for the eye is the life of the picture.'[43] Aubrey again and again provides vivid and distinctive descriptions of the eyes of his subjects, something scarcely found at all in earlier English biography. He tells us that James Bovey had 'a dark hazell eie, of a midling size, but the most sprightly that I have beheld,' James Harrington had 'quick-hott-fiery hazell eie,' William Harvey had 'little eie, round, very black, full of spirit,' Robert Hooke had 'eie full and popping, and not quick; a grey eie,' and Ben Jonson had 'one eie lower than t'other, and bigger.' He informs us that John Tombes had 'a little quick searching eie, sad, gray,' Edmund Waller a 'full eye, popping out and working,' and that Sir Walter Ralegh, to judge by his portrait, was 'sour eie-lidded' with 'a kind of pigge-eie.' He records that Thomas Hobbes had 'a hazel, quick eie,' 'full of life and spirit, even to the last,' in which 'there shone (as it were) a bright live-coale' when he was earnest in discourse.[44]

Aubrey observes the ways in which the eyes sometimes appear to the advantage and sometimes to the disadvantage of the subjects, and the ways in which they may suggest the personality. He comments that Sir John Birkenhead had 'great goggli eies, not of a sweet aspect,' and that Richard Head, even worse, 'looked like a knave with his gogling eies.' In contrast, he notes, Lady Petty had 'glorious eies,' and those of her husband Sir William were also attractive: 'His eies are a kind of goose-grey, but very short sighted, and, as to aspect, beautifull, and promise sweetnes of nature, and they doe not decieve, for he is a marveillous good-natured person.' Like many of his contemporaries, Aubrey was interested in theories of physiognomy, and he often sees the eyes as a clue to character, but he does not falsify or oversimplify. Thus while he records Harvey's report that Bacon's eyes were like those of a viper he does not conclude from this that Bacon's character was viper-like, as Lytton Strachey was later to do.[45]

Aubrey displays an interest too in the hair of his subjects characteristic of portrait painters such as Durer, who had been particularly famous for his skill in painting hair. Showing his painterly eye for precision in colour, he tells us that Mary Herbert, Countess of Pembroke, had 'reddish yellowe' hair, while her brother Sir Philip Sidney had hair 'not red, but a little inclining, viz. a darke amber colour.' He records that Suckling's hair was sandy coloured, that Harrington had 'thick moyst curled haire,' Thomas Willis 'darke red haire (like a red pig),' and Lord Falkland 'blackish haire, something flaggy.' He informs us that

Hobbes had when young hair black as a crow and that his whiskers naturally turned up, which Aubrey notes, showing his interest in physiognomy, is the mark of a brisk wit. He was fortunately able to see many of his subjects before the male fashion for wearing wigs became widespread. In his *Numismata* in 1697 John Evelyn noted regretfully that the physiognomist could no longer inspect men's hair: 'those manly Distinctions being now no more the *Mode*, chang'd universally into the *Peruke*.'[46]

Aubrey shows the painter's eye also in his descriptions of the colour and texture of the skin and facial complexion of his subjects. As he works by an implicit comparative method, these descriptions do much to differentiate his subjects one from another and to establish their individuality. He tells us that William Prynne, the Puritan controversialist, had a strange saturnine complexion, while among the poets Katherine Philips had a red, pimpled face (but a good disposition) and Thomas Randolph was pale, ill complexioned, pock marked. In contrast, Venetia Digby's cheeks were just the colour of the damask rose, and Sir John Danvers's complexion was so fine that during his youthful travels people would cross the street just to admire him. He makes us aware of the importance these sensual aspects had in the lives of his subjects as he recounts the amatory career of Venetia Digby and writes of the surprising marriage of the middle-aged widow Magdalen Herbert to Danvers, even though she was 'old enough to have been his mother' and the union was opposed by his family.[47]

While the various features of Aubrey's physical descriptions can be separated for such listing and analysis, they really of course make their impact cumulatively. After an earlier note that Sir John Denham was 'unpolished with the small-pox: otherwise a fine complexion,' his main portrait of this poet begins: 'He was of the tallest, but a little incurvetting at his shoulders, not very robust,' and passes to the description of his hair: 'thin and flaxen, with a moist curle,' his gait: 'slow,' 'rather a stocking (he had long legges),' and his eyes: 'a kind of light goose-gray, not big' but with 'a strange piercingness' so that 'when he conversed with you he look't into your very thoughts.' Often his details reinforce each other so that he achieves a fine unity of impression, for example in his description of Francis Potter as looking like a monk, long visaged with pale grey eyes, and his account of Ralph Kettell as providing a spectacle comic but terrifying to the students of his college: a menacing figure of 'terrible gigantique aspect,' with sharp grey eyes, who dragged his right foot, giving warning like a rattlesnake.[48]

Aubrey's descriptions of the appearance of his subjects often include information about their clothing. This is another area in which he moves well beyond his predecessors. Castiglione in his *Courtier* had stated that clothing is a good index to a person's character, and it has already been noted that some English biographers had provided conventional symbolic or iconic descriptions of clothing as exemplifying high rank, magnificence, or pride, as in Cavendish's life of Wolsey and the anonymous life of Perrot, or conversely as demonstrating humility, as in hagiographical works like the lives of Bedell, the bishop in brogues. But apart from such occasional symbolic developments, of which Walton's life of Herbert provides a particularly fine example, the biographers rarely described or attached significance to their subjects' clothing.[49]

Aubrey, in contrast, no more ignores clothing than would a portrait painter. He mentions that Ben Jonson wore a coachman's cloak, and that Sir Henry Spelman, the country gentleman turned antiquary, wore a sword until he was seventy or older. He gives such precise details as the information that John Hales wore 'a kind of violet-colourd cloath gowne, with buttons and loopes,' and that Hobbes in cold weather wore a black velvet coat lined with fur, and all year round boots of Spanish leather. He tells us that Dr John Dee, who was reputed to be a conjurer and believed to have inspired Jonson's *The Alchemist*, 'wore a gowne like an artist's gowne, with hanging sleeves, and a slitt.'[50]

Aubrey often uses such information about clothing to convey aspects of his subjects' characters, for example Sir Kenelm Digby's wearing a mourning cloak as part of his elaborately theatrical manner of displaying his grief for the death of his wife, the beautiful Venetia, or Isaac Barrow's negligence of dress marking his absorption in scholarship. He informs us that another scholar, William Oughtred, after studying late lay abed with his doublet on until eleven or twelve, and then to receive visitors dressed himself in an old russet cassock that had once been black. In contrast to such scholars, Aubrey notes, the courtier Sir Walter Ralegh even as a prisoner in the Tower wore a fine gown and appears in a portrait in a white satin doublet embroidered with rich pearls. Another courtier, Sir John Suckling, 'the greatest gallant of his time, and the greatest gamester,' after his heaviest losses in gambling 'then would make himselfe most glorious in apparell, and sayd that it exalted his spirits, and that he had then best luck,' and when he raised a troop for one of Charles I's expeditions against the Scots he clad his men in 'white doubletts and scarlett breeches, and scarlet coates,' so that they were said to be 'one of the finest sights in those days' but attracted some satire.[51]

While Aubrey's remarkable visual sense caused him to wish he had been a painter, his portraits benefit in many ways from the fact that he is not confined to a visual medium. He exploits his literary resources to reveal aspects of his subjects that would be impossible for a painter. Rather than representing his subjects in a fixed pose, he is able to describe them in motion, as is illustrated by his account of Denham's gait and Kettell's manner of dragging his foot. And rather than being limited to silent images of his subjects, he describes their manner of speech and gives us their words.

Aubrey has a good ear as well as a fine eye, and he tells us how his subjects' voices sounded. Here again he is an innovator, for few earlier biographers had provided information on this subject, except in the special case of the clergyman whose voice was a particular asset or liability. Aubrey mentions Ralegh's small voice and tells us that he spoke with a Devonshire accent to the end of his days and that Hobbes retained a little of his Wiltshire accent. He tells us of Thomas Willis's stammering and of the 'squeaking' voice in which Kettell preached an absurd funeral sermon. He describes the singing voices of Kettell, Richard Corbet, and Milton: Kettell sang in a high shrill treble; Corbet had a rare good voice, which he once put to use by becoming a seller of ballads. It is to Aubrey, rather than Milton's other early biographers, that we owe the description of the poet's 'delicate tuneable voice' and the information, which he obtained from Dryden, about Milton's hard pronunciation of the letter R.[52]

Aubrey's recording of speech is inevitably on a small scale, at the opposite extreme from Boswell's reporting of Johnson's speech, but considering the brevity of his lives he is remarkably successful in conveying the characteristic quality of the conversation of his subjects. He moves beyond the conventional listings of wise or favourite sayings that some earlier biographers had provided. He has the ability to select what is distinctive and display it concisely and dramatically. Establishing the appropriate contexts and settings, he communicates splendidly through his examples the absurd speech and '*hasty-pudding*' mind of Kettell, and by way of contrast conveys equally well the wit of Corbet and Henry Marten. For example, he cites the occasion when Marten, a libertine among the Puritans of the Long Parliament, countered a proposal that all unsanctified members should be expelled from the House of Commons by moving that all fools should be expelled too. This reproduction of verbal wit appears deceptively easy but it requires dramatic skill, for wit is fragile and many biographers have failed lamely in their attempts to communicate it, while Aubrey's renditions remain fresh and pointed. It is significant that he was the author of an uncompleted play and an admirer of the dramatic characterization of Shakespeare and Jonson.[53]

Aubrey's ability in recording conversation is closely linked to his special skill in the handling of anecdotes: the two things are virtually inseparable, since his anecdotes usually include speech. His skill in gathering and telling anecdotes scarcely needs to be emphasized, since this is an element in the *Brief Lives* that has always been appreciated. The lives indeed have often been read as an anthology of entertaining anecdotes. Aubrey has sometimes been considered frivolous or unduly digressive because of his love of a good story, but the anecdote is integral to the lives. As John Collier points out, Aubrey has the special ability to give just two or three episodes that reveal the man or woman. They represent what Boswell termed 'characteristical circumstances': they show the character in action and in relation to other people, concretely and vividly.[54]

V

A high proportion of Aubrey's anecdotes relate to his subjects' private lives, including intimate aspects. Nowhere do his *Brief Lives* mark a more striking and important advance over most earlier English biographies than in this area, since few previous biographers had given much prominence to private life, apart from exemplary details designed to demonstrate the saintliness of the subjects in religious biographies. It has been noted in earlier discussion that the practice of virtually excluding most of private life was so strongly established in seventeenth-century biography that we sometimes learned whether the subject was married and had children only when the deathbed scene was described at the end. Aubrey, in contrast, specially excels in providing the kind of detail neglected by most earlier English biographers, regarding the habits and tastes of his subjects, their personal relations, their domestic lives, their sexual lives, and their recreations. It is characteristic of him that in his life of Milton, as has been seen, he provides more intimate detail, including accounts of the habitual pattern of the poet's day and of his friendships, than any of Milton's other early biographers including even his nephew.[55]

The personal details recorded by Aubrey that have become best known are those relating to the sexual lives, loves, and marriages of his subjects. His unprecedented candour in this area has given special fame or notoriety to the *Brief Lives*. It is certainly very striking in contrast to the reticence displayed even by the best other biographers, for example by Rawley on Bacon's marriage or by Burnet on Hale's two marriages. Aubrey provides a rich store of scandal in his accounts of the sexual licence of such figures as Venetia Digby, Mary, Countess of Pembroke, and Dean Overall's beautiful wanton wife. He tells us of Selden's amours, quoting the great lawyer's saddler: he 'got more by his Prick then he had done by his practise,' and adding after reference to his aristocratic wife: 'they did talk also of my Lady's Shee Blackamore.' He records that William Harvey 'kept a pretty young wench to wayte on him, which I guesse he made use of for warmeth-sake,' and that Sir Henry Lee never married but kept women to read to him when he was in bed, and evidently to do more than read.[56]

Aubrey took pride in this candour as one of the special merits of his lives, while recognizing that he had included much that could not be immediately published. In a letter to Wood on 22 May 1680, he declared, making an allusion to Dryden's *The Conquest of Granada*: 'I am like Almansar in the Play, that spare neither friend nor Foe.' In his letter three weeks later on 15 June he stated that he had set down 'the naked and plaine trueth, which is here exposed so bare that the very *pudenda* are not covered, and affords many passages that would raise a blush in a young virgin's cheeke,' and he cautioned Wood that he would need to 'castrate' his work before publishing from it.[57] Even in the case of Hobbes, where his information about personal habits and tastes is relatively innocuous, he makes a proviso of confidentiality about his remark that the philosopher had no abhorrence to women and wine: ' – this only *inter nos*.' But his portraits are not slanted unduly toward the scandalous; rather, he provides a full picture of human variety and individuality in sexual relations and marriage as in other things. The unhappy marriage of Thomas Goffe to a shrewish wife and the licentiousness of Mrs Overall are balanced by the ideally happy marriages of William Holder and William Penn.[58]

In later times the scandalous passages in the *Brief Lives* have often been extracted and given a prominence they do not possess in their context. Aubrey simply represents the sexual behaviour of his subjects as one among the various aspects of life to be recorded. This element occupies only a small proportion of the lives and it is introduced unsensationally in a matter-of-fact way. Aubrey is in reality strikingly free from any tendency to make sex the whole key to character. He mentions Bacon's reputed homosexuality just as one of many matters of interest concerning him. An account of the rumour of incest between the Countess of Pembroke and her brother Sir Philip Sidney prompts a remark on heredity. Aubrey's viewpoint is eminently balanced and tolerant. Far from giving an undue prominence to sex, he might be criticized from a Freudian or post-Freudian viewpoint as not regarding it as sufficiently critical to character. In this matter as in others Aubrey refuses to simplify human complexity.

Aubrey frequently gives as much attention to his subjects' friendships as to their sexual and domestic lives. As well as listing their friends he even records negatives, telling us that Marvell had no general acquaintance and that Milton and Hobbes were not friends. He describes their tastes and preferences, both likes and dislikes, in many areas beyond the sexual, ranging from Laud's love of cats to Bushell's fondness for caves and walking at night, even to Bacon's aversion to the smell of neat's leather and Kettell's hatred of long hair, so great that he carried scissors to shear long-haired scholars in his college.[59] He gives attention to his subjects' habits of eating and drinking, aspects of life ignored by most previous biographers unless as evidence of saintly austerity. He shows that they may be significant in relation to character: he tells us much about Hobbes's character in his discussion of the philosopher's manner of drinking, and suggests Marvell's secretive and unsociable nature by reference to his solitary drinking.

The extent to which Aubrey takes biography into private and intimate areas is suggested by the amount of information he gives us about his subjects in bed, which is by no means confined to their sexual lives. He does not merely distinguish between those who arise at unusually early hours, like John Hoskyns at four a.m., and those who arise late, like Oughtred in bed until noon, but he shows that his subjects carry on a surprising variety of activities in bed: Hobbes sings in bed, Sir Henry Lee is entertained by his reading women, and Suckling, the great gambler, practises cards in bed by himself. He records that Harvey's working mind often kept him from sleeping: 'he told me that then his way was to rise out of his bed and walke about his chamber in his shirt till he was pretty coole.'[60]

Aubrey does not undertake extensive or systematic analysis of the writings and scholarly or scientific achievements of his subjects: this could scarcely be expected in view of the brevity of his lives and their origin as supplementing information Wood could obtain from written sources.

But he seeks to indicate in general terms the nature of their achievements, and he displays a great interest in their habits of work. This interest was no doubt intensified by his consciousness of his own great difficulty in bringing his diverse works to completion. He records that Isaac Barrow, viewed by a contemporary as 'the veriest scholar' he had ever encountered, was so intent upon study that he would not notice his bed being made and would go out sometimes without a hat, and that he was matched by Thomas Fuller, who had 'a very working head' and would eat a penny loaf without knowing it. He tells us that James Bovey kept a candle burning all night by his bed so as never to lose a thought, that Hobbes carried a tablet and made notes while he walked, and that Harvey preferred the dark to daylight because he could then best contemplate. We learn from him that William Prynne, 'a learned man, of immense reading' but 'much blamed for his unfaithfull quotations,' had a highly individual manner of study: he wore a cap over his eyes as an umbrella against light, and he had a roll and a pot of ale brought to him every three hours to avoid interruption for meals, a fact that no doubt helps explain the enormous output of this prolific Puritan controversialist and pamphleteer.[61]

Aubrey values most highly innate originality and practical achievements, and takes more interest in the new science and mathematics, invention and technology than in older, more traditional kinds of learning. The favourite word in his vocabulary is 'ingeniose': it is as central to his writing as 'felicity' is to Traherne's. For him it represents a value as dominant as holiness in religious biographies, and it tends to replace such secular values as courage and loyalty, prominent in aristocratic biographies, and even the regard for learning for its own sake common in the biographies of scholars. He notes that such original thinkers as Hobbes and Petty read little and considered that an advantage. Again and again his highest praise for a person is that he is 'ingeniose,' and this word occurs with special frequency in his accounts of such radically original figures as Harrington. He praises Hobbes as one who even when he errs 'erres so ingeniosely.' He notes in his life of Seth Ward that King Charles II loved ingenuity and ingeniose men, and his own fondness for this word marks him unmistakably as belonging to the Restoration world of the Royal Society.[62]

Aubrey's interest in the achievements and skills of the ingeniose is not confined to important contributions in philosophy, science, and literature, but includes a wide range of lesser accomplishments. He comments on Kenelm Digby's ingeniose conversation, and notes that Henry

Birkhead was ingeniose in diatribe, like Kettell, who had special skill in Latin imprecation, and he even credits Harry Marten with being 'an honest ingeniose Fornicator.'[63] He admires Bishop Richard Corbet for the skill he once showed in selling ballads at Abingdon Cross, and Sir Robert Moray, the Scottish courtier and statesman, for knowing as a Highlander how to make his own clothes. Among the noteworthy achievements he lists is that of Elizabeth Danvers, who had the works of Chaucer at her fingertips. He specially admires versatility, and praises Bacon on the basis of his estate at Gorhambury as being ingeniose in gardening as well as in greater things. On the other hand, he is scornful of those of high rank lacking worthy accomplishments, like the current Earl of Pembroke in 1680, who (in contrast to the earlier members of his family famous as patrons of artists and writers) 'has at Wilton 52 mastives and 30 grey-hounds, some beares, and a lyon, and a matter of 60 fellowes more bestiall than they.'[64]

Aubrey should certainly not be regarded as a mere chronicler of human eccentricity, since he cultivated the acquaintance of Hobbes, Harvey, and many of the other great intellectual figures of his day, and gave them prominence in his biographies, but he was as much interested in originality of character as in other achievements. Hence he gave more attention to figures like Kettell because of the individuality and idiosyncrasies of their character and ways of life than their scholarly or other accomplishments would warrant. He was fascinated by the variety of Renaissance self-fashioning, and valued the range of human individuality for its own sake.

Aubrey's fascination with the variety of individuality has as its natural corollary a remarkable toleration and freedom from prejudice. In striking contrast with the fierce religious and political prejudices of his friend Anthony Wood, who continued to fight the Civil War, Aubrey's toleration developed partly as a reaction against the bitter conflicts of that period. He writes in letters to Wood in 1681: 'God graunt us Peace. I thinke upon honest G. Ents saying, a Pox on Parties,' and 'I never medled with Controversy in my Life, nor ever shall.'[65] His affinities are closest with Fuller among other seventeenth-century biographers, but while Fuller's toleration is linked with Anglican latitudinarianism, Aubrey's is more radically secular in its basis, as is indicated by his decision to leave study of the church fathers to the divines, and by his special admiration for Hobbes, demonstrated by his making this philosopher, who was generally vilified by the orthodox as an atheist, the subject of his fullest biography. While Aubrey was formally Anglican, he was unusually detached and undogmatic in religious matters: he describes himself as a 'peeper' at the church doors of Anglican services.[66] He included among his friends not only Anglicans but Roman Catholics, many varieties of nonconformists, and sceptics, and he treated them all impartially in his biographies.

Aubrey is as tolerant in political as in religious matters. While he was formally a Royalist, he was a friend of the republican Harrington and free of animosity toward the leading figures of the Commonwealth and Puritan regime. Writing in the Restoration when the regicides were generally reviled, he gives them a relatively sympathetic treatment in his biographies, viewing Sir John Danvers and Harry Marten as imprudent rather than evil. The life of Milton that has already been considered is typical of the objectivity and sympathy he brings to figures usually condemned bitterly at the time for political and religious reasons. His remarkable degree of detachment is indicated by his declaration regarding his attempt to obtain copies of Milton's panegyrics on Cromwell and Fairfax: 'Were they made in commendation of the devill, 'twere all one to me.'[67]

Aubrey's tolerance in these matters is matched by his broad-mindedness about moral failings. He is sometimes critical of vanity and dishonesty, of failures in generosity and charity, but he is tolerant of weaknesses of the flesh. He writes sympathetically of the beautiful but wanton Venetia Digby, and declares of Dean Overall's promiscuous wife that her beauty was so great that one must have a hard heart not to admire her. This breadth of sympathy and freedom from rigidity and dogmatism are essential to his success as a brief biographer ranging widely over persons of the most diverse characters, beliefs, and ways of life.

How intrinsic these qualities are to Aubrey's character appears in his personal relations. When he recognized that faults were balanced by scholarly merit and shared enthusiasm, he was ultimately willing to overlook even such injustice and ingratitude as he himself had sometimes suffered at the hands of Anthony Wood. He wrote in a letter in 1696 a few months after the death of 'my deare Freinde and old correspondent' that though Wood's 'spleen used to make him chagrin and to chide me,' 'yet we could not be asunder, and he would always see me at my Lodgeing, with his darke Lanthorne, which should be a Relick.'[68] This letter, which serves as the elegy marking the end of the long relationship so fruitful for biographical writing, displays the same tolerance and magnanimity that underlies the *Brief Lives* and gives them much of their special character.

VI

Aubrey was well aware not only of the distinctive merits of his lives but also of their limitations, arising partly from the very nature of brief biography as a form and partly from their unfinished state, but he was skilful at working within and around the limitations and even in turning them to advantage. Although the constrictions of length did not allow him to provide any extended chronological account of his subjects' development through the various stages of life, even within brief scope he often succeeds in showing these figures in the dimension of time. More than most seventeenth-century biographers he has a sense of the importance of the early years. While other biographers took the view that all children are alike, Aubrey in his remarkably enlightened and humane treatise on education, which has been published from his manuscript only in relatively recent years, recognizes that each child has its own particular genius, individual nature, and propensities.[69] We find him frequently making inquiries about the early years of his subjects, about Milton from the poet's brother Christopher and about Katherine Philips from the cousin with whom she lived from her infancy. At the other end of life, he gives us many views of the changes, often unexpected and often melancholy, brought about by old age: he records his last visit to the old and blind Francis Potter, who found his servants kinder to him than his relatives, and describes Harrington in his aged madness.

Like Montaigne, who gives pictures of himself at various ages in his essays, Aubrey recognizes the need to provide portraits of an individual at different periods of life. He records that Sir William Petty was very slender when young but very plump when old, and he traces John Selden from student days, when he appeared 'a long scabby-pold boy,' all the way to his funeral and burial. He not only describes various phases of the lives of William Harvey and Samuel Butler but reports that he served as a pallbearer at their funerals. In the life of Hobbes, where he is freest of the constraints of brevity, he describes the changes in the philosopher's appearance from the 'ill yellowish complexion' of an unhealthy youth to the 'fresh, ruddy, complexion' (said by the physiognomists to be 'the most ingeniose complexion') of a healthier middle age, and from the crow-black hair of early years to a bald old age, 'which claymed a veneration.' He tells us of the changes in Hobbes's habits and ways of life as he moved from one stage of life to another. He provides memorable accounts too of some of Hobbes's intellectual developments, such as his discovery of a mathematical mode of reasoning upon his accidentally looking at a copy of Euclid at the age of forty.[70]

Despite the brevity of his biographies, Aubrey manages to display the individuality of his characters not only during the various earlier phases of their lives but even on their deathbeds. The variety of his deathbed scenes is in striking contrast to the highly standardized aspects of the conventionally pious, edifying deathbed scenes so prominent in seventeenth-century exemplary religious biography: here as in other matters Aubrey's interest is not in what can be made to fit traditionally approved patterns but in what does not fit ordinary patterns. While Burnet elaborated on the Earl of Rochester's death as a great example of the repentant sinner, Aubrey records the incongruous detail that Rochester, never shy of publicity, sent at his death for all his servants, even the piggard boy, to hear his palinode. He records that Lord Herbert of Cherbury, despite his unorthodoxy as 'the father of English deism,' had a tranquil death, and that this enthusiastic horseman mentioned his horses in his will. While in the conventional religious biographies of the period there was often no variation at all in the final words, 'Come, Lord Jesus,' traditionally established (from Revelation 22:20) as the proper last words of the dying Christian, Aubrey's characters conform to no such pattern. He tells us that Bishop Corbet's last words, addressed to an old friend, were 'Good night, Lushington.' Barrow's dying words as reported by Aubrey, 'I have seen the glories of the world,' were regarded as so unorthodox even by a twentieth-century biographer that he proposed emending them to 'I have seen through the glories of the world.'[71]

The most obvious and serious of Aubrey's limitations is of course his inability to complete his work. Yet he brought the fullest and most important of his biographies closer to a finished state than the surface disorder of his manuscripts might suggest. Helen Darbishire observed that the life of Milton, which has probably been subjected to closer scrutiny than any other, is really quite methodical beneath its apparently chaotic appearance. She concluded from her analysis that Aubrey deserves praise not only for the extent and intelligence of his researches and for his accuracy but for his ordering of the life and his care in revision.[72] Although his notes for many of his subjects are slight and fragmentary, at his best Aubrey achieves comprehensiveness even within relatively little space. Sir Geoffrey Keynes after making a close examination of Aubrey's life of William Harvey concluded that it was remarkable for its completeness as well as its vividness and accuracy. He declared that Aubrey was for Harvey 'the only recorder of what he looked like, of what he said, of his personal habits and foibles, and of the manner of his death.' In contrast to the modern scholars who have recoiled in dismay from Walton upon discovering his inaccuracies and distortions of his subjects' characters, Keynes concluded that Aubrey, although perhaps misled by contemporary gossip into belittling Harvey as a practising doctor, formed a very just estimate of his character and source of greatness, and altogether 'bequeathed to us the most life-like portrait of Harvey that we possess.'[73]

Aubrey's brief lives moreover gain special merits from their unfinished state. As he comments in a letter to Richard Blackburne, he is well aware that a painter's early drafts of a subject may possess values lacking in more finished versions. Not only do his biographies exhibit the liveliness and freshness of the sketch as opposed to the formal portrait but they often possess a special interest from their self-reflexive nature. In some cases, above all in the most ambitious and largest in scale of the lives, that of Hobbes, they can be read as biographies about the problems of writing biography. Aubrey's manuscripts of this life contain comic instances of his digressiveness, as when he mentions an inscription for a portrait of Hobbes he has presented to the Royal Society, and writes a note to himself: 'Gett a brasse wyer to hang it by.' But on a more serious level the biography provides a valuable, highly self-conscious, consideration of problems, which shows Aubrey's strong awareness of the degree to which lives of real people resist ordering into simple definitive patterns.[74]

In his drafts of the life of Hobbes and his letters to Wood and Blackburne about this project, Aubrey considers what sources to draw upon. He meditates upon problems of selection and propriety. Should he be as minute in information as Sir William Petty advised? He asks himself how far he should go in candour. He notes that he has been advised that on grounds of dignity he should omit mentioning that Hobbes had served as a page, and he decides that the king's calling Hobbes '*the beare*' was '*too low* witt' to be published. He discusses at some length the question of where to begin, and considers the possibility of opening with 'a pleasant description of Malmesbury, etc., (all new and untoucht),' that is his own and Hobbes's native area where he first met Hobbes when he was a schoolboy twelve years old.[75]

Aubrey expresses envy that Hobbes when he composed always knew where everything should be fitted in a work, and he worries over his own problems of organization, asking himself where particular pieces of information would best come in. But Aubrey's problems arise partly from the great abundance and diversity of the information he has gathered. He has even anticipated Boswell in staging scenes involving his subject, working to arrange for Hobbes to meet Charles II at the studio of Samuel Cooper, the painter.[76] Despite all his hesitations and uncertainties, he achieves a remarkably full and comprehensive biography as he ranges over such subjects as Hobbes's family and youth, his changes with aging, his methods of study and his intellectual development, his appearance, dress, temperament, tastes, habits of eating and drinking, recreations, his speech, sayings, writings, letters, his friends, critics, and opponents.

Among the questions Aubrey raised about his life of Hobbes was: 'Is my English style well enough?' Wood, although he was notoriously hard to please, scribbled the reply, "Tis well.'[77] His reply was the right one, for Aubrey's style even in his unfinished writings is far superior to Wood's own. Aubrey often expressed dissatisfaction about his style and wished for an Aristarchus to polish his writings, but he wisely rejected Blackburne's view that he should put the Hobbes into a 'High Style.' His style has the merits that his description of his method of writing in his letter to Wood on 15 June 1680 suggests: 'I fancy my selfe all along discourseing with you ... so that you make me to renew my acquaintance with my old and deceased friends.'[78] He writes as one talking to a friend, frequently about friends. His style is not only marked by conversational informality, liveliness, and freshness, but it conveys such infectious interest and enthusiasm that he often seems almost incapable of writing a dull sentence, and yet it is generally quite compressed, economical, and pithy. Even in an age of highly individual prose styles, his style stands out as distinctive, so that one can often spot by style alone when Wood in the *Athenæ Oxonienses* is following Aubrey, even though he rarely acknowledges his borrowings.

The *Brief Lives* are full of memorable phrases, like the description of Milton: 'his harmonicall and ingeniose soul did lodge in a beautifull and well-proportioned body.'[79] Aubrey has a poet's gift for apt comparison and evocative imagery, as when he terms Barrow as pale as the candle he studied by or compares the menace of the sound of Kettell's dragged leg with the noise of a rattlesnake about to strike. As well as displaying flashes of poetry, his biographies are enlivened by humour and irony of a quiet unforced kind. He comments on the enigmatic General Monck, who without revealing his purpose led into London on horseback the army which brought about the Restoration in 1660, that he no more intended the king's restoration than did his horse.

Aubrey's literary sense and critical discrimination are such that he recognizes Chaucer, Shakespeare, and Jonson as the supreme English masters of the arts of observing, understanding, and giving life to characters. In his *Idea of Education* he writes of Chaucer: 'one gift he has above all other authors and that is by excellency of his descriptions, to possess his readers with a more forcible imagination of seeing (as it were) done before their eyes, which they read, than any other that has ever written in any other tongue.'[80] Chaucer and the other great creative writers are in Aubrey's mind as ultimate models, so far as is possible and appropriate in the form of the brief life, for his attempts to practise what he terms the art of the conjurer.

It is a testimony to Aubrey's literary skills that, even though academic critics and historians have tended to underrate his work as a biographer, novelists including Anthony Powell and John Fowles have admired the *Brief Lives*.[81] They have recognized that Aubrey possesses to a high degree the novelist's interest in what makes one human being different from another. Powell not only wrote a standard biography of Aubrey but introduced into his novels character sketches that seem modelled on Aubrey's. Among later biographers, Lytton Strachey, who was not often generous in his comments on his predecessors, praised Aubrey for his 'unfailing eye for what was interesting,' his 'natural gift of style,' and his ability to give 'the pure essentials – a vivid image, on a page or two.'[82] He concluded: 'A biography should either be as long as Boswell's or as short as Aubrey's,' a recognition that for one type of biography Aubrey's work possesses a classic quality: it provides a model of excellence that has never been surpassed.

CHAPTER 10

Biography as Family History

I

In his classic *Civilization of the Renaissance in Italy*, Jacob Burkhardt suggested that the family histories that evolved at an early period in Florence and were said to survive there as manuscripts in some numbers might be important for the development of biographical writing.[1] His perceptiveness in drawing attention to this area is confirmed by the development of biography in England. The seventeenth century there gave rise not only to such advanced but relatively conventional and impersonal works of aristocratic genealogy as Sir William Dugdale's *The Baronage of England* (1675), notable for the accuracy of its antiquarian scholarship, but also to a more novel type of family history that incorporated extensive biographies with much fuller personal detail. The lives embodied in these family histories constitute one of the most interesting and neglected types of biographical writing in England during this period.[2]

A reason for the neglect is that many of these works, written for private family purposes, remained in manuscript hidden in private archives until long after they were written. This is the case with three works that represent the most innovative developments and finest achievements of the genre: John Smyth's lives of the Berkeleys, written mainly by 1618 but not published until the nineteenth century, Sir Hugh Cholmley's lives of the Cholmleys, written about 1655–7 but printed only privately in 1787, and the most remarkable of these, Gervase Holles's history of the Holles family, completed about 1657 but not published until 1937.[3] This is a field in which unknown specimens may still emerge from family muniment rooms and local archives.

In certain ways these biographies anticipate the work of Aubrey, different though they are in form. By its very nature biography as family history tends to bring out in the writers some of the same qualities that distinguish Aubrey, even if they may lack his brilliance. Smyth and Holles display much of Aubrey's historical sense, not only because they are well-trained antiquaries but because the kind of double vision he possesses, at once backward and forward looking, develops naturally in family historians writing about earlier and current generations for the benefit of descendants in later times. And they exhibit an interest like Aubrey's in minute personal details and intimate private matters, because these things seem natural and allowable in works written for private family use: as Lord Herbert of Cherbury declares of the information about his body and health in his autobiography: 'All which I doe in a familiar way mention to my Posterity though otherwise they may bee thought scarce worth the writing.'[4]

In the family context the biographer could often break through the sense of decorum that so frequently inhibited those writing for publication. This context may sometimes prompt uncritical praise and undue reverence, but it often fosters candid criticism. The biographer can write with candour when what he writes is all going to be within the family. Moreover, the family biographer tends naturally to work by a comparative method: he is interested not only in identifying common traditional or hereditary qualities in the family but also in displaying all the variations from generation to generation. Interest in diversity and individuality is furthered by comparison of ancestors and later family members with each other. Smyth states an essential principle of biography shaped as family history when he exhorts the young Lord Berkeley: 'Compare you these and other your Ancestors past with your self present.'[5]

Because it is shaped primarily by secular aristocratic traditions and values, seventeenth-century family history represents a marked break with the conventions of the predominant exemplary religious biography of the period. The religious biographers indeed often make a point of declaring quite explicitly that they attach little importance to the family lineage of their subjects. Thus John Barlow in his funeral sermon for Lady Strode in 1619 declines to praise her high birth and pedigree, because 'we are all of one blood' and 'they are most honourably (as I perswade my selfe she was) descended, that are borne againe by the word and spirit.' The biographer of the nonconformist divine Vavasor Powell in 1671 likewise expresses the view common in authors of religious lives when he emphasizes that, although his subject was descended from ancient Welsh and Yorkshire families, 'his best pedegree and highest discent was that which he derived from the most honourable Family of *Abraham.* For the unworthiest persons many times pretend to the highest worldly discents, the new born being only the best born.'[6]

Like the religious biographers, the family historians often display an exemplary aim, an intention of showing descendants what to emulate or shun by the examples of their forebears: Smyth lists 'uses' following each of his lives of the Berkeleys; but the values are much more secular, and the emphasis falls very differently from the religious lives, even when the author is, like Gervase Holles, a man of exemplary Anglican piety. The difference is shown well in Holles's description of his father: 'In his devotions he was constant morning and evening, having ever most humble and pious affections to Godward; but he could by no meanes brooke a man y^t desired to appear holy: he would say such men looked too like hippocrites.'[7] Characteristically in family history the emphasis is not on piety or learning, though both may have their place, but on family status and alliances, management of estates, and public and military service. It is instructive to compare the subjects indexed in a collection of exemplary religious biographies such as Samuel Clarke's *Lives of Sundry Eminent Persons in this Later Age* with the subjects central in biographies incorporated in family histories. The two have almost nothing in common.

II

Many of the common elements in the family biographies clearly spring from social factors rather than from established generic traditions and conventions, since most of the histories incorporating the biographies remained unpublished and each writer worked without much reference to existing models. Both Smyth and Holles have a strong sense of novelty, of the unprecedented nature of their transformation of conventional family genealogies and chronicles into works that include biographies and character portraits with much personal detail. By his priority in date Smyth deserves special credit as the pioneer of the type in England, since his work was largely completed by 1618, although he made some later additions. His claim to be an innovator in his lives of the Berkeleys seems to be entirely justified: 'Though I know that this and other like noble families have been in divers ages served with many worthy men and minds, yet none have ventured on the history of their lords or masters lives; whereby for ought I have observed, I am the first and alone that hitherto have run this course of a genealogike history of any patrimoniall family.'[8]

John Smyth (1567–1640) was not a member but a retainer of the family about which he wrote. He was Steward of the Hundred and Liberty of Berkeley, with the duty of presiding over the manor court. At the same time he was a gentleman, educated at Oxford and the Middle Temple, who accumulated a substantial estate of his own. He early developed antiquarian interests and skills and, as he tells us, he worked on his history of the Berkeley family for forty years, using extensive family muniments at Berkeley Castle and elsewhere. He wrote particularly to instruct the young lord, George (b. 1601), and his mother and sister.[9]

The Lives of the Berkeleys is remarkable for its vast scope: a family history extending from 1066 to 1618, for twenty generations and 550 years, as the author proudly claims. As full as forty years of dedicated research could make them, the lives are organized under such headings as Birth and Manner of Education, Employments in War, Foreign Employments, Husbandries and Hospitalities, Wives, Issue, Purchase or Sale of Lands, Seals of Arms, Alms and Devotions, Recreations and Delights, Death and Place of Burial. Smyth's primary concern is with the successive lords Berkeley, heads of the family, but he provides lives also of their wives and some other family members.

Inevitably the earlier lives, those of the lords Berkeley and their wives during the Middle Ages, are without much personal detail, since the existing records related mainly to such matters as estates and expenditures, but the more recent lives include fuller personal information, as Smyth was able to draw on oral tradition together with his own observations and those of others. One of the fullest biographies is the life of Henry, Lord Berkeley (d. 1613). As one might expect in a biography written by a steward, much of the material still consists in estate records, and in financial affairs, which were unfortunate for most of this lord's life: there are eighty-five pages in Smyth's manuscript, nearly seventy-five printed pages, on his law suits. Law suits indeed are extraordinarily prominent in the family histories of the gentry and aristocracy during this period. David Lloyd in his *Memoires* considers it worth recording as an unusual fact that one Sir Edward Berkeley never either sued or was sued.[10]

In addition to such dry matters as law suits, however, Smyth provides some good personal detail about Henry, including physical description and information about his abilities, tastes, and habits, and about his marriages and family relations. For example, the section on his 'recreations and delights' tells us not only that hunting and hawking were his chief pleasures but even gives the names of his falcons; it informs us that he spent much, perhaps too much, time in bowls, tennis, cock-fighting, cards, and dice. Smyth comments: 'And I will, without blemish to his honor, tell his posterity, That his longe and slender lady-like-hand knew a dye as well and how to handle it as any of his ranke and time,' and illustrates this point with an anecdote.[11] This concreteness extends to the account of Henry's death, with details about his sickness caused by a surfeit of small custards and his difficulty in pronouncing his last words.

Smyth also gives an interesting character of Henry's first wife, Lady Katherine (d. 1596), who was a daughter of Henry Howard, Earl of Surrey. This is developed as a study in aristocratic grandeur and cultivated accomplishments. Smyth recalls that in her aristocratic stateliness and love of ceremony she required him as a boy to curtsy to her and taught him how. He tells us that she had a complexion 'lovely both in the springe and autumne of her life, but a little inclining towards an high colour.' He records that in speech she was 'passing Eloquent and ready; whom in many years I could never observe to misplace or seem to recall one mistaken, misplaced or mispronounced word or sillable.' She was skilful in French and Italian. She played the lute and sang so admirably that her husband and servants listened secretly outside the door. After the execution of her brother, the Duke of Norfolk, her habits changed; she sought solitude, and studied natural philosophy and astronomy with the aid of a globe and instruments. Smyth writes of her with admiration but sustains his claim to avoid flattery: he suggests that she was too dominant in her husband's affairs.[12]

When he comes close to the present Smyth sometimes becomes more evasive. Discretion overrules candour and he refrains from full disclosure. He states that the ways followed by Sir Thomas, the father of the current lord, seemed 'somwhat foule,' so he leaps over rather than wades through them, and leaves it to the widow to decide how much to tell the son.[13] In lives like those of Henry, Lord Berkeley, and Lady Katherine, however, biography begins to emerge in an interesting way from family history. Although he is primarily an antiquarian, Smyth displays the interests and impulses of the true biographer.

III

In contrast to Smyth, Cholmley and Holles were both members of the families about which they wrote. They illustrate the way in which the

Civil War stimulated this branch of biographical writing, because both were Royalist gentlemen who turned to family history and biography during the enforced leisure brought about by the defeat of their cause. Sir Hugh Cholmley (1600–57) had special reason for writing about his own life, because his part in the Civil War had been controversial: beginning as a Parliamentarian, he had switched sides and become a Royalist military leader; but he states that his starting point for family history was his desire to commemorate his wife, who died in 1655.[14] His *Memoirs*, written soon after that date, are addressed to his two sons, intended for them and their descendants, not for publication.

Cholmley's work is on a smaller scale and has a much shorter time span than Smyth's, but he provides several well-realized short biographies. He begins at the period of the planting of his family in Yorkshire with his great-great-grandfather, but his chief subjects are his great-grandfather, Sir Richard Cholmley, his father, who was also Sir Richard, and himself in an autobiographical section, which includes a fine character study of his wife, Elizabeth (née Twisden). He carries out his declared purpose in treating these figures: 'not only mentioning their births, matches, fortunes, and times of their deaths, which may be useful for pedigrees and evidences of titles; but also describing and deportraiting their persons, conditions, and humours.'[15] As well as some account of the main events of the lives, he provides character sketches, including good physical description, and finely balanced and candid analyses of the personalities.

As usual in family history of the gentry and aristocracy, Cholmley's dominant subjects are such matters as lineage, marriage alliances, public service as justices of the peace, sheriffs of the county, and members of Parliament, and financial details about estates and law suits, but he provides considerable detail also about the more intimate private aspects including the sexual lives of his subjects. He tells us that his great-grandfather, the first Sir Richard, was extraordinarily given to the love of women and had a perhaps justifiably jealous side to his character. He refused Henry VIII's request to bring his beautiful second wife to the royal court, and he put his second son, Roger, last in the entail and left him no portion in his will, 'because Sir Richard doubted whether he was his own son, as it has been told to me.'[16] His amorous propensities were inherited by his children, and one of his daughters married her singing and dancing master.

Cholmley opens his biography of his father with the following detailed and individual description of this second Sir Richard's appearance and physical characteristics:

> He was of the tallest stature of men, about the height of his father, but slender and well-shaped. His mother was a very beautiful woman, contributing, as did his grandmother, to the whitening of those black shadows formerly incident to the family; for when he was very young, his hair was of a light colour, and his complexion fair; and acting the part of a woman in a comedy at Trinity College, in Cambridge, he did it with great applause, and was esteemed beautiful; yet, being grown to be a man, his complexion grew brown, and something inclinable to swarthy, which yet may be ascribed rather to his riding in the sun, and much using of field sports, in his youth, than to nature; for the skin of his body was a passing white, and of a very smooth grain, and he had a most incomparable sweet breath, insomuch as many times one would have thought it had carried a perfume or sweet odoriferous smell with it. The hair of his head was chestnut-brown, and the ends of his locks curled and turned up very gracefully, without that frisling which his father Sir Henry's was inclined to; his beard a yellowish brown, and thin upon the chin, as was his father's; his eyes grey, his face and visage long, with a handsome Roman nose; of a very winning aspect, a most manly and graceful presence. He had also a rare voice, being both sweet and strong, nature affording him those graces in singing, which others endeavoured to attain to by art and practice; all which rendered him famous among the female sex.[17]

Cholmley's portrait of his father nicely balances the positive and negative aspects of his character. That he possessed the courage proper to his order is shown in a finely told anecdote of a quarrel, which began on the stage of the Blackfriars Theatre. The son reveals that his father, like many of his class, suffered from perplexed and mismanaged financial affairs. He incurred heavy debts partly as a result of law suits brought by an exceptionally litigious neighbour, Sir Thomas Hobby, and when he attempted to recoup his fortune, his funds were further drained by a cousin, Gascoigne, in London, engaged in the search for the philosopher's stone. Furthermore, the son comments: 'One other cause of this debt, as some would conjecture, was his amorous humour, which was conceived might be costly; but I have heard him protest it was not.' He refers to other faults in his father including his imperious manner and harsh language to servants and country folk, which made him unpopular, and his 'ill custom to swearing, especially in his anger or sports, when they went cross to his mind.' While he does not lack respect and affection for his father, he writes with a degree of objectivity in keeping with his statement in his dedication that he desires to 'forget my relation' and write as a historian.[18]

IV

While Sir Hugh Cholmley wrote his *Memoirs* when he took refuge with his wife's family in Kent after his party's defeat, his fellow Royalist Gervase Holles wrote his *Memorials of the Holles Family* during the same period of the 1650s in more distant exile in Holland. His work displays qualities similar to Cholmley's, on a larger scale and with greater distinction. It is the masterpiece of biography in the context of family history, at least until the appearance of Roger North's *Lives of the Norths*.

Gervase Holles (1607–75) inherited family estates in and around Grimsby, Lincolnshire, at an early age. He pursued legal studies at the Middle Temple, engaged in antiquarian activities, and took part in public life. He served as mayor of Grimsby and member of Parliament, and when the Civil War broke out he raised a regiment which he led as colonel, until captured and imprisoned, and then after the Royalist defeat forced into exile in Holland.[19] When he wrote his family history he had suffered not only defeat and impoverishment but a series of personal catastrophes, including the deaths of his wife and two of his three children. He declares in an autobiographical section of the history that his life had been for the most part 'nothing els but a varied scene of infelicity,' and his writing is permeated by a gentle but pervasive melancholy.[20]

In exile Holles turned to literary and antiquarian studies, since, as he states, 'banished men finde very litle busines besides bookes.'[21] He had earlier made large collections for a history of Lincolnshire, but most of these had been lost during the Civil War, so he confined himself to the writing of family history, aided by the remnant of his collections which he managed to bring to Holland, and by English friends including Sir William Dugdale who answered his inquiries. This was a natural move for one of his antiquarian interests, because he belonged to a minor branch of a family that had been prominent for several generations and had risen by the seventeenth century to a position of considerable wealth and eminence.

Holles is concerned primarily with four or five generations of his family, extending from the early sixteenth to the mid-seventeenth century.

He begins with some discussion of the family's obscure earlier origins, moves to the life of the ancestor who raised it to prominence, Sir William Holles, a rich merchant who became Lord Mayor of London, and then goes on to the different branches of the family springing from Sir William's sons, including a branch ennobled as earls of Clare, two military heroes, and many country gentlemen. He provides histories also of allied families: Sheffield, Frescheville, Clifton, and Kingston. The history includes, as one might expect, dry pages of genealogy and details relating to estates, but as a whole it is remarkably vital, and it incorporates numerous lives. These are not full-scale biographies, but some are quite substantial: they include an account of the chief events or phases of the subject's life and often conclude with a fine 'description' of the subject's appearance, character, and accomplishments.

In a dedication to his surviving son Frescheville, Holles not only emphasizes that he intends his history for private family use — he desires that it should not be published but be copied on vellum so that it might last for many generations in the family — but he also defines the innovative quality of his work: 'you shall not only know the names, the qualities, the services and the matches of your ancestors, but in many of them their very features and dispositions (a designe I dare boldly say wch in any private family hath not hitherto beene undertaken).' He promises not merely to provide his son and descendants with an accurate record of genealogy and descent 'but also to set the right stamp and value upon every person, wch indeed is the true life of this part of venerable antiquity.' He conceives it as an act of piety to those who are dead and threatened with oblivion to ensure that his family and descendants 'may beholde both the features and dispositions of their deceased ancestors and retrive (as it were) a conversation and entercourse with those whome death hath silenc'd.'[22]

While he moves beyond conventional antiquarian aspects of family history, Holles's *Memorials* is nevertheless shaped in many ways by the traditions of the genre represented by such figures as Dugdale. As one would expect in an aristocratic family history, his basic structure and his principles of inclusion and emphasis are determined largely by pedigree and genealogy. He states that he writes little of families that intermarried with his own without leaving descendants in his branch, but that he writes at length of the Freschevilles, for example, because through them he and his posterity are linked to many streams of the oldest gentry and nobility. But he is critical of those who display narrow aristocratic pride. In discussing the merchant Sir William Holles he condemns the folly of many English gentry who consider the calling of merchant unworthy. His liberal views were evidently derived from his father, Frescheville Holles, who consented to become an alderman of Grimsby despite family criticism for connecting himself with 'meane and mechanicke fellowes.' Gervase, who similarly became mayor of Grimsby, declares that he would not scrape out of his pedigree a chimney sweep who conveyed to him his being.[23]

Far from neglecting the normal antiquarian aspects of family history, Holles brings to his work the most advanced antiquarian principles and practices of his day. The great contemporary master of the scholarly study of genealogy, Dugdale, termed him 'that judicious Antiquary (my worthy friend).'[24] In his dedicatory epistle Holles claims for his history: 'You will like two thinges in it: Truth and Modesty. I affirme nothing but what I have warranted by record; what I do offer from tradition I represent only as tradictory.' He displays in his work painstaking search for relevant records, careful citation and quotation of authorities, and critical examination and skilled interpretation of evidence drawn from such sources as inquisitions, heraldic visitations, pipe rolls, charters, church monuments, armorial glass, wills, and letters. Like Dugdale, he is highly sceptical about many of the allegedly aristocratic pedigrees to be found in the Heralds' Office. He criticizes or treats with gentle irony persons who unhistorically claim long pedigrees, and questions even the Earl of Clare's claims of exalted ancestry. He comments on one such case: 'But theis romances are but too frequent.'[25]

Following the best antiquarian precedents, Holles shuns elaboration of style, although he displays a sophisticated knowledge of literature and incorporates in his writing occasional allusions to classical biographers, historians, and poets. He states that 'Antiquity is a matron grave and venerable, not a virgin elegant and beautifull,' and that truth is more often found 'sitting upon a rude and time-eaten stone then upon a new and polished marble.' Accordingly he develops a serviceable plain style, but one that is frequently enlivened by laconic wit and gentle irony (qualities that evidently ran in his family, for he tells us that his father 'had a short lackonicke way of witt wch well became him'), and that is capable of rising to a height of simple eloquence, as when he describes movingly the death of his son George at the age of two or delivers an elegy for his talented cousin William Holles, killed during his youth in the Civil War.[26]

Admirable though his scholarship and style are, if Holles had confined himself to his skilled but relatively conventional antiquarian researches he could have produced no more than a dryly factual genealogical work like Dugdale's *Baronage*. What gives his work special interest from a biographical point of view is that he sought out personal detail, not only in written records but also in informal and oral sources. He was highly aware of the dangers of 'hear say' and second- or third-hand reports, but he frequently made judicious use of such sources, giving cautions about their reliability where appropriate. Fortunately he was ideally placed in his youth for gathering such information. He was brought up by a father and grandfather whose memories extended far into the past, and the family connections included figures like Sir Francis Coke, who would spend a whole night telling stories about family members and forebears. Such sources, combined with his own direct observation, provided him with much of the human detail that was essential to his reconstruction of the portraits of his ancestors and relatives.

These portraits are developed partly as expansions of the traditional topics of aristocratic family history. In dealing with the careers, occupations, and accomplishments of his subjects, Holles gives much attention to military service, roles at court and in Parliament, work in local administration, and management of estates, since most of the male members of his family possessed avocations and concerns typical of the gentry and aristocracy of their times. Thus he describes the part his relatives took in all the major expeditions and theatres of war: the defeat of the Spanish Armada, the Islands Voyage, and campaigns in the Netherlands and Ireland. He provides full accounts of the military careers of the two heroes of warfare in the Netherlands, Sir George and Thomas Holles, and celebrates those who served the Royalist cause in the Civil War, like his cousin William Holles.

Holles shows that as well as upholding the family honour in military service some of his relatives were remarkable for versatility, notably the first Earl of Clare, whom Lord Brooke described as the most accomplished gentleman he had met in his wide travels, and one of Gervase's grandfathers, an earlier Gervase Holles, who exemplified the Castiglione ideal of the well-rounded gentleman amateur. For a surprising number of members of the family, their accomplishments included the writing of poetry. Gervase tells us that his mother, for example, wrote a verse history of her life, and he informs us that the talented and precocious William Holles, killed young in the Civil War, wrote many poems in Latin, Greek, and English, and two comedies, apparently lost in the war.[27]

Holles's work is typical of aristocratic family history, however, in that many of his subjects showed little inclination toward learning and letters. In the small space they give to academic studies, many of his lives are at the opposite pole to some other branches of seventeenth-century biography such as the lives of learned clergymen, but they have their precedents in other lives of gentry and aristocracy, for example the late sixteenth-century biography of Sir Peter Carew by John Vowell, alias Hooker, which informs us that Carew in his youth was 'more desyrouse of libertie then of learnynge' and that his schoolmaster 'in noe wise coulde frame the younge Peter to smell to a bocke, or to licke of anye schollinge.'[28] Among Holles's representative figures are his grandfather Kingston, who proceeded no further in school than Ovid's *Metamorphoses* before he threw away his books and got a kennel of hounds, and Thomas Holles, who abandoned his studies at Cambridge and went to trail a pike in the Low Countries. The active life of the soldier and the practical occupations of the estate manager loom much larger than the study of books among the occupations of Holles's subjects.

Even in his handling of such conventional subjects of aristocratic family history as the management of estates, however, Holles provides a wide range of interesting personal detail. The comparative method of family history is very much at work as he examines a variety of patterns and brings out the individuality of various members of the family partly by showing their different attitudes to family property and their different degrees of success and failure in managing it. The patterns include the accumulation of great fortune by the first Sir William Holles, the merchant, the enjoyment of spending it in a magnificent and luxurious lifestyle by his son, the second Sir William, the total dissipation of fortune and reduction to penury of the elder branch of the family through extravagance, and the amassing and careful guarding of vast revenues by the financially prudent first Earl of Clare. Holles writes of all this with a degree of detachment and objectivity, but he makes it clear that he disapproves of members of the family dominated by narrowly mercenary motives. He shows that he bears no ill will to those like his grandfather Kingston, who recklessly or carelessly dissipated estates that might have been inherited by Holles himself. His ideal, which is similar to Ben Jonson's in 'To Penshurst,' is exemplified by Sir Peter Frescheville, who is praised as the best landlord in England, one who manages his estates with a view to social responsibility and social benefit rather than the maximizing of financial profit.[29]

V

While in his concern with military service and estate management as well as with pedigree and genealogy Holles follows the conventional forms of aristocratic family history, at the same time he fulfils his promise to move beyond the usual limitations of such works and provide his descendants with the 'very features and dispositions' of their ancestors. He accomplishes this partly through well-chosen anecdotes to illustrate the characters of his subjects. At every point his narratives are rich in significant and memorable anecdotes. These range from serious stories of military life illustrating the courage of Sir George Holles to more comic episodes demonstrating the reckless early years of his grandfather Sir Gervase Holles, known in his youth as 'wild Holles,' and to anecdotes showing the ambition, youthful haughty spirit, and later prudence of the first Earl of Clare. Holles's methods of displaying the 'very features and dispositions' of his subjects may be further shown by considering his representation of such aspects as their appearance, dress, speech and mannerisms, and marriages.

Holles customarily opens his 'description' of his subjects with some account of their appearance. He provides more precise and detailed depictions than are to be found in most earlier biographies, and anticipates Aubrey in his concern with the visual and physical. His description of John Holles, first Earl of Clare, begins:

> He was a personage of a gallant presence. He was full six feet high, straight and of a strong limbe. In his youth he was somewhat leane, but in his later days he grew well in flesh, but not corpulent. His hayre was of a light browne, something towardes an aburne; his eyes were grey, he had a white skin, and his cheekes were rosy. He carried a majesty in his countenance, and in his face there was a strange mixture of severity and sweetnes. His motion was stately, befitting so great a person.[30]

Holles then proceeds to give illustrations of the earl's youthful grace in dancing, his skill in riding and fencing, and his other physical activities continuing even in old age.

How far Holles goes in providing minute detail about his subjects' appearance may be illustrated by his description of his father's hair:

> His hayre was then [in youth] a bright flaxen (but it after turned into a light browne) wch curled naturally and so becomingly as if nature had used art in the ornament. Out of wch he nourished a locke on the left side wch voluntarily cast itselfe into wreathes and was the most becomming one y^t I have seene: untill about some two yeares before he died the gentlewoman I last mentioned (who might best be bold with him for he loved and honoured hir for hir worth) finding him one day asleep in his chayre shee tooke a payre of sissers and cut it of. When he wakened he was in a very

great chaff untill he heard who did it; he sayd then only 'Shee did well, it was full of grey hayres.'[31]

This minuteness is not random but significant for what it reveals of the father's character, of his aging and attitude toward aging.

Like Aubrey, Holles shows how the individual characteristics of his subjects are manifested even in their clothing. He tells us that his father's unostentatious modesty was apparent in his dress: 'In his habit he loved plainnes wch he embroider'd with his neatnes, and in him was very becoming because it was wthout affectation.' Gervase informs us that the military hero Thomas Holles, who had his share of excesses in youth but then became 'a great example of piety and temperance,' was known in his later years for his old-fashioned clothes, and 'he was not more usually described by anything than by his long poled hatt.' In contrast to these two figures Gervase describes his grandfather, Sir Gervase Holles, who never entirely cast off the love of rich clothing he had acquired as a soldier in his youth: 'If he had any vanity it was a disposition he had (even to his last) to weare costly apparell. I remember not above two yeares before his death he made him a tawney sattin suit and bestowed neare thirty pounds upon the embrodery.' Gervase gives an anecdote about this grandfather when at the age of eighty he was persuaded to have his portrait painted: he put on 'a white sattin doublet embroidered wth flowers of silke and golde,' saying 'that he did not like theis fooleries, but, seeing we would have it so, and that he could be drawne with no better face, he would be drawne in a good doublet.'[32]

Holles establishes the individuality of his subjects also through mannerism and speech when he has an opportunity to observe them. He tells us, for example, that the first Earl of Clare displayed a felicity of conversation beyond other men. He does not record extended passages of dialogue but he gives characteristic remarks and favourite sayings or oaths: his father's 'Pres God,' his grandfather Kingston's 'Body of our Lord,' and the second Sir William Holles's 'Sake of God.' He establishes his grandmother Kingston's charity of nature both by her actions and by the only words of hers he records: 'I always observed of hir that if a poore creature begged food shee would bid her servantes fetch it, but if they asked for drinke shee would hast for it hir selfe, saying thirst was an importunate thing.' He shows very well the character of the second Sir William Holles, who lived in great style, comfort, and contentment on his country estate and sought no great alliances, in recording a speech in which Sir William commented on a proposal that his daughter marry George Clifford, Earl of Cumberland: '"Sake of God" (that was his usuall word of asseveration) "I do not like to stand wth my cap in my hand to my son in law. I will see hir married to an honest gentleman wth whome I may have friendship and conversation."'[33]

Holles's ability to convey the individuality of human character and temperament and the variety of patterns of life is well shown in his accounts of marriages of members of his family. In contrast to the slight treatment of the subject in many exemplary religious biographies, marriage is a leading subject of family histories of the gentry and aristocracy, because of the characteristic concern with alliances and blood-lines, genealogy, property settlements, and inheritances. Here as in other areas Holles moves beyond these conventional aspects to provide much information about personal character, circumstances, and relationships in marriage. While he commonly gives most prominence to male members of his family, as one would expect in the representation of an aristocratic society in which titles and entailed estates descended in male lines, he includes many character sketches, sometimes affectionate and sometimes critical, of the female members, as he writes of their marital lives.

Holles describes a great variety of marriages, good and bad, marriages undertaken from romantic impulses and from prudential motives, even marriages prompted by a whim or a fit of passion. Among the bad marriages are those of two relatives to maids of honour at the royal court, who proved proud and extravagant. Gervase comments: 'slips transplanted from that soyle for the most part make but ill proofe in the country.' One of the patterns he describes is the marriage that begins romantically but ends badly. His grandfather Sir Gervase during his spirited youth eloped with the beautiful heiress Frances Frescheville, but her father refused ever to see her again and contrived to disinherit her, and her husband did not remain faithful to her. Gervase gives a picture of her in old age, grown corpulent, and melancholy because of her father's rejection of her and her husband's unfaithfulness.[34]

Gervase shows that other marriages in the family followed the opposite pattern, with less romantic beginnings but happier outcomes. He tells us that his grandfather Kingston after getting in debt through youthful extravagance declared: 'Body of our Lord! I will go marry this olde widdow and pay my debts. Then when I have buried hir will I marry a young wench and get children!' In this case the irony of the outcome was more comic than tragic. The old widow 'held him tug above 38 yeares and lived near 12 years after him.' She lived to be eighty-nine, and according to Gervase proved an excellent wife, and discreetly bore her husband's infidelities, although she was a woman of spirit.[35]

As well as showing the contrasting patterns of marriage in different members of his family, Holles records the variations that sometimes appeared in the successive marriages of individuals. He tells us that his father's youthful love was so strong that in the face of opposition he endured a wait of seven years before his first marriage could take place, but that he married a second time much more precipitously 'in a pet.' Holles reports that the record for number and variety of marriages among his family connection was held by Sir Gervase Clifton, who was still alive at the time of writing:

> For one thing more he is remarkable (having in y^t gone beyond any of our nation y^t I have yet heard of) wch is this: he hath already buried six wives and married a seaventh about two yeares since when he was neare 70 yeares olde. He would say y^t he had married just as his chapleine used to begin his sermons when my Lord of Cumberland was at his house, v^{izt} Right Honourable, most Worshipfull and Welbeloved: his first two being Earle's daughters, his two second grave widdows, and the last couple young gentlewomen. He hath begun againe as he began at the first, his seaventh wife being a virgin and the Earl of Huntingdon's daughter. I will not wish y^t he may run the same course over againe least the weomen should be angry wth me, but I heartily pray that he may live a very long life and a happy.[36]

As Holles's handling of such subjects as marriage illustrates, his special merits include a remarkable candour, carried much further than it could have been if he were writing for publication. While he is moved by family piety, he recognizes that honesty is essential. He declares: 'neither my nearnes of bloud or perticular affection to any person whome I shall here discourse of, shall sway me anything from the exact rule of truth and justice,' and he promises his family readers that he will show 'the virtues, and imperfections too, of your ancestors and nearest relations.'[37]

The one fault that was commonly admitted in the subjects of religious biography, choler, seems to have been just as widespread in the secular world if the Holles family is at all typical. Few members of the family, among the males at least, escaped this fault: it comes up again and again in every generation. It appears even in Holles's father, a man of very virtuous character, as 'an hereditary evill derived from his ancestors.' Gervase writes that his uncle Francis Holles was exceptional among soldiers for his affability, and did not quarrel or fight duels with his fellows: 'yet (that he might show of what family he is) I have seene him sometimes very cholerique.' When the first Earl of Clare is described as reddening in anger we recognize him as a true Holles, and his career is shown to be marked by a long series of quarrels and bloody feuds.[38]

While religious biography provides abundant precedent for admission of the fault of choler, it provides little for admission of sexual incontinence, unless in conversion narratives where such failings can be consigned to an unregenerate past. But Holles, in advance of Aubrey, freely moves into this area. He tells us that Denzil Holles, father of the first Earl of Clare, was so well known for his 'immoderate love to weomen' that he became the butt of satirical verses beginning: 'Hollys hits in every hole'; he built a house for his mistress, and left illegitimate children, as did other members of the family, including both Gervase's grandfathers. Gervase reports that an elder who knew the family history told him as a schoolboy: 'take but after either of thy grandfathers and thou wilt neither run from man nor woman!' He comments that sexual looseness was so general in the family that his father's chastity stood out as a rare exception, and writes with ironic understatement that exemplary continence was 'a crowne the males of our family have not bene commonly too ambitious of.'[39]

In his accounts of such matters as illicit sexual liaisons, mistresses, and illegitimate children, Holles displays a tolerant spirit. He has a generous view of human nature and human weakness, and writes of the sins of the flesh without undue severity. He reserves his more serious condemnation for failures in loyalty, honour, and courage, as appears in his criticism of John Frescheville, who he believes during the Civil War twice surrendered Royalist strongholds to the rebels without adequate reason. While he is candid about many other matters, he passes rapidly over the younger Denzil Holles, second son of the Earl of Clare, who initially at least supported the 'rebel' or Parliamentary cause. He regards the aristocratic conceptions of honour and loyalty as harmonious with religious values, although he recognizes that a conflict arises in the matter of duelling: 'Indeed this is that onely wch threatens to devide the union betwixt a Christian and a gentleman.'[40]

While Holles writes as a devout Anglican and praises religious devotion where he finds it in his subjects, he does not give special prominence to religion.[41] He provides none of the elaborate deathbed scenes that are so prominent in exemplary religious biography, but he displays the variety of ways death comes to his subjects and in which they respond to its coming. In this as in other matters the implicit comparative principle of family history is at work. He tells us that his father when dying asked three times to have the passing bells tolled, which he heard with contentment, but that the military hero Sir George Holles regretted dying in bed rather than in battle, and complained of 'this lazy death.' He gives poignant accounts of the deaths of children and youths who died unfulfilled, and in contrast a description of the honour awarded Sir George Holles in a grand state funeral: 'the greatest and most solemne that I have yet seene.'[42]

VI

The way in which Holles's biographies benefit from the context of family history which does much to shape them becomes evident if one compares two of his fullest character studies, those of the second Sir William Holles and his grandson, the first Earl of Clare (who were respectively Gervase's own great-grandfather and the first cousin of his father). These are contrasting figures, and the contrast which helps define their characters emerges more clearly and naturally from the family context than it would if they were viewed in isolation from it. Sir William, second son of the rich merchant who founded the family fortune, inherited great revenues, and lived on his estate at Houghton or Haughton, Nottinghamshire, in much prosperity and state, with a large body of retainers, his own company of stage players, and even his own fool. As Epicurean as Chaucer's Franklin in his way of life, he was famous for the splendid scale of his housekeeping, and his hospitality was 'a wonder': he roasted an ox on each of the twelve days of Christmas. He was so charitable that he was long remembered by the folk of his area as 'the good Sir William.' He neither advanced nor retarded his estate very much, and he refused to add to it at the expense of others. Nor did he seek advancement in position, as was shown by his refusal to allow his daughter to marry a great nobleman, the Earl of Cumberland. Gervase, writing in more troubled times, comments enviously that Sir William's life was wholly pleasant and happy. This is a simply drawn but memorable portrait of a figure who represents the traditional Tudor ideal of the great housekeeping country gentleman.[43]

Sir William Holles's grandson, the first Earl of Clare, is a much more complex character, contrasting greatly with his grandfather in his ambitious nature, his wide range of abilities and accomplishments, and the troubles and turmoils as well as the successes of his drive to rise to high position. He displayed precocious intellectual abilities at Cambridge, where he entered university at the age of thirteen, and showed equal physical prowess in the action against the Spanish Armada, but his aristocratic pride and unruly nature involved him in feuds which resulted in bloodshed and a long period of exile on the Continent. He engaged in disputes with the most mighty in the land, including Lord Burghley and the Duke of Buckingham. Favoured by Queen Elizabeth but not by James, he was a friend of Sir Walter Ralegh, for whom he wrote an elegy. He became alienated from court but bought peerages, a barony and an earldom, from Buckingham, whom he despised. Combining financial prudence with his pride and unruliness, he husbanded his estates and increased them to an enormous value, but in striking contrast to his grandfather he was criticized for his lack of expenditure on his household. He complained that his grandfather's revenues went down the privy, a remark and an attitude of which Gervase disapproves. While Gervase shows respect and admiration for the Earl of Clare's talents in raising his family in rank and fortune, his portrait is candid rather than flattering. He depicts him as accomplished and formidable, but he represents the grandfather as more likeable, good-hearted and generous.[44]

As comparison of these two figures shows, in Holles's work the parts gain from the whole. The family history in which the individual characters are embodied constitutes a study in human mutability and vicissitudes, displaying great contrasts both in character and fortune. Writing in exile and poverty at a low point in his own fortunes, Holles, who sometimes quotes Boethius on the mutability of life, has a strong awareness that as families rise so do they fall. This awareness, reinforced by his historical studies, is one of the things that makes against excessive family pride. He states that while he can trace his descent through his Frescheville and Clifton ancestry from Edward III and most of the old sovereign princes of Christendom, he knows a tanner in Mansfield who is likewise descended from most of the royal houses of Europe.[45]

While Holles traces the rise of one branch of his family, which had acquired the historic royal title of Earl of Clare and was already well on the way to the ducal rank it subsequently achieved, he shows that another branch, in fact the eldest in descent from the first Sir William Holles, who founded the family fortunes, had undergone an equally striking decline. In this branch great estates were quickly dissipated; its eventual heir was found as a boy begging for bread in the streets, and seen by Gervase when he had been put to turning spits in the kitchen by servants of the first Earl of Clare. The earl then apprenticed the boy to a jeweller, but he stole from his master and disappeared for the last time from the scene.[46] In so tracing the similarities and differences in character and fortune, the parts played by inheritance, heredity, individual qualities, and accident, Holles's work has close affinities with the series of family biographies Roger North wrote at the end of the seventeenth century and beginning of the eighteenth century, and anticipates many qualities of historical and family chronicle novels that developed in later times. It is not surprising that Sir Walter Scott, although he did not know Holles's work, edited one of the Scottish examples of the same type of seventeenth-century aristocratic family history, James Somerville's *Memorie of the Somervilles*, in 1815, close to the time he embarked on his career as a historical novelist.

In the form it appears in Holles, however, biography written as family history must be considered a distinctively seventeenth-century type, just as much as Aubrey's kind of brief life. The type seems to belong to a period of balance and transition between older aristocratic and newer middle-class orders. As Smyth's *Lives of the Berkeleys* so strongly demonstrates, it is shaped by an aristocratic sense of family, defined by noble rank, ancient genealogy, and grand alliances, and asserts exalted lineage at a time when much power is shifting to a more commercial middle class. Holles's lives, later in the century, gain much of their interest from the representation of the interrelation between the older and newer orders. Holles takes pride in his descent from noble and even royal families, but he is critical of those who attach exaggerated importance to inherited distinctions, and he emphasizes rather than hides the commercial foundation of the fortunes of his branch of the family; he declares: 'For my owne part I shall ever esteeme it more honour to be descended from a merchant ... then from any civill profession whatever,' and he accepts office as mayor of Grimsby.[47] At the end of the century and beginning of the next, Roger North's subject is the members of an old aristocratic family who made their way in the professions, especially law, and in commerce, as well as in public service: the worlds of the lawyer and merchant loom larger in his lives than the world of the aristocrat. This biographical type does not seem to continue as a vital form in England past the early years of the eighteenth century, perhaps because even though the aristocracy long remained powerful the aristocratic sense of family was already in decline.

CHAPTER 11

Roger North: Lives of the Norths

I

Roger North's *Lives of the Norths* are not only in many ways the culmination of the seventeenth-century type of biography shaped as family history represented by Gervase Holles, but they are the first in which new biographical principles of the kind that had been developed by John Aubrey are comprehensively applied to the writing of full-scale lives. While Aubrey did not aim for completeness, and even the longest of his and Holles's biographical sketches are relatively brief, Roger North at the end of the seventeenth and in the early years of the eighteenth century wrote, together with his autobiography, long, full, and rounded lives of his three brothers: the lawyer and statesman Francis, who became Lord Keeper and was ennobled as Lord Guilford, the merchant Dudley, who made his fortune in trade and was a notable economist and public official, and the scholar John, who was Master of Trinity College, Cambridge.[1]

Roger North emphasizes his aim as a biographer for completeness of representation of his subject at the opening of his life of Francis: 'I hope to give a clear account of all I know or can gather of his lordship's life, interior and exterior, whereby in one place or other there may be found a great man's life and entire character.'[2] North achieves this aim for comprehensiveness in the writing of lives to an unprecedented degree. He does not often display such flashes of brilliance as Aubrey, but he possesses much of Aubrey's concern for the individual and intimate, much of his sense of the importance of minute detail, and much of his candour, while he gives, as Aubrey does not, extensive and ordered accounts both of the private lives and the professional and public careers of his subjects. In many respects he provides fuller depictions of his subjects than any previous English biographer.

Roger North's composition of his biographies extended from the last decades of the seventeenth century into the early decades of the eighteenth century. He did not complete the lives in their final forms until the 1720s, when in his later years he was living in retirement on his country estate at Rougham in Norfolk, and they were not published until 1742–4, when a posthumous edition prepared by his son Montagu North appeared; but the biographies were gradually shaped and revised over many years, and Roger's first composition of them began in the 1680s and 1690s.[3] Most of Roger's own life (1651–1734) belongs to the seventeenth century, and his three subjects all died well before the end of the century.[4] While his work has attracted some interest in recent years as an anticipation of Johnson and Boswell,[5] his lives are as truly seen as the climax of the seventeenth-century movement toward a new kind of biography.

North often expressed the sense that he was an innovator in biography, and he had good reason for making such claims. Although in the most radical aspects of his lives, his concern for individuality, intimacy, and candour, he had been anticipated by Aubrey and to some extent by Holles, their work remained unpublished and unknown. He had some acquaintance with Aubrey; he describes him as a 'professed virtuoso,' 'always replete with new discoveries,' and tells us that Aubrey frequently visited his brother Francis, 'who encouraged him by his attention';[6] but Roger appears to have developed his biographical principles and methods quite independently. Despite its radical aspects, however, in many ways his work grows out of traditions well established in the course of the seventeenth century and his lives belong to easily recognizable types of the period: not only biography as family history, but biography as defence of controversial public figures, and biography as an exemplary form.

Although North writes primarily of members of a single generation, the affinities of his biographies with the seventeenth-century tradition of aristocratic family history are apparent in many ways. The North brothers were members of a noble family long prominent in English history, which had its own tradition of biographical writing. An earlier member of the family had produced the North translation of Plutarch's lives, and Roger tells us that his father, Dudley, Lord North, wrote an autobiography and a life of Edward, first Baron North. Roger indicates in a letter that he began his first biography, the life of Francis, for the instruction of Francis's son, the second Lord Guilford, and he states in prefaces that he writes in large part from family motives, for the information of descendants.[7]

These motives were fused with affection for the brothers he desired to commemorate and with special gratitude to Francis, the second son among the many children of their noble house, for raising the fortunes of the family, which had fallen low, and for providing the foundation for his own prosperity, since, as he states, he made his fortune as a lawyer in three years when Francis was Lord Keeper. He comments near the end of his life of Francis: 'I have here showed how a half-decayed family with a numerous brood and worn-out estate, of the Norths, by the auspicious character of one child of ten was re-edified; and all the rest lifted into the world with wonderful success.'[8] Like Holles's lives, North's gain from their aspect as family history qualities of intimacy and candour that develop naturally in lives written by a member of the family for other members of the same family. Like Holles also, North works in terms of a comparative method, implicitly or explicitly developing parallels and contrasts between his subjects in a way that arises naturally in family history.

North writes, however, with public as well as private family purposes, especially in defence of the character and career of Francis. The defence was necessary because the Norths were adherents of a party and political philosophy that had been defeated and fallen into disrepute, supporters of the royal prerogative in the reigns of Charles II and James II. Francis and John died before the Revolution of 1688, but Dudley and Roger, who lived beyond it, retained Jacobite sympathies. Roger is much concerned in the lives to defend the principles and integrity of Francis and Dudley as public officials, for, as he states in his prefaces, he finds that they are either slandered or ignored by the current 'Whig' historians. In response to criticism of Francis in White Kennett's *A Complete History of England* (1706) and similar works, he reshaped his life of the Lord Keeper to give it a more public dimension than he evidently intended in his original purpose of writing for members of the family.[9] Thus the *Lives of the Norths* takes its place in the long list of biographies written in defence of adherents of apparently defeated causes, which includes Cavendish's *Wolsey*, Roper's *More*, and the lives of Anglican ecclesiastics and Royalists written during the Interregnum.

Ultimately, however, North conducted his most detailed defence of Francis's part in public life in a separate work, the *Examen*,[10] and he evidently conceived his biographies in their final versions as having a broadly exemplary more than a narrowly political aim, even though he was highly critical of the defects of the type of exemplary tradition that dominated much seventeenth-century biography. His vigorous condemnation of falsity in the exemplary religious tradition as represented by Burnet's lives of Hale and Rochester has already been noted. While he commends his subjects for their good religious principles where appropriate, like Holles he dislikes ostentatious piety. In his life of Dudley he declares that in historical relations no man can be a hero as in romance, and he makes it plain that his subjects are far from being saints.[11] Yet rather than breaking so fully with the exemplary tradition in biography as Aubrey does, he broadens and secularizes it. Thus he provides much detail about Francis's legal studies and conduct of law business for the instruction of the young man of good family embarking on a legal career, and much in his life of Dudley is intended to show the young merchant the route to success. He offers negative as well as positive lessons, showing in his life of John excessive timidity and lack of self-confidence as errors to be avoided. Maintaining the exemplary value of biography in private and domestic as well as public and professional life, he aims to provide through the lives of his brothers models and instruction also in such areas as family life and education of children.

II

As his criticism of the defects of exemplary religious biographies suggests, North has the kind of self-consciousness about biographical principles and methods that appears earlier in Aubrey and later in Johnson and Boswell. This is an aspect of his work that has deservedly begun to attract increased attention in recent years, particularly with the publication for the first time of his manuscript 'General Preface.' He states his principles and describes his innovations fully in this 'General Preface' as well as in the three biographies themselves. He sets out his key principles thus in a passage in the life of Francis:

> If the history of a life hangs altogether upon great importances such as concern the church and state, and drops the peculiar economy and private conduct of the person that gives title to the work, it may be a history and a very good one; but of any thing rather than of that person's life. Some may think designs of that nature to be, like the plots of Mr. Bays, good only to bring in fine things: but a life should be a picture; which cannot be good if the peculiar features whereby the subject is distinguished from all others

are left out. Nay, scars and blemishes as well as beauties ought to be expressed; otherwise it is but an outline filled up with lillies and roses.[12]

Nearly all the essential principles of the 'new biography' are here: the central concern with individuality: 'the peculiar features whereby the subject is distinguished from all others,' the insistence on the distinction between biography and history, the concern for private life, and for candour, honesty, and balance.

Making the proper distinction between biography and history is a leading concern of North's, reiterated in many of his statements of principles. He complains in the 'General Preface': 'in all our bibliothecs we scarce find a book writ of lives, but what is done chiefly to introduce the history of the time, or for some other special by-end or purpose. And if any pages are spent upon the person, or his ordinary behaviour, it is perfunctory.' As well as emphasizing the need for the biographer to keep his eye on his proper subject, he repeatedly insists on the importance of giving full treatment to private and domestic life in addition to the public career. He declares that among existing biographies, 'I have scarce found a person taken up and set down again in a private capacity.'[13]

Recognizing like Aubrey the value of minute and apparently trivial details, in his 'General Preface' he defends his inclusion of them against critics, particularly in relation to private life: 'some will say what pleasure can there be in reading the account of a private man's economy, how he was educated, matched, governed his family, conducted his affairs or passed his time?' In his life of Francis he answers such objections first by the argument of utility, stating he has set down things which some may complain are too trivial but the smaller incidents in the life of a busy man are often as useful to be known as the greater. Later in this life he provides his most eloquent statement of the fundamental value of minute detail in biography and history:

> Some may also allege that I bring forward circumstances too minute. ... [B]ut I fancy myself a picture-drawer and aiming to give the same image to a spectator as I have of the thing itself which I desire should here be represented. As for instance a tree, in the picture whereof the leaves and minor branches are very small and confused, and give the artist more pain to describe than the solid trunk and greater branches. But if these small things were left out it would make but a sorry picture of a tree. History is as it were, the portrait or lineament and not a bare index or catalogue of

things done; and without the how and why all history is jejune and unprofitable.[14]

North's insistence on fullness and completeness, including extensive accounts of private life and well-informed analysis of character, requires exceptionally close knowledge of the subject. He anticipates Johnson and Boswell in holding that such knowledge can be gained only by prolonged and intimate acquaintance with the subject, and that such intimacy is essential for the biographer.[15] In his 'General Preface' he states: 'a life-writer in education, friendship, conversation, and all commerce of life ought to be the nearest of any allied to his subject, and not a contingent gatherer or compiler only.' Biographers, he holds, must have been

> in almost continual conversation or converse with the subjects, and so attached to the very persons, that little of importance in their whole lives could escape their notice. Such friendships often happen between persons who live almost at bed and board together, and communicate to each other their most recondite thoughts and designs, and profit each other by mutual counsel. Such as these are so far qualified to be authors of lives. But where this intimacy is not found, men (as I said) may gather and compile what is called a life, but is in truth anything else rather than that of which it bears the name.

In keeping with this emphasis on the importance of intimate biography, North doubts the possibility of writing satisfactory lives of persons long dead. He states at the opening of his biography of John North that in such cases 'the life-scraps come out very thin and meagre. And after great length of time how should it come off better?'[16]

Roger North himself possessed the intimate knowledge of his subjects that these statements postulate for the biographer. He and three brothers remained close to each other all their lives. When Francis rose in the law he made Roger his assistant and protégé. Roger writes they were so near allied in family, education, and profession 'that we were almost inseparable,' and tells us: 'I passed almost all the active time of my life in his company.' He had a similarly close knowledge of Dudley during the earlier and later parts of this brother's life, although no first-hand knowledge of the middle years when Dudley was a merchant in Turkey. He was able to fill this gap not only by means of letters but through conversations after Dudley's return to England, when their intimacy was so great that Dudley's good-humoured wife sometimes complained of it. He was in fact really closer to Dudley than to Francis, by whom he was over-awed. The life of John was a special problem, for this brother suffered from such acute despondency and sense of failure that, as Roger laments, he took 'express care that nothing real should remain whereby in after times he might be remembered.' Fortunately, Roger's memory was well stocked: he had been in the same college at Cambridge as John and had his company at times in London.[17]

Roger's other qualifications as a biographer include a very wide range of interests and experiences. He was a Restoration virtuoso with interests as diverse as Aubrey's, in mathematics, science, invention, philosophy, history, politics, painting, and agriculture. Although he published only a few minor works, among the writings he left in manuscript are important discourses on music and an interesting treatise on architecture.[18] He took advantage of all opportunities to observe public events like the proclamation of the accession of James II in a way that sometimes reminds one of Pepys. With the help of Francis he gained wide experience not only of law but of public affairs, government, and royal courts. In contrast to Aubrey, who was unable to hold on to his inherited properties, Roger North possessed sufficient practical abilities to enable him, with the aid of his family connections, to acquire a substantial estate. He declares in his autobiography that his legal practice and life on the circuit gave him knowledge of men. This range of experience provided him with the essential foundation, both the knowledge and perspective, for his representation and judgment of his brothers and their achievements.

III

Perhaps the greatest of all Roger's assets as a biographer is one that he does not say much about in his statements of principles: his knowledge and understanding of character, psychology, and motive. He writes at one point in his life of John that he proposes to 'consider his natural temper and propensities, such as of one kind or another all men living have, and which came into the world with them, and are in their power to alter no more than complexion or stature.'[19] He has the ability to analyse and describe the propensities of his subjects, to show the ways in which their characters are shaped throughout their lives by these qualities, and also the ways in which they learn to overcome or at least restrain certain tendencies. He identifies such qualities without oversimplifying: while he shows action as generally inseparable from character, he sometimes records surprises that seem to contradict the essentials of character.

North not only analyses the special propensities of each of the three brothers but he uses their characters to shed light on each other. It has sometimes been suggested that one life be read in preference to the others. F.P. Wilson recommended the life of John, and this was the first to be edited and republished in recent years. Donald Stauffer preferred the life of Dudley, and others have considered the life of Francis to be the best.[20] But such a debate misses the point that the three gain much of their interest from being read together, as is implied by the 'General Preface' Roger wrote for the three lives collectively. They are parts of a larger design, and the whole is greater than its parts, in a way that is characteristic of biographies written in the context of family history.

Although Roger's comparisons between his three brothers are more implicit than explicit, so that each biography can be read independently of the others, the lives of the Norths are really most notable as a trilogy, or as a quartet if we include Roger's autobiography, developed on the principle of comparative biography, studies in similarities and differences. The similarities are important. Roger shows that the three brothers faced the same problems, as the younger sons of an impoverished noble family. The similarities include not only politics, which as Roger says often runs in families,[21] but tastes, such as the love of music they derived from their parents. All were under certain pressures from the family background as well as being helped in other ways by it. We see that the demands and oppressions of the tyrannical old lord, their grandfather, may help explain the diffidence Roger and two of his brothers (but not Dudley) suffered from. But Roger shows that divergences between his three brothers also appeared early, even in childhood. In contrast to many of those exemplary biographers he criticizes, he differentiates well both the characters and careers of his subjects, and he clearly distinguishes the different patterns of their lives. With Francis the pattern is brilliant success followed by tragedy; Dudley, the happiest of the three, experiences success without tragedy; the life of John is almost unmitigated tragedy.

Roger represents Francis as the most complex of the three characters. He shows that this brother's natural inclination was toward the life of a cultured gentleman of leisure. Francis possessed broad interests in art, literature, and science, as well as a liking for country sports and other pleasurable activities; and he told Roger that he would never have become a lawyer if he had a hundred pounds a year. But he knew from an early time that he must make his own way in the world. A realist, he took to the study of law with great diligence, although relieving this dry study with more agreeable recreations.

Roger shows that the essential and dominating quality of Francis's character was always prudence, and that his success was founded on his self-knowledge, self-control, and shrewd understanding of human nature. All the Norths were choleric, Roger states, and at bottom Francis may have been as subject to passion as the others, but he learned to restrain himself. He sensed that men were most honest when most passionate, and he was careful never to give himself away in speech or manner. Recognizing and controlling his own weaknesses, Francis had the same understanding of others, and the ability to exploit their weaknesses. Roger comments, 'next to Machiavel, none ever understood human nature better.' He insists much on Francis's integrity as judge, showing that on occasion he delivered judgments against his brother Dudley and in favour of his enemy, Lord Macclesfield, but reveals he was not above making use of the prejudices of other judges.[22]

In Francis's character, Roger shows, prudence was combined with a second dominant quality, one weakness he never learned to overcome: timidity, diffidence, lack of self-confidence. As a young lawyer he was too bashful to enter the hall of his Inn of Court except in the company of others, and he waited at the door until others came along. This natural timidity remained a permanent part of his character and affected his life to the end. Roger holds that this weakness, in combination with his integrity, brought about the tragedy of the later part of his life. Ironically his greatest success, his elevation to the position of Lord Keeper, was the ruin of his happiness. This office, which he accepted from a sense of duty, proved to be a disease like consumption, cured only by death. His prudence was not enough to preserve him in the world of the royal court into which he was then plunged. He was no courtier, and his bashfulness and timidity made him out of place in the courts of Charles II and James II. He was uneasy in attendance there, he resented the importunities of the courtiers, and he became a completely isolated figure.

After the accession of James II, as Roger shows, Francis's situation became even more difficult than under Charles II. He was distrusted at the new court because, although he was a supporter of the royal prerogative, he was equally a supporter of the Church of England, and he could not accede to James's Roman Catholic designs. But Roger holds that this tragic period was Francis's finest hour. His principles, which he refused to abandon, caused him to cease being a 'Tory' and become a 'Trimmer,' although he was under constant attack from the notorious Chief Justice Jeffreys. Yet he did not resign the Great Seal, although he often meditated it, and the strains of his position contributed to his fatal sickness. Roger comments at the end of Francis's life that his brother's distemper was caused by his taking things too much to heart and his conscientiousness in business: he lacked the apathy necessary for tranquillity.[23]

Roger represents Dudley's character as simpler, more extrovert and happier than Francis's. He shows that Dudley had much of Francis's industry and desire for worldly success but was less inhibited, with none of his older brother's bashfulness and timidity. Optimism, forwardness and confidence, both flexibility and decisiveness were prominent in his character from childhood.

Like Francis, Dudley recognized from his youth that he must make his own way in the world, but law and learning were not for him. His interest was in practical matters, and accordingly his parents wisely decided he should become a merchant. Lacking Francis's prudence, he sometimes went astray. As a boy learning his trade in London, he took advantage of opportunities for dissipation, and gambled and got in debt, while later in Turkey he took to drinking too much, but in all such cases he corrected himself by making what he called a 'short turn' to bring himself back to a proper course. He was not so concerned as Francis to hide his real nature, for example the choler that ran in the family, but would lose his temper with knaves; and after his return to England he would sometimes fall back into Turkish because he found the language so adapted to scolding.[24]

Roger shows that during Dudley's years as a merchant in Turkey his aim was always to build up a fortune so that he could return to England and enjoy it. In his time there he worked hard and lived economically, although taking the opportunities life offered for pleasure. His extrovert character and affability, that easiness Francis lacked in getting on with all manner of people, were essential to his success. His flexibility and versatility were shown in his willingness not only to learn the Turkish language but to adjust himself to Turkish ways of life and even to adopt Turkish dress.

At every stage of his life Dudley appears as a much bolder and more decisive character than Francis. As Roger comments about a hazardous voyage this brother made in youth to Archangel, once Dudley was resolved on a course he was not deterred by any difficulty. He had some failures, but whenever he had good luck he seized upon it and made the most of it. His great opportunity came when he was taken into an English firm in Constantinople, and there he quickly made his fortune. He was equally resolute in abandoning unsuccessful ventures, leaving an earlier post in Smyrna when after some years it became clear he would not make a fortune there, and leaving the firm in Constantinople finally when it became more advantageous for him to set up in business for himself. He took this course rather than palliate inconveniences, in striking contrast to Francis's retention of the Great Seal in intolerable circumstances.

These qualities of character were combined in Dudley with skill in accountancy and bookkeeping, and a mastery of economics that was eventually embodied in a notable treatise on the subject. Roger describes how, after making his fortune in Turkey, Dudley returned to England and took an important part in the royal service, in the management of customs and taxation, and shows that his boldness of character appeared in his remaining in England after the Revolution of 1688, although he had been urged to flee because of his official role under James II. In his later years as in his earlier ones he enjoyed a happiness denied his brothers Francis and John. This sprang, as Roger suggests, from his philosophy of life: he had learned a most useful principle: 'to lay nothing to heart which he could not help.'[25]

While Dudley stands on one side of Francis, bolder, more extrovert, and happier, John stands very much on the other side. Roger shows that the timidity which was a part of Francis's character appeared even more strongly in John, indeed to an extraordinary degree. As John was the most studious and introverted of the brothers even in his schooldays, he was destined from early years for the church. He adopted an academic career at Cambridge, and lived austerely, dedicating himself to books and allowing himself little diversion. Helped to preferment by his aristocratic family and by the influence of Francis after the latter had risen to high place, he became Master of Trinity College. But this advancement proved an even greater personal catastrophe for him than the elevation to Lord Keeper for Francis. His nature was so retiring and lacking in self-confidence that his public position caused him the utmost misery. He suffered such unpopularity with students upon whom he tried to impose discipline that on one occasion Roger describes a stone was hurled through his window; and his college's fellows so quarrelled with him that at the end of his life he asked to be buried in the antechapel, 'that the fellows might trample upon him dead, as they had done living.'[26] These miseries, combined with over-studiousness and excessive scrupulousness, brought upon him both physical and psychological disorders. He was stricken by paralysis and passed his last years in a most pitiable condition, infirm both in body and mind.

Roger North's life of his brother John is a concrete representation of those miseries of scholars so vividly described by Robert Burton in his digression on the subject in *The Anatomy of Melancholy*. Thanks to his family connections and preferments, John did not suffer the poverty of Burton's typical scholar, but he suffered acutely from most of the other miseries, including solitude and ill health. Roger North holds with Burton that the sedentary life is unhealthy, and suggests that a life of action would not have allowed time for such anxieties as John developed. He comments that John lacked spirit, courage, and even philosophy to fill the gap, and shows that his diffidence affected his scholarly work as well as other aspects of his life: he was never satisfied with what he had written but published little of it and ordered his manuscripts destroyed on his death.

Nothing in the *Lives of the Norths* is more vividly described than John's extraordinary timidity and fearfulness. Roger suggests that this timidity sprang from a feeble constitution of body, inclining to the effeminate:

> One would have expected that a youth at the university, no freshman, nor mean scholar, should have got the better of being afraid in the dark; but it was not so with him, for when he was abed, if alone, he durst not trust his countenance above the clothes. For some time he lay with his tutor, who once coming home found the scholar abed, with only his crown visible. The tutor (indiscreetly enough) pulled him by the hair, whereupon the scholar sank down, and the tutor followed, and at last with a great outcry, the scholar sprang up, expecting to see an enorme spectre.

Timidity and the increasing sense of failure were linked in John's character with extreme self-effacement. Roger tells us that his brother had the strange practice of effacing even the mark his body left on his bed after he rose, and that the only portrait surviving of him was as a schoolboy, because he would never afterwards allow one to be made, even though Sir Peter Lely wished to paint him. Finally he desired to be utterly forgotten.[27]

Roger North is conscious of the paradoxical nature of this biography of a figure who wished to be forgotten, but he succeeds in making this study of failure just as memorable as the studies in success in the other two biographies. The psychological depth and penetrating analysis of the neurotic character of John make this biography worthy to stand with the other two lives as completing a trilogy remarkable not only for North's combination of fullness and complexity but also for his skill in bringing out the individual differences between the three brothers, rather than blurring distinctions in order to emphasize similarities in the manner of Walton and Fell.

IV

North is successful in these lives partly because, in keeping with his statements of his principles, he maintains the proper distinction between biography and history better than many earlier seventeenth-century biographers. In his 'General Preface' he emphasizes his adherence to this distinction, even though his three brothers all had 'considerable posts of preferment, and two of them concerned deep in affairs of the public': 'yet I stand to my point, that the lives I write are private; for I shall not go out of my way to fall upon foreign affairs or national concerns, at least not so much as may be expected, and indeed no more than in the lives of those persons is absolutely necessary to account for their passing their time, and what they immediately transacted, and no further.'[28] In contrast to such biographers as Heylyn in the life of Laud, North is careful in his lives of Francis and Dudley not to allow the individuals to become submerged in general or political history.

This is not to say that North's concern with the private dimensions of life causes him to neglect the more public and professional aspects. In fact he gives greater prominence to the public and especially the professional than to the intimately private aspects. He provides detailed narratives and analyses of Francis's career both in law and politics, showing the interrelation between the two spheres. He deserves indeed to be credited with providing the first full English biography of a lawyer, in contrast to earlier lives of figures like More and Bacon which really gave little attention to their legal careers and attainments.[29] The public aspects of life naturally loom largest in this biography, but it helps Roger to maintain the distinction between biography and history that he can separately place his more general commentary on the history of the period in his *Examen*.

Roger deals in appropriate ways also with the careers of Dudley and John. In his account of Dudley's period in Turkey he takes his eyes off his subject more than elsewhere, and introduces a long digression on Turkish life and history, but despite his limitations of knowledge he succeeds in providing the first extensive biography of an English merchant. For this brother's later life, although he tells us little of the important treatise on economics for which Dudley North is now chiefly remembered,[30] Roger gives a good account of his abilities as a public official in customs and revenue. While the life of John North differs from the other two, both because he did not take any prominent part in public life and because his professional career, as scholar and academic administrator, was a tragic failure, Roger provides as full an account of his academic activities as this brother's deliberate destruction of the evidence permits, and the psychological depth he brings to this study makes it perhaps the most memorable of the many lives of scholars that had been produced for a century or more in England, just as in the lives of Francis and Dudley he achieves fuller and more satisfactory biographies of a lawyer and a merchant than any previous English writer.

Much more fully than many earlier biographers, Roger North recognizes that public and private life are inseparable. He shows that the same qualities of character predominate in both and that neither is comprehensible without an understanding of the other. He brings out many of the special links between the personal and the professional and political levels in the lives of his brothers. Thus he reveals the importance of Francis's family connections and personal friendships, like one with the son of Attorney-General Sir Geoffrey Palmer, as factors in this brother's success as a lawyer and rise to high office. Similarly he reveals Francis's influence, after he had gained power, in furthering the careers of Dudley and John, as well as Roger's own career, and shows that both Francis and John were aided by friendship with the Duke of Lauderdale. This is in contrast to earlier biographies like Harris's life of Arthur Lake, which narrates Lake's advancement to a bishopric without mentioning the influence of his brother as Secretary of State.[31]

In the life of Francis, Roger complements his account of his brother's legal and public career with systematic accounts of the private life from time to time. He introduces one such passage with the promise to give a description of 'all his lordship's concerns and reflections, as well of those in which himself alone was interested as others which might affect and influence the public; such as matching, residences, fortunes, entertainments, reflections, doubts, melancholies, confidences, with his arts of governing himself and his passions.' He carries out this program most elaborately in a section of the life where he moves first from the public to the domestic sphere, and then finally takes his brother from domestic life into the privacy of solitude, with this announcement: 'But now I must cashier all those matters and retire with his lordship into his solitudes, and show him there as he was both a moral philosopher and a good Christian.'[32] In the life of Dudley, Roger marks a similar movement from the public career into domestic and private life with the declaration: 'But now we have our merchant, sheriff, alderman, commissioner, &c. at home with us, a private person divested of all his mantlings; and we may converse freely with him in his family and by himself without clashing at all against any concern of the public. And possibly, in this capacity I may show the best side of his character.'[33]

Roger does not always provide us with as much information as we might like about his brothers' domestic lives, but he shows us that their marriages were in keeping with their characters. In Francis's choice of a wife, as one might expect, prudential considerations of family and fortune predominated, but the marriage appears to have been happy enough until the early death of his wife. Dudley, in accordance with his combination of worldly prudence and liking for a pleasurable life, chose a wife who had some fortune and was good humoured. Roger brings out well Dudley's fondness for her and their children. He tells us that his brother enjoyed her company and spent much time with her, and he gives memorably intimate pictures of their family life: 'If time lay on his hands he would assist his lady in her affairs. I have come there and found him very busy in picking out the stitches of a dislaced petticoat. But his tenderness to his children was very uncommon, for he would often sit by while they were dressing and undressing and would be assisting himself, if they were at any time sick or out of order.'[34] In the strongly contrasting case of John, Roger suggests that the failure to marry contributed to his unhappiness and ill health.

Roger recognizes the importance of providing information about his subjects' friendships as well as about their domestic lives. He gives systematic accounts of Francis's friendships at more than one period in his life, not only those that helped advance his career but others that reflect his various cultural interests, with such figures as the painter Sir Peter Lely and the architect Hugh May and virtuosos like John Aubrey. But the friendships he describes most fully are those between the four North brothers themselves.

Roger is excellent on the habits of his subjects in both work and leisure. He gives us typical schedules of their days, an element rarely found in earlier biographies. He provides such schedules for Francis at the various stages of his life, showing how the daily pattern was affected by his official positions and by his domestic status as single, married, or widower, and how it varied according to the seasons of the year and the legal terms. Roger's accounts of Dudley's habits serve to demonstrate this brother's skill in balancing business and pleasure, in contrast to John's austere and restricted way of life.

In order to bring out their individual characters, Roger displays quite fully his brothers' personal interests and recreations. He shows that Francis, as his friendship with artists demonstrates, had like himself the wide-ranging interests of a Restoration virtuoso, which included a passionate love of music all his life, and an enjoyment of all forms of shows and entertainments: on one occasion, Roger tells us, Francis even went 'so low as to hear Hugh Peters preach.' He shows that Dudley was less interested in art and literature, and more inclined to extroverted activities and practical subjects, in youth such recreations as swimming in the Thames and cock-fighting, and in mature years pursuits in science and technology, as well as in business and commerce. He describes how Dudley in his later years carried out scientific experiments in spare rooms in his London house and fitted up outbuildings on Francis's estate at Wroxton for working as a blacksmith and carpenter.[35]

Roger North at times anticipates Samuel Johnson and Sir Joshua Reynolds, who according to Boswell agreed that 'the real character of a man was found out by his amusements.'[36] He reveals much of the contrast between the four brothers by showing the favourite recreations of each. Francis's greatest joy was as a musician; Dudley was happiest when working as a carpenter and blacksmith at Wroxton, while Roger's own happiest moments were spent on a yacht: he informs us that for him a day spent yachting came closest to perfection. In the case of John, Roger deplores the unhealthy lack of recreation. He tells us that such pleasures as this brother had were closely connected with his studies and gives a memorable description of John's joy in book-collecting: 'He courted as a fond lover all best editions, fairest characters, best bound and preserved. ... His soul was never so staked down as in an old Latin-boo[k]seller's shop.' Roger tells us that John shared Francis's love of music, and brought retaliation on himself from his neighbours by playing an organ in his college rooms, but his other amusement was a curious and unexpected one: 'keeping of great house spiders in wide-mouthed glasses, such as men keep tobacco in.' He delighted to observe the spiders making webs and eating their prey, and he sometimes caught flies to feed them. In Roger's narrative the spiders and flies assume symbolic value, representing John's confined and fearful life.[37]

V

More fully than earlier English biographers, Roger shows his characters in the dimension of time. He emphasizes the importance of this aspect of biography in his 'General Preface': 'I should gladly meet with an author that in the course of a written life delineates to us in lively examples the precipitous steps and dangerous meanders of youth, the difficulties of riper years, and the fondnesses of old age, and where one may see distinctly the early application of some persons to proper employments, with the eventual prosperities attending them.'[38] Aubrey had earlier recognized the need for a series of portraits to reflect a character's changes through time, and he applied this principle most notably in his life of Hobbes, but only on a relatively small scale. Many biographers like Cavendish and Hacket had of course depicted the rise and fall of their subjects, but none had attempted to show so fully as North the effects of time on their subjects: changes not only in circumstances but in appearance, in habits, in health, and in ideas and outlook.

This is not to say that North provides much chronological precision. In fact he gives few dates and seems to recognize their importance no more than do many earlier seventeenth-century biographers: in his life of Francis he does not state clearly the date even of Francis's marriage or of his elevation to the office of Lord Keeper.[39] Roger represents his characters' development in what he regards as the main periods of their lives rather than year by year: four phases in Francis's life and three in Dudley's. He shows the effects of time largely in the broad terms of these phases.

North does not provide very full accounts of the early years of his subjects but he goes further than many earlier biographers in recognizing the importance of childhood. Since Francis was fourteen years older than himself he had no first-hand knowledge of this brother's childhood, and he writes apologetically: 'We have little to say of him during his minor years, but shall make amends afterwards.' He does better in the cases of Dudley and John. He demonstrates that Dudley showed his extrovert, gregarious, and confident character from his earliest years: when taken outside for airing as a child at the Norths' London house, 'by his forward familiarities, he had made himself known to most people that had to do thereabouts; and nothing so common as his being at his post with an audience in the street to share his conversation.' In schooldays at Bury St Edmunds, Dudley revealed other essential qualities of his character: he was little interested in books but he 'had a strange bent to traffic and, while he was at school, drove a subtle trade among the boys by buying and selling.' Roger shows that John's quite opposite character was also apparent during his schooldays: he was less vigorous and athletic than his brothers, and had a 'reserved and studious' temper and a 'non-natural gravity.' While Dudley as a child was too active for books, John was just the reverse.[40]

In all the lives Roger does 'make amends' for the brevity of his treatment of childhood, not only by giving full accounts of manhood and maturity but also by providing memorable pictures of the later years of his subjects, when they were afflicted by age or illness. Dudley, who had never expected to live to an old age, died relatively young with unimpaired faculties, but Francis and John, although they did not survive to a great age either, were both much afflicted by declines in health and spirits in later years. Roger vividly conveys the pathos of John's mental condition, when after suffering the stroke that left him impaired in body and mind he decided he had earlier been too severe with himself, demanded merry tales from those around him, and 'often laughed, but (as his visage was then distorted) most deformly'; and he gives a horrifying account of John's suffering at the hands of ignorant and barbarous physicians. He shows that old age and ill health, rather than bringing out the best, may often aggravate defects of character. He describes how in Francis's final sickness, 'All that was pecularly good in his humour left him,' and his life-long prudence turned into avarice, and how John in his afflicted condition also developed increasingly avaricious tendencies. Thus the lives of Francis and John provide a strong contrast to the edifying pictures of the final days of life developed by biographers in the exemplary religious tradition.[41]

Although he lacks Aubrey's special genius in rendering visual details, the appearance, clothing, and gestures of his subjects, Roger recognizes their significance, and he shows the way they change with time and age. He describes Francis's appearance early in his career, when he wore the deliberately unostentatious dress of a young lawyer, and shows that the 'spider-kind of life' of the lawyer made him increasingly hypochondriac, so that he later wore broad stomachers on his chest and commonly a leather skullcap, which in his prosperous years he used as a money bag for coins. In the life of Dudley, Roger describes the change from the athletic youth to the middle years in Turkey, when this brother grew fat, was well whiskered, and made the kind of jolly appearance the Turks approved of in a man; and he gives a memorable picture of Dudley's exotic dress and appearance on his return to England: 'with his mustachios, according to the Turkish manner, *Cordubee* hat and strange out-of-the-way clothes, just as if one had been dressed up to act Captain Dangerfield in the play.' In contrast, Roger conveys the unhealthy, timid, and introspective nature of John in a description of his method of walking, weak and shuffling, often crossing his legs as if tipsy, even before he was afflicted by the terrible disabilities of his later years.[42]

VI

North's frank treatment of the afflictions of age illustrates the candour he brings to his biographies. The closeness to his subjects that provides intimate knowledge obviously rules out complete objectivity, but he is very much aware of the dangers of bias and suppression, and he carries candour further than most seventeenth-century biographers, with the notable exception of Aubrey. His lives demonstrate his determination to break free of the limitations he criticizes in exemplary religious biography. They reflect the view he states in his discussion of biographical principles that in historical relations no man can be a hero as in romance and that the biographer must show his subjects' scars and blemishes. In his life of Dudley, for example, as well as describing this brother's youthful dissipations, he states that he supposes Dudley in Turkey employed the normal tricks of trade and that like other English merchants there he enjoyed certain sexual 'diversions.' In the life of Francis he declares that he writes 'as if I were sworn; entirely assured that all the good is true and the evil of him no other, nor more in any respect, than in this work I have expressed.' There were few dissipations to be chronicled in the case of this prudent brother, but Roger makes us sufficiently aware of the Machiavellian aspects of his character and methods, and reveals the conflicts and controversies that arose from his ambitious nature and drive to advancement and wealth.[43]

It is in the life of John that Roger shows most fully his candour and his break with the biographical tradition of dignified formality. Episodes like the one that depicts John cowering beneath his bedclothes in fright from an imaginary ghost are a refreshing departure from the decorum of dignity that had crippled so many seventeenth-century biographies, as in a different way is the picture of Dudley picking stitches from his wife's petticoat. In the later part of the life of John, after Roger embarks on the 'uneasy task' of describing this brother's mental decay, 'according to the profession I make of truth, for better or worse,' he leaves us with the sense that he has indeed concealed very little.[44]

North's rejection of the decorum of vague dignified generalization that prevailed in much exemplary religious biography is shown in many aspects of his work. He understands the importance of the anecdote and the concrete example. In demonstrating the young Francis's skill as a lawyer he states that he will provide examples of his conduct in particular matters: 'because his character may better appear by such than by general eulogies, I will subjoin one or two of his dexterous exploits.' His minuteness of detail and lack of false reticence appear in the information he gives us about the financial affairs of his subjects. He tells us the exact amount of the allowance Francis received in youth from his family, the amounts of his annual income at various stages of his career, and the value of his estate at his death. Few precedents exist in earlier English biography for this fullness of financial detail, important though such matters must be in many lives.[45]

Despite his achievement of such valuable qualities as this concreteness in his writing, Roger North like Aubrey was never satisfied with what he had written, as he states in his autobiography: 'For I was ever pleased to be wrighting somewhat or other, and striving at method, and clearness, but could not attaine, so as to perfect any one designe.' However, although he agreed with Aubrey that sketches are more lively than finished paintings, he left better-ordered manuscript drafts of his lives than Aubrey, and his biographies have much more the quality of the finished work. It seems appropriate that while Aubrey was the friend of Samuel Cooper, the painter of vividly lifelike and individual miniatures, North, much as he valued intimacy in portraiture, was the friend and executor of Sir Peter Lely, whose portraits are larger in scale, often full length, and more formal and finished in style.[46]

North provides a number of statements of his stylistic principles. In his 'General Preface' he maintains: 'the same ingredients that are usually brought to adorn fiction may come forward, and be as well applied to the setting forth of truths; that is, choice of words, charming periods, invention of figures, interspersion of sentences, and facetious expressions.' In the life of John he declares he has adopted a conversational style: 'I chose to proceed in a style of familiar conversation, and as one engaged to answer such questions concerning our doctor as may be obviously demanded.'[47] In practice he most commonly employs a quite plain style, without so much artifice as the first statement might lead one to expect or so great an informality as the second might suggest. He does not display such lively colloquial vigour as Aubrey, and in contrast to the smoothly polished styles of such biographers as Fell and Sprat his phrasing and sentence structure are often marked by a certain awkwardness or oddity, which no doubt helps account for his dissatisfaction with his writing: he states that he attempts to rectify or compensate for the want of style by '*copia* of matter.' Among the stylistic oddities that give his writing a strongly individual flavour is the occasional Browne-like coinage of vocabulary from Latin: 'clancular,' 'funest,' 'luculent.'[48] This individuality of style and absence of neoclassical decorum are among the features of his work that mark him as a man of the seventeenth century, whose earliest formative years antedated the Restoration.

Although he advocates the 'invention of figures,' North is sparing in his introduction of imagery. More examples are to be found in the life of John than in the others. He compares John to a flourishing fruit tree which blossomed fairly and then was blighted, and describes him in his later years as like a high-flying owl with one wing cut off. While he provides relatively little such invented imagery, like Cavendish and Walton he has the ability, in a manner appropriate to the biographical mode, to fix upon symbolic objects, actions, and habits in the lives of his subjects, such as John's practice of keeping spiders in jars, and Francis's possession of a skullcap, which is at first the mark of his hypochondria, and later the sign of his growing avarice, when it is used as a bag for coins. He fully matches the biographers of earlier Lord Chancellors and Lord Keepers, Wolsey, More, and Williams, in showing the symbolic value of the Great Seal in the life of Francis. Charles II tells Francis in giving the seal to him: 'you will find it heavy,' and we learn that the weight deprives Francis of all happiness, so that he never afterwards has an easy moment, and finally brings him to the grave. Roger recounts the journey he and Dudley made after Francis's death from his country seat of Wroxton to the royal court to return 'that pestiferous lump of metal.'[49]

Roger North maintains a fine unity of tone throughout the biographies, not unlike that of Holles's *Memorials*: a quiet and mild but pervasive melancholy, which is no doubt related to his decision to withdraw from the city and public life to the more retired life of the country gentleman, and prompted partly by the disillusionments of age and political defeat. There is in his work a strong sense of life as Vanity Fair, but balance and humour, and little bitterness. He is a Thackeray among biographers.

Although there has been some rediscovery and revival of interest in

Roger North in recent years, his lives are still not as well known as they should be. The 'Tory' principles of the North brothers, and their combination of aristocratic and prudential values, have not endeared them to posterity. Roger himself comments on the way in which party politics and prejudices run in families,[50] and the later reputation of his work has no doubt been affected by the dominance of the Whig view of history. His biographies are certainly not without faults and limitations. As his own dissatisfaction with his work suggests, he is not always successful in putting his admirable biographical principles into practice: he does not always achieve as good a balance between the public, professional, and private aspects of life as his theoretical statements postulate, or solve very well his problems of organization.[51] His sometimes rather awkward and clumsy style lacks the liveliness of Aubrey's, the special charm of Walton's, and the magisterial dignity of Fell's. Yet his biographies are much more truly full and complete than Walton's or Fell's, and he goes much further than they do in establishing individuality, in demonstrating 'the peculiar features whereby the subject is distinguished from all others.'[52]

While North's lives are notable for the fullness of the representation of the central figures, they are remarkable also for the excellence of the briefer biographical sketches they contain, and these are a prominent feature also of his autobiography and the *Examen*. They range from fine, balanced pictures of Charles II to the characters even of Francis's and Dudley's horses. At the beginning of his life of Francis, Roger provides some good sketches of members of his family, including his grandfather, the tyrannical and vindictive 'old lord,' and he gives memorable pictures of some family retainers. He inserts in this life an extensive series of brief biographies of those involved with Francis in legal and public life, for which he uses the term 'petit biography.'[53]

North's 'petit biographies' of legal figures are specially good. Among those in the life of Francis are vivid portraits of the notorious Chief Justice Jeffreys, revealing his pathological qualities, and of the curious figure of Chief Justice Edmund Saunders, whose 'character and his beginning were equally strange.' He describes the remarkable way in which Saunders raised himself to legal eminence from the most humble origins, 'no better than a poor beggar boy,' and provides an extraordinary picture of the man's mixed qualities: his repellently ugly, diseased, and stinking body: 'corpulent and beastly; a mere lump of morbid flesh'; his dissipated, sottish style of life; his fine mental abilities; his great goodness of nature; and his great integrity: 'he was as honest as the driven snow was white' and had 'no regard for money or desire to be rich.' In the space of three paragraphs North combines these apparently incongruous elements into an unforgettable whole.[54]

North's special brilliance in this most distinctive and distinguished biographical form of the seventeenth century, the brief life, is one of the features that mark his work as a culmination of that century's achievements. In his fine pioneering study of eighteenth-century biography, Donald Stauffer commented that North's character sketches are 'more finished and thoughtful than the comparable side-panels in Boswell.'[55] While there is much in North's full-scale lives that anticipates the great later biographers, in the art of brief biography he is among those like John Aubrey who have not been excelled by later writers but deserve to be recognized as possessing a classic status. His lives, belonging as they do to two centuries, demonstrate the enduring value of seventeenth-century achievements in biography, as well as providing a notable initiation of eighteenth-century developments.

Notes

Introduction

1 Donald Stauffer, *English Biography before 1700* (Cambridge, Mass.: Harvard University Press, 1930). In a second volume, *The Art of Biography in Eighteenth Century England* (Princeton: Princeton University Press, 1941), Stauffer includes discussion of one important figure who belongs partly to the seventeenth century, Roger North. Vivian de Sola Pinto's *English Biography in the Seventeenth Century: Selected Short Lives* (London: George G. Harrap and Co., 1951) is primarily an anthology but includes a perceptive introduction.
2 See, for example, Paul Delany, *British Autobiography in the Seventeenth Century* (London: Routledge and Kegan Paul, 1969). Like Delany, I view autobiography as a form separate from biography, and do not include it in the present study.
3 For example, David Novarr gives few of the five hundred pages of his otherwise valuable study, *The Making of Walton's Lives* (Ithaca: Cornell University Press, 1958), to examination of the context of seventeenth-century biography. The attempt to examine Walton in this context seems scarcely to have begun until Jessica Martin's *Walton's Lives: Conformist Commemorations and the Rise of Biography* (Oxford University Press, 2001), which is so recent that it did not reach me until I had concluded my own study; it provides approaches and views different from my own. It is indicative of the general neglect of lives written during the period that even well-informed scholars continued in the later twentieth century to produce papers with titles like Robert Halsband's 'The Penury of English Biography before Samuel Johnson,' in *Biography in the Eighteenth Century*, ed. J.D. Browning (New York and London: Garland, 1980), 112–27.

4 Because of the lack of modern editions, more summary and quotation have been provided in this study than would otherwise have seemed necessary. In quotations spelling and punctuation of the originals have been retained, but the amount of italic type has sometimes been reduced when it loses its point outside the original context.
5 See especially Burckhardt's 'Biography in the Middle Ages and in the Renaissance,' in Part IV, 'The Discovery of the World and Man,' in *The Civilization of the Renaissance in Italy*, trans. S.G.C. Middlemore (London: Penguin, 1990), 213–22. Burckhardt stated that the first idea for his great book, published in 1860, came to him in Rome in 1847 on reading a copy of the late fifteenth-century biographies of Vespasiano da Bisticci, as Myron P. Gilmore points out in his introduction to *The Vespasiano Memoirs: Lives of Illustrious Men of the XVth Century*, trans. W. George and E. Waters, Renaissance Society of America Reprint (Toronto: University of Toronto Press, 1997), xi.
6 Peter Burke, Introduction to the Penguin edition of Burckhardt's *The Civilization of the Renaissance in Italy* (1990), 14. Wallace Ferguson's *The Renaissance in Historical Thought* (Cambridge, Mass.: Houghton Mifflin, 1948) is a classic older account of Burckhardt's influence and reactions against him. John Martin provides a critical analysis of some of the more recent reactions in 'Inventing Sincerity, Refashioning Prudence,' *American Historical Review* 102 (1997), 1309–42. Among Burckhardt's modern defenders are William Kerrigan and Gordon Braden in *The Idea of the Renaissance* (Baltimore: Johns Hopkins University Press, 1991).
7 Here of course the word 'men' reflects a common linguistic bias of the 1880s and 1890s when the first parts of the *OED* were published as the *New English Dictionary*.
8 North, *The Life of the Right Hon. Francis North, Lord Guilford, Lives of the Norths*, ed. Augustus Jessopp (London: George Bell and Sons, 1890), I, 100. Cf. North, *The Life of the Lord Keeper North*, ed. Mary Chan (Lewiston: Edwin Mellen Press, 1995), 207.
9 *Johnsonian Miscellanies*, in James L. Clifford, ed., *Biography as an Art: Selected Criticism 1560–1960* (London: Oxford University Press, 1962), 49.
10 See Foucault, *The Order of Things* (New York: Vintage, 1973), 55; and Bush, *English Literature in the Earlier Seventeenth Century*, second edition (Oxford: Clarendon Press, 1962), 1.
11 See David Tylden-Wright, *John Aubrey, A Life* (London: HarperCollins, 1991), 51, 67.
12 Virginia Woolf, 'The Art of Biography,' *The Death of the Moth and Other Essays* (London: Hogarth Press, 1942), 120.
13 I use 'religious biography' here to include not only lives of clerical figures

but also those of secular or lay persons represented by their biographers primarily in religious terms.

Chapter 1

1 *The History of that Most Eminent Statesman, Sir John Perrott* (published belatedly, 1728), viii. *The Twoo Bookes of Francis Bacon. Of the Proficience and Advancement of Learning* (1605), II, 13ᵛ.
2 *A Treatise of Death; The Last Enemy to be Destroyed* (1661), 249. 'To the Reader,' in Clarke, *Lives of Sundry Eminent Persons* (1683), a3.
3 'To the Christian Reader,' *Mistris Shawe's Tomb-Stone* (1658), B9. *The Life and Death of Mrs. Margaret Andrews* (1680), 9–10. Among other lives of children is the anonymous *The Compleat Scholler; Or, A Relation of the Life, and Latter End Especially, of Caleb Vernon* (1666), the subject of which died at the age of twelve years and six months.
4 See p. 44 below.
5 The works mentioned here and in the next paragraph are all considered in subsequent chapters.
6 See G.R. Owst, *Preaching in Medieval England* (Cambridge: Cambridge University Press, 1926), 265–8; Fisher, *Funeral Sermon of Margaret Countess of Richmond and Derby* (1509, reprinted 1708); and Thomas White, *A Godlie Sermon Preached at the Buriall of Sir H. Sidney* (1586).
7 *Memoirs of the Verney Family*, ed. Frances Parthenope Verney (1892; reprinted New York: Barnes and Noble, 1970), IV, 454. Sparke, *A Sermon Preached ... at the Buriall of ... the Earle of Bedford* (1585), Aij. Walker, Εὑρηκα, εὑρηκα. *The Virtuous Woman Found* (1678), 41. The 1693 edition of Calamy's *The Godly Mans Ark*, which includes his funeral sermon on Elizabeth Moore, is described by the publisher as 'The 17th Edition Corrected and Amended.' In his preface, 'The Author to the Reader,' in his funeral sermon for Dr Samuel Bolton, *The Saints Transfiguration* (1655), Calamy refers to the unauthorized publication of that work. Some of Benjamin's Whichcote's sermons are among those published from copies made by auditors; see his *Select Sermons* (1698), A8ᵛ.
8 'A Catalogue of the Printed Books of Sir William Musgrave, Barᵗ,' British Library, Add. MSS 25403–4.
9 See David Cressy, *Birth, Marriage, and Death: Ritual, Religion, and the Life-Cycle in Tudor and Stuart England* (Oxford: Oxford University Press, 1997), 421–55, 572n39, and Ralph Houlbrooke, *Death, Religion, and the Family in England, 1480–1750* (Oxford: Clarendon Press, 1998), 295–330, 386–7. The figures given are likely to be underestimates, since forms of titles in the STCs do not always make it clear which works are funeral sermons.

10 Harrison and Leygh, *Deaths Advantage Little Regarded*; Eaton, *A Sermon Preached At the Funeralls of ... Master Thomas Dutton*; Fenton, *A Sermon Preached at the Funerall of Mr. John Newman*; and Denison, *The Monument or Tombe-Stone*.
11 Hyperius, *The Practis of Preaching* (1577), 154–5. Among those who state the same principles is Anthony Burgess in his funeral sermon for Thomas Blake, *St Pauls Last Farewell* (1658), 18.
12 See Ashe's sermons for the funerals of Robert Strange and Rev. Ralph Robinson, *The Efficiency of Gods Grace* (1654), 39, and *The Good Mans Death Lamented* (1655), 25.
13 On Williams's sermon see below, pp. 42–4. Boteler, *The Worthy of Ephratah* (1659), a3^v. Stubbs, *The Hopes of a Resurrection Asserted and Applied* (preached 1700, published 1701). See the younger John Carter's biography of his father in *The Tomb-Stone, and a Rare Sight* (1653), 26–7; however a commemoration sermon for the elder Carter was nevertheless preached. For Fuller's report of Sir Richard Hutton's prohibition, see the Cumberland section of the *Worthies* (1662), I, 219.
14 See the first edition of Wood, *Athenæ Oxonienses* (1691–2), II, 134, 615, 854; and the second edition (1721), II, 922.
15 Bodleian, MS Wood F 39, 344, 405.
16 Donne's sermon on Lady Danvers (better remembered as Magdalen Herbert), which is actually a commemoration sermon preached later than the funeral, was first published in 1627, and Taylor's sermon on Lady Carbery was published in 1650. Both have frequently been included in anthologies of seventeenth-century prose, as well as in editions of their authors' works. Abbot's *A Sermon Preached ... at the Funerall Solemnities of ... Thomas Earle of Dorset*, and Parsons's *A Sermon Preached at the Funeral of ... John Earl of Rochester* (first published in Oxford) have rarely been reprinted.
17 Buckeridge, *A Sermon Preached at the Funeral of ... Lancelot Late Lord Bishop of Winchester*; Rust, *A Funeral Sermon, Preached at the Obsequies of ... Jeremy Lord Bishop of Down*.
18 L.P. Smith's Introduction in his edition, *The Golden Grove: Selected Passages from the Sermons and Writings of Jeremy Taylor* (Oxford: Clarendon Press, 1955), xviii.
19 *Funerals Made Cordials ... Robert Rich*, and *A Sermon ... at the Funeral of Dr Brounrig, late Lord Bishop of Exceter. With an Account of his Life and Death*.
20 See Walton's statement at the opening of his life of Donne, prefaced to Donne's *LXXX Sermons* (1640).
21 Toland's biography was prefaced to Harrington's *Oceana*, Sir Edward Coke's life of Littleton was prefaced to *The First Part of the Institutes of the Lawes of England. Or, A Commentarie upon Littleton*, Edward Vaughan's life of his father

was prefaced to his edition of *The Reports and Arguments of ... Sir John Vaughan,* and Smith's life was prefaced to *Catalogus Librorum Manuscriptorum Bibliothecæ Cottonianæ* (Oxford).
22 Ursula Quarles's life was prefaced to her husband's *Solomons Recantation.* An anonymous life of Rochester (attributed to Robert Wolsey) was prefaced to *Valentinian* in 1685, and anonymous lives of Cleveland were attached to *Clievelandi Vindiciæ* in 1677 and of Aphra Behn to her *Histories and Novels* in 1696.
23 See the more detailed discussion of the work of Fuller and Wood below in chapter 8.
24 Leland's mid-sixteenth-century *Commentarii de Scriptoribus Britannicis* survived largely in manuscript until the eighteenth century. For a recent discussion of Bale's work on literary figures see Anne Hudson, 'Visio Baleii: An Early Literary Historian,' in *The Long Fifteenth Century, Essays for Douglas Gray,* ed. Helen Cooper and Sally Mapstone (Oxford: Clarendon Press, 1997), 313–29.
25 Lloyd, *Memoires of the Lives, Actions, Sufferings & Deaths of Those Noble, Reverend and Excellent Personages, That Suffered ... In our Late Intestine Wars.* Lloyd's other biographical collections include *State-Worthies. Or, the States-men and Favourites of England Since the Reformation* (1665, 1670).
26 North, *The Life of the Right Hon. Francis North, Lord Guilford, The Lives of the Norths,* ed. Augustus Jessopp (London: George Bell and Sons, 1890), I, 46.
27 *The General History* was first published in 1624 as *Γυναικεῖον: or, Nine Bookes of Various History Concerning Women.* Heywood's *The Exemplary Lives and Memorable Acts of Nine the Most Worthy Women of the World* was published in 1640.
28 Ken, *A Sermon Preached at the Funeral of ... Lady Margaret Mainard.*
29 Dobson, *A Sermon Preacht at the Funeral of ... Lady M. Farmor* (1670), 32–3. Fuller, *The Mourning of Mount Libanon* (1628), 29–30. Ken, *Lady Margaret Mainard* (1682), 29.
30 Rainbowe, *A Sermon Preached at ... the Interring of the Corps of ... Susanna, Countesse of Suffolke,* and *A Sermon Preached at the Funeral of ... Anne Countess of Pembroke, Dorset and Montgomery.* I have provided some discussion of the former in 'Additional Seventeenth-Century Allusions to George Herbert,' *George Herbert Journal* 11 (Spring, 1988), 38–40.
31 Prude, *A Sermon at the Funeral of the Learned and Ingenious Mrs. Ann Bayard.*
32 See chapter 7 of Fuller's introduction to the *Worthies* (1662), I, 20, and the preface to *Biographia Britannica,* I (1747), xii. For North's comments on Burnet, see below, pp. 51–2.
33 Bodleian, MS Wood D 19, vol. 4, contains Wood's extensive biographical notes on English musicians, including references to some 250 figures.
34 Graham, 'A Short Account,' 231.

35 Prince's *Worthies* was published in Exeter in 1701 but evidently completed a few years earlier. The epistle 'To the Reader' quoted here is dated 1697. See sig. B.
36 This work was anonymously published but is identified as Heywood's in the Pollard and Redgrave *Short-Title Catalogue*.
37 *Human Nature Displayed in the History of Myddle ... Antiquities and Memoirs of the Parish of Myddle* (Fontwell, Sussex: Centaur Press, 1968), first published in 1834. In his introduction to the 1968 edition, W.G. Hoskins points out that it was mainly written in 1700–1, with some slightly later additions.
38 *Myddle*, 1968 edition, 87, 64, 133, 122.

Chapter 2

1 Foxe, *Actes and Monuments* (1563), B6^v. In addition to the more specialized modern studies of John Foxe, Helen C. White's *Tudor Books of Saints and Martyrs* (Madison: University of Wisconsin Press, 1963) remains a useful survey of sixteenth-century English religious biography.
2 Burnet, *The Life and Death of Sir Matthew Hale* (1682), A5^v–A6.
3 Featley, 'The Life of the Worthie Prelate and Faithfull Servant of God John Jewel,' prefaced to Jewel's *Works* (1609), sig. ¶¶5^v.
4 'Preface,' *Wadsworth's Remains* (1680), 87. Newcome, *A Faithful Narrative of the Life and Death of ... Mr. John Machin* (1671), A5–A5^v, published anonymously.
5 Bagshaw, 'The Life and Death of Mr. Bolton,' *Mr. Boltons Last and Learned Worke of the Foure Last Things* (1635), 1–2.
6 Bèze, *A Discourse ... Containing the Life and Death of M. John Calvin*, translated by I.S. (John Stubbs?). Humphrey, *J. Juelli Episcopi Sarisburiensis vita et mors*.
7 Fuller, 'The Life of Bishop Ridley,' *Holy State* (1642), 292.
8 Featley's manuscript version of this life in the Bodleian Library has the heading 'collected out of Dr Humfrey's large treatise,' but, in an accompanying letter to Dean Thomas Morton, Featley quite justifiably makes larger claims for the originality of his work (MS Rawl. D 47, 194, 209).
9 Paule, *The Life of ... John Whitgift, Lord Archbishop of Canterbury*.
10 Carleton's *The Life of Mr. Bernard Gilpin* (1629) was translated by William Freake. Featley's 'The Life and Death of John Reinolds' was included in Thomas Fuller's *Abel Redevivus* (1651).
11 *Lycidas*, ll. 114–15. Harris, 'A Short View of the Life and Vertues of the Authour,' prefaced to Lake's *Sermons with some Religious and Divine Meditations*. Isaacson, *An Exact Narration of the Life and Death of ... Lancelot Andrewes*.
12 Oley in his life of Herbert declared openly that the church had few such

clergy as Herbert and that the church's afflictions resulted from its corruption. It is significant that Harris, the biographer of Lake, later went over to the Puritan side, and that the important Anglican biographer Featley also compromised in some respects with the Puritan regime.
13 Vaughan, 'The Life and Death of the Venerable Dr. Jackson,' prefaced to *A Collection of the Works of that Holy Man and Profound Divine Thomas Jackson*. Walton, 'The Life of Mr. Richard Hooker,' *Lives*, World's Classics (London: Oxford University Press, 1973), 170–1. For the anonymous life of Fuller, see below, pp. 124–7.
14 Fell, *The Life of the Most Learned, Reverend and Pious Dr H. Hammond*, first published separately in 1661, was included with revisions and additions as a preface to Hammond's *Workes* in 1674. Fell's life of Allestree was published as a preface to Allestree's *Forty Sermons* (1684).
15 David Lloyd's *Memoires of the Lives, Actions, Sufferings & Deaths* ... (1668) is a folio volume of over 700 pages of biographies and briefer accounts of those who suffered in the Anglican and Royalist causes. Charles I and Laud were of course regarded by Royalists as martyrs, but even Royalist biographers and historians generally recognized that few suffered death for reasons of religion under the Puritan regime: Cromwell was no maker of martyrs in England. Peter Barwick in *The Life of the Reverend Dr. John Barwick* (written in Latin in the 1670s and published in an English translation in 1724) emphasizes his brother's heroism in the Anglican and Royalist service but states that on an occasion when he was imprisoned by the rebels they refrained from torture, which would be 'a Barbarity in this Age unheard of in *England*' (1724 edition, 124).
16 Fell emphasizes that Hammond, who died on the eve of the Restoration, dreaded the evils prosperity would bring more than he had feared the previous afflictions, and he laments, 'Persuasions to Piety nowadayes are usually in scorn call'd Preaching' (*Hammond*, 1661 version, 204–5, 243).
17 Burnet, *Some Passages of the Life and Death of ... John, Earl of Rochester, The Life and Death of Sir Matthew Hale*, and *A Sermon Preached at the Funeral of the Honourable Robert Boyle*, 21, 37. Evelyn, *The Life of Mrs. Godolphin*, first published in 1847, edited by Samuel Wilberforce. Walker, Εὑρηκα, εὑρηκα. *The Virtuous Woman Found* (1678).
18 The most important of Clarke's biographical collections are *A General Martyrologie* (1651, 1677) and *The Lives of Sundry Eminent Persons in this Later Age* (1683).
19 For Ball's life of Preston, see below, pp. 97–9. Carter's life of his father, first printed in *The Tomb-Stone, and a Rare Sight* (1653), is included in Clarke's *A Collection of the Lives of Ten Eminent Divines* (1662), and in his *General Martyrol-*

ogie (1677), which also contains Gower's life of Rothwell. Lightfoot's life of Broughton, first published as a preface to Broughton's *Works* (1662), is included in Clarke's *Lives of Sundry Eminent Persons*. Baxter's *Breviate of the Life of Margaret, the Daughter of Francis Charlton ... and Wife of Richard Baxter* was separately published in 1681.

20 Baxter, *Reliquiæ Baxterianæ* (1696), I, 124, and 'To the Reader,' in Clarke (1683), a3.
21 *The Life & Death of the Most Reverend and Learned Father of our Church Dr. James Usher* (1656).
22 Oley, 'A Prefatory View of the Life and Vertues of the Authour,' Herbert, *Remains* (1652), a10, b12ᵛ.
23 Hinde, *A Faithful Remonstrance of the Holy Life and Happy Death of John Bruen* (1641), 13. I. Mather, *The Life and Death of Mr. Richard Mather* (Cambridge, Mass., 1670), 26. Gauden, 'The Life and Death of Mr. Richard Hooker,' Hooker, *Works* (1662), 32. Dillingham, *Vita Laurentii Chadertoni* (Cambridge, 1700), 31. Mayo, *The Life & Death of Edmund Staunton* (1673), 19. The Anglican William Fulman criticized such comparisons in the nonconformist Mayo's biography, in *A Short Appendix to the Life of Edmund Stanton* (1673).
24 See St Gregory of Nyssa, *Encomium ... on his Brother Saint Basil*, ed. Sister James Aloysius Stein (Washington: Catholic University of America, Patristic Studies, XVII, 1928), par. 23, etc.
25 Whitefoote, Ἰσραὴλ ἀγχίθανης. *Deaths Alarum* (1656), 65.
26 Williams, *Great Britains Salomon* (1625), 37–9, 67. The '*verse*, before my *Text*' is 1 Kings 11:41–3.
27 Dawbeny, *Historie & Policie Re-Viewed, In the Heroick Transactions of his Most Serene Highnesse, Oliver, Late Lord Protector* (1659), a3ᵛ.
28 Harris, 'A Short View of the Life and Vertues of the Authour,' prefixed to Lake's *Sermons with Some Religious and Divine Meditations* (1629), sig. †2. See Walton's life of Sanderson, *Lives*, World's Classics (London: Oxford University Press, 1973), 357.
29 Whitefoote, Ἰσραὴλ ἀγχίθανης. *Deaths Alarum* (1656), A7. Baddeley and Naylor, *The Life of Dr. Thomas Morton, Late Bishop of Duresme* (York, 1669), 167–8. Stubbs, *The Hopes of a Resurrection Asserted and Applied* (1701), 29; a sermon preached in 1700.
30 Featley, *Ancilla Pietatis* (1626), A4ᵛ. Wood, *Athenæ Oxonienses*, II (1692), 38. In the later part of his career Featley directed his polemical weapons also against some of the Puritan sects, most notably in *The Dippers Dipt: Or, the Anabaptists Duck'd and Plunged over Head and Eares at a Disputation in Southwark* (1645).

31 Wood, *Athenæ Oxonienses*, II (1692), 184.
32 The son's *Life and Death of William Bedell*, first published in 1871, was edited by E.S. Shuckburgh in *Two Biographies of William Bedell* (Cambridge: Cambridge University Press, 1902). Burnet's *The Life of William Bedell*, derived partly from Clogie's manuscripts, was published in 1685. Clogie's *Speculum Episcoporum; Or the Apostolick Bishop: Being a Brief Account of the Life and Death of ... Dr. William Bedell*, first published in 1862, is included in Shuckburgh's *Two Biographies*. Bernard's 'A Character of Bishop *Bedell*' is appended to James Ussher's *The Judgement of the Late Archbishop of Armagh* (1659). Cf. Walton's life of Wotton, *Lives*, World's Classics (London: Oxford University Press, 1973), 136–9.
33 Burnet, *The Life of William Bedell* (1685), b2.
34 One late seventeenth-century biography of a clerical figure which stands apart because of its author's concern with entertaining as much as instructing the reader is Walter Pope's life of Seth Ward, Bishop of Salisbury, published in 1697, the work not of a clergyman but of an astronomer. See below, p. 165.
35 Barnard, *Theologo-Historicus, Or the True Life of the Most Reverend Divine and Excellent Historian Peter Heylyn* (1683), 22. Cf. Vernon, *The Life of the Learned and Reverend Dr Peter Heylyn* (1682).
36 Fell, *The Life of ... Dr H. Hammond* (1661), 241–2. Burnet, *The Life and Death of Sir Matthew Hale* (1682), 118.
37 Burnet, *Hale*, 11.
38 Burnet, *Hale*, 25.
39 Burnet, *Hale*, A7, b^v.
40 North, *Notes of Me, The Autobiography of Roger North*, ed. Peter Millard (Toronto: University of Toronto Press, 2000), 171. *Life of ... Francis North, Lord Guilford, Lives of the Norths*, ed. Augustus Jessopp (London: George Bell and Sons, 1890), I, 79–91.
41 Aubrey, *Brief Lives*, ed. Andrew Clark (Oxford: Clarendon Press, 1898), I, 278. Baxter, *Additional Notes on the Life and Death of Sir Matthew Hale* (1682), A4.
42 North, *General Preface and Life of Dr John North*, ed. Peter Millard (Toronto: University of Toronto Press, 1984), 77.

Chapter 3

1 Johnson, *Johnsonian Miscellanies*, in James L. Clifford, ed., *Biography as an Art: Selected Criticism 1560–1960* (London: Oxford University Press, 1962), 49.
2 See Harris's life prefaced to Lake's *Sermons* (1629), Vaughan's life prefaced

to Jackson's *A Collection of the Works* (1653), and the opening of Fuller's life of Henry Smith, prefaced to Smith's *Sermons* (1657), unsigned preliminaries.
3 Isaacson, *Saturni Ephemerides, Sive Tabula Historico-Chronologica* (1633), A4, and *An Exact Narration of the Life and Death ... of Lancelot Andrewes* (1650). Two further dates are added in a list of Andrewes's works at the end of the life.
4 For Wood's criticism of Walton, see below, p. 160.
5 Featley, 'The Life of ... John Jewel,' Jewel, *Works* (1609), sig. ¶¶ᵛ.
6 Nicolls, *The Life and Death of Mr. Ignatius Jurdain*, second edition (1655), 6. Lloyd, *Memoires* (1668), 579.
7 Featley, 'Jewel,' Jewel, *Works*, sig. ¶¶ᵛ. Vaughan, 'Jackson,' Jackson, *Works*, (a2)ᵛ.
8 Boswell, *Life of Johnson*, ed. G. Birkbeck Hill, rev. L.F. Powell (Oxford: Clarendon Press, 1934), III, 191–2.
9 See, for example, Ralph Houlbrooke, *Death, Religion, and the Family in England, 1480–1750* (Oxford: Clarendon Press, 1998), 147–219.
10 King, *A Sermon Preached at the Funeralles of the Most Reverend Father, John, Late Arch-bishoppe of Yorke*, preached 1594, appended to King's *Lectures upon Jonas* (Oxford, 1597), 681; cf. Eccl. 11:3. Taylor, *A Sermon Preached ... At the Funeral of ... John, Late Lord Archbishop of Armagh* (1663), 33.
11 I. Mather, *The Life and Death of Mr. Richard Mather* (Cambridge, Mass., 1670), 28. Bagshaw, 'The Life and Death of Mr. Bolton,' in Bolton, *Foure Last Things* (1635), 29. Plume, 'An Account of the Life and Death of the Author,' in Hacket, *A Century of Sermons* (1675), liii. Anon., life prefaced to Mead's *Works* (1664), LXII.
12 Janeway, *Invisibilities, Realities, Demonstrated in the Holy Life and Triumphant Death of Mr. John Janeway* (1673), 117.
13 King, *Sermon* in *Lectures upon Jonas* (1597), 680. Jenkyn, *A Shock of Corn Coming in its Season* (1654), 43. Clogie, *Speculum Episcoporum*, in *Two Biographies of William Bedell*, ed. Shuckburgh, 197–8. Bates, *A Funeral-Sermon for the Reverend, Holy and Excellent Divine, Mr. Richard Baxter* (1692), 123.
14 Featley, 'The Life and Death of John Reinolds,' in Fuller, *Abel Redevivus* (1651), 488. Plume, 'Life,' in Hacket, *A Century of Sermons* (1675), lii.
15 Taylor, *A Funerall Sermon, Preached at the Obsequies of ... Frances, Countess of Carbery* (1650), 36. Fenton, *A Sermon Preached at the Funerall of Mr. John Newman* (1616), 217. Pierce, Εμψυχον νεκρον ... *A Sermon Preached at the Funerall of Edward Peyto* (1659), 28.
16 Lightfoot, Preface, Broughton, *Works* (1662), a.
17 Anon., *The Life of that Reverend Divine and Learned Historian, Dr. Thomas Fuller* (1661), 76. Howes, *Real Comforts ... A Sermon Preached at the Funeral of that Reverend Divine Mr. Thomas Ball ... With a Narrative of His Life and Death* (1660),

42. Durham, *The Life and Death of that Judicious Divine and Accomplished Preacher, Robert Harris* (1660), 73.
18 Bates, *A Funeral Sermon ... Dr. Thomas Manton* (1678), 50. Denison, *The Monument or Tombe-Stone* (1631), 43; preached in 1619. J. Ferrar, 'A Life of Nicholas Ferrar,' *The Ferrar Papers*, ed. B. Blackstone (Cambridge: Cambridge University Press, 1938), 66.
19 Walton, *Lives*, World's Classics (London: Oxford University Press, 1973), 49. Isaacson, *Andrewes* (1650), sig. [★★4]. Anon., 'The Life and Death of Mr. Samuel Fairclough,' in Clarke, *Lives of Sundry Eminent Persons in this Later Age* (1683), 164. Rust, *Funeral Sermon ... Jeremy Lord Bishop of Down* (1668), 14.
20 Gauden, life prefaced to Hooker, *Works* (1662), 30. Walton, *Lives*, World's Classics, 216; cf. Fuller, *The Church-History of Britain* (1655), IX, 216. Burnet, *A Sermon Preached at the Funeral of ... John ... Lord Archbishop of Canterbury* (1694), 13–14.
21 Heywood, *A Narrative of the Holy Life and Happy Death of ... Mr. John Angier* (1685), 6. Ashurst, *Some Remarks upon the Life of that Painful Servant of God Mr. Nathanael Heywood* (1695), 68. Anon., *The Life of ... Dr. Thomas Fuller* (1661), 14–15. Fuller, 'The Life of Mr. Perkins,' *The Holy State* (1642), 90.
22 Baxter, *Faithful Souls Shall Be with Christ* (1681), 53.
23 Donne, 'Preached at the Funerals of Sir William Cokayne' (1626), *The Sermons of John Donne*, ed. George R. Potter and Evelyn M. Simpson (Berkeley: University of California Press, 1962), VII, 257–78. Reynolds, *Deaths Advantage Opened* (1657); see Thomason's copy, British Library, E 912 (6). Bagshaw, *A Sermon Preacht in Madrid* (1667). Brady, *A Sermon Preached at the Funeral of Thomas Shadwell* (1693).
24 For North's criticism of Burnet's *The Life and Death of Sir Matthew Hale*, see above, pp. 51–2.
25 See Phillipe Ariès, Introduction, *Passions of the Renaissance, A History of Private Life*, III, ed. Roger Chartier, trans. Arthur Goldhammer (Cambridge, Mass.: Harvard University Press, 1989).
26 Paule, *Whitgift* (1612), 86. Vaughan, life prefixed to Jackson, *Works* (1653). Burnet, *Hale* (1682), A7–A7^v.
27 Ferrar, *Ferrar Papers*, ed. Blackstone, 76.
28 Burnet, *Hale* (1682), 149, 164. Hinde, *A Faithfull Remonstrance of the Holy Life and Happy Death of John Bruen* (1641), 28–49. Anon., 'The Life and Death of Mr. Richard Blackerby,' in Clarke, *The Lives of Sundry Eminent Persons in this Later Age* (1683), 64. Ashe, *The Faithfull Christians Gain* (1659), 41.
29 Thomas Hayne's translation from the Latin original of Adamus's biography (Heidelberg, 1620) was published as *The Life and Death of Dr Martin Luther* in London in 1641.

30 Featley, 'Jewel,' Jewel, *Works* (1609), sigs. ¶¶ᵛ–¶¶2. T. Gouge, 'A Narrative of the Life and Death of Doctor Gouge,' prefaced to William Gouge, *A Learned and Very Useful Commentary on the Whole Epistle to the Hebrews* (1655), c2. P. Barwick, *The Life of the Reverend Dr. John Barwick* (1724), written c. 1670.
31 Howes, *Real Comforts ... A Sermon Preached at the Funeral of that Reverend Divine Mr. Thomas Ball ... With a Narrative of his Life and Death* (1660), 48–9.
32 Boate, *The Character of a Trulie Vertuous and Pious Woman, as it hath Been Acted by Mistress Margaret Dungan (Wife to Doctor Arnold Boate)* (Paris, 1651), 47–8.
33 Parr, *The Life of the Most Reverend Father in God James Usher* (1686). Fell, *Hammond* (1661), 62–3.
34 Evelyn, 'A Digression Concerning Physiognomy,' *Numismata. A Discourse of Medals Ancient and Modern* (1697), 336.
35 Fell, 'Life,' Allestree, *Sermons* (1684), c2–c2ᵛ.
36 See Burnet, *The Life of William Bedell* (1685), 219.
37 Anon., 'The Life of Mr. Henry Wharton,' Wharton, *Fourteen Sermons* (1697), A6. Fell, *Hammond* (1661), 84–5.
38 T. Gouge, 'Narrative,' in W. Gouge, *Commentary* (1655), cᵛ. Clarke, 'The Life and Death of Mr. Richard Vines,' *Lives of Sundry Eminent Persons in this Later Age* (1683), 50. Baddeley and Naylor, *Morton* (1669), 157.
39 J. Ferrar, 'Life,' *Ferrar Papers*, ed. Blackstone, 10. Donne, 'A Sermon of Commemoration of the Lady Danvers,' *Sermons*, ed. Potter and Simpson, VIII, 89. Burnet, *Hale* (1682), 20.
40 Anon., 'The Life and Death of Dr. Samuel Bolton,' in Clarke, *Lives of Sundry Eminent Persons* (1683), 45. Bedell, 'Life,' in *Two Biographies of William Bedell*, ed. Shuckburgh, 15. Anon, *The Life of ... Edward Rainbow, D.D. Late Lord Bishop of Carlisle* (1688), 19.
41 Anon., 'The Life and Death of Mr. Samuel Fairclough,' in Clarke, *Lives of Sundry Eminent Persons* (1683), 154. Walker, *The Holy Life of Mrs Elizabeth Walker* (1690), 13. Anon., 'Preface,' *Wadsworth's Remains* (1680), 4.
42 Bagshaw, 'The Life and Death of Mr Bolton,' prefixed to Bolton, *Foure Last Things* (1635), 12. Burnet, *Hale* (1682), 6. Hart-On-Hi [John Hart], *Trodden Down Strength By the God of Strength, Or Mrs Drake Revived* (1647), 26–7. Anon., 'Life and Death,' appended to William Gouge, *Funeral Sermon ... Mrs Margaret Ducke* (1646), 26–7. See my 'Puritans and the Blackfriars Theater: The Cases of Mistresses Duck and Drake,' *Shakespeare Quarterly* 45 (Spring, 1994), 92–5. Anon., *A Summary Account of the Life of ... Dr. Anth. Horneck* (1697), 34.
43 Hinde, *Bruen* (1641), 176–7.
44 Walker, Εὑρηκα, εὑρηκα. *The Virtuous Woman Found* (1678), 108. T. Gouge, 'Narrative,' in W. Gouge, *Commentary* (1655), c–cᵛ. Burnet, *Bedell* (1685), 153.

45 Fuller, *Abel Redevivus* (1651), 444. Featley, 'Jewel,' Jewel, *Works* (1609), sig. ¶¶3.
46 Mayo, *Staunton* (1673), 47. Barnard, *Theologo-Historicus, Or the True Life of ... Peter Heylyn* (1683), 11–12, 17. Vernon's *The Life of the Learned and Reverend Dr Peter Heylyn* was separately published in 1682, preceded by a version prefaced to one of Heylyn's works in 1681.
47 A translation of Basil's homily was included in a publication titled *The Fathers Not Papists* in London in 1634; see p. 47.
48 J. Featley, *Featlæi παλιγ γενεσια: or Doctor Daniel Featley Revived ... With a Succinct History of his Life and Death* (1660), 8. John was Daniel Featley's nephew. Wood reveals that Daniel's father was a college cook, in *Athenæ Oxonienses* (1691-2), II, 37. Wood also comments on Cavendish's omission regarding Wolsey's father, in *Athenæ*, I, 569. On Hammond's relatives, see *Athenæ*, II, 162. Compare Harris's life of Lake prefixed to Lake's *Sermons* (1629) with accounts of the brother, Sir Thomas Lake, in the *DNB* and standard histories of the period.
49 Clogie, *Speculum Episcoporum*, in *Two Lives of William Bedell*, ed. Shuckburgh, 117–18. Burnet, *Bedell* (1685), 86–7.
50 For North's criticism of Burnet, see especially pp. 51–2 above.
51 Burnet, *Hale* (1682), 80. Wordsworth, 'Walton's Book of Lives,' *Ecclesiastical Sonnets*, III, v. For Hacket's life of Williams, see below, pp. 99–104.
52 John Ayre, 'Biographical Memoir of John Jewel,' in Ayre's edition, *The Works of John Jewel* (London: Parker Society, 1845–50), IV, v–xxx.
53 Fell, *Hammond* (1661) 3–4, 193, 105.
54 Southcomb, *A Sermon at the Funeral of the Reverend Mr. John Culme* (1690), 20. Fell, *Hammond*, 125, 209–10, 94, 228, 216, 5, 85.
55 See Aubrey, *Brief Lives*, ed. Andrew Clark (Oxford: Clarendon Press, 1898), I, 19, 343–6; and Michael Hunter, *John Aubrey and the Realm of Learning* (London: Duckworth, 1975), 35.

Chapter 4

1 There is no edition of the lives that records the variants resulting from Walton's successive additions and revisions. Except where otherwise indicated, references in this chapter are to the World's Classics *Lives* (Oxford: Oxford University Press, 1973), which prints the text of the biographies of Donne, Wotton, Hooker, and Herbert from the 1675 collected *Lives* and that of the biography of Sanderson from the first edition (1678).
2 *Lives*, 98, 142.
3 *Lives*, 170, 183, 206, 311–12, 351, 402.
4 See especially *Lives*, 179.

5 *Lives*, 275, 288, 319.
6 See especially *Lives*, 382, 401–2, 406–7.
7 Logan Pearsall Smith, *The Life and Letters of Sir Henry Wotton* (Oxford: Oxford University Press, 1907), I, iii.
8 Empson, *Some Versions of Pastoral* (New York: New Directions, n.d.), 23.
9 Camden, *The History of the Most Renowned and Victorious Princess Elizabeth*, ed. W.T. MacCaffrey (Chicago: University of Chicago Press, 1970), 6. Anon., Appendix to 'Life,' Mead, *Works* (1664), LXXVI. Gumble, *The Life of General Monck, Duke of Albemarle* (1671), 143. Milton, *The History of Britain* (1670), Book II, 66.
10 *Lives*, 345.
11 *Lives*, 213. Frederick Pamp shows that Walton had evidently not read the *Ecclesiastical Polity*, in 'Walton's Redaction of Hooker,' *Church History* 17 (June, 1948), 96, 101.
12 Gauden, 'The Life & Death of Mr. Richard Hooker,' prefaced to Hooker's *Works* (1662), 14. Fuller, *The Church-History of Britain* (1655), Book IX, 216.
13 In addition to David Novarr, *The Making of Walton's Lives* (Ithaca: Cornell University Press, 1958), see especially R.C. Bald, 'Historical Doubts Respecting Walton's *Life of Donne*,' in *Essays in English Literature ... Presented to A.S.P. Woodhouse*, ed. Millar MacLure and F.W. Watt (Toronto: University of Toronto Press, 1964), 69–84, and *John Donne: A Life* (Oxford: Clarendon Press, 1970); C.J. Sisson, *The Judicious Marriage of Mr. Hooker and the Birth of the Laws of Ecclesiastical Polity* (Cambridge: Cambridge University Press, 1940); Joseph Summers, *George Herbert: His Religion and Art* (London: Chatto and Windus, 1954); and Amy Charles, *A Life of George Herbert* (Ithaca: Cornell University Press, 1977).
14 See especially Sisson, xiii and 45 ff., and Novarr, 274. In a review of Novarr's book, John Butt and Peter Ure point out, however, that evidence shows that a large part of Hooker's estate actually did consist of books: *Modern Language Review* 54 (1959), 588–9.
15 On Wotton's diplomatic policy in Venice, see L.P. Smith, *Life and Letters*, I, 76, etc.
16 On the invented episode, see Novarr, 471. In a letter to Anthony Wood in February 1693, Walter Getsius noted that Sanderson retained his benefice until the Restoration 'but was never censur'd as a sider with the usurper for this' (Bodleian, MS Wood F 42, 18).
17 See Charles, *Herbert*, 148.
18 Donne, 'A Sermon of Commemoration of the Lady Danvers,' *The Sermons of John Donne*, ed. George R. Potter and Evelyn M. Simpson (Berkeley: University of California Press, 1962), VIII, 88.

19 See Herbert, *The Life of Edward, First Lord Herbert of Cherbury, Written by Himself*, ed. J.M. Shuttleworth (London: Oxford University Press, 1976), 9; and Baxter, *Reliquiæ Baxterianæ* (1696), II, 363; cf. II, 357. *The Compleat Angler* concludes with the exhortation from 1 Thes. 4:11: '*Study to be quiet.*'
20 *Lives*, 21.
21 *Lives*, 270, 275, 288, 291, 305.
22 Gauden, 'Hooker,' Hooker, *Works* (1662), 9; contrast Walton, *Lives*, 171–3, 214–15, 221. Cotton, 'To my Old and most Worthy Friend, Mr. Izaak Walton,' *Lives*, 8–13. *Lives*, 21.
23 *Lives*, 83, 397, 285, 107, 216.
24 *Lives*, 378, 219. John Butt, 'Izaak Walton's Collections for Fulman's Life of John Hales,' *Modern Language Review* 29 (1934), 267.
25 Stephen, 'John Donne,' *National Review* 34 (1899), 595–6, cited by Novarr, 13. Walton's methods, however, have recently been defended by Jessica Martin in *Walton's Lives: Conformist Commemorations and the Rise of Biography* (Oxford: Oxford University Press, 2001), which reached me after I had completed my study. It makes a better case for Walton as a devotional and political writer than as a biographer and has not altered my view of his limitations.
26 For Wood's criticism of Walton, see below, p. 160. See Woolf, 'The Art of Biography,' in *The Death of the Moth and Other Essays* (London: Hogarth Press, 1942), 119–26, and 'The New Biography,' in *Granite and Rainbow* (London: Hogarth Press, 1958), 149–55. Cf. *The Diary of Virginia Woolf*, ed. Anne Olivier Bell (Harmondsworth: Penguin, 1979), I, 235–6: 24 January 1919.
27 Walton, *The Compleat Angler*, World's Classics (London: Oxford University Press, 1974), 6. The phrase 'or rather was' is an addition in the 1661 edition, reflecting the impact on Walton of the Civil War and its aftermath.
28 Preface, *Sylvæ*, *The Works of John Dryden*, ed. H.T. Swedenberg, E. Miner, and V.A. Dearing (Berkeley and Los Angeles: University of California Press), III (1969), 6. This remark is generally assumed to refer to Lely, although the painter is not mentioned by name.

Chapter 5

1 Burnet, *Dukes of Hamilton* (1677), a^v.
2 Fulke Greville, Lord Brooke, *The Life of the Renowned Sr Philip Sidney* (1652), 239–40.
3 Fuller, 'To the Reader,' *Holy State* (1642), A2–A2^v. Gumble, *The Life of General Monck, Duke of Albemarle* (1671), 411. The phrase Gumble quotes is best known from Ralegh's use of it, but Gumble refers to it as an ancient (or classical) saying. On Wood's problems with censorship, see below, pp. 161–2.

258 Notes to pages 93–8

4 Dryden, Dedication to Duke of Ormond, 'The Life of Plutarch,' prefixed to *Plutarch's Lives Translated ... by Several Hands* (1683), *The Works of John Dryden*, XVII, ed. S.H. Monk (Berkeley and Los Angeles: University of California Press, 1971), 235–6.
5 One of the partial exceptions is Henry Fletcher's *The Perfect Politician* (1680), an unusually objective life of Oliver Cromwell, but it is primarily a history of public events.
6 Montaigne, 'On Books,' *Essays*, trans. J.M. Cohen (Harmondsworth: Penguin, 1963), 167. Johnson's statement from *The Rambler* no. 60, 13 October 1750, is included by James Clifford in his *Biography as an Art: Selected Criticism 1560–1960* (London: Oxford University Press, 1962), 42.
7 George Cavendish, *The Life and Death of Cardinal Wolsey*, ed. Richard Sylvester, Early English Text Society (Oxford: Oxford University Press, 1959), 11. Dryden, 'Life of Plutarch,' *Works*, XVII, ed. Monk, 275. Lloyd, 'To the Reader,' *State-Worthies. Or, The States-men and Favourites of England Since the Reformation*, second edition (1670), A2^v.
8 Camden's *Elizabeth* was in fact an English translation of his Latin *Annales* (1615–25). English translations at first retained but later dropped the word 'Annales' or 'Annals' from the title.
9 Wotton, *Buckingham* (1642), 17.
10 References here are to the first edition, Heylyn, *Cyprianus Anglicus: Or, the History of the Life and Death, of the Most Reverend and Renowned Prelate William ... Lord Archbishop of Canterbury* (1668).
11 Wood, *Athenæ Oxonienses*, II (1692), 184. Coleridge's annotated copy of the 1671 edition of *Cyprianus Anglicus* is in the British Library, Ashley 4776; see *Marginalia*, II, ed. George Whalley, *The Collected Works of Samuel Taylor Coleridge*, XII, pt. 2 (London: Routledge and Kegan Paul, 1984), 1095–1104.
12 *Cyprianus Anglicus*, A2, B.
13 *Cyprianus Anglicus*, 176.
14 *Cyprianus Anglicus*, 345. Aubrey's manuscript, 'Containing Discourses Chronological,' quoted by Michael Hunter, *John Aubrey and the Realm of Learning* (London: Duckworth, 1975), 164. Edward Hyde, Earl of Clarendon, *The History of the Rebellion and Civil Wars in England*, ed. W.D. Macray (Oxford: Clarendon Press, 1888), I, 120, 196. Fuller, *Church-History* (1655), XI, 217. In his *Examen Historicum* (1659), 217, Heylyn displayed his own anger at this criticism of Laud by Fuller.
15 Burnet, *Dukes of Hamilton* (1677), a^v, 2.
16 Ball's *Life of the Renowned Doctor Preston* was included in an abridged version in Samuel Clarke's *A General Martyrologie* in 1651 and 1677, and printed more fully in 1885 from a manuscript in his possession by E.W. Harcourt, who was

evidently unaware of the earlier publications. All references here are to Harcourt's edition (Oxford: Parker). According to Harcourt's title-page the work was written in 1628, but some internal evidence suggests a date around the middle of the century, for example a statement that Charles I thought he would be absolved if he adhered to the prelates: 'but those that have read ye commentaryes that have since bin writ in red Letters will have occasion to beleeve the contrary' (156).

17 *Preston*, 9–10, 16–19.
18 Harcourt, 'Introduction,' *Preston*, xv. Fuller, *The History of the Worthies of England* (1662), Part II, Northamptonshire, 291.
19 References are to the first and only edition, Hacket, *Scrinia Reserata: A Memorial Offer'd to the Great Deservings of John Williams* (1693). Heylyn's life of Laud, written a few years after Hacket completed his work, has a greater number of folio pages but fewer words per page.
20 *Scrinia Reserata*, I, 207, 69, 2.
21 *Scrinia Reserata*, II, 182. Hacket states that, as Camerarius divides his biography into two parts with the death of Luther, he divides his own with the death of James (II, 3).
22 *Scrinia Reserata*, I, 2.
23 Gardiner, *History of England from the Accession of James I to the Outbreak of the Civil War 1603–42* (London: Longmans, Green and Co., 1884), VI, 340. In the preface to the second edition of his *Archbishop Laud 1573–1645* (London: Macmillan and Co., 1962), H.R. Trevor-Roper stated that he had come to view Williams's policies more favourably than when he published the first edition in 1940.
24 *Scrinia Reserata*, I, 58; II, 63. Coleridge, *Marginalia*, II, ed. Whalley, *Collected Works*, XII, pt. 2, 940.
25 *Scrinia Reserata*, I, 8.
26 *Scrinia Reserata*, I, 76. Coleridge, *Specimens of the Table Talk of the late Samuel Taylor Coleridge*, ed. H.N. Coleridge (London: John Murray, 1835), II, 196.
27 *Scrinia Reserata*, II, 229.
28 *Scrinia Reserata*, II, 130. Philips, *The Life of John Williams* (Cambridge, 1700), A3^v.
29 Johnson, 'Ambrose Philips,' *Prefaces, Biographical and Critical, To the Works of the English Poets*, VIII (1781), 3.
30 *The History of that Most Eminent Statesman, Sir John Perrott*. Reference here is to the first and only edition (1728) but a manuscript of the life in an early hand, perhaps that of the author, is in the Bodleian Library (MS Wood D 33).
31 *Perrott*, 18, 199.

32 Walker, 'A Short View of the Life of the Most Noble and Excellent Thomas Howard Earl of Arundel and Surrey,' dated June 1651, published in Walker's *Historical Discourses Upon Several Occasions* (1705), 209–23; see especially 214, 221–3. The story about Cromwell and Lely, as recorded by George Vertue, appears in Horace Walpole's *Anecdotes of Painting in England* (1786), III, 30.

33 John Hutchinson was a 'regicide,' who had signed the death warrant of Charles I, and the biography remained unpublished until 1806. In James Sutherland's edition (London: Oxford University Press, 1973) see especially 32, 264.

34 Fanshaw, *Memoirs*, first published in 1829; included in *The Memoirs of Anne, Lady Halkett and Ann, Lady Fanshawe*, ed. John Loftis (Oxford: Clarendon Press, 1979).

35 Cavendish, *The Life of the Thrice Noble, High and Puissant Prince William Cavendishe, Duke, Marquess, and Earl of Newcastle* (1667). As part of the large literature concerned with Royalist sufferings and losses in the Civil War and its aftermath, the biography takes its place with works like David Lloyd's *Memoires*.

36 Pepys, *The Diary of Samuel Pepys*, ed. R. Latham and W. Matthews (London: G. Bell and Sons, 1970–6), IX, 123: 18 March 1668.

37 Lamb declared, 'no casket is rich enough, no casing sufficiently durable, to honour and keep safe such a jewel' as this book: 'Detached Thoughts on Books and Reading,' *The Last Essays of Elia, The Works of Charles and Mary Lamb*, ed. E.V. Lucas (London: Methuen and Co., 1903–5), II, 174. Virginia Woolf provided a much more mixed and judicious view of Margaret Cavendish and her writings, in 'The Duchess of Newcastle,' *The Common Reader* (London: Hogarth Press, 1925).

38 Walsingham, *Britannicæ Virtutis Imago. Or the Effigies of True Fortitude, Expressed to the Life, in the Famous Actions of that Incomparable Knight, Major General Smith* (Oxford, 1644), *Alter Britanniæ Heros: Or the Life of the Most Honourable Knight, Sir Henry Gage* (Oxford, 1645), and *Life of Sir John Digby*, ed. George Bernard, *Camden Miscellany*, XII (London: Camden Society, 1910).

39 In 'The Author, to censure,' 28, at the conclusion of his life of Sir John Smith, Walsingham quotes the well-known passage from *The Advancement of Learning* (1605), II, 13^v.

40 This is one of the neglected works, like the anonymous life of Sir John Perrot, to which Donald Stauffer rightly drew attention in his *English Biography before 1700*, 150–1.

41 *Perrott*, v–vi.

42 Quoted here from *Characters from the Histories & Memoirs of the Seventeenth Century*, ed. David Nicol Smith (Oxford: Clarendon Press, 1920), 71, 139–40.

This text follows the manuscripts more closely than most printed versions of Clarendon's *History* and *Life*.
43 Firth, 'Burnet as Historian,' *Essays, Historical and Literary* (Oxford: Clarendon Press, 1938), 203–6.
44 Reprinted from Burnet's *History of His Own Time*, I (1724), in Smith, *Characters from the Histories & Memoirs*, 228.
45 Reprinted from Warwick's *Memoirs* (1701) in Smith, *Characters from the Histories & Memoirs*, 141–2.
46 Quoted here from the second edition, Weldon, *The Court and Character of King James* (1651), 164–5.

Chapter 6

1 Phillips, 'The Life of Mr. John Milton,' prefixed to *Letters of State, Written by Mr. John Milton* (1694), (ii).
2 Stanley, 'Socrates,' *History* (1655), pt. 3, 1–58.
3 See Stanley's dedicatory epistle to John Marsham in the first volume of the *History* (1655), and the extracts from Bacon and Montaigne at the opening of the third volume (1660).
4 The fuller title of Gassendi's work is *The Mirrour of True Nobility & Gentility. Being the Life of the Renowned Nicolaus Claudius Fabricius Lord of Peiresk*.
5 *The Mirrour of True Nobility & Gentility* (1657), 160, 161, 165–6, 164.
6 Johnson, 'Cowley,' *Prefaces, Biographical and Critical, To the Works of the English Poets*, I (1779), 1.
7 Rawley, 'The Life of the Honourable Author,' prefixed to *Resuscitatio, Or, Bringing into Publick Light Severall Pieces of the Works ... of the Right Honourable Francis Bacon*, 1657, reissued with slight additions in the 1661 edition of *Resuscitatio*. Both issues of the life have the same confusingly over-heavy punctuation. Quotations are from the 1661 text, cited as Rawley. On Rawley see the *DNB*.
8 For Aubrey's life of Bacon, see below, pp. 174–5.
9 Rawley, (c), (c)–(c)^v, (c2).
10 Rawley, (c)^v, (c2).
11 Rawley, (c), (c3).
12 Spedding, 'History and Plan of this Edition,' *The Works of Francis Bacon*, ed. James Spedding, Robert Ellis, and Douglas Heath, I (London: Longman and Co., 1857), ix.
13 Such eulogies as Gilbert Burnet's *A Sermon Preached at the Funeral of the Honourable Robert Boyle* (1692), which treat their subjects as religious figures, give very little information about their work as scientists. Quotations from

Hill's life of Barrow are given here from the revised version, 'Some Account of the Life of Dr. Isaac Barrow,' prefixed to the 1716 edition of Tillotson's *The Works of the Learned Isaac Barrow*, cited as Hill.

14 Hill, a^v, b2.
15 Hill, a2, a2^v, b^v.
16 Hill, a^v, a2^v.
17 Hill, b3, b2^v–b3. For Aubrey on Barrow, see below, p. 175.
18 Hill, b3^v.
19 On the seventeenth-century antiquarian movement, see David C. Douglas, *English Scholars 1660–1730* (London: Eyre and Spottiswood, 1951), and Graham Parry, *The Trophies of Time: English Antiquarians of the Seventeenth Century* (Oxford: Oxford University Press, 1995).
20 In addition to the lives of Spelman and Somner considered in the next paragraphs, see Edmund Gibson's life of Camden, prefixed to the English translation of the *Britannia* (1695), and Thomas Smith's Latin life of Cotton, prefixed to *Catalogus Librorum Manuscriptorum Bibliothecæ Cottonianæ* (Oxford, 1696).
21 References are to the first edition of Kennett's 'The Life of Mr. Somner,' prefixed to James Brome's edition of Somner's *A Treatise of the Roman Ports and Forts in Kent* (Oxford, 1693), cited as Kennett. A later edition of the life, with additions of no special importance, was prefixed to Somner's *A Treatise of Gavelkind*, second edition, in 1726.
22 Kennett, 9–10, 11, 10.
23 Kennett, 12–13.
24 *The Life of that Reverend Divine, and Learned Historian, Dr. Thomas Fuller*, published in London in 1661, was reissued in Oxford in 1662. References here are to the London publication of 1661, cited as *Fuller*.
25 *Fuller*, 15.
26 *Fuller*, 27, 28.
27 *Fuller*, 71–2, 59, 61.
28 *Fuller*, 72, 69.
29 *Fuller*, 65–6, 66, 67.

Chapter 7

1 See Speght, life prefixed to *The Workes of our Antient and Lerned English Poet, Geffrey Chaucer* (1598), and Greville, *The Life of the Renowned Sr Philip Sidney* (1652).
2 Such standard works as Richard Altick's *Lives and Letters: A History of Literary Biography in England and America* (New York: Alfred Knopf, 1966) give rela-

tively little attention to the seventeenth century. The postmodern interest in canon formation and the construction of the author has stimulated more recent studies of the development of English literary biography, for example Kevin Pask's *The Emergence of the English Author: Scripting the Life of the Poet in Early Modern England* (Cambridge: Cambridge University Press, 1996), but few seventeenth-century biographies have yet entered into these discussions.

3 Davies, 'Account of the Author of this Translation, and his Works,' cited here as Davies. On Davies in addition to the *DNB* see Joseph E. Tucker, 'John Davies of Kidwelly (1627?–93), Translator from the French,' *Papers of the American Bibliographical Society* 44 (1950), 119–52.
4 Davies, a8^v, A.
5 Davies, b–b^v, b6, b8^v.
6 Davies, b6^v, b7^v.
7 Davies, b8.
8 Davies, b7^v–b8.
9 Davies, b3.
10 Davies, b8, A, A^v.
11 Davies' accuracy is attested, for example, by P.S. Havens, 'A Tract Long Attributed to Milton,' *Huntington Library Bulletin* no. 6 (November, 1934), 109–14.
12 References here are to the English version of Sprat's life prefixed to *The Works of Mr Abraham Cowley* (1668), cited as Sprat. The Latin version was prefixed in the same year to *Abrahami Couleij Angli, Poemata Latina.*
13 Johnson, 'Cowley,' *Prefaces, Biographical and Critical, To the Works of the English Poets,* I (1779), 1–2.
14 On the suppressed passage of the 1656 preface, see Sprat, a^v–a2, and A.H. Nethercot, *Abraham Cowley, The Muse's Hannibal* (Oxford: Oxford University Press, 1931), 158–9. Nethercot prints Cowley's will, 296–7.
15 Sprat, A2, c2^v. Johnson, 'Cowley,' 2. Nethercot points out that the poet's father may actually have been a stationer rather than a grocer, in his *Cowley,* 1–3.
16 Sprat, d2.
17 Sprat, d. For Coleridge's comment, see A.H. Nethercot, 'The Letters of Abraham Cowley,' *Modern Language Notes* 43 (1928), 369–70.
18 On Fell's lives, see above, pp. 37–8, 47, 50, 68–9, 76–7.
19 Sprat, e2^v.
20 Sprat, c.
21 Sprat, e2. Samuel Johnson gives this report about Sprat in his life of Milton as told him by Dr Gregory: *Prefaces, Biographical and Critical, To the Works of the English Poets,* II (1779), 131.

22 Helen Darbishire's edition, *The Early Lives of Milton* (London: Constable, 1932), is useful, but some aspects need to be critically examined, such as the attribution of the anonymous life to John Phillips. In addition to that life it includes the biographies by Aubrey, Wood, Edward Phillips, Toland, and Jonathan Richardson (1734).
23 Aubrey, *Brief Lives*, ed. Andrew Clark (Oxford: Clarendon Press, 1898), II, 67, 69, 70.
24 First edition of Wood, *Athenæ Oxoniensis*, I (1691), 880–4; see especially I, 881.
25 See Wood's lives of George Morley in the first edition of the *Athenæ*, II (1692), 582, and of Edward Phillips in the second edition, II (1721), 1118, and his copy of *Theatrum Poetarum* in the Bodleian Library, Wood 88, 114.
26 References here are to the text of the anonymous 'Life of Mr. John Milton' as given in Helen Darbishire's edition, *The Early Lives of Milton*, although her attribution of this life to John Phillips has not been generally accepted. On the attribution to Cyriack Skinner, see J. Milton French, *The Life Records of John Milton* (New Brunswick, NJ: Rutgers University Press, 1949–58), V, 276–8.
27 Anon, 'Life,' *Early Lives*, ed. Darbishire, 30, 32, 33.
28 Phillips, 'The Life of Mr. John Milton,' prefixed to *Letters of State, Written by Mr. John Milton* (1694), xliii; cited below as Phillips.
29 Phillips, xx.
30 Phillips, xx–xxi.
31 Phillips, iii, viii, ix, xxxv.
32 Phillips, xxxv–xxxvi.
33 Darbishire, Introduction, *The Early Lives of Milton*, vii.
34 Toland, 'The Life of John Milton' (1698), in *The Early Lives of Milton*, ed. Darbishire, 84–5.
35 Toland, 'Life,' *Early Lives*, ed. Darbishire, 126, 192. Toland's biography of Harrington was prefixed to his edition, *The Oceana of James Harrington and his Other Works* (1700).
36 See especially Toland, 'Life,' *Early Lives*, ed. Darbishire, 120, 156–8, 171–4, 127.
37 Toland, 'Life,' *Early Lives*, ed. Darbishire, 182, 179, 96, 178.
38 Johnson, 'Milton,' *Prefaces, Biographical and Critical, To the Works of the English Poets*, II (1779), 142. Boswell, *The Journal of a Tour to the Hebrides*, 22 September 1773, in James L. Clifford, ed., *Biography as an Art: Selected Criticism 1560–1960* (London: Oxford University Press, 1962), 47. Johnson, 'Milton,' 1.

Chapter 8

1. See above, pp. 22–4.
2. Finch, dedication to James, Earl of Abingdon, Nepos, *Lives* (Oxford, 1684), a5–a5ᵛ.
3. See above, pp. 124–7.
4. References in this chapter are to the first edition of Fuller, *The History of the Worthies of England* (1662).
5. *Worthies*, I, 40.
6. Fuller, 'Of Tombes,' *The Holy State* (1642), 189.
7. Fuller, *The Holy State* (1642), 74. *Worthies*, I, 297–8, 59.
8. *Worthies*, II, 130, 256.
9. *Worthies*, III, 126.
10. *Worthies*, I, 332; II, 305, 137; I, 334–5; III, 61, 28, 130; II, 115.
11. See the anonymous life of Fuller (1661), 16, 23. Coleridge commented on the *Church-History*: 'Fuller was incomparably the most sensible, the least prejudiced, great man of an age that boasted a galaxy of great men': *The Literary Remains of Samuel Taylor Coleridge*, ed. H.N. Coleridge (London: William Pickering, 1836–9), II, 390.
12. *Worthies*, I, 2. Patrick Garland's stage version of Aubrey's *Brief Lives*, acted as a one-man show by Roy Dotrice, ran in leading theatres in London and New York in 1967.
13. *Worthies*, I, 182, 337; II, 320.
14. Kennett, life prefixed to Somner, *A Treatise of the Roman Ports and Forts* (Oxford, 1693), 114; Kennett, the future Bishop of Peterborough, also laments that serious works of scholarship are unpublishable, while 'Plays and Pamphlets reward the trifling writers' (81). See Heylyn, *Examen Historicum* (1659), aᵛ–b2. William Addison provides a good account of Heylyn's attack and Fuller's response, in his *Worthy Dr Fuller* (London: J.M. Dent, 1951), 204–15.
15. Pepys, *The Diary of Samuel Pepys*, ed. R. Latham and W. Matthews (London: G. Bell and Sons, 1970–6), III, 26–7.
16. Wood, 'To the Reader,' *Athenæ Oxonienses* (1721), I, a. According to the prefatory address, 'The Booksellers to the Reader,' in 1721, this epistle of Wood's had previously been included in only a few copies of the first edition. In an edition in four volumes (London: F.C. and J. Rivington, 1813–20), Philip Bliss generally followed the 1721 text; he added notes from various sources but did not make full use of Wood's manuscripts. References in the present chapter are to the first and second editions of *Athenæ Oxonienses*, by volume and column number, with dates included to distinguish between the two editions.

17 *Athenæ*, II (1692), 619; Harrington's Introduction, II (1692), A2. In the first edition Harrington contributed both the Preface to the first volume and the Introduction to the second volume.
18 I have provided some discussion of Wood's lives of literary figures in a two-part article, 'According to Wood: Sources of Anthony Wood's Lives of Poets and Dramatists,' *Review of English Studies* n.s. 28 (August and November, 1977), 268–89, 407–20.
19 Aubrey, letter to Wood, 21 October 1693, Bodleian, MS Wood F 51, 6.
20 1721 edition, I, 74, 230–3; *Fasti* 202; II, 884. Wood makes special acknowledgment of Andrew Allam's assistance with the *Athenæ*, II (1692), 594–5, and he laments that after William Fulman's death he was refused use of the latter's valuable collections, II (1692), 624–5.
21 1691-2 edition, I, 411; II, A2.
22 Wood's diary-autobiography, *The Life and Times of Anthony Wood*, ed. Andrew Clark, Oxford Historical Society (Oxford: Clarendon Press, 1891–1900), I, 326. On Wood's assistance to others, see Nicolas K. Kiessling, 'Anthony Wood, Thomas Gore and the Use of Manuscript Material,' *Library* sixth series 21 (June, 1999), 108–21.
23 These letters are mainly classified as Bodleian, MSS Wood F39–51. I have discussed their nature and Wood's use of them in the *RES* article, 'According to Wood: Sources of Anthony Wood's Lives of Poets and Dramatists.'
24 Bodleian, MS Wood E 10, v; MS Wood F 45, 128. On Wilkinson, see the *DNB*.
25 Bodleian, MS Wood F 39, 165. See also Andrew Clark's edition of Aubrey's *Brief Lives* (Oxford: Clarendon Press, 1898), II, 313. Wood, perhaps playing a trick of his own, appears to have told Aubrey he was uncertain of the year of his own birth (Aubrey's 'Collectio Geniturarum,' Bodleian, MS Aubrey 23, 77).
26 White to Wood, 2 and 12 April 1692, Bodleian, MS Wood F 45, 106–13. On White, see the *DNB*.
27 Thornton to Wood, 12 April 1692, Bodleian, MS Wood F 45, 19. Aubrey to Wood, MS Wood F 39, 347–347^v.
28 *Athenæ*, I (1721), a.
29 See Wood's lives of James Heath and Henry Savage, II (1692), 226, 366. Burnet's criticism of Wood appeared in his *Letter writ ... to the Lord Bishop of Cov[entry] and Litchfield* (1693), which was primarily a response to an attack on his *History of the Reformation* by Henry Wharton (under the pseudonym of Anthony Harmer). *A Vindication of the Historiographer of the University of Oxford, and his Works, from the Reproaches of the Lord Bishop of Salisbury* was first published as a separate pamphlet in 1693, and subsequently included in the second edition of the *Athenæ*, I, a2^v–b2^v; see especially b2. In both cases it

carried the statement '*Written by E.D.*' It has usually been attributed to Anthony Wood's nephew, Thomas Wood, a lawyer who served as his counsel in the Clarendon libel case, but Anthony Wood himself claimed the authorship in his life of Henry Wharton, appended to that of Henry Maurice in the second edition of the *Athenæ*, II, 874–5.

30 Wood's copy of Walton's *Lives* is classified as Bodleian, Wood 229. See *Athenæ* (1691–2), I, 264, 475, 531; II, 266.

31 Wood's bibliographical notes and listings in Bodleian, MSS Wood D 18 (2), E 2, E 4, and E 10 record many of his searches in private collections as well as in institutional libraries.

32 *Athenæ*, II (1692), 278.

33 Fuller, *Worthies*, I, 73. *Athenæ* (1691–2), I, a^v; II, A2. Andrew Clark provides a concise account of the Clarendon libel case in his life of Wood in the *DNB* and much fuller details in his edition of Wood's *Life and Times*, IV, 1–50.

34 *Athenæ*, II (1692), 546; I (1691), 466, 795; II (1692), 681; II (1721), 1041–2; II (1692), 816.

35 *Athenæ*, II (1692), 490.

36 *Vindication* reprinted in the *Athenæ*, I (1721), b2; this defends Wood against Burnet's charge that he had been made a tool by Roman Catholics 'to reproach all the greatest Men of our Church' (b^v). After 1688 Wood was often viewed as a Jacobite.

37 *Athenæ*, II (1721), 898; II (1692), 646; II (1721), 1014. For Wood on Milton, see above, pp. 137–8.

38 Bodleian, MS Wood F 49, 175, and F 45, 118. Mather's letters of information to Wood in 1691–2 are in MS Wood F 43, 114–38, and MS Tanner 26, 48, also in the Bodleian Library.

39 *Athenæ*, I (1691), 479; II (1692), 370–2, 409–12, 493–5. Toland, 'The Life of James Harrington,' prefixed to *The Oceana of James Harrington and his Other Works* (1700), xviii.

40 *Athenæ*, I (1691), 150, 196; I (1721), 576; II (1721), 899; I (1691), 768; II (1692), 90. The entry on Hayman is phrased a little differently in I (1691), 494, than in I (1721), 576.

41 *Athenæ*, II (1692), 821; II (1721), 1094–6. Pope, *The Life of the Right Reverend Father in God Seth, Lord Bishop of Salisbury* (1697); see the edition by J.B. Bamborough (Oxford: Luttrell Society, 1961) for a fuller account of the quarrel of Anthony and Thomas Wood with Pope. Thomas Wood, *An Appendix to the Life of ... Seth Lord Bishop of Salisbury; Written by Dr. Walter Pope* (published anonymously, 1697), 4, 6–7.

42 T. Wood, *An Appendix*, 30.

43 Wood or his nephew Thomas responded to this criticism in the *Vindication* reprinted in the *Athenæ*, I (1721), b2.
44 See for example Wood's criticism of the poor index of Bulstrode Whitelocke's *Memorials of the English Affairs*, 'which is a disadvantage to the book in many respects,' in *Athenæ*, II (1692), 401.
45 Wood had attached a brief and not very favourable account of James Wright to his biography of his father, Abraham Wright, in *Athenæ*, II (1692), 642. Wright's criticism, written into a book he once owned, is printed in an unsigned article, 'A Critic of Anthony Wood,' *Bodleian Quarterly Record* 7 (1932), 176–8. Other early critical responses to the *Athenæ* are to be found in letters addressed to Wood himself, for example an anonymous letter dated 15 July 1691 (Bodleian, MS Wood F 51, 13–14^v).
46 *Athenæ*, I (1691), 62, 115.
47 Aubrey, *Brief Lives*, ed. Clark, I, 225. *Athenæ*, II (1692), 239.
48 *Athenæ*, I (1691), a; II (1692), A2.
49 *Athenæ*, II (1692), 497; I (1691), 232; II (1692), 584; II (1721), 966; II (1692), 658, 750.
50 *Biographia Britannica*, I (1747), xi.
51 On 10 October 1782, Johnson wrote to John Nichols urging him to prepare a supplement to Wood's *Athenæ Oxonienses*; see *The Letters of Samuel Johnson*, ed. Bruce Redford (Princeton: Princeton University Press, 1992–4), IV, 78–9.

Chapter 9

1 Aubrey, letter to Wood, 27 October 1691, Bodleian, MS Wood F 39, 435. On Aubrey's life see Anthony Powell, *John Aubrey and His Friends* (New York: Charles Scribner's Sons, 1948), and David Tylden-Wright, *John Aubrey: A Life* (London: HarperCollins, 1991). For his early biographical plans see Powell, 71, and Tylden-Wright, 109.
2 On the basis of a statement by Wood in his *Life and Times*, Powell (127–30) considers that the first meeting between Wood and Aubrey took place in August 1667, but Tylden-Wright (142) believes the correct date is the summer of 1665.
3 Aubrey, letter to Wood, 27 March 1680, Bodleian, MS Ballard 14, 131.
4 Wood, however, had destroyed parts of the manuscripts of the *Brief Lives* when they were in his hands, in reaction to his prosecution for libel.
5 See Andrew Clark's discussion of the publication of *Lives of Eminent Men by John Aubrey* attached to *Letters Written by Eminent Persons* in 1813, in his edition of Aubrey's *Brief Lives* (Oxford: Clarendon Press, 1898), I, 21–3. John Collier's *The Scandal and Credulities of John Aubrey* was published in London by

Peter Davies in 1931. Oliver Lawson Dick's edition, *Aubrey's Brief Lives*, first published in London by Secker and Warburg in 1949, has frequently been republished; when it is cited here, reference is to the same publisher's third edition (London, 1960). A recent addition is John Buchanan-Brown's edition of the *Brief Lives* (London: Penguin, 2000), which aims to provide 'the essential Aubrey.' A full-scale critical edition of the *Brief Lives* is understood to be currently under way. Except where otherwise indicated, references to the *Brief Lives* in the present chapter are to the two volumes of Andrew Clark's edition of 1898, which at the time of writing remains essential, cited here as *BL*.

6 See especially Michael Hunter, *John Aubrey and the Realm of Learning* (London: Duckworth, 1975), an admirable study more concerned with Aubrey's other scientific and antiquarian activities than with his work as a biographer.

7 *Aubrey's Brief Lives*, ed. Dick (London: Secker and Warburg, 1960), civ. Sutherland, *English Literature of the Late Seventeenth Century* (Oxford: Clarendon Press, 1969), 255. Stauffer, *English Biography before 1700* (Cambridge, Mass.: Harvard University Press, 1930), 165.

8 Bodleian, MS Wood F 39, 206.

9 Some of Aubrey's scientific limitations, on the other hand, are pointed out by Hunter (23–4, 132–6, etc.) and Tylden-Wright (139).

10 This is not to suggest that the relation between Aubrey and Walton was an unfriendly one. Walton in his old age in 1680 assisted Aubrey with some of his biographical inquiries: see *BL*, II, 14–16.

11 *Aubrey's Brief Lives*, ed. Dick, 34–5, 262, 59–60. Cf. *BL*, ed. Clark, I, 116–19, 156–7.

12 Aubrey to Wood, 27 March 1680, Bodleian, MS Ballard 14, 131. Blackburne (or Blackbourne) wrote a Latin life of Hobbes, based largely on materials supplied him by Aubrey.

13 In addition to Aubrey's life of Bacon in Clark's edition, *BL*, I, 66–84, see Wood's note printed by Clark, *BL*, I, 394.

14 Hill's request was made on his behalf by his friend and publisher, the bookseller Brabazon Aylmer, and Aubrey in a letter of 10 May 1683 asked Wood to provide Aylmer with a transcript of the manuscript, which was then in his hands (Bodleian, MS Ballard 14, 136).

15 *BL*, I, 91.

16 *BL*, I, 91.

17 This letter is printed in full by Clark, *BL*, I, 10–12.

18 *BL*, I, 10. Cf. Wood's epistle 'To the Reader' in the second edition of *Athenæ Oxonienses* (1721), I, a, quoted above, p. 160.

19 In his correspondence Aubrey urges Wood to provide precise dates, espe-

cially nativities, for astrological purposes: for example in November 1670 and June 1671, Bodleian, MS Wood F 39, 128, 131. Cf. Aubrey's 'Collectio Geniturarum,' Bodleian, MS Aubrey 23.
20 See for example Aubrey's complaint in *Wiltshire. The Topographical Collections of John Aubrey*, ed. John E. Jackson (Devizes: Wiltshire Archaeological and Natural History Society, 1862), 17.
21 *BL*, I, 189–90.
22 Thomas Hearne, *Remarks and Collections*, ed. C.E. Doble, III (Oxford: Clarendon Press, 1889), 35. On Aubrey's originality as an antiquary, see especially Hunter, *John Aubrey and the Realm of Learning*, 191–208.
23 Johnson, *The Rambler*, no. 60, 13 October 1750, in James L. Clifford, ed., *Biography as an Art: Selected Criticism 1560–1960* (London: Oxford University Press, 1962), 42.
24 *BL*, I, 349–50.
25 Aubrey to Wood, 1681, Bodleian, MS Wood F 39, 397. Ray's letter is quoted by Hunter in *John Aubrey and the Realm of Learning*, 133.
26 See Wood's *Life and Times*, August 1667, quoted by Powell, and see also Powell's account of Wood's quarrel with Aubrey, in *John Aubrey and His Friends*, 129–30, 221–5.
27 *BL*, I, 210; II, 83.
28 *BL*, I, 220; II, 14.
29 8 September 1680, quoted in *BL*, I, 3.
30 *BL*, II, 140.
31 Toland, *Miscellaneous Works* (1747), quoted by Hunter, *John Aubrey and the Realm of Learning*, 212; cf. 205n.
32 22 May 1680, Bodleian, MS Wood F 39, 340.
33 Connolly, 'Letters of Horace Walpole,' *Previous Convictions* (London: Hamish Hamilton, 1963), 140–2.
34 Aubrey, *Wiltshire. The Topographical Collections*, 314, and *BL*, I, 43, 36.
35 Aubrey, *Wiltshire. The Topographical Collections*, 4.
36 See Dick's introduction to his edition, *Aubrey's Brief Lives*, xxxi, and Aubrey's *Wiltshire. The Topographical Collections*, 14, 148, 339.
37 See *BL*, I, 18, 11. This historical sense is not so well developed even in Fuller as in Aubrey. Fuller writes in the *Worthies* of Sir William Doddington: 'What *Tragedies* have since happened in his household, is generally known' (II, 14), and does not recognize the need to provide more information for readers of later times.
38 Aubrey, *An Essay Towards the Description of the North Division of Wiltshire*, quoted by Powell, *John Aubrey and His Friends*, 275–6.
39 See *BL*, I, 43, 152, 136. It is significant that one of the few academic studies to

take Aubrey very seriously as a biographer and recognize the extent of his originality is specially concerned with visual representation, Richard Wendorf's *The Elements of Life: Biography and Portrait Painting in Stuart and Georgian England* (Oxford: Clarendon Press, 1990), 108–23.
40 See above, p. 68.
41 *BL*, I, 347.
42 *BL*, II, 159.
43 Hilliard, *A Treatise Concerning the Arte of Limning*, ed. Philip Norman, Walpole Society, First Annual Volume (Oxford: Oxford University Press, 1912), 24.
44 *BL*, I, 113, 293, 300, 411; II, 14, 260, 276, 184; I, 347–9.
45 *BL*, I, 105, 305; II, 143, 145; I, 72. See Strachey, *Elizabeth and Essex: A Tragic History* (New York: Harcourt, Brace, 1929), 44, 52, 250, 258.
46 *BL*, I, 311; II, 247, 242; I, 293; II, 303; I, 152, 329, 348. Evelyn, 'A Digression Concerning Physiognomy,' *Numismata. A Discourse of Medals Ancient and Modern* (1697), 334.
47 *BL*, I, 196. Regarding Danvers see also *Aubrey's Brief Lives*, ed. Dick, 81.
48 *BL*, I, 216, 220; II, 164, 17, 22.
49 See above, pp. 70, 85–6, 106.
50 *BL*, I, 280, 214.
51 *BL*, II, 240–2.
52 *BL*, II, 20, 67. Wood in *Athenæ Oxonienses* borrows Aubrey's phrasing for Milton's voice.
53 *BL*, II, 17–26, 45–6. For Aubrey's play, 'The Countrey Revell,' see Clark's appendix, *BL*, II, 333–9. For his views of Shakespeare and Jonson, see his *Idea of the Education of Young Gentlemen*, ed. J.E. Stephens, with the title *Aubrey on Education* (London: Routledge and Kegan Paul, 1972), 57, 118, as well as *BL*, especially II, 226.
54 Collier, *The Scandal and Credulities of John Aubrey*, x. Boswell, *Life of Johnson*, ed. G. Birbeck Hill, rev. L.F. Powell (Oxford: Clarendon Press, 1971), I, 256.
55 On Aubrey's life of Milton, see above, p. 137.
56 In his edition, *Aubrey's Brief Lives*, 271, Dick gives parts of the life of Selden expurgated by Clark. For Harvey and Lee see Clark's edition, *BL*, I, 299; II, 31.
57 Bodleian, MS Wood F 39, 340, and *BL*, I, 11.
58 *BL*, I, 350. Regarding Goffe see *Aubrey's Brief Lives*, ed. Dick, 113.
59 Aubrey's comment on Laud and cats does not occur in the *Brief Lives* but in his manuscript, 'Containing Discourses Chronological,' quoted by Hunter, *John Aubrey and the Realm of Learning*, 164.
60 *BL*, I, 301.
61 *BL*, I, 91, 257; II, 174.

62 *BL*, I, 333. Aubrey's notes for lives of English mathematicians are in Bodleian, MS Aubrey 8, Pt. III, 69 ff. In his new edition of the *Brief Lives* (2000) John Buchanan-Brown prints together these lives, which have usually been dispersed among the others by editors.
63 Aubrey makes this comment on Marten in a letter to Wood, 11 October 1673, Bodleian, MS Wood F 39, 231.
64 *BL*, I, 317; the reference is to Philip Herbert, seventh Earl of Pembroke.
65 13 January and 2 April 1681, Bodleian, MS Wood F 39, 351, 358.
66 See Aubrey's proposal regarding a monument for himself, quoted by Powell, *John Aubrey and His Friends*, 246.
67 *BL*, II, 70.
68 Letter to Thomas Tanner, 19 March 1696, quoted by Powell, *John Aubrey and His Friends*, 242.
69 First published in 1972 as *Aubrey on Education*, ed. J.E. Stephens (see n. 53 above). On the importance of the individual genius or propensity, see for example pp. 53, 86.
70 *BL*, II, 220; I, 347, 332.
71 *BL*, I, 187, 91. See Percy Osmond, *Isaac Barrow, His Life and Times* (London: SPCK, 1944), 221–2.
72 See Darbishire's introduction to her edition, *The Early Lives of Milton* (London: Constable, 1932), xxxv–xxxviii. John Buchanan-Brown in his edition of the *Brief Lives*, xxii–xxiii, maintains that Andrew Clark did a disservice to Aubrey by exaggerating the disorder of the manuscripts.
73 See Keynes, *Harvey through John Aubrey's Eyes*, Harveian Oration, Royal College of Physicians. Reprinted from the *Lancet*, with additions (n.p., 1958), 6, 22.
74 *BL*, I, 20, 355.
75 *BL*, I, 340, 20.
76 *BL*, I, 339–40.
77 *BL*, I, 21, 21n.
78 Aubrey to Wood, 22 May 1680, Bodleian, MS Wood F 39, 340; and 15 June 1680, in Clark's edition of the *Brief Lives*, I, 11.
79 *BL*, II, 67.
80 *Aubrey on Education*, ed. Stephens, 57; cf. 118. See also *BL*, II, 226.
81 In addition to Powell's biography, *John Aubrey and His Friends* (1948), see his edition of Aubrey's *Brief Lives and Other Selected Writings* (London: Cresset Press, 1949). John Fowles edited Aubrey's *Monumenta Britannica* (Sherborne: Dorset Publishing, 1980–2). Robertson Davies gave the title 'The New Aubrey' to the final part of his novel, *The Rebel Angels* (Toronto: Macmillan 1981).

82 Strachey, 'John Aubrey,' *Biographical Essays* (New York: Harcourt Brace Jovanovich, n.d.), 15–16; first published 1923.

Chapter 10

1 Burckhardt, *The Civilization of the Renaissance in Italy*, trans. S.G.C. Middlemore (London: Penguin, 1990), 217, referring primarily to autobiography.
2 The examples considered in this chapter are English, but it is to be noted that aristocratic family history was a flourishing genre also in Scotland during the seventeenth century. Sir Robert Gordon of Gordonstown wrote in 1639 *A Genealogical History of the Earldom of Sutherland* (published in Edinburgh in 1813); David Hume of Godscroft wrote in 1625–30 his *History of the Houses of Douglas and Angus* (published in Edinburgh in 1644); and James Somerville completed in 1679 his *Memorie of the Somervilles* (published in Edinburgh in Sir Walter Scott's edition in 1815).
3 John Smyth's *Lives of the Berkeleys* was partly published in 1821, and more fully in 1883 as volumes I and II of *The Berkeley Manuscripts*, edited by Sir John Maclean, for the Bristol and Gloucestershire Archaeological Society (Gloucester: John Bellows), cited in this chapter as Smyth. *The Memoirs of Sir Hugh Cholmley* was printed from manuscripts in the possession of Nathaniel Cholmley in 1787 (place of publication not given), cited here as Cholmley. Gervase Holles's *Memorials of the Holles Family, 1493–1656* was edited from manuscripts at Longleat and Welbeck by A.C. Wood, and published in 1937 by the Camden Society, Third Series, vol. 55, cited here as Holles.
4 Herbert, *The Life of Edward, First Lord Herbert of Cherbury, Written by Himself*, ed. J.M. Shuttleworth (London: Oxford University Press, 1976), 102.
5 Smyth, II, 443.
6 Barlow, *The True Guide to Glory* (1619), 48. *The Life and Death of Mr. Vavasor Powell*, attributed to Edward Bagshaw the Younger (n.p. [actually London], 1671), 106.
7 Holles, 201.
8 Smyth, II, 440.
9 Smyth is included in the *DNB* (XVIII, 481–2) as 'Smith or Smyth, John.' See also James H. Cooke, 'The Berkeley Manuscripts and Their Author – John Smyth,' *Transactions of the Bristol and Gloucester Archaeological Society, 1880–81*, V, 212–21. Cf. *Lives of the Berkeleys*, II, 442.
10 Lloyd, *Memoires* (1668), 109.
11 Smyth, II, 363.
12 Smyth, II, 382–8.
13 Smyth, II, 400.

14 On Cholmley see the *DNB*, IV, 268–9. Cf. his *Memoirs*, 3–4.
15 Cholmley, 3.
16 Cholmley, 10.
17 Cholmley, 17–18.
18 Cholmley, 26–7, 4.
19 On Holles, in addition to the *DNB*, IX, 1061–2, see R.E.G. Cole's edition of Holles's *Lincolnshire Church Notes* (Lincoln: Lincolnshire Record Society, 1911); Richard F. Goulding, 'Gervase Holles, "A Great Lover of Antiquities,"' *Transactions of the Thoroton Society* 26 (1922), 36–70; A.C. Wood's introduction to his edition of *Memorials of the Holles Family*, and his 'The Holles Family,' *Transactions of the Royal Historical Society* fourth series 19 (1936), 144–65.
20 Holles, 227.
21 Holles, 2.
22 Holles, 2, 8–9.
23 Holles, 19, 197, 12.
24 A.C. Wood quotes Dugdale's praise in his introduction, Holles, vii; cf. Holles, 133.
25 Holles, 3, 150, 135. In his edition A.C. Wood points out that Holles did not always achieve complete accuracy, but this is understandable in a work written in exile.
26 Holles, 5, 202, 235–6, 189–90.
27 See especially Holles, 190, 219.
28 Vowell, 'The Lyffe of Sir Peter Carewe,' ed. Sir Thomas Phillipps, *Archaeologia* 28 (1840), 98.
29 Holles, 160.
30 Holles, 111.
31 Holles, 200.
32 Holles, 200, 86, 127, 125.
33 Holles, 195–6, 217, 41, 226, 41.
34 Holles, 30, 116–18, 183.
35 Holles, 215.
36 Holles, 194–5, 181.
37 Holles, 9, 2.
38 Holles, 202, 191.
39 Holles, 67, 227, 202.
40 Holles, 160–1, 81.
41 Like Walton, both as an Anglican and as an antiquary Holles laments the Puritan destruction of church monuments (e.g., 56).
42 Holles, 190–200, 76, 77.

43 Holles, 37–47.
44 This life of the Earl of Clare is a substantial biography, running to twenty-six pages in the edition by A.C. Wood (88–114).
45 Holles, 181–3, 4.
46 Holles, 34–5.
47 Holles, 4, 19.

Chapter 11

1 For the biography of Francis, references are to the first volume of Roger North, *The Lives of the Right Hon. Francis North, Baron Guilford; the Hon. Sir Dudley North; and the Hon. and Rev. Dr. John North*, ed. Augustus Jessopp (London: George Bell and Sons, 1890), cited as Jessopp, I; and North, *The Life of the Lord Keeper North*, ed. Mary Chan, Studies in British History, vol. 41 (Lewiston: Edwin Mellen Press, 1995), cited as Chan. For the biography of Dudley, references are to the second volume of Jessopp's edition of the *Lives*, cited as Jessopp, II. For North's 'General Preface' and biography of John, references are to *General Preface & Life of Dr John North*, ed. Peter Millard (Toronto: University of Toronto Press, 1984), cited as Millard. The editions of Chan and Millard are more faithful to North's manuscripts than previous ones like Jessopp's based on the first editions, published after Roger's death by his son Montagu North in 1742–4. Chan provides the first complete and accurate text of Roger's final manuscript version of the life of Francis. She shows that Montagu's text is a composite, amalgamating parts of an earlier version with parts of the final version, and bringing into the main narrative material which Roger had placed in a series of thematic essays on various aspects of Francis's life in a separate section of the biography. Montagu North's text, however, has a special place in literary history as the form in which the life was known for two hundred and fifty years, and is still the one that is most readily available in many locations. It is less burdened with extraneous and marginally relevant material than the version edited by Chan; it contains valuable passages not in that version, and in some respects shows Roger North as biographer to better advantage. I have made use of it here in Jessopp's edition, while also utilizing Chan's edition as a highly important work of North scholarship. I have followed established tradition in referring to the biographies collectively as *Lives of the Norths*, although editions have rarely had exactly that title.
2 Jessopp, I, 15.
3 On the dating of North's numerous manuscript versions of the lives, see

Peter Millard, 'The Chronology of Roger North's Main Works,' *Review of English Studies* n.s. 24 (1973), 283–94, and Mary Chan, 'Roger North's *Life* of Francis North,' *Review of English Studies* n.s. 42 (1991), 190–211.

4 On North's life see especially *Notes of Me: The Autobiography of Roger North*, ed. Peter Millard (Toronto: University of Toronto Press, 2000), cited below as *Notes of Me*, while this editor's *General Preface & Life of Dr John North* is cited throughout as Millard.

5 James Clifford was the pioneer in the modern revival of interest in North. He included extracts from the manuscript of North's 'General Preface' in his *Biography as an Art: Selected Criticism 1560–1960* (London: Oxford University Press, 1962), 27–37, describing it as a 'a remarkable document' and an 'astonishing ... anticipation of the later work of Johnson and Boswell' (xii); and he developed his views further in 'Roger North and the Art of Biography,' *Restoration and Eighteenth-Century Literature: Essays in Honor of Alan Dugald McKillop*, ed. Carroll Camden (Chicago: University of Chicago Press, 1963), 275–85. He argued that North thought more deeply about biography than any writer before Johnson.

6 Jessopp, I, 374; cf. Chan, 243.

7 See Jessopp, I, 6, 8–9; Millard, 94–5; and the letter quoted by Chan, 'Roger North's *Life*,' 197–8. Roger's strong family sense was shown in his later years when he acted as executor of his elder brothers and guardian of their children.

8 Jessopp, I, 405.

9 See 'General Preface' in Millard, 81; Jessopp, I, 3–4, 10–11; and Mary Chan's discussion in her *RES* article.

10 North, *Examen: Or an Enquiry into the Credit and Veracity of a Pretended Complete History ... Together with some Memoirs* (1740).

11 See above, pp. 51–2, and cf. Jessopp, II, 80.

12 Jessopp, I, 100; cf. Chan, 207.

13 Millard, 62, 64.

14 Millard, 59; Jessopp, I, 15, 327.

15 Boswell reports that in 1772 Johnson said 'nobody can write the life of a man, but those who have eat and drunk and lived in social intercourse with him': *Life of Johnson*, ed. G.B. Hill, rev. L.F. Powell (Oxford: Clarendon Press, 1934), II, 166.

16 Millard, 77–8, 80, 94.

17 Jessopp, I, 12–13; Millard, 95.

18 Half a dozen editions of North's writings on music were published between 1846 and the end of the twentieth century, and *Of Building; Roger North's*

Writings on Architecture, ed. H. Colvin and J. Newman, was published in 1981 (Oxford: Clarendon Press).
19 Millard, 102.
20 See F.P. Wilson, *Seventeenth Century Prose* (Berkeley and Los Angeles: University of California Press, 1960), 65–6, and Stauffer, *The Art of Biography in Eighteenth Century England* (Princeton: Princeton University Press, 1941), 362. Mark Longaker in his *English Biography in the Eighteenth Century* (Philadelphia: University of Pennsylvania Press, 1931; reprinted New York: Octagon Books, 1971), 173, considered the life of Francis the 'most engaging' of the three.
21 Regarding politics, see Millard, 99.
22 Jessopp, I, 242, 268–71.
23 Jessopp, I, 360–1.
24 Jessopp, II, 6, 77, 51, 248.
25 Jessopp, II, 56.
26 Millard, 149. John North's wish was carried out: a stone on the floor of the antechapel at Trinity College is marked with his initials and the date of his death.
27 Millard, 103, 138.
28 Millard, 82.
29 The final manuscript version of the life of Francis edited by Chan contains many sections and much detail on legal matters likely to be of interest primarily to lawyers or law students of Roger's period or to specialized legal historians of later times. Montagu North reduced the amount of this material in the version he edited to produce a more balanced and readable biography.
30 Dudley North's *Discourses upon Trade; Principally Directed to the Cases of the Interest, Coynage, Clipping, Increase of Money* was published in 1691.
31 See above, p. 73.
32 In Montagu North's version of the life of Francis, the quoted passages are inserted with discussions of Francis's private life in the main narrative, Jessopp, I, 99–100, 418. In the final manuscript version edited by Chan, they appear in a separate section titled 'Retiredments' among the thematic essays in the second part of the biography that follows the main narrative, 206–40; see especially 207, 222.
33 Jessopp, II, 234.
34 Jessopp, II, 241–2.
35 Jessopp, I, 38; II, 4–5, 243–4. Peters was a popular Puritan preacher, executed in 1660 for having advocated the execution of Charles I.

36 Boswell, *Life of Johnson*, IV, 316.
37 Jessopp, I, 388–9; *Notes of Me*, 107; Millard, 106, 109.
38 Millard, 64.
39 Roger himself comments on his weakness in dating, Chan, 9.
40 Jessopp, I, 15; II, 2–3; Millard, 98.
41 Millard, 155; Jessopp, I, 349; Millard, 104.
42 Jessopp, I, 44–5, 117; II, 77, 170; Millard, 139. On Thomas Dangerfield see the *DNB*.
43 Jessopp, II, 80; I, 100; II, 158; I, 252. In the 'General Preface' Roger discusses the dangers of partiality and suppression, Millard, 78–9.
44 Millard, 155.
45 Jessopp, I, 61, 40, 125; II, 218–19.
46 *Notes of Me*, 96, 246–7. North's prolonged work as Lely's executor is the subject of the final section of this autobiography, 237–52.
47 Millard, 59–60, 95.
48 Jessopp, I, 4, 102, 330; Chan 9. In her edition of the life of Francis, Mary Chan includes an extensive glossary which extends beyond special legal terms.
49 Millard, 127, 156; Jessopp, I, 255, 352. In the version edited by Chan, 130, the last phrase reads 'that pestilent lump of mettall.'
50 Millard, 99.
51 Although Montagu North's editorial practices are open to criticism by modern standards, it can be argued that his selection from and rearrangement of the manuscript versions of the life of Francis were an understandable response to problems in the material his father left him.
52 Jessopp, I, 100; Chan, 207.
53 Jessopp, I, 329–30; *Examen* (1740), 656; Jessopp, I, 65; II, 242; I, 5–7, 29–36, 69. Many of the brief biographies dispersed in Montagu North's edition of the life of Francis appear together in Roger's final manuscript version in a chapter on Francis's 'Cotemporaries.' See Chan, 424–64.
54 Jessopp, I, 288–90, 293–6; cf. Chan, 441–3, 454.
55 Stauffer, *The Art of Biography in Eighteenth Century England*, 357.

Select Bibliography

The English biographical writings of the seventeenth century are so numerous that a full list would form a book in itself. The following short list represents the major figures together with a good range of biographical types, including some histories and memoirs which incorporate biographies. Bibliographical information for many other biographies of the period considered in this study and for many other works cited is provided in the notes. References for the most important manuscript sources, the Aubrey and Wood MSS in the Bodleian Library, are given in chapters 8 and 9 and the attached notes.

I Seventeenth-Century English Biographies

Abbot, George. *A Sermon Preached ... at the Funerall Solemnities of ... Thomas Earle of Dorset.* 1608.
Aubrey, John. *Aubrey's Brief Lives.* Ed. O.L. Dick. London: Secker and Warburg, 1960.
– *Brief Lives.* Ed. John Buchanan-Brown. London: Penguin, 2000.
– *Brief Lives.* Ed. Andrew Clark. 2 vols. Oxford: Clarendon Press, 1898.
Bacon, Francis. *The Historie of the Raigne of King Henry the Seventh.* 1622.
Bagshaw, Edward. 'The Life and Death of Mr. Bolton.' Preface to Robert Bolton. *Mr. Boltons Last and Learned Worke of the Foure Last Things.* 1635.
Ball, Thomas. *The Life of the Renowned Doctor Preston.* Ed. E.W. Harcourt. Oxford: Parker, 1885.
Baxter, Richard. *A Breviate of the Life of Margaret, the Daughter of Francis Charleton ... and Wife of Richard Baxter.* 1681.
Bedell, William. *Life and Death of William Bedell.* In *Two Biographies of William Bedell.* Ed. E.S. Shuckburgh. Cambridge: Cambridge University Press, 1902. 1–75.

Bernard, Nicholas. *The Life and Death of ... Dr. James Usher ...* 1656.
Boate, Arnold. *The Character of a Trulie Vertuous and Pious Woman, as it hath Been Acted by Mistress Margaret Dungan (Wife to Doctor Arnold Boate).* Paris, 1651.
Buckeridge, John. *A Sermon Preached at the Funeral of ... Lancelot* [Andrewes] *Late Lord Bishop of Winchester.* 1631.
Burnet, Gilbert. *History of His Own Time.* 2 vols. 1724. 1734.
– *The Life and Death of Sir Matthew Hale.* 1682.
– *The Life of William Bedell.* 1685.
– *Memoires of the Lives and Actions of James and William Dukes of Hamilton and Castleherald.* 1677.
– *Some Passages of the Life and Death of ... John, Earl of Rochester.* 1680.
Camden, William. *The Historie of ... Elizabeth, late Queene of England.* 1630.
Carleton, George. *The Life of Mr. Bernard Gilpin.* 1629.
Cavendish, Margaret, Duchess of Newcastle. *The Life of ... William Cavendishe, Duke, Marquess, and Earl of Newcastle.* 1667.
Cholmley, Sir Hugh. *The Memoirs of Sir Hugh Cholmley.* 1787.
Clarke, Samuel. *A General Martyrologie.* 1651. 1677.
– *The Lives of Sundry Eminent Persons in this Later Age.* 1683.
Clogie, Alexander. *Speculum Episcoporum; Or the Apostolick Bishop: Being a Brief Account of the Life and Death of ... Dr William Bedell.* In *Two Biographies of William Bedell.* Ed. E.S. Shuckburgh. Cambridge: Cambridge University Press, 1902. 78–213.
Davies, John. 'An Account of the Author of this Translation, and his Works.' Preface to John Hall, trans. *Hierocles Upon the Golden Verses of Pythagoras.* 1657.
Dawbeny, Henry. *Historie & Policie Re-Viewed, In The Heroick Transactions of his Most Serene Highnesse, Oliver, Late Lord Protector.* 1659.
Donne, John. *A Sermon of Commemoration of the Lady Danvers.* 1627.
Dryden, John. 'Life of Plutarch.' Preface to *Plutarch's Lives Translated ... by Several Hands.* 1683.
Dugdale, Sir William. *The Baronage of England.* 1675.
Evelyn, John. *The Life of Mrs. Godolphin.* London: William Pickering, 1847.
Fanshawe, Ann, Lady. *Memoirs.* In *The Memoirs of Anne, Lady Halkett and Ann, Lady Fanshawe.* Ed. John Loftis. Oxford: Clarendon Press, 1979. 101–92.
Featley, Daniel. 'The Life and Death of John Reinolds.' In Thomas Fuller et al. *Abel Redevivus.* 1651. 477–98.
– 'The Life of ... John Jewel.' Preface to Jewel. *Works.* 1609.
Fell, John. *Life of ... Dr. H. Hammond.* 1661. Republished as preface to Henry Hammond. *Workes.* 1674.
– 'Preface.' In Richard Allestree. *Forty Sermons.* 1684.

Ferrar, John. 'A Life of Nicholas Ferrar.' In *The Ferrar Papers*. Ed. B. Blackstone. Cambridge: Cambridge University Press, 1938. 9–94.
Fuller, Thomas. *Abel Redevivus*. 1651.
– *The Church-History of Britain*. 1655.
– *The History of the Worthies of England*. 1662.
– *The Holy State*. 1642.
Gauden, John. 'The Life and Death of Mr. Richard Hooker.' Preface to Hooker. *Works*. 1662.
Gough, Richard. *Human Nature Displayed in the History of Myddle ... Antiquities and Memoirs of the Parish of Myddle*. Fontwell, Sussex: Centaur Press, 1968.
Greville, Fulke, Lord Brooke. *The Life of the Renowned Sr Philip Sidney*. 1652.
Gumble, Thomas. *The Life of General Monck, Duke of Albermarle*. 1671.
Hacket, John. *Scrinia Reserata: A Memorial Offer'd to the Great Deservings of John Williams*. 1693.
Harris, John. 'A Short View of the Life and Vertues of the Author.' Preface to Arthur Lake. *Sermons*. 1629.
Herbert, Edward, Lord Herbert of Cherbury. *The Life and Raigne of King Henry the Eighth*. 1649.
Heylyn, Peter. *Cyprianus Anglicus: Or, the History of the Life and Death, of the Most Reverend and Renowned Prelate William* [Laud] *... Lord Archbishop of Canterbury*. 1668.
Hill, Abraham. 'Some Account of the Life of Dr. Isaac Barrow.' Preface to Barrow. *Works*. Ed. J. Tillotson. 1683. 1716.
Hinde, William. *A Faithfull Remonstrance of the Holy Life and Happy Death of John Bruen*. 1641.
The History of that Most Eminent Statesman, Sir John Perrott. 1728.
Holles, Gervase. *Memorials of the Holles Family, 1493–1656*. Ed. A.C. Wood. Camden Society, Third Series, vol. 55. 1937.
Hutchinson, Lucy. *Memoirs of the Life of Colonel Hutchinson*. Ed. James Sutherland. London: Oxford University Press, 1973.
Hyde, Edward, Earl of Clarendon. *The History of the Rebellion and Civil Wars in England*. Ed. W.D. Macray. 6 vols. Oxford: Clarendon Press, 1888.
– *Life of Edward Earl of Clarendon ... Written by Himself*. Oxford: Clarendon Press, 1827.
Isaacson, Henry. *An Exact Narration of the Life and Death of ... Lancelot Andrewes*. 1650.
Kennett, White. 'The Life of Mr. Somner.' Preface to William Somner. *A Treatise of the Roman Ports and Forts in Kent*. Oxford, 1693.
'The Life of Mr. John Milton.' In *The Early Lives of Milton*. Ed. Helen Darbishire. London: Constable, 1932. 17–34.

The Life of that Reverend Divine, and Learned Historian, Dr. Thomas Fuller. 1661.
'The Life of the Reverend and most Learned Joseph Mede.' Preface to Joseph Mead (or Mede). *Works.* 1664. 1672. 1677.
Lightfoot, John. 'The Preface Giving Some Accompt of the Authors Life and Writings.' In Hugh Broughton. *Works.* 1662.
Lloyd, David. *Memoires of the Lives, Actions, Sufferings & Deaths of Those Noble, Reverend and Excellent Personages, That Suffered ... In our Late Intestine Wars.* 1668.
– *State-Worthies. Or, the States-men and Favourites of England Since the Reformation.* 1665. 1670.
Mather, Increase. *The Life and Death of Mr. Richard Mather.* Cambridge, Mass., 1670.
North, Roger. *Examen: Or An Enquiry into the Credit and Veracity of a Pretended Complete History ... Together with some Memoirs.* 1740.
– *General Preface & Life of Dr John North.* Ed. Peter Millard. Toronto: University of Toronto Press, 1984.
– *The Life of the Lord Keeper North.* Ed. Mary Chan. Lewiston: Edwin Mellen Press, 1995.
– *The Lives of the Right Hon. Francis North, Baron Guilford; the Hon. Sir Dudley North; and the Hon. and Rev. Dr. John North.* Ed. Augustus Jessopp. 3 vols. London: George Bell and Sons, 1890.
Oley, Barnabas. 'A Prefatory View of the Life and Vertues of the Authour.' Preface to George Herbert. *Remains.* 1652.
Parr, Richard. *The Life of the Most Reverend Father in God James Usher.* 1686.
Parsons, Robert. *A Sermon Preached at the Funeral of ... John Earl of Rochester.* Oxford, 1680.
Paule, Sir George. *The Life of ... John Whitgift, Lord Archbishop of Canterbury.* 1612.
Phillips, Edward. 'The Life of Mr. John Milton.' Preface to *Letters of State, Written by John Milton.* 1694.
– *Theatrum Poetarum.* 1675
Pinto, V. de Sola, ed. *English Biography in the Seventeenth Century. Selected Short Lives.* London: George G. Harrap and Co., 1951.
Plume, Thomas. 'An Account of the Life and Death of the Author.' Preface to John Hacket. *A Century of Sermons.* 1675.
Pope Walter. *The Life of the Right Reverend Father in God Seth* [Ward], *Lord Bishop of Salisbury.* 1697.
Prince, John. *The Worthies of Devon.* Exeter, 1701.
Rainbowe, Edward. *A Sermon Preached at ... the Interring of the Corps of ... Susanna, Countesse of Suffolke.* 1649.
– *A Sermon Preached at the Funeral of ... Anne Countess of Pembroke, Dorset and Montgomery.* 1677.

Rawley, William. 'The Life of the Honourable Author.' Preface to *Resuscitatio, Or, Bringing into Publick Light Severall Pieces of the Works ... of the Right Honourable Francis Bacon*. 1657.

Rust, George. *A Funeral Sermon, Preached at the Obsequies of ... Jeremy* [Taylor] *Lord Bishop of Down*. 1668.

Smith, D. Nicol, ed. *Characters from the Histories & Memoirs of the Seventeenth Century*. Oxford: Clarendon Press, 1920.

Smyth, John. *Lives of the Berkeleys*. Vols. I and II of *The Berkeley Manuscripts*. Ed. Sir John Maclean. Gloucester: Bristol and Gloucestershire Archaeological Society, 1883.

Sprat, Thomas. 'An Account of the Life and Writings of Mr Abraham Cowley.' Preface to *The Works of Mr Abraham Cowley*. 1668.

Stanley, Thomas. *The History of Philosophy*. 1655. 1656. 1660. 1662.

Taylor, Jeremy. *A Funerall Sermon, Preached at the Obsequies of ... Frances, Countesse of Carbery*. 1650.

Toland, John. 'The Life of John Milton.' Preface to *A Complete Collection of the Historical, Political, and Miscellaneous Works of John Milton*. London with false Amsterdam imprint, 1698.

Vaughan, Edmund. 'The Life and Death of the Venerable Dr. Jackson.' Preface to *A Collection of the Works of that Holy Man and Profound Divine Thomas Jackson*. 1653.

Vowell, John, alias Hooker. 'The Lyffe of Sir Peter Carewe.' Ed. Sir Thomas Phillipps. *Archaeologia* 28 (1840), 96–151.

Walker, Sir Edward. 'A Short View of the Life of the Most Noble and Excellent Thomas Howard Earl of Arundel and Surrey.' *Historical Discourses upon Several Occasions*. 1705. 209–23.

Walsingham, Edward. *Alter Britanniæ Heros: Or the Life of the Most Honourable Knight, Sir Henry Gage*. Oxford, 1645.

– *Britannicæ Virtutis Imago. Or the Effigies of True Fortitude, Expressed to the Life, in the Famous Actions of that Incomparable Knight, Major General Smith*. Oxford, 1644.

– *Life of Sir John Digby*. Ed. George Bernard. *Camden Miscellany*, vol. 12. Camden Society, 1910. 65–125.

Walton, Izaak. 'The Life and Death of Dr Donne, Late Deane of St Pauls London.' Preface to John Donne. *LXXX Sermons*. 1640.

– *The Life of Dr. Sanderson, Late Bishop of Lincoln ... To which is added some short Tracts or Cases of Conscience written by the said Bishop*. 1678.

– *The Lives of Dr. John Donne, Sir Henry Wotton, Mr. Richard Hooker, Mr. George Herbert*. 1670.

– *The Lives of John Donne, Sir Henry Wotton, Richard Hooker, George Herbert and Robert Sanderson*. World's Classics. London: Oxford University Press, 1973.

Weldon, Sir Anthony. *The Court and Character of King James.* 1650. 1651.
Williams John. *Great Britains Salomon.* 1625.
Winstanley, William. *The Lives of the Most Famous English Poets.* 1687.
Wood, Anthony. *Athenæ Oxonienses.* 2 vols. 1691. 1692.
– *Athenæ Oxonienses.* 2 vols. 1721.
– *Historia et Antiquitates Universitatis Oxoniensis.* 2 vols. Oxford, 1674.
Wotton, Sir Henry. *A Short View of the Life and Death of George Villiers, Duke of Buckingham.* 1642.

II Other Primary Works

Aubrey, John. *Aubrey on Education.* Ed. J.E. Stephens. London: Routledge and Kegan Paul, 1972.
Bacon, Francis. *The Twoo Bookes of Francis Bacon. Of the Proficience and Advancement of Learning.* 1605.
Baxter, Richard. *Reliquiæ Baxterianæ.* 1696.
Boswell, James. *Life of Johnson.* Ed. G. Birkbeck Hill, rev. L.F. Powell. 6 vols. Oxford: Clarendon Press, 1934.
Cavendish, George. *The Life and Death of Cardinal Wolsey.* Ed. Richard Sylvester. Early English Text Society. Oxford: Oxford University Press, 1959.
Evelyn, John. *Numismata: A Discourse of Medals Ancient and Modern.* 1697.
Foxe, John. *Actes and Monuments.* 1563.
Gassendi, Pierre. *The Mirrour of True Nobility & Gentility. Being the Life of the Renowned ... Lord of Peiresk.* Trans. W. Rand. 1657.
Herbert, Edward, Lord Herbert of Cherbury. *The Life of Edward, First Lord Herbert of Cherbury, Written by Himself.* Ed. J.M. Shuttleworth. London: Oxford University Press, 1976.
Heylyn, Peter. *Examen Historicum.* 1659.
Hilliard, Nicholas. *A Treatise Concerning the Arte of Limning.* Ed. Philip Norman. Walpole Society. First Annual Volume. Oxford: Oxford University Press, 1912.
Humphrey, Laurence. *J. Juelli Episcopi Sarisburiensis vita et mors.* 1573.
Johnson, Samuel. *Lives of the Poets.* 10 vols. 1779–81.
Montaigne, Michel de. *Essays.* Trans. J.M. Cohen. Harmondsworth: Penguin, 1963.
North, Roger. *Notes of Me: The Autobiography of Roger North.* Ed. Peter Millard. Toronto: University of Toronto Press, 2000.
Pepys, Samuel. *Diary.* Ed. R. Latham and W. Matthews. 11 vols. London: George Bell and Sons, 1970–83.
Roper, William. *The Lyfe of Sir Thomas Moore.* Ed. Elsie V. Hitchcock. Early English Text Society. London: Oxford University Press, 1958.

Walton, Izaak. *The Compleat Angler.* Ed. Jonquil Bevan. Oxford: Oxford University Press, 1983.
Wood, Anthony. *Life and Times of Anthony Wood ... Described by Himself.* Ed. Andrew Clark. 5 vols. Oxford: Oxford Historical Society, 1891–1900.

III Secondary Works

Altick, Richard. *Lives and Letters: A History of Literary Biography in England and America.* New York: Alfred Knopf, 1966.
Anderson, Judith. *Biographical Truth: The Representation of Historical Persons in Tudor-Stuart Writing.* New Haven: Yale University Press. 1984.
Ariès, Philippe. Introduction. *Passions of the Renaissance.* Vol. III of *A History of Private Life.* Ed. Roger Chartier. Trans. Arthur Goldhammer. Cambridge, Mass.: Harvard University Press, 1989.
Bald, R.C. 'Historical Doubts Respecting Walton's *Life of Donne.*' In *Essays in English Literature ... Presented to A.S.P. Woodhouse.* Ed. Millar MacLure and F.W. Watt. Toronto: University of Toronto Press, 1964. 69–84.
– *John Donne: A Life.* Oxford: Clarendon Press, 1970.
Burckhardt, Jacob. *The Civilization of the Renaissance in Italy.* Trans. S.G.C. Middlemore. London: Penguin, 1990.
Charles, Amy. *A Life of George Herbert.* Ithaca: Cornell University Press, 1977.
Clifford, James L., ed. *Biography as an Art: Selected Criticism 1560–1960.* London: Oxford University Press, 1962.
Coleridge, S.T. *Marginalia.* Ed. George Whalley. Vol. XII, pt. 2, of *The Collected Works of Samuel Taylor Coleridge.* London: Routledge and Kegan Paul, 1984.
Costa, Francisque. *L'Oeuvre d'Izaak Walton.* Paris: Didier, 1973.
Cressy, David. *Birth, Marriage, and Death: Ritual, Religion, and the Life-Cycle in Tudor and Stuart England.* Oxford: Oxford University Press, 1997.
Delany, Paul. *British Autobiography in the Seventeenth Century.* London: Routledge and Kegan Paul, 1969.
Douglas, David C. *English Scholars 1660–1730.* London: Eyre & Spottiswood, 1951.
Firth, C.H. 'Burnet as Historian.' *Essays, Historical and Literary.* Oxford: Clarendon Press, 1938. 174–230.
France, Peter, and William St Clair, eds. *Mapping Lives: The Uses of Biography.* Oxford: Oxford University Press for the British Academy, 2002.
Gurevich, Aaron. *The Origins of European Individualism.* Trans. K. Judelson. Oxford: Blackwell, 1995.
Halsband, Robert. 'The Penury of English Biography before Samuel Johnson.' In *Biography in the Eighteenth Century.* Ed. J.D. Browning. New York: Garland, 1980. 112–27.

Houlbrooke, Ralph. *Death, Religion, and the Family in England, 1480–1750.* Oxford: Clarendon Press, 1998.
Hunter, Michael. *John Aubrey and the Realm of Learning.* London: Duckworth, 1975.
Kerrigan, William, and Gordon Braden. *The Idea of the Renaissance.* Baltimore: Johns Hopkins University Press, 1991.
Keynes, Sir Geoffrey. *Harvey through John Aubrey's Eyes.* Harveian Oration, Royal College of Physicians. Reprinted from the *Lancet*, with additions. N.p., 1958.
Longaker, Mark. *English Biography in the Eighteenth Century.* Philadelphia: University of Pennsylvania Press, 1931.
Martin, Jessica. *Walton's Lives: Conformist Commemorations and the Rise of Biography.* Oxford: Oxford University Press, 2001.
Nethercot, A.H. *Abraham Cowley, The Muse's Hannibal.* Oxford: Oxford University Press, 1931.
Novarr, David. *The Making of Walton's Lives.* Ithaca: Cornell University Press, 1958.
Parry, Graham. *The Trophies of Time: English Antiquarians of the Seventeenth Century.* Oxford: Oxford University Press, 1995.
Pask, Kevin. *The Emergence of the English Author: Scripting the Life of the Poet in Early Modern England.* Cambridge: Cambridge University Press, 1996.
Powell, Anthony. *John Aubrey and His Friends.* New York: Charles Scribner's Sons, 1948.
Sisson, C.J. *The Judicious Marriage of Mr. Hooker and the Birth of the Laws of Ecclesiastical Polity.* Cambridge: Cambridge University Press, 1940.
Smith, Logan P. *The Life and Letters of Sir Henry Wotton.* 2 vols. Oxford: Oxford University Press, 1907.
Stanwood, P.G. *Izaak Walton.* New York: Twayne, 1998.
Stauffer, Donald. *The Art of Biography in Eighteenth Century England.* Princeton: Princeton University Press, 1941.
– *English Biography before 1700.* Cambridge, Mass.: Harvard University Press, 1930.
Strachey, Lytton. 'John Aubrey.' *Biographical Essays.* New York: Harcourt Brace Jovanovich, n.d. 11–16.
Summers, Joseph. *George Herbert: His Religion and Art.* London: Chatto and Windus, 1954.
Trevor-Roper, H.R. *Archbishop Laud 1573–1645.* London: Macmillan, 1962.
Tylden-Wright, David. *John Aubrey: A Life.* London: HarperCollins, 1991.
Wendorf, Richard. *The Elements of Life: Biography and Portrait Painting in Stuart and Georgian England.* Oxford: Clarendon Press, 1990.

White, Helen C. *Tudor Books of Saints and Martyrs*. Madison: University of Wisconsin Press, 1963.
Wilson, F.P. *Seventeenth Century Prose*. Berkeley and Los Angeles: University of California Press, 1960.
Woolf, Virginia. 'The Art of Biography.' *The Death of the Moth and Other Essays*. London: Hogarth Press, 1942. 119–26.
– 'The Duchess of Newcastle.' *The Common Reader*. London: Hogarth Press, 1925. 98–109.
– 'The New Biography.' *Granite and Rainbow*. London: Hogarth Press, 1958. 149–55.

Index

Abbot, George, 18, 178
Adamus, Melchior, 66
Allam, Andrew, 156
Allen, William, 151
Allestree, Richard, 20, 37–8, 47, 50, 55–6, 65, 68, 72, 76
Ambrose, St, 16
Andrewes, Lancelot, 18–19, 36, 54–5, 60, 62, 74
Andrews, Margaret, 11
Aneley, Samuel, 168
Angier, John, 62
Ariès, Philippe, 64
Arundel, Earl of. *See* Howard, Thomas Ashe, Simeon, 17, 65
Ashmole, Elias, 148, 171
Ashurst, Henry, 63
Ashurst, Sir Henry, 62
Athanasius, 45
Aubrey, John, 4–5, 6, 13, 18, 22–3, 51, 77, 96, 118, 137, 146, 151–3, 160, 167, 170–98, 219–20
Augustine, St, 25, 33, 41, 54, 65, 86

Bacon, Francis, 9, 94, 117–20, 174–5, 184, 190, 192
Baddeley, Richard, 45, 65, 69

Bagshaw, Edward, 33, 41, 58, 66, 71
Bagshaw, Henry, 63
Baker, Elizabeth, 11
Bale, John, 23, 156
Ball, Thomas, 39, 61, 66, 97–9
Bancroft, Richard, 34
Barksdale, Clement, 17, 24
Barlow, John, 200
Barnard, John, 49, 73
Barrow, Isaac, 69, 120–2, 174–5, 191, 195
Barwick, John, 38, 66
Barwick, Peter, 38, 66
Basil, St, 15, 41, 42, 73
Bates, William, 59, 61
Baxter, Margaret, 25, 39, 67
Baxter, Richard, 11, 25, 39, 40, 51, 59, 63, 67, 85
Bayard, Ann, 27
Bedell, William (father), 48–9, 59, 60, 68, 70, 72, 74, 78
Bedell, William (son), 48–9, 60, 70
Bedford, Earl of. *See* Russell
Behn, Aphra, 21
Berkeley, Sir Edward, 202
Berkeley, Henry, Lord, 202–3
Berkeley, Lady Katherine, 203

Berkeley, Sir Thomas, 203
Bernard, Nicholas, 41, 48, 66, 69, 74
Bèze, Théodore de, 33
Biographia Britannica, 27, 168
Birkenhead, Sir John, 184
Birkhead, Henry, 191–2
Blackburne, Richard, 174, 180, 196, 197
Blackerby, Richard, 65
Boate, Arnold, 66–7
Boate, Margaret, 66–7
Bolton, Robert, 33, 41, 58, 66, 71, 164
Bolton, Samuel, 70
Boswell, James, 57, 143, 241
Boteler, Edward, 17
Bovey, James, 184, 191
Boyle, Robert, 38
Bradshaw, John, 163
Brady, Nicholas, 63
Bramhall, John, 58
Bretterg, Katherin, 16
Brideoake, Ralph, 162
Brightman, William, 159
Brinton, Thomas, 15
Broughton, Hugh, 39, 60, 66
Bruen, John, 42, 65, 71–2
Brownrig, Ralph, 19
Buckeridge, John, 18–19
Buckingham, Duke of. *See* Villiers, George
Bull, John, 164
Bunyan, John, 39–40, 57, 66, 154
Burgess, Anthony, 18
Burckhardt, Jacob, 5–6, 199
Burnet, Gilbert, 31, 38, 47–52, 56–7, 62–5, 68, 70–2, 74–5, 91, 96–7, 111–12, 162–3, 165
Bush, Douglas, 7

Calamy, Edmund (the elder), 15, 17

Calamy, Edmund (grandson), 24
Calvin, John, 33, 41
Camden, William, 82, 94
Camerarius, Joachim, 100
Carbery, Countess of. *See* Vaughan, Frances
Carleton, George, 36, 44
Carter, John, 17, 39
Carew, Sir Peter, 210
Cary, Lucius, Viscount Falkland, 111, 184
Cavendish, George, 12, 70, 73, 93, 100–2
Cavendish, Margaret, Duchess of Newcastle, 107–8
Cavendish, William, Duke of Newcastle, 107–8
Caxton, William, 30
Cervantes, Miguel de, 165
Chaderton, Laurence, 42
Chaloner, Thomas, 166
Charles I, 12, 44, 93, 101
Charles II, 113, 120, 135, 191, 197, 240
Chaucer, Geoffrey, 198
Cholmley, Elizabeth, 204
Cholmley, Sir Hugh, 199, 203–6
Cholmley, Sir Richard (I), 204
Cholmley, Sir Richard (II), 204–6
Chrysostom, St John, 173
Clare, Earl of. *See* Holles, John
Clarendon, Earl of. *See* Hyde, Edward
Clarke, Andrew, 171
Clarke, Samuel, 11, 24–6, 39, 40, 65, 69, 156
Clifford, Anne, Countess of Dorset, Pembroke and Montgomery, 26–7
Clifford, Martin, 132, 134
Clifton, Lady Francis, 26
Clifton, Sir Gervase, 214

Cleveland, John, 21–2
Clogie, Alexander, 48–9, 59, 74
Cokayne, Sir William, 63
Coke, Sir Francis, 209
Coleridge, S.T., 95, 102–3, 134, 151
Collier, John, 171–2, 188
Connolly, Cyril, 181
Conopius, Nathaniel, 168
Cooper, Anthony Ashley, Earl of Shaftesbury, 162
Cooper, Samuel, 183, 197
Corbet, Richard, 187, 192, 195
Cotton, Charles, 88
Cotton, Sir Robert, 123
Couper, Thomas, 168
Cowley, Abraham, 132–6, 155, 177
Cranmer, Thomas, 45
Cromwell, Oliver, 12, 44, 93, 111–12, 155
Cromwell, Richard, 159
Culme, John, 76

Daniel, Samuel, 148–9
Danvers, Elizabeth, 192
Danvers, Sir John, 84, 185
Danvers, Magdalen (Herbert), Lady, 69, 84, 185
Darbishire, Helen, 141, 195
Davies, John, 128–32, 161
Dawbeny, Henry, 44
Dee, Arthur, 179
Dee, John, 179, 186
Denham, Sir John, 179, 185
Denison, Stephen, 16, 61
Dick, Oliver Lawson, 171, 173–4
Digby, Sir John, 108–10
Digby, Sir Kenelm, 167, 186, 191
Digby, Venetia, Lady, 185, 189
Dillingham, William, 42
Diogenes Laertius, 114–15

Dobson, John, 26
Donne, John, 12–13, 17, 18, 21, 32, 55, 59, 61–3, 69, 78, 85, 86–90, 128
Drake, Joan, 71
Dryden, John, 90, 93, 94
Duck, Margaret, 71
Dugdale, Sir William, 179, 199, 208
Durham, William, 61
Dutton, Thomas 16

Eaton, Richard, 16
Elizabeth I, 94
Empson, William, 82
Erasmus, Desiderius, 68
Eusebius, 31
Evelyn, John, 38, 68, 183, 185

Fairclough, Samuel, 62, 71
Falkland, Viscount. *See* Cary
Fanshawe, Ann, Lady, 107
Fanshawe, Sir Richard, 63, 107
Farmor, Mary, Lady, 26
Featley, Daniel, 20, 32, 34–6, 46, 54, 56, 59, 66, 69, 72–3, 75–6
Featley, John, 73
Fell, John, 20, 37–8, 47, 50, 61, 65, 68–9, 72, 75–7, 135
Fenton, Roger, 16, 59
Ferrar, John, 61, 65, 69
Ferrar, Nicholas, 41, 61, 65, 69, 78, 80
Fiennes, William, Viscount Saye and Sele, 166
Finch, Leopold, 146
Firth, C.H., 111
Fisher, John, 15
Fisher, John, S.J., 46
Fisher, Payne, 164
Fletcher, John, 178
Foucault, Michel, 7
Fowles, John, 198

Fox, George, 40
Foxe, John, 30–2, 34–5, 44–5, 54, 65, 148–9, 156
Frescheville, John, 215
Frescheville, Sir Peter, 210
Fuller, Thomas, 13–14, 17, 22, 27, 35, 54, 62–3, 69, 72, 83, 92, 96, 99, 124–7, 145–53, 156, 191, 192
Fuller, William, 26

Gage, Sir Henry, 108–10
Gardiner, S.R., 102
Gascoigne, George, 164
Gassendi, Pierre, 115–16
Gauden, John, 19, 42, 62, 83, 88
Gibson, Edmund, 123
Gilbert, William, 150
Gilpin, Bernard, 36, 44
Glanvill, Joseph, 168
Godolphin, Margaret, 38
Gordius, 73
Gouge, Thomas, 66, 69, 72
Gouge, William, 59, 66, 69, 72
Gough, Richard, 24, 29
Gower, Stanly, 39
Graham, Richard, 27–8
Gregory of Nazianzus, 17, 25, 33, 44–5, 58, 68, 70
Gregory of Nyssa, 15, 33, 48, 52
Greville, Fulke, Lord Brooke, 92, 98, 128
Guidott, Thomas, 24
Gumble, Thomas, 82, 92

Hacket, John, 13, 58–9, 66, 75, 99–104
Hale, Sir Matthew, 31, 38, 50–2, 63–5, 70–2, 75
Hales, John, 89, 186
Halifax, Marquis of. *See* Savile, George

Hall, John, 128–32
Hall, Joseph, 45
Hamilton, James, Duke of Hamilton, 91, 96–7
Hamilton, William, Duke of Hamilton, 91, 96–7
Hammond, Henry, 37–8, 47, 50, 55, 61, 65, 67, 69, 73, 76–7
Hammond, Robert, 73
Hammond, Thomas, 73
Harcourt, E.W., 99
Harpsfield, Nicholas, 48
Harington, Sir John, 150
Harrington, James (political scientist), 184, 194
Harrington, James (lawyer), 154, 156–7, 162, 167–8
Harrington (or Harington), John, Lord, 150
Harris, John, 36, 45, 54, 65, 73, 75
Harris, Robert, 61
Harrison, William, 16
Harvey, William, 184, 189, 190, 194–6
Hayman, Robert, 164
Head, Richard, 184
Henry VII, 94
Henry VIII, 94, 151
Herbert, Edward, Lord Herbert of Cherbury, 85, 94, 149, 195, 200
Herbert, George, 32, 37, 41, 59, 66, 68, 70, 78–86, 87–90
Herbert, Magdalen. *See* Danvers, Magdalen
Herbert, Mary, Countess of Pembroke, 184, 190
Herbert, Philip, Earl of Pembroke, 162, 192
Heylyn, Henry, 95
Heylyn, Peter, 47, 49, 73, 95–6, 147, 152

Heywood, Nathaniel, 62
Heywood, Oliver, 62
Heywood, Thomas, 25, 28
Hill, Abraham, 69, 120-2, 174-5
Hilliard, Nicholas, 183-4
Hinde, William, 42, 65, 71-2
Hobbes, Thomas, 129, 168, 180-7, 189, 191, 194, 196-7
Holdsworth, Richard, 150
Horneck, Anthony, 18, 71
Hooke, Robert, 183-4
Hooker, Richard, 42, 62, 68, 78-84, 88-90
Holles, Denzil (I), 215
Holles, Denzil (II), 215
Holles, Elizabeth, 209
Holles, Frances, 213
Holles, Francis, 215
Holles, Frescheville (I), 201, 208, 211-12, 214-16
Holles, Frescheville (II), 207
Holles, George, 208
Holles, Sir George, 209, 216
Holles, Gervase, 13, 199, 201, 206-18
Holles, Sir Gervase, 209, 211-13
Holles, John, Earl of Clare, 209, 211, 215-17
Holles, Thomas, 209-10, 212
Holles, William, 209
Holles, Sir William (I), 207
Holles, Sir William (II), 212-13, 216
Howe, John, 15, 163
Howell, James, 160
Howes, John, 61, 66
Howard, Susanna, Countess of Suffolk, 26-7
Howard, Thomas, Earl of Arundel, 106
Humphrey, Laurence, 33, 35, 54

Hutchinson, John, 67, 107
Hutchinson, Lucy, 67, 107
Hyde, Edward, Earl of Clarendon, 13, 96, 111, 162
Hyperius, Andreas, 16

Isaacson, Henry, 19, 36, 54-5, 60, 62, 69, 74
Isham, Zacheus, 18

Jackson, Thomas, 37, 54, 57, 64-5, 72, 149
Jacob, Henry, 165
James I, 42-4, 83, 98, 101, 112-13
Janeway, James, 58
Janeway, John, 58
Jeffreys, George, Lord, 240
Jerome, St, 25
Jenkyn, William, 59
Jewel, John, 20, 32-5, 54, 56, 59, 66, 72, 75-6
Johnson, Samuel, 6, 53, 57, 93-4, 104, 117, 133, 136, 143, 168-9, 178, 234
Jonson, Ben, 150, 179, 184, 186
Junius, Francis, 72
Jurdain, Ignatius, 56
Juxton, Elizabeth, 16, 61

Ken, Thomas, 26
Kennett, White, 123-4, 152
Kettell, Ralph, 185, 187, 190, 192
Keynes, Sir Geoffrey, 195-6
Killigrew, Anne, 153
King, John, 57-9
Kingston, Catherine, 212-14
Kingston, John, 210, 213

Lake, Arthur, 36, 45, 54, 65, 73
Lamb, Charles, 108

Langbaine, Gerard, 24
Laud, William, 12, 32, 47, 85, 95–6, 101, 152
Lauderdale, Duke of. *See* Maitland, John
Lee, Sir Henry, 189
Leland, John, 23
Lely, Sir Peter, 90, 238
Leygh, William, 16
Lightfoot, John, 39, 60, 66
Lilly, William, 154
Littleton, Sir Thomas, 21
Lloyd, David, 23, 38, 56, 94, 156, 202
Luther, Martin, 41, 66

Machiavelli, Niccolo, 102
Machin, John, 32
Maitland, John, Duke of Lauderdale, 111–12
Manchester, Countess of. *See* Montagu, Essex
Manton, Thomas, 61
Marlowe, Christopher, 154
Marten, Henry, 164, 187, 192
Marvell, Andrew, 154, 190
Mather, Increase, 42, 58, 163–4
Mather, Richard, 42, 58
Matilda, Queen, 152
May, Robert, 22
Maynard, Margaret, Lady, 26
Mayo, Richard, 42, 72–3
Mead, Joseph, 20, 58, 82, 150
Milton, John, 36, 67, 82, 136–44, 155, 163, 178, 187, 193–4
Monck, George, Duke of Albemarle, 82, 92
Montagu, Essex, Countess of Manchester, 65
Montaigne, Michel de, 93
Moray, Sir Robert, 192

More, Sir Thomas, 10, 12, 48, 56, 68, 70, 179
Morley, George, 34
Morton, Thomas, 34, 45, 65, 69
Mulgrave, Earl of. *See* Sheffield, Edmund
Musgrave, Sir William, 16, 18

Naylor, Joseph, 45, 65, 69
Nepos, Cornelius, 146
Newcome, Henry, 32
Newman, John, 16, 59
Nicolls, Ferdinando, 56
North, Dudley, Lord, 220
North, Sir Dudley, 219, 221–2, 224–6, 228–9, 231–9
North, Francis, Lord Guilford, 219–24, 226–8, 231–9
North, John, 219, 224–6, 229–39
North, Montagu, 220
North, Roger, 4, 25, 31, 51–2, 74, 94, 219–41
Nowell, Alexander, 151

Oley, Barnabas, 37, 41
Osborne, Penelope, Lady, 15
Oughtred, William, 186
Overall, Anne, 189, 193
Overall, John, 150

Parr, Richard, 67
Parr, Thomas, 28, 148
Parsons, Robert, 18
Patrick, Simon, 18
Paul, St, 44–5, 64
Paule, Sir George, 35, 55, 64
Peiresc, Nicolas-Claude F. de, 115–16
Pembroke, Earl and Countess of. *See* Herbert, Mary; Herbert, Philip
Pepys, Samuel, 108, 153

Perkins, William, 63, 150
Perrot, Sir John, 9, 105–6, 110
Petty, Sir William, 180, 184, 194
Peyto, Edward, 60
Philips, Ambrose, 104
Philips, Katherine, 155, 185
Phillips, Edward, 24, 114, 137, 139–41
Pierce, Thomas, 60
Piers, John, 57–9
Pits, John, 23
Plume, Thomas, 58, 59, 66
Plutarch, 91, 94
Pope, Walter, 165
Popham, Sir John, 183
Possidius, 33, 41, 54, 58, 65
Potter, Francis, 185
Poultney, John, 150
Powell, Anthony, 198
Powell, Vavasor, 200–1
Preston, John, 12, 39, 97–9
Price, John, 157
Prince, John, 24, 28
Prude, John, 27
Prynne, William, 45, 95, 159, 185, 191

Quarles, Francis, 21
Quarles, Ursula, 21

Rainbowe, Edward, 26–7, 70
Ralegh, Sir Walter, 92, 152, 184, 186–7
Randolph, Thomas, 154, 164, 185
Rawley, William, 117–20, 122, 174–5
Ray, John, 179
Reynolds, Edward, 63
Reynolds, John, 36, 54, 59
Rich, Mary, Countess of Warwick, 16, 38, 72
Rich, Robert, 19
Rochester, Earl of. *See* Wilmot

Roper, William, 10, 12, 48, 56, 70
Rothwell, Richard, 39
Russell, Francis, Earl of Bedford, 15
Rust, George, 18–19, 62

Sackville, Thomas, Earl of Dorset, 18
Saltmarsh, John, 151
Sanderson, Robert, 21, 78–85, 88
Saunders, Sir Edmund, 240–1
Savage, Henry, 160
Savile, George, Marquis of Halifax, 113
Saye and Sele, Viscount. *See* Fiennes, William
Scott, Sir Walter, 218
Selden, John, 100, 178, 189, 194
Shadwell, Thomas, 63
Shaftesbury, Earl of. *See* Cooper, Anthony Ashley
Shakespeare, William, 21, 143–4, 148–50, 178
Shawe, Dorothy, 11
Shawe, John, 11
Sheffield, Edmund, Earl of Mulgrave, 17
Sidney, Sir Henry, 15
Sidney, Sir Philip, 92, 128, 184, 190
Smith, Henry, 54
Smith, Sir John, 108–9
Smith, Logan P., 19, 82
Smith, Thomas, 21
Smyth, John, 199–203
Socrates, 115
Somerville, James, 218
Somner, William, 123–4
South, Robert, 162
Southcomb, Lewis, 76
Southey, Robert, 109
Sparke, Thomas, 15

Spedding, James, 119–20
Speght, Thomas, 21, 128
Spelman, Sir Henry, 123, 186
Sprat, Thomas, 117, 132–6, 177
Spring, Mary, Lady, 25
Stanley, Thomas, 13, 114–15
Stauffer, Donald, 3, 171, 226, 241
Staunton, Edmund, 42, 72–3
Stephen, Sir Leslie, 89
Sternhold, Thomas, 166
Strachey, Lytton, 90, 184, 198
Strode, Lady, 200
Stubbes, Katherine, 25
Stubbes, Philip, 25
Stubbs, Philip, 17, 46
Suckling, Sir John, 184, 186–7
Suetonius, 91, 106
Suffolk, Countess of. *See* Howard, Susanna
Sutherland, James, 171

Taylor, Jeremy, 18–19, 58–9, 62
Taylor, John, 28, 154
Thomason, George, 63
Thornton, W., 159
Tillotson, John, 62
Toland, John, 21, 137, 141–3, 164, 180
Tombes, John, 164, 184

Ussher, James, 32, 41, 66–7, 74

Vasari, Giorgio, 28
Vaughan, Edmund, 37, 47, 54, 57, 64–5, 72, 75, 149
Vaughan, Frances, Countess of Carbery, 58
Vaughan, Sir John, 21
Vernon, George, 49, 73

Villiers, George, first Duke of Buckingham, 94–5, 99, 101
Vines, Richard, 69
Vowell, John, 210

W., W., 21
Wadsworth, Thomas, 32, 71
Walker, Anthony, 16, 38, 71–2
Walker, Sir Edward, 106
Walker, Elizabeth, 71
Waller, Edmund, 183–4
Wallis, John, 162
Walsingham, Edward, 108–10
Walton, Izaak, 4, 12–13, 20–1, 32, 34, 37–8, 47–8, 55, 59, 62, 66–7, 70, 72, 74–5, 78–90, 128, 154, 160, 173
Ward, Seth, 165
Warwick, Countess of. *See* Rich, Mary
Warwick, Sir Philip, 112
Weldon, Sir Anthony, 112–13
Whalley, Peter, 63
Wharton, Henry, 69
White, Jeremiah, 159
Whitefoote, John, 42
Whitgift, John, 35, 55, 64, 78
Wilkins, John, 164
Wilkinson, Henry, 158, 163
Williams, John, 12, 17, 42–4, 99–104, 151
Willis, Thomas, 184, 187
Wilmot, John, Earl of Rochester, 18, 21, 38, 57, 162–3, 195
Wilson, F. P., 226
Winstanley, William, 24
Wither, George, 161
Wolsey, Thomas, 12, 70, 73, 93
Wood, Anthony, 13, 17–18, 22, 24, 27, 46–7, 55, 73, 92–3, 95, 136–8,

153–69, 170, 176–9, 189, 192–3, 197
Wood, Thomas, 165
Wordsworth, William, 75
Wren, Sir Christopher, 158–9
Wright, James, 166
Wright, Thomas, 17

Woolf, Virginia, 7, 90
Wotton, Sir Henry, 20, 78–85, 88–90

Yorke, James, 148

Zanchy, Heirome, 168

www.ingramcontent.com/pod-product-compliance
Lightning Source LLC
Chambersburg PA
CBHW030306080526
44584CB00012B/459